FROM PETRARCH TO LEONARDO BRUNI

FROM PETRARCH TO LEONARDO BRUNI

Studies in Humanistic and Political Literature

by HANS BARON

Published for The Newberry Library by
THE UNIVERSITY OF CHICAGO PRESS
Chicago and London

Library of Congress Catalog Card Number: 68-16686

The University of Chicago Press, Chicago 60637
The University of Chicago Press, Ltd., London W.C. 1

ACKNOWLEDGMENTS

In the course of critical investigations such as those which form the major part of this book, an author incurs obligations to many people for advice and the procurement of documents. I cannot thank all these helpers individually, although I have acknowledged some of my debts at the proper places in the discussion. Here I wish to express my gratitude to those colleagues and friends without whose persistent interest this work could not have been published now, when the problems with which it deals are in the forefront of scholarly debate.

Like so many of my previous publications, the present book has been made possible by the sympathetic aid of The Newberry Library, especially that of its Director and Associate Director, Dr. Lawrence W. Towner and Mr. James M. Wells. This refers not only to the granting of every possible working facility while my studies were in progress; it refers above all to the open-mindedness with which Dr. Towner accepted the successive changes and extensions needed to draw the various strands of investigation into a book that focuses on a number of crucial questions. I owe a very great debt of gratitude to Mr. Wells for his editorial patience in helping to prepare for press a manuscript that, on account of its heterogeneous origin and the incorporation of an appended Latin text, posed some unusual problems. I am also most grateful to Dr. Donald W. Krummel, Associate Librarian of the Newberry, for his unfailing readiness to help in expediting my labors.

Warmest thanks are due to Professor Denys Hay of the University of Edinburgh, whose criticism of my manuscript was extremely useful and constructive. I am profoundly indebted to Professor Eric Cochrane of the University of Chicago for taking time from a busy schedule to read, and comment on, the manuscript.

Finally, as often in the past, I had the selfless collaboration of my daughter and son-in-law, Renate and Marcel Franciscono, in the revision of my English. Their contribution at many points went far beyond matters of language and style.

H. B.

Chicago, March 1968

CONTENTS

vii

INTRODUCTION

These studies form a sequel to *Humanistic and Political Litera-*
ture in Florence and Venice at the Beginning of the Quattrocento,
published in 1955 as a companion volume to *The Crisis of the*
Early Italian Renaissance.[1] But they are meant to be more than
merely an extension of the discussion to adjacent areas, such
as Petrarch's Humanism. Even in 1955, I did not look upon
the kind of critical investigation offered here simply as a
means of buttressing the interpretation of the intellectual
transition from the Trecento to the Quattrocento that I had
given in a number of essays and in the *Crisis.* Rather, I also
hoped to help keep alive a method which in our day, it
seems to me, is not practiced with the persistence and frequency needed in Renaissance research.

Nobody will question that, with the ever-increasing facility
of access to manuscript libraries and archives, it has become
the most pressing task for the next few generations of scholars
to broaden as rapidly as possible the documentary basis for
the study of Renaissance Humanism. Nonetheless, the present
overwhelming interest in accumulating new source material
has not been wholly beneficial. There are many critical questions which we cannot relegate to second place even temporarily, above all those concerned with the nature and value of
the documents and writings already known. As the amount
of material at our command increases, so must our knowledge
of what scholars have of late begun to call the biographies of
the more significant works—how, during their composition,
they were influenced by changes in the lives and minds of
their authors and how they were transformed from their first
conception to their final forms.

This knowledge is especially needed in understanding the

---

[1] *Humanistic and Political Literature in Florence and Venice at the Beginning of the Quattro-*
cento: Studies in Criticism and Chronology (Cambridge: Harvard University Press, 1955;
Reprint edition, with a new "Introductory Note", New York: Russell & Russell,
1968).
The Crisis of the Early Italian Renaissance: Civic Humanism and Republican Liberty in an
Age of Classicism and Tyranny, 2 vols. (Princeton, N.J.: Princeton University Press, 1955;
Revised one-volume edition, 1966).

I

Renaissance because of the important role played by rhetoric in humanistic literature, in the historiography, and even in the political writings of the period. Unless we know exactly when, where, and under what conditions a work was written, and whether it was composed all of a piece or emerged little by little, we cannot judge the author's intention, the seriousness or merely oratorical character of his statements, or the relationship of his work to the actual life of his time. These questions often challenge all our ingenuity, yet only in a limited number of cases do we find manuscripts which provide physical evidence of how the structure of a work may gradually have been changed; and rarely are the surviving versions sufficient to tell the full story. Even autographs often fail to bear sure indications of the moment when they were written, and their correct dating and understanding remain dependent on our critical appraisal of other factors. We should, therefore, soon find ourselves in a quandary if, strengthened by the growing historical skepticism of our time, the opinion should become prevalent that, where manuscript documentation is scarce, definitive results are unobtainable because the methods of textual analysis by themselves have often failed in the past. If, in consequence of such distrust, our willingness and ability to explore the structure of important writings for traces of complicated composition histories should permanently decline, the acquisition of more and more material would merely weaken our capacity to judge the value of our sources and to establish foundations on which a scholarly consensus can be reached, irrespective of differences in historical interpretation.

Since the publication of my first collection of critical investigations in 1955, I have become more and more convinced that the palpable decrease of interest in objective structural analyses of this kind has had a deleterious effect on Renaissance studies. It has played a part in the emergence of a situation in which endless controversies over contradictory interpretations have led to a desperate feeling that we may never have at our command a nucleus of knowledge that is firmly and soundly based. Because of this situation, I have made every possible effort to free my own conclusions from reliance on arguments whose force might depend on the acceptance of particular views or evaluations. This is not to suggest that I now believe that fundamental new results in the field of historical criticism can often derive from the method of textual and philological investigation used in a purely technical fashion; I am still convinced that the perceptiveness required for reading a text in a new light comes as a rule when a document, or the movement which it represents, is viewed from a new historical perspective. Nevertheless, as far as possible the critical results must afterwards be freed from their initial connection with a specific interpretative approach if they are to be generally useful. This I have tried to do in the first four studies of the present book. If, as a consequence, my labors should prove to be of help in extending the area where adherents of different approaches can agree on the progress made, the primary purpose of this volume will have been attained.

The first study tries to show that Petrarch scholarship, during the past few decades, has already undergone a crucial, though probably not yet sufficiently acknowledged shift. There are available results that permit us to draw definitive conclusions regarding the structure, genesis, and chronology of a considerable number of Petrarch's humanistic works. As the study suggests, it has thus become possible to form a concrete idea of the development of certain trends in Petrarch's thought, no matter how one may appraise the psychological component of his famous vacillations and waverings or the role of the persistent rhetorical element in his Humanism.

The second study, an attempt to detect successive stages in the composition of Petrarch's *Secretum*, applies the methods of structural analysis to a work which in the past has defied such efforts. The outcome is that substantial interpolations can be discerned beyond doubt and that their causes may at least be conjectured. In other words, the *Secretum*, like most of Petrarch's works, continued to evolve long after its initial draft. We are delivered thereby from the former dilemma of a contradiction between apparent testimonies for Petrarch's early thought found in the *Secretum* and the evidence encountered in some of his other early writings.

Turning from Petrarch's Humanism to the intellectual transition at the beginning of the Quattrocento, we reach the crucial test for the methods used—and, I hope, refined—in this book.

3

The history of the crisis which separates Quattrocento culture from the world of the Trecento is bound to look entirely different according to the chronology and genesis that we ascribe to each of our three most important literary sources: Bruni's *Laudatio* of the city of Florence, his two *Dialogi*, and Gregorio Dati's *Istoria* of the Florentine war against Giangaleazzo Visconti. In 1955, I proposed that these three works (or, more precisely, the *Laudatio, Dialogus II*, and the *Istoria*) closely followed upon Florence's trial and triumph in the struggle with Giangaleazzo and, consequently, that they allow us to measure the influence of that confrontation on the Florentine mind.

How sure is this chronology when taken out of its original framework, the historical appraisal of the role of the war as given in the *Crisis*? In studies 3 and 4, I recast and enlarge my critical argument of 1955. As a result, I now feel more sure than ever that we have attained complete certainty regarding the chronological relationship of those three key works to the Florentine triumph. Unless I grievously deceive myself, there should no longer be any dispute about this basic point in any future debates on the early Renaissance.

These four methodologically related studies have two minor sequels in the last two studies (6 and 7) which may help to illustrate how in the absence of sufficient external evidence the application of an analytical method to individual manuscripts can assist us in the identification of their time and genesis and in filling in an incomplete historical picture. In study 6, an unknown Venetian chronicle which proves to be a missing link in the filiation of the narratives already known makes possible a brief review of our present knowledge concerning the nature and relationship of the chronicles written in Venice during the early Quattrocento. I trust that the inclusion in the present volume of this unpretentious contribution to Venetian historiography in Bruni's and Dati's generation will not appear out of place. The subsequent discussion (study 7) of the date, place, and significance of a roughly contemporaneous copy of an ancient work which became for the first time fully known during that generation—Aulus Gellius' *Noctes Atticae*—may seem a somewhat less appropriate choice. It is reprinted here mainly for the reason that, apart from offering the critical discussion of the manuscript from which it starts, it has proved useful, since its first publication in a periodical, to students of the classical influence on Humanism. No other appraisal of the transmission to the Renaissance of Gellius' storehouse of ancient knowledge and opinions has thus far been attempted.

Finally, this volume serves to redeem a promise I made years ago: it presents, in an appendix, the first printed edition of one of the major humanistic sources discussed in so many of the studies here included—Bruni's *Laudatio Florentinae Urbis*. Why its publication has had to wait until now is explained on pages 228–30 below.

In bringing out this work of Bruni, I felt I should add a more balanced estimate of its historical importance, its relationship to its forerunners, and its effect on Quattrocento thought than I was able to give in my 1955 analysis of the contemporaneous political and intellectual crisis. One of the questions not fully considered in the *Crisis* concerns the relationship of the *Laudatio* to its Greek model, Aelius Aristides' *Panathenaicus*, seen in the light of the effect of the revival of Greek studies on intellectual change around 1400; another problem is the significance of the *Laudatio* when it is compared with what we have gradually come to know about the early emergence of historical criticism and humanistic philology during the Trecento. In study 5, subsequent to the chronological discussion of Bruni's and Dati's works, attention is directed to these and other not yet sufficiently appreciated aspects of Bruni's panegyric, whereas less emphasis is placed on its political tenor, which has been analyzed in the *Crisis*. When examining this new essay on the *Laudatio* and the preceding chronological studies on Bruni and Dati, readers, I hope, will have the *Crisis* at hand and look upon the present volume, *inter alia*, as an attempt to continue the search for solutions to some of the problems first posed there.

It remains to be stated that studies 1, 2, and 7 have previously been published in periodicals and study 6 in a Festschrift. Some alterations will be found in the title, on the first three pages, and in the paragraph sequence of the study on Venetian chronicles (6), and there are occasional insertions of new evidence in the footnotes of the Aulus Gellius study (7), some pages of which have been reorganized. The frequent other changes, some quite extensive, in the text of the republished pieces are stylistic.[2]

---

[2] The four studies were originally published in *Bibliothèque d'Humanisme et Renaissance*, *Studies in Philology*, and *Essays in History and Literature Presented by Fellows of The Newberry Library to Stanley Pargellis*. I am grateful to the editors of the two journals and to the Trustees of the Newberry Library for permission to reprint these pieces in a slightly different form. The exact place and date of previous publication are given in an unnumbered footnote on the first page of each chapter.

1 THE EVOLUTION OF PETRARCH'S THOUGHT: Reflections on the State of Petrarch Studies

I. Students of Humanism have grown increasingly wary of the abstractions that necessarily result from presenting the thought of a leading figure or phase of the Renaissance in "cross-sections". Many have come to realize how much more can be learned by viewing life in its flux as it passes through crises and develops in reaction to concrete situations. At the same time, the basis for observing such reactions has been constantly broadened by the discovery of manuscripts reflecting successive stages of important works and by the critical revision of epistolary collections and their chronologies. Indeed, the trend toward a genetic and evolutional approach seems to have firmly taken root everywhere—except in Petrarch studies.

Not that the textual and chronological study of Petrarch's writings has at any time been neglected. Quite the contrary, thanks to the recovery of some of the autograph manuscripts of his works and of many volumes of his library with his own marginal notes, Petrarch scholarship has in many respects set the pace and served as a model for critical studies of Humanism. But in the case of Petrarch's life and work, the great advance of textual criticism and manuscript research appears to have checked rather than encouraged hopes for a truly evolutionary understanding. For one of the results has been the disappointing realization that most of Petrarch's Latin and vernacular works are known to us only in the final form in which Petrarch left them late in his life or at his death. He constantly refused to release the master copies of his writings; even after their relative completion, he kept on making changes and additions that reflected the events and thoughts of subsequent years. Only in the last decade of his life did he occasionally allow copies to be made for a friend,[1] and even then he

---

This study first appeared in *Bibliothèque d'Humanisme et Renaissance*, XXIV (1962), 7–41.

[1] I am thinking of the copy of the *De Vita Solitaria* for Filippo di Cabassole, and of the tentative release of the *De Remediis*, both in 1366.

7

did not afterwards refrain from making further changes. In a few, equally rare situations, copies of successive versions of some of his writings were made by his scribes.[2] But in most cases we know merely the state of the texts as they were left at his death; and, consequently, we can determine the date of origin of individual pages or passages only when and where we have succeeded in establishing a relationship to some otherwise known, datable events, writings, or ideas.

This applies even to the two works which earlier students had thought were especially reliable biographic documents revealing the course of Petrarch's emotional and intellectual life from his youth: the *Canzoniere* and the several collections of his letters. Like the known texts of the major Latin works, the three successive forms of the *Canzoniere* which have survived belong to the last part of Petrarch's life, the oldest—the so-called Chigi form—stemming from a time no earlier than about 1360, fourteen years before his death.[3] Consequently, the endless pains taken by scholars of past generations to establish dates and circumstances of the poems which echo situations in Petrarch's younger years are valuable only within narrow limits. By 1360, not only had the wording of probably a large number of the early poems been retouched, but some had certainly been entirely reshaped for the benefit of the final architecture of the *Canzoniere*. Other sonnets and *canzoni*, though made to look as if they were composed during certain definite moments of Petrarch's love, were actually written years or decades afterwards, during the composition of the book edition. Even the apparent acid test of distinguishing between poems presupposing that Laura was still alive, and poems presupposing her death, has not proved wholly reliable. For the sake of the artistic balance of his work, Petrarch was able to recapture his frame of mind of years long passed, and to express his feelings for Laura as if she were still alive long after death had given a different meaning to his love.

Observations of a similar nature have been made regarding Petrarch's correspondence—ever since Vittorio Rossi began to

---

[2] Especially of the *Vita Scipionis* and of some portions of the *Trionfo della Fama*, as we shall see.

[3] See E. H. Wilkins' fundamental work, *The Making of the Canzoniere and Other Petrarchan Studies* (Rome, 1951), esp. pp. 236 f.

scrutinize the manuscripts for his edition of the *Epistolae Familiares* in the "Edizione Nazionale". Here, too, separate pieces were substantially altered when Petrarch selected and assembled them to form a book. Only a little less than a quarter of the *Familiares* letters have also been preserved in their original texts as actual missives. The vital part of the revision took place between 1351 and 1353, but Petrarch continued to make alterations and to add new letters until 1366.[4] As long ago as 1932, Rossi was able to give a foretaste of the revelations which critical scholarship was soon to make about the thoroughness of the changes that Petrarch permitted himself in reworking his early correspondence. Letters ostensibly belonging to the 1330's and 1340's (so Rossi found out) frequently use and quote classical authors actually unknown to Petrarch at the time, or not available to him in his library until the middle of the 1340's or even 1350's—authors such as Plautus and Quintilian or the anonymous compilers of the *Historia Augusta*. Following the procedure also used in the making of the *Canzoniere*, Petrarch added letters which certainly or very probably had never been sent to any addressee. Such letters, specifically composed for the book form of the correspondence during the early 1350's, or possibly still later, were added either in order to round out his portrait of himself in his younger years, or for the benefit of the symmetry and artistic balance of the emerging book.[5]

Since 1932, critical research has steadily undermined the belief that the *Epistolae Familiares* are reliable autobiographical documents, and the unmasking of garbled texts may continue for some time to come. Not long ago, the extent of these alterations was carefully assessed for one of the cases in which the original missive form is still available, thus permitting comparison. In the eighth book of the *Familiares*, Petrarch reports the tragic circumstances which, in 1349, caused the fail-

---

4 See, in addition to the basic investigations into the history of the *Familiares* by V. Rossi and G. Billanovich which we are going to discuss in detail, the "Nota critica" in *F. Petrarca: Prose* (see note 11, below), p. 1178, by E. Bianchi, who states that "il lavoro vero e proprio di ordinamento cominciò tra il 1351 e il 1353," and the descriptions of the successive phases of Petrarch's work on the collection of the letters by E. H. Wilkins in his *Studies in the Life*, pp. 165–67 and 170–81, and in his *Eight Years*, pp. 236–37 (for these works, too, see note 11, below).

5 V. Rossi, "Sulla formazione delle raccolte epistolari petrarchesche," *Annali della Cattedra Petrarchesca*, III (1932), 62 ff.

ure of a plan that might have changed the further course of his life. At that time he had intended not to return from northern Italy to the Vaucluse, but to settle down in Parma for the rest of his life in a household shared with two intimate friends —a scheme which, if carried out, would have made his *vita solitaria* in the Vaucluse and its impact on his thought a much shorter episode in his life than it was in fact to be. The plan was still-born because the two friends at that very moment were attacked by bandits on a road in Tuscany, and one of them was killed in the assault. Petrarch had explained his intentions in a long letter which on account of the catastrophe did not reach his friends; afterwards he gave the grim news to Ludwig van Kempen (the "Socrates" of the *Familiares*) in another long missive. In the collected edition of the *Familiares*, these two original letters were broken down into not fewer than seven shorter pieces (VIII 2–5 and 7–9); in retrospect, he apparently felt this matter to be of such significance for his life and at the same time to lend itself so well to a clearly organized, impressive narrative that he found the two lengthy original texts inadequate. This process of alteration involved so many changes and transpositions that only a single sentence of the original letters remained unmodified; about one-fifth of the wording was omitted altogether, and twice as much was newly added. Even the basic tenor did not remain untouched: indignation and spontaneous reaction to the reported events were replaced by indications of deep discouragement, perhaps because this was in greater harmony with that general sense of the futility of much of human life which the Petrarch of the 1350's was trying to convey.[6]

It has seemed advisable to recall this incident in some detail not only because it alerts us to the degree of interference for which we must be prepared, but also because it shows that the extensive changes which Petrarch made here were due to an unusual, specific circumstance. Such sizable alterations need not therefore necessarily be typical of every section of the *Familiares*. The fact remains, however, that alterations of this magnitude do occur. When coupled with the knowledge that

---

[6] See the careful analysis by A. S. Bernardo, "Letter-splitting in Petrarch's *Familiares*," *Speculum*, XXXIII (1958), 236–41.

in the *Canzoniere*, too, the autobiographical fact was touched up in places, and that many of Petrarch's Latin works were subjected to often indiscernible changes until the end of his life, it is readily understandable that the earlier hopes for an insight into the development of Petrarch's mind have been disappointed. Indeed, the last serious effort to depict the history of his work and thought in a chronological and evolutionary order was Luigi Tonelli's *Petrarca* of 1930. Since then—with the exception of a few special studies which we shall discuss presently—every scholarly appraisal of Petrarch's position in intellectual and spiritual history has resorted to some kind of cross-section of one or several areas of his work, for which it is maintained that no evidence for lasting development can be found. An early example of a book about Petrarch composed of such cross-sections, each using material from all periods of Petrarch's life, is H. W. Eppelsheimer's *Petrarca* (Bonn, 1926), a work that has largely determined the view of Petrarch held by German readers. A similar neglect of evolutionary factors characterizes the only recent general appraisal in English, J. H. Whitfield's *Petrarch and the Renascence* (Oxford, 1943), as well as the most widely read Italian synthesis, U. Bosco's *Petrarca*, first published in 1946. The same is true of most recent monograph discussions of specific aspects of Petrarch's humanistic thought:[7] each of these authors tells us that, in the present state of our studies, cross-sections that avoid the pitfalls of Petrarch chronology offer the best, if not the only possible, opening for research.

In the influential opinion of Umberto Bosco, not only is this presentation in cross-section required by the nature of a literary lifework of which too little has survived unchanged, but the avoidance of any genetic aspects is in harmony with the peculiar bent of Petrarch's mind. As Bosco argues, we find it so difficult to reconstruct *"la storia della sua anima,"* not only

---

[7] R. De Mattei's *Il Sentimento Politico del Petrarca* (Florence, 1944), W. Rüegg's essay on Petrarch and the concept of *humanitas* (in Rüegg's *Cicero und der Humanismus* [Zurich, 1946]), M. Seidlmayer's survey of Petrarch's statements on many aspects of his Humanism ("Petrarca, das Urbild des Humanisten," *Archiv für Kulturgeschichte*, XL [1958]), and even K. Heitmann's incisive treatise on Petrarch's moral philosophy (*Fortuna und Virtus: Eine Studie zu Petrarcas Lebensweisheit* [Cologne, 1958]), which is in substance an analysis of the *De Remediis Utriusque Fortunae* indifferently rounded out with citations from writings from all periods of Petrarch's life.

because we must depend on texts phrased or rephrased late in Petrarch's life, but also for the more profound reason that Petrarch's mind was unusually "immovable" and "static," "without growth" and preoccupied with the same inner struggles and perplexities "from the beginning to the end" of his life. It is for this reason, says Bosco, that every attempt, from Leopardi to De Sanctis and Carducci, to write the history of Petrarch's love and poetry, has eventually foundered, as has every subsequent effort to point out a pattern of evolution capable of being applied to the analysis of his thought. "The truth is that in no way can we recognize a line of growth—a development—not only in Petrarch's *Canzoniere*, but anywhere in Petrarch. His mind has no history, provided one thinks of him, as one must, in terms of his entire lifework."[8]

This, or something very similar, has remained the prevailing judgment of literary historians and students of Humanism. In W. Binni's surveys on the course of literary research in Italy, *I Classici Italiani nella Storia della Critica* (1954), the author of the section on Petrarch expresses his agreement with Bosco's skepticism concerning any evolutionary approach to Petrarch's work and attributes to Bosco a crucial place in Petrarch scholarship because he has destroyed the old illusion "that one can harmonize the history of Petrarch's life and the history of his works."[9] Among German scholars, Heitmann adopts the Bosco verdict that "Petrarch's mind has no history" and lacks "any line of growth, any development," adding as the result of his own investigation of Petrarch's moral philosophy that the latter, in substance, was "a chaos of contradictions," an unresolved struggle in which the antagonistic points of view "constantly negate each other [*sich beständig selbst aufheben*]."[10]

The pages which follow propose to ask whether these judg-

---

[8] "Il vero è che noi non possiamo in alcun modo ravvisare una linea di sviluppo, uno svolgimento, non solo nel canzoniere, ma in tutto il Petrarca. Egli è senza storia, se lo si considera, come si deve, nel concreto di tutta l'opera sua." U. Bosco, *Petrarca* (Turin, 1946), pp. 9–12.

[9] E. Bonora, "Francesco Petrarca," in Binni's *Classici Italiani*, I, 159–60.

[10] K. Heitmann, *Fortuna und Virtus*, pp. 249–50. Seidlmayer, "Petrarca . . . ," considers the alleged contradictions in Petrarch's ideas so grave as to conclude that Petrarch's Humanism was of real significance only in its psychological—not its intellectual—consequences (pp. 189–92).

ments do not transcend the need for caution and occasional resignation. It may be granted that we incur a risk in making inferences regarding Petrarch's thought in periods about which we do not have as much reliable information as we may desire. But is it not more dangerous to suggest that any changes, not only of the mood reflected in his lyric poetry, but also of his view of man and life, from his youthful conception of Roman *virtus* in the *Africa* to his late philosophy in the *De Remediis Utriusque Fortunae*, were so insignificant that his outlook may be regarded as having been "without a history"? Furthermore, by abandoning our efforts to give reality and meaning to single utterances by relating them to situations from which they may have sprung, we exchange one difficulty for another in still another respect. Can we believe it possible that all the views and judgments that are found in a text of Petrarch published late or posthumously had actually existed simultaneously in his mind as conscious convictions? In view of his habit of keeping his manuscripts for years and even decades and of adding occasional supplements, often in marginal notes, while leaving the bulk of the text untouched, is it not more reasonable to assume that there is much unchanged material in the preserved wording of each work that Petrarch would not have written in the same way at the time of the eventual publication? It may well be a greater distortion of the truth to deal with all such opinions as if they had actually coexisted in Petrarch's mind, than to attempt to assign them their proper origins in spite of the danger of occasional mistakes.

II. Moreover, do our efforts at chronological identification really look so hopeless as long as the intention is not so much ideally to determine the date of every passage in a piece of writing, but rather to collect enough evidence to decide whether Petrarch's views in certain areas changed during successive phases of his life? It is true that Petrarch's habit of keeping his writings indefinitely in his desk usually deprives us of our normal chance of establishing from the year a work left its author's hands for publication whether a certain passage was already in the text by that time. On the other hand, the frequency of Petrarch's correspondence and the preservation of numerous autographs allow us to determine the time and circumstances of the first conception of most of his writings with more accuracy than is possible for any other writer of the Middle Ages and the early Renaissance. In more technical language, while for a given sentence or paragraph we are only too often unable to indicate the date *before* which it must have been written (the *terminus ad quem*), we can nearly always establish a close approximation to the date *after* which it was written (a *terminus a quo*).

That we know exactly the date of the first conception and composition of almost every literary work of Petrarch's is no small matter, and is perhaps the greater part of what is needed for the reconstruction of the course of his thought. There is no doubt about the sequence of the first conception of each of Petrarch's major Latin works—the *Africa* and the *De Viris Illustribus* coming before the autobiographical confessions in the *Secretum;* the *De Vita Solitaria* and the *De Otio Religioso* following, and the *De Remediis Utriusque Fortunae* and the *De Sui Ipsius et Multorum Ignorantia* still later. In every case, the underlying plan of the work allows us to recognize that certain views and evaluations must have been part of it from its inception. The same consideration applies to Petrarch's three great *Invectivae* and to scores of datable letters dealing with matters of significance.[11] We have more often than not, therefore, a chance to ascertain by comparison whether some key ideas of Petrarch's major works were already present in his previous writings. In addition, there are among Petrarch's Latin works a few that for some reason have entirely or essentially escaped his usual changes and revisions. For it is one of the by-products of the critical efforts of the past thirty years

---

[11] It is hardly necessary to say that, in the study of any of Petrarch's works, the safe guides to all chronological questions now are the "Note critiche ai testi" in the two volumes of the series "La Letteratura Italiana: Storia e Testi" (Riccardo Ricciardi Editore): *Francesco Petrarca: Prose* (Milan, 1955), pp. 1161–79, and *Francesco Petrarca: Rime, Trionfi e Poesie Latine* (Milan, 1951), pp. 857–66; and, for the letters, E. H. Wilkins' two manuals: *Petrarch's Correspondence* (Padua, 1960) and *The "Epistolae Metricae" of Petrarch* (Rome, 1956), together with Wilkins' biographical-chronological outline, *Life of Petrarch* (Chicago, 1961), as well as his "intimate biography" of Petrarch from 1351 to his death, presenting a day-to-day study of Petrarch's life, chiefly based on the reconstruction of his correspondence, and divided into three monographs: "Petrarch in Provence, 1351–1353" in Wilkins' *Studies in the Life and Works of Petrarch* (Cambridge, Mass., 1955), pp. 81–181; *Petrarch's Eight Years in Milan* [*1353–1361*] (Cambridge, Mass., 1958); and *Petrarch's Later Years* (Cambridge, Mass., 1959).

that for practically every period of Petrarch's life a small number of such exceptions has been definitively established. A few important examples are: the coronation oration on the Roman Capitol, one of the principal documents of the period preceding the crisis of the *Secretum*, neglected by the author himself during his later years and not published until the nineteenth century; the *Rerum Memorandarum Libri* from his middle years, begun in 1343 shortly after the *Secretum*, but abandoned in 1345 and hardly touched again;[12] the *Vita Scipionis Africani* in the *De Viris*, a biography of which we have no fewer than three datable, successive versions of *ca.* 1339, 1341–43, and post-1352;[13] and from the last period of Petrarch's life (in addition to the *De Ignorantia*) the *De Gestis Caesaris*, not composed before 1366,[14] as well as that storehouse of many of Petrarch's late humanistic and political ideas, the *Invectiva Contra Eum Qui Maledixit Italiae*, conceived and written about a year before Petrarch's death. The same kind of help, of course, can also be obtained from all the *Epistolae Familiares* whose original missive versions have been preserved. Their number is by no means negligible—about 80 letters out of the 350 in the collection of the *Familiares*—even though, unfortunately, too many come from the later periods of Petrarch's life.[15] These are augmented by the surviving missive texts of a few of the *Epistolae Seniles*.[16]

This brings us to another point, one too rarely noted by students in recent years: the most disquieting features detected by the critics of the *Familiares*—the artificial fabrication of entire letters and the rewriting in a changed spirit of substantial portions of others—have few, if any, parallels in Petrarch's other epistolary collections. In the *Epistolae Familiares*, the

---

[12] Cf. the emphasis on this fact in G. Billanovich's preface to his "Edizione critica" of the *Rerum Memorandarum Libri* (Florence, 1943), pp. lxxxii ff., xc ff., cxii ff.

[13] All three are published in *La Vita di Scipione l'Africano*, ed. G. Martellotti (Naples, 1954), pp. 130 ff., 210 ff. See also pp. 29, 35, below.

[14] Cf. U. Bosco, "Il Petrarca e l'umanesimo filologico," *Giornale Storico della Letteratura Italiana*, CXX (1942), 84, 88 ff.

[15] All these original texts are now accessible in the appendices and notes to V. Rossi's edition of the *Epistolae Familiares* in the "Edizione Nazionale." A survey of the pieces available in the missive form is given in the first volume, pp. ciii–cix.

[16] On these, see Martellotti's note in *F. Petrarca: Prose*, p. 1179, and Wilkins, *Later Years*, pp. 305 ff.

interference with the essence of certain pieces results from Petrarch's intention not only to give heightened literary distinction to the collected letters but to create an integrated portrait of his own personality, work, and outlook on life as they existed during the early period in which he had not yet kept copies of his letters and which he viewed after 1350 in a changed light. In the case of the *Epistolae Metricae*, which include much material from the 1330's and 1340's, Petrarch's plan had originally run parallel to the program for the *Familiares*, and he did start work on their revision about 1350 (roughly at the time he began assembling the *Familiares*). This work, however, was not carried very far, as is proven by several facts: promises made in the preface to the intended edition are not fulfilled in the letters; there are striking disparities in the length of the letters and in the space apportioned to the various periods of Petrarch's life (an indication of a lack of elaboration); and finally, unlike the *Familiares*, the *Metricae* were not published in Petrarch's lifetime.[17] As for the *Epistolae Seniles*, which with few exceptions belong to the last two decades of Petrarch's life, the time for possible subsequent, profound transformations of his outlook had then already passed. Scholars have shown[18] that the letters selected for the book edition of the *Seniles* were adapted with moderation, and that the number of newly written pieces and of references to later events is very small.[19] Of course, many lesser alterations were made (as suggested by the preserved missive texts of seven *Seniles*): constant stylistic changes, suppressions of what seemed to Petrarch of merely private interest, and cancellations of names, dates, and places in letter

---

[17] See E. Bianchi's critical note on the text of the *Metricae* in *F. Petrarca: Rime, Trionfi*, p. 865.

[18] Martellotti in *F. Petrarca: Prose*, p. 1179; Wilkins, *Later Years*, pp. 303, 313.

[19] It seems to amount to the inclusion in the book edition of the *Seniles* of one, easily recognizable essay on old age (addressed "ad amicos," not to an individual addressee, *Sen.* VIII 2), and to the re-elaboration of the subjects of two genuine letters in two immediately preceding or following pieces: *Sen.* VI 7 and 8 (of which the latter is not a real letter, but rather a philosophical treatise on "avaritia" that has found its way into the *Seniles*, lacking any indication of an addressee, place, and date) and *Sen.* XVI 6 and 7. On two other occasions, a war and a death of later years are prematurely mentioned, indicating insertions, possibly after the time of the literary polishing: *Sen.* XIII 7 and 8. See Wilkins' *Later Years*, pp. 200 f., 213 f. A passage in *Sen.* X 2, suspected by Foresti to stem from a much earlier letter, has been shown by Wilkins to be an integral part of X 2 (see *Later Years*, p. 131).

headings and subscriptions. But this is only what we must expect in book editions of nearly every humanistic correspondence, and nobody would for such minor instances of unreliability despair of tracing the histories of the intellectual and spiritual development of their authors—provided that in cases of doubt we gave a belabored literary letter second place to the testimony preserved in missive texts or in any other surviving piece of unadulterated information.

Therefore, when everything has been considered and weighed, it appears that the two crucial discoveries of recent critical research—that most of Petrarch's works have only reached us in versions from the later part of his life, and that the *Epistolae Familiares* as well as the *Canzoniere* contain outright inventions—will cause serious embarrassment only in studies of Petrarch's youth,[20] and even this is proving to be a challenge that can be met by the resources at our disposal. For the elimination of those *Familiares* letters which are products of the 1350's or a still later time has given us an opportunity to reconstruct the world of Petrarch in the 1330's and 1340's on a more reliable, if narrower, basis.

III. The portrait of Petrarch during the 1330's and 1340's which can be drawn today with the help of the *Familiares* owes most to Vittorio Rossi, who formulated essential new criteria as early as 1932; to Giuseppe Billanovich, who implemented Rossi's program in a chapter of his *Petrarca Letterato* in 1947; and to Ernest H. Wilkins, who assessed the strength and limitations of the new approach. An attempt to reconstruct Petrarch's outlook in his youth must start from the critical observations of these three scholars.

Rossi, who had been the first to recognize the thorough changes made in many older *Familiares* after 1350, also became the first to recognize the weakness of some of the bases on which the picture of Petrarch's beginnings had rested—among them the belief in the genuineness of Petrarch's famous letter on his ascent of Mont Ventoux in 1336. Naturally, Rossi ar-

---

[20] Of letters later than the 1340's, *Fam.* XII 14 and 16 have been suspected of being fictitious, namely, by Rossi, "Sulla formazione . . . ," p. 67; but Wilkins, *The Making*, p. 317 n. 1, and *Studies in the Life*, pages listed on p. 320, has pronounced both letters most probably genuine.

gued, the long report in *Fam.* IV 1 could not possibly have been written in the evening of the day of the ascent while Petrarch was waiting for his meal in his rustic lodgings, as he contends. The letter is a carefully designed piece of art, an elaborate symbolic interpretation of Petrarch's life and human life in general, *"allegoria dell'uomo che faticosamente vince su questa terra il dominio delle passioni"*—the theme of the *Secretum* of 1342–43. And since, in Petrarch's narrative, his long, aimless wanderings in the valleys are contrasted with his brother Gherardo's straight climb to the mountain top, the letter, as we have it, cannot have been written before Gherardo became a monk in a Carthusian monastery about 1342.[21]

This does not necessarily mean that the entire event described in *Fam.* IV 1 must be mere fiction, including the fact itself that an ascent of Mont Ventoux was made in 1336 and left a deep and lasting impression on Petrarch's mind. There are, however, some suspicious signs which could seem to point in this direction. As Billanovich was later to suggest, the date of *Fam.* IV 1 appears to have been freely chosen because of its symbolic meaning,[22] and—a particularly perplexing observation—the letter itself (one of Petrarch's most fascinating letters!) seems to have remained unknown to his most eager disciples. For when Boccaccio, not yet on terms of personal friendship with Petrarch, during the 1340's obtained a small collection of Petrarch's *"opuscula"* from Naples—where Dionigo da Borgo San Sepolcro, the alleged addressee of *Fam.* IV 1, was the center of a group of Petrarch's friends—the two other known letters from Petrarch to Dionigi (*Fam.* IV 2 and *Metr.* I 4) as well as some letters which Petrarch had sent to other friends in Naples formed part of that collection, but not so *Fam.* IV 1. Is it not improbable that this outstanding piece would have been excluded unless it was unknown to Dionigi and his circle?[23]

---

[21] Rossi, "Sulla formazione . . . ," pp. 68–73.

[22] G. Billanovich, *Petrarca Letterato*, Vol. I: *Lo Scrittoio del Petrarca* (Rome, 1947), p. 195. On the alleged date of the ascension, April 26, 1336, it may be noted that Petrarch was in his 32d year—the same age as Augustine at the end of his conversion. And as for the day, Petrarch says on the mountain top, addressing himself: "hodie decimus annus completur, ex quo puerilibus studiis dimissis, Bononia excessisti."

[23] Billanovich, *Petrarca Letterato*, pp. 88 ff., 192 ff. As early as 1929, E. Carrara, in another context, had drawn attention to the Neapolitan collection consulted by Boccaccio; reprinted in Carrara's *Studi Petrarcheschi* (Turin, 1959), pp. 8 ff.

To be sure, these observations pertain only to the letter and do not necessarily imply that Petrarch's ascent of the mountain and the alleged profound impression made by the experience were mere fable. Like Rossi, Ernest H. Wilkins, in appraising the validity of Billanovich's findings, preferred to conclude that the wealth of personal details included in the letter makes the event itself and the existence of a *"nucleo primordiale dell'epistola, un cenno dell'ascensione"* "written at the time of the ascent," rather "probable."[24] Moreover, it is difficult to consider as mere fiction the story in the letter according to which Petrarch, on the top of Mont Ventoux, opened his copy of Augustine's *Confessions* at random, and chanced upon the words, so appropriate and so provoking in his situation, that "men go abroad to admire the heights of mountains, . . . and themselves they neglect." For unless this story had some kernel of truth, can we believe that Petrarch would have dared to affirm: "I invoke God as my witness, as well as the one who was present [that is, his beloved and admired saintly brother], that on the page where I first turned my eyes I found written . . ."? But while it is important to note that Billanovich's skepticism may have gone too far and that, consequently, one

---

[24] Wilkins, *The Making*, pp. 312, 317. It should be noted that Billanovich, using the same criteria as for *Fam.* IV 1, pronounced IV 3, too, a fabrication of the early 1350's. Wilkins' convincing proof (*The Making*, pp. 320–23) that IV 3 cannot be mere fiction further weakens the hypothesis of the total fictitiousness of IV 1.

While reading the proofs, I received a new paper by Billanovich—"Petrarca e il Ventoso," *Italia Medioevale e Umanistica*, IX (1966), 389–401—in which his former and some new arguments for the completely imaginary nature of the Mont Ventoux episode have been forcefully restated. There is nothing in them, however, to allay the objections to a radical denial of Petrarch's veracity that are listed above on this page. Also, the increasing discovery of classical models for the phrases and literary motifs in Petrarch's letter does in itself not throw any doubt on Petrarch's truthfulness. To make the language and the expressions of recognized literary models one's own and to clothe experiences from one's own life in an inherited guise is the very heart of the humanistic program of rhetorical culture. To some extent, our judgment of how far Petrarch may have gone in outright deception while invoking God and everything sacred to him as witness does not depend on what we regard as proper and usual in rhetorically minded authors, but on our total vision of Petrarch's personality and piety; it is, therefore, bound up with the future development of our views of Petrarch. At present, as Billanovich himself says at the end of his reflections, "the essential thing is to discern for what reasons and at what time" the text which we have was composed in its present structure. On this score, Billanovich's proof of the late origin of the *Fam.* IV 1 (the date is now even more accurately placed in the proximity of the year 1353) is all-decisive for our nascent ability to distinguish Petrarch's early Humanism from the attitudes and values of his later years. This lasting result of Billanovich's new and original approach has been consistently used as a guideline in the course of our discussions.

of the most impressive episodes of Petrarch's life need not, after all, be entirely written off, it has also been conclusively demonstrated that the symbolism and spirit of the report in *Fam.* IV 1 reflects the state of Petrarch's mind during the early 1350's, about ten years after the *Secretum*—and not, as had always been thought, his attitude during the period preceding the *Secretum*. The major features of *Fam.* IV 1 as we have it are evidently *in nuce* the themes of the *Secretum:* a striving for dominion over man's passions, for triumph over worldly dissipations, and a spiritual conversion under the influence of Augustine. The customary view of *Fam.* IV 1 as a testimony to Petrarch's state of mind in 1336 had in effect caused students to read the spirit of the *Secretum* phase of his life into the period of his youth. Now we are for the first time released from this embarrassment, and as a consequence the interpretation of the stages of Petrarch's development is bound to change. In whatever fashion we may try to reconstruct the Ventoux event in detail, it has inevitably lost much of its significance for 1336, and the *Secretum* crisis of 1342–43 must proportionally appear more unique and more important. In other words, it has not become more difficult to recognize a trend and direction in Petrarch's life from the pre-*Secretum* period to the time of crisis introduced by the *Secretum*, but, on the contrary, the difference between these two periods can today be more clearly charted.

The revaluation, and in a sense devaluation, of the famous letter in Book IV of the *Familiares* is only one of the implications of the new criticism connected with the names of Rossi, Billanovich, and Wilkins; perhaps an even more far-reaching consequence is the recognition of the unreliability of a great number of letters in Books I and II. In both of these books Billanovich has noted an obviously artificial arrangement of the dates; an apparently fictitious selection of the group of people to whom the letters are said to be addressed; and the suspicious circumstance that not a single letter of the first book survives in a missive version (although complete absence of missive texts is found elsewhere in the twenty-four books of the *Familiares* only in the case of Books XIII–XIV). From these and similar criteria Billanovich inferred the following bold theory. In preparing the book form of the *Familiares* during the early 1350's, Petrarch first freely invented all the twelve letters of the first book. Then, in Book II, he placed letters actually sent to the persons to whom they are addressed, but—with the exception of II 1 and the very brief last four or six letters which look essentially "genuine"—profoundly transformed, enlarged, and made into *"una lunga catena di 'consolatoriae' e di 'hortatoriae', secondo la suggestione . . . degli maestri d'arte epistolare."* So it is only in the third and fourth books—and even there a few further fictitious pieces (III 1–2, IV 1, and IV 3) must be excepted—that the series of Petrarch's "real correspondence" begins.[25]

Now in this case again one need not accept the thesis without reservations in order to recognize its tremendous significance. Or, rather, this significance becomes even more manifest after some possible exaggerations of the basic idea have been removed. If we focus on the third letter of the first book, for instance, we find a piece that despite its title, "On the inconstancy of the flower of youth," is different from the neighboring *consolatoriae* and *hortatoriae* in that it is a highly personal letter talking continuously of Petrarch's own present youth. Had it actually been written twenty years after its ostensible date, Petrarch would be guilty of several outright acts of deception. For if the letter was not written until the early 1350's, what can one possibly think of Petrarch's saying in 1360 (in *Fam.* XXIV 1, 1–4) that he had written *Fam.* I 3 "thirty years ago," "ages ago" as it seemed to him now; that *Fam.* I 3 was a letter which by virtue of its early origin had to be placed in the first book of the epistolary collection; and that it reflected faithfully his state of mind at that time? In 1373–74, Petrarch once more commented that *Fam.* I 3 had been written "in the period of my youth," about forty years previously.[26] Is it not probable—or virtually certain—that he made these later statements because he was keenly aware that *Fam.* I 3 was one of very few letters which had been preserved from his early years?[27] And there are in Book 1 other cases in

[25] Billanovich, *Petrarca Letterato*, pp. 48–54.

[26] In *Sen.* XVI 1 (XV 1 in *Opera* [Basel, 1581], p. 948), where Petrarch refers to Raimond Subirani, "ad quem, ante hos XL annos, scripta iuvenilis mea quaedam nunc etiam extat epistola."

[27] It may be noted, in further support of the above opinion, that we do not find in *Fam.* I 3 quotations from three classical authors, Horace, Plautus, and Quintilian, who

which free invention of the letters is very improbable, as Wilkins has shown. According to Wilkins' argument, none of Billanovich's criteria actually applies to *Fam.* I 4–6, which are descriptive travel accounts from Petrarch's journeys through France and western Germany and in many details represent too immediate a reaction to the personal experiences of those years to have been written twenty years after the events.[28]

But these are exceptions, and after their elimination the nature of the remaining, suspicious letters becomes more easily recognizable: in addition to the report on the Mont Ventoux ascent, it is most, if not all, of the alleged *consolatoriae* and *hortatoriae* of the young Petrarch that turn out to be the products of a later period, either *in toto* or in essential parts. As long as the series of *consolatoriae* and *hortatoriae* in the first few books of the *Familiares* were still regarded as genuine sources of Petrarch's thinking in his early years, they seemed to demonstrate that a pervasive mood of resignation and pessimism, almost identical with the outlook of the late *De Remediis*, had enveloped Petrarch's life from the beginning. This impression was produced especially by the letters found in the first half of the second book (II 2–8). Here the superscription to every letter, reminding the reader of the wisdom known from the *De Remediis*,[29] directs him to the wearisomely uniform teaching of the letters themselves: that a true sage, proud and immovable in his ataraxy, is not affected by exile, loss of property, or the death of beloved friends; that he may wish not to have been born into this wretched world, but will not highly regard or lament fortune and will never succumb to

---

did not become well known to Petrarch until the late 1340's and are copiously quoted in the allegedly early *consolatoriae* and *hortatoriae* that were actually written later. (See Rossi's "Sulla formazione . . . ," pp. 62–63, and Billanovich's *Petrarca Letterato*, p. 49, on such quotations in the other letters.) After these observations had been written, I noticed that Wilkins, who in *The Making*, p. 314, had called the composition of I 3 in 1350–51 a "probability," revised his opinion in *Eight Years*, p. 241 n. 5, on account of the reference to the letter found in *Fam.* XXIV 1, which "seems to prove that *Fam.* I 3 is an actual letter, though it may well be that it was substantially revised. . . ."

[28] *The Making*, pp. 314–17.

[29] Cf. the "rubricae" of *Fam.* II 2, "Consolatoria super casu amici mortui et insepulti . . ."; II 3 and 4, "Consolatoria super exilio"; II 5, "Multa pati animos ex societate corporis"; II 6, "Absentiam amicitiis non obesse"; II 7, "Expectationes anxias amputandas ut tranquille vivatur"; II 8, "Toleranda equo animo que naturaliter contingunt et ab inutilibus querimoniis abstinendum."

passion. To most of the passages and letters in the early books of the *Familiares* marked by this outlook we may now assign the beginning of the 1350's as the earliest possible time of origin.

IV. It is perhaps too rarely noticed that the epistolary studies just discussed have a close parallel in recent research into the gradual growth of some of Petrarch's historiographical works. Here, too, traditional views have been shattered by the discovery that certain traits, long accepted as characteristic of Petrarch's outlook in his youth, actually belong to his later years and have been read into his early literary works erroneously.

The center of Petrarch's occupation with history was the slow, lifelong preparation of his *De Viris Illustribus*. Pierre de Nolhac seemed to have established a secure basis for the study of this work in 1890 by discovering in a Paris manuscript a version that presented a selection from the great men of action "of all ages and nations"[30] and so included, in addition to the lives of great Romans, a number of figures from both the Orient and the Old Testament. Nothing had been known of the text of this version, to which there were a few vague references in Petrarch's other works. In studying it for the first time, Nolhac concluded that this more inclusive text represented the original plan and that it had preceded the *De Viris* scheme otherwise known from the manuscripts, referred to in the *Secretum*, and presupposed in Books II and IX of the *Africa* —a scheme limited to Rome's political leaders from Romulus to Titus, and among non-Romans including only Alexander, Pyrrhus, and Hannibal.[31]

---

[30] This is how Petrarch himself characterizes the more inclusive form of the *De Viris* in *Fam.* VIII 3 and in the *Invectivae Contra Medicum* (see p. 26, note 38, below). In the preface to the more inclusive text (republished in *F. Petrarca: Prose*, pp. 218–26), he refers to the universal scope of his plan only indirectly, by saying that in a selection of great men of action according to the standard of "virtus" and "gloria" there was no room for the kings of the Parthians, Macedonians, Goths, Huns, Vandals, "atque aliarum gentium" whose rulers have been forgotten.

[31] P. de Nolhac, "Le *De viris illustribus* de Pétrarque. Notice sur les manuscrits originaux," *Notices et extraits des manuscrits de la Bibliothèque Nationale et autres bibliothèques*, XXXIV (1891), 61–148, esp. 99. (For another recently found manuscript of the twelve *vitae* of patriarchs and legendary oriental figures, lacking the preface, see W. Simpson, "A New Codex of Petrarch's *De Viris Illustribus*" [Vat. Lat. 1986], *Italia Medioevale*

Before Nolhac's find, it was thought[32] that Petrarch had originally started out with a Roman project and that this was later enlarged to include the worthies of other nations about the time when he referred to such a plan in the *Epistola Fam.* VIII 3, apparently written in 1349, where we are told that the solitude of the Vaucluse had inspired him "to bring together illustrious men from all countries and ages [*ex omnibus terris ac seculis illustres viros in unum contrahendi*]." The seemingly neat documentation of this sequence—use of the Roman "Titus plan" in the *Africa* and in the *Secretum* about 1340, and reference to an "all-ages plan" in 1349—would appear to have posed an obstacle to the acceptance of Nolhac's thesis, but he succeeded in making such a chronology suspect by suggesting that Petrarch's description of an "all-ages" plan in the letter of 1349 did not refer to the state of the *De Viris* in that year but rather to its original design during Petrarch's first stay in the Vaucluse in 1337–41. As for the *Secretum* reference to the Roman "Titus plan", this did not necessarily refute Nolhac's thesis, provided it was assumed that the mention of the *De Viris* had been inserted as late as 1353–58, when the *Secretum* was thought to have been retouched, or enriched with insertions, at some points.

For the next half-century after Nolhac it was generally considered that Petrarch's historical views had passed from a phase during which he still shared the diffuse and encyclopedic interests of the late Middle Ages (as found in comparable contemporary works like those by Guglielmo da Pastrengo and Giovanni Colonna) to a subsequent concentration on the beloved Roman past.[33] This notion of a slow advance from the medieval outlook to the humanistic idea of history still persisted during the 1940's, when Theodor E. Mommsen made it the basis of his widely read characterization of "Petrarch's

---

e *Umanistica,* III [1960], 267–70.) On the historical scheme presupposed in the *Africa,* see *Africa* II 266–76, where the vision of the history of Rome ends with Titus, and IX 257–62, where the *De Viris* is characterized as a work which deals with Romans— "fortes Romulidas"—and in which "in medio effulgens" and "magnus erit Scipio."

[32] Cf. the conclusion reached by G. Kirner, *Sulle opere storiche di Francesco Petrarca* (Pisa, 1889), esp. p. 8, published one year before Nolhac's *Notice.*

[33] An early example: A. Viertel, *Petrarcas "De Viris Illustribus"* (Göttingen, 1900), pp. 9 f. A late example: E. Carrara in his article on Petrarch in the *Enciclopedia Italiana,* Vol. XXVII (1935), and republished in book form, *Petrarca* (Rome, 1937), pp. 37 f.

Concept of the Dark Ages," a paper which maintained that the "decisive change" in Petrarch's relationship to the past and "a new concept of history" could not have come to pass until his interest in Rome had reached its apogee with his coronation on the Capitol in 1341. Before that time, Mommsen decided, Petrarch had not yet dislodged the "principles" of "medieval historiography."[34] Thus the continuity of the medieval and the gradual rise of the humanist ideas seemed to have been confirmed.

By 1942, however, when Mommsen made this statement, an entirely new school of thought was developing. Since the 1930's Carlo Calcaterra had been suggesting that Petrarch's spiritual crisis of 1342 exerted a more profound influence on his mind than had usually been supposed. Calcaterra had hinted at the possibility that the more inclusive version of the *De Viris* with its introductory discussion of the effects of Adam's fall on human history, and with its string of biblical *vitae*, might have originated in this more religious atmosphere.[35] In 1949 Guido Martellotti, starting not from general reflections on the trend of Petrarch's life, but from a number of exact textual and critical observations, arrived at similar conclusions about the chronology of the *De Viris*. By using various works of Petrarch of which successive, datable ver-

---

[34] *Speculum*, XVII (1942), 226–42, esp. 230, 233, 237. Reprinted in Theodor E. Mommsen, *Medieval and Renaissance Studies*, ed. E. F. Rice, Jr. (Ithaca, N.Y., 1959), pp. 106–29, esp. 112, 117, 122.

[35] Although not clearly suggesting a changed chronology, C. Calcaterra in his paper "La concezione storica del Petrarca"—first published 1939, reprinted in his *Nella Selva del Petrarca*, 1942—had actually placed the more inclusive version of the *De Viris* after the "Titus plan" (in *Nella Selva*, pp. 418 f.); and orally he had reasoned outright in favor of a change in the accepted sequence of the two versions (see Martellotti's report in "Linee . . . ," pp. 52 f.). It is a different question whether or not Calcaterra was right in believing "che il cammino generale dello spirito petrarchesco va proprio nella direzione cristiana," and whether or not we should accept "la tesi principale di Calcaterra, d'un umanesimo petrarchesco progrediente dal paganesimo letterario al cristianesimo" (as Bosco, with personal assent, defined Calcaterra's view of Petrarch's life and Humanism, *Studi Petrarcheschi*, V [1952], 10, 11). The decision will have to depend on what we consider original and historically significant in the second half of Petrarch's life. For when the later phases of Petrarch's work are duly considered, a characterization of Petrarch's development as "progrediente dal paganesimo letterario al cristianesimo" will prove too exclusive. Nevertheless the school of thought of which Calcaterra is representative has helped greatly to open our eyes to the differences between the period of crisis midway in Petrarch's life (the decade initiated by the *Secretum*) and the preceding years of his youth. Here, among other things, Calcaterra's approach has smoothed the path for a more correct understanding of the succession of Petrarch's plans for the *De Viris*.

sions have become available (chiefly thanks to Martellotti's own investigations), Martellotti could show that, contrary to the conjectures of Nolhac and his school, all testimonies to the encyclopedic "all-ages plan" of the *De Viris* point to the years 1351–53. The phases of Petrarch's thought, therefore, said Martellotti, occurred in an order leading from a single-minded interest in Rome to an outlook in closer touch with the ideas of preceding medieval writers. "We see Petrarch starting from the study of some [ancient] texts, contemptuously scorning any help of the medieval tradition; but afterwards, slowly in the course of this study, he accepts, and re-creates in his thought, attitudes and judgments that had also been those of the Middle Ages. . . ."[36] *Epistola Fam.* VIII 3, although originally written in 1349, that is, earlier than 1351–53, does not place any obstacle in the way of these conclusions. For since its missive version is known and the letter in this form does not contain the passage on the *De Viris*,[37] it should always have been clear that the words *"ex omnibus terris ac seculis illustres viros in unum contrahendi"* were not written before the preparation of the book edition of the *Familiares* in 1351–53. We may add that, on the other hand, the reference in the *Secretum* to a history leading from Romulus to the emperor Titus must belong to the *Secretum's* first draft, of 1342–43, and not to a revision in 1353–58, because, in addition to the final text of *Fam.* VIII 3, we have a testimony of Petrarch's plans about 1353 in the second book of his *Invectivae Contra Medicum* (written in early 1353 and sent to Boccaccio in 1355), where the great figures of the *De Viris* are again characterized as "ex omnibus seculis illustres."[38] And to this chain of interlocking cross-references another link has lately been added by the exploration of Petrarch's library: in a Suetonius manuscript,

---

[36] "Noi vediamo il Petrarca partire dallo studio di alcuni testi [antichi], rifiutando sdegnosamente ogni ausilio della tradizione medievale, e poi a poco a poco, attraverso quello studio, accogliere o ricreare in sè atteggiamenti e giudizi ch'erano stati anche del Medioevo." Martellotti in his "Linee di sviluppo dell'umanesimo petrarchesco," *Studi Petrarcheschi*, II (1949), 51–82, esp. 67.

[37] *Le Familiari*, ed. Rossi, II, 198, line 167. (Compare this with the insertion in the book version, p. 160, line 84.) The missive form had already been published by Fracassetti as part of the letter *Variae* 53.

[38] *Invective contra Medicum*, ed. P. G. Ricci (Rome, 1950), p. 45. For the date, see U. Bosco, "Precisazione sulle *Invective contra Medicum*," *Studi Petrarcheschi*, I (1948), 98, 103 f.

used between 1338 and 1342, Petrarch speaks in a marginal note of his *"liber de viris illustribus populi romani"*[39]—precisely what we would expect if that was the time of the "Titus plan."

The thesis of a development from concentration on a Rome distinct from the worlds of the Bible and the Middle Ages to a program more akin to the traditional commixture of the biblical and the Roman past, is more than just another plausible theory. We may put down as fact that critical research, here as in the exploration of the *Familiares*, has definitively discovered a pattern of growth in one area of Petrarch's thought that may be henceforth used as a point of departure.[40]

As Martellotti showed, his findings gain a still wider significance in connection with inquiries about Petrarch's subsequent development. Thus, in discussing the history of the *De Viris*, Martellotti traces three, largely parallel, lines in Petrarch's historical outlook with the help of the *Trionfo della Fama*, of which successive versions have long been known.

One of these lines allows us to trace the appearance of biblical figures in Petrarch's writings in more detail. In an early draft of the first chapter of the *Trionfo della Fama*, datable shortly after 1350, we encounter among many classical heroes three from the Old Testament: David, Judas Maccabaeus, and Joshua. They are the only biblical personages in the pageant, oddly placed among the representatives of Greece. The final version of the *Trionfo*, written probably in the mid-fifties or a little later,[41] includes, however, nearly all the patriarchs and other biblical figures who are portrayed in the 1351–53 version of the *De Viris;* and they appear in an arrangement of the triumphal procession that divides Roman and biblical personalities into separate groups, each shown as an independent historical cycle.[42] The implications are interesting: here, again, there has been a strengthening of the trend toward

---

[39] Cf. Billanovich, "Uno Suetonio della Biblioteca del Petrarca (Berlinese Lat. Fol. 337)," *Studi Petrarcheschi*, VI (1956), 29.

[40] Cf. P. G. Ricci's agreement with Martellotti's conclusions, *Rinascimento*, VI (1955), 166 f., and also Wilkins' detailed assent in the chapter "The *De viris illustribus*" in *Later Years*, pp. 283 ff.

[41] Cf. F. *Petrarca: Rime, Trionfi*, p. 860.

[42] The passage of the earlier draft is in F. *Petrarca: Rime, Trionfi*, p. 570; that of the final version, *ibid.*, pp. 538 ff.

biblical representation during the early 1350's. Furthermore, the process has a distinct articulation: in the stage shortly after 1350, the biblical world intrudes into the world of the ancient heroes, producing a mixture that resembles the medieval mingling of the two worlds; but in the final version, the groups of classical figures have managed to maintain a separate identity from the group of biblical representatives, although the latter now have a somewhat larger share in Petrarch's imagination and thought.

The same successive versions of the *Trionfo della Fama* show that a comparable development occurred in Petrarch's views of the relations between ancient Rome and the early medieval Empire. During his early days, in the *Africa* and in the first scheme of the *De Viris*, the genuine Roman emperors had seemed to him to be only those who were blood descendants of the Roman patriciate; and so he ended the record of the "Roman" Empire with Titus. In the draft of the *Trionfo della Fama* written shortly after 1350, the circle of the rulers of the Empire is so greatly enlarged that it includes not only the later emperors from Trajan to Marcus Aurelius, but even Theodosius and, consequently, reaches the Christian Empire. And again the definitive text of the *Trionfo* does both things: it renders even fuller justice to the Christian element, but also draws a distinct boundary line between the Roman and the non-Roman eras. For while, in the final version, the Christian emperors, Theodosius and Charlemagne, have found their places in a non-Roman group, the group of the Roman heroes has regained a separate identity, presenting figures from the beginnings of Rome to the emperor Marcus Aurelius. [43]

---

[43] Cf. Martellotti, "Linee . . . ," pp. 59–64. The non-Roman group, it is true, does include one Roman emperor, Septimius Severus. But this exception does not impair the definiteness of the distinction between the two groups, because Septimius Severus, as is well known, was the first emperor from a province to show frank contempt of Rome and Italy. Consequently, his exclusion from the group of Roman leaders and inclusion among the "pellegrini egregi" only helps to emphasize the difference between Roman and non-Roman or anti-Roman. The distinction would be less clear and meaningful, to be sure, if Martellotti's assumption (p. 64) were correct that Septimius Severus has been assigned to the non-Roman group because, as a native of Africa, he was racially not a Roman. But this cannot be Petrarch's reason because Trajan appears in the Roman group in spite of his Spanish origin; the mere circumstance that Septimius Severus, in the *Trionfo*, is called an emperor "d'Affrica," just as Theodosius "uno di Spagna" and Charlemagne "un Lottoringo," does not tell us *why* those "Roman emperors" are associated with the non-Roman illustrious.

Finally, a very similar trend is encountered in the history of Petrarch's views of Scipio Africanus Maior and Caesar. It has long been common knowledge, of course,[44] that Petrarch started out by celebrating, in the *Africa*, the elder Scipio as the embodiment of Roman greatness, whereas Caesar, as the destroyer of the republic, was at that time the object of his bitter criticism; and that the same Caesar, in all the relevant works of Petrarch's old age—in the *De Gestis Caesaris* as well as in the *Invectiva Contra Eum Qui Maledixit Italiae* and in the Mirror for Princes addressed to Francesco da Carrara of Padua—appeared as the supreme model and the very apex of Roman history. But Martellotti added the striking observation that in the draft of the *Trionfo della Fama* written shortly after 1350 Caesar obscures Scipio's figure, because he stands resplendent at Fama's right, whereas Scipio, flanked by the younger Scipio, is merely one in a crowd led by Augustus and Drusus. In the final version of the *Trionfo*, however, Scipio and Caesar are placed together at Fama's right at so equal a distance from the deity that the poet feels "*a gran pena,*" as he says, to decide which of the two was nearer to the goddess. The treatment of Scipio and Caesar in the different versions of the *De Viris* essentially corresponds to these phases of evaluation. As Petrarch tells in his *Africa*, the *De Viris* had originally been planned as a history in which "*in medio effulgens . . . Magnus erit Scipio,*" and Scipio's *Vita* seems to have been the first portion of the history which was worked out.[45] During the 1350's and 1360's, however, after Caesar's star had risen on Petrarch's horizon, the biographies of both Scipio and Caesar grew equally beyond the size and significance of all the other *vitae*, with the result that the work eventually had two high points—the figure of Scipio, the symbol of all that had been sacred to Petrarch at the time of his first work on the *Africa*,

---

[44] Or, should be common knowledge. For Gundolf, in his otherwise brilliant picture of Petrarch's attitude toward Caesar, has entirely obscured this development by giving a static mosaic, a mixture of utterances from all periods of Petrarch's life; see Martellotti's appropriate criticism in his "Il Petrarca e Cesare," *Annali della R. Scuola Normale Superiore di Pisa*, Ser. II, vol. XVI (1947), p. 152.

[45] The passages on Caesar and Scipio from the earlier draft of the *Trionfo della Fama* are in *F. Petrarca: Rime, Trionfi*, p. 565; those from the final version, *ibid.*, pp. 531 f. For Petrarch's statement in the *Africa* on the *De Viris*, see *Africa* IX 257-67. On the Scipio *Vita* as the first part of the work done on the *De Viris*, cf. *F. Petrarca: Prose*, p. 1163. Cf. also note 31, above.

balanced against the figure of Caesar, who had become the center of his political ideals and whom he admired personally during the second half of his life.[46]

In all three lines of change in Petrarch's historical outlook, therefore, we find that a trend characteristic of his younger years was overshadowed by contrary tendencies and by the early 1350's at times almost obliterated, but that it was subsequently revived, so that the earlier attainments were not lost, and finally a kind of equilibrium emerged.

Why, one wonders, did these many analogous changes occur in Petrarch's thoughts and convictions?

V. To Martellotti, the final cause appeared to be the gradual expansion of Petrarch's reading, the growth of his learning. There may have been contributing elements, Martellotti said: Petrarch may have become more ready to listen to the voice of the medieval past because of his spiritual crisis during the 1340's and his increased familiarity with early Christian Rome during the jubilee of 1350. He may have taken a more favorable view of Caesar and the Empire after making contact with Ghibelline circles in Milan and elsewhere in Italy; he may have softened his originally almost racial view of *"romanitas"* when he began to hail Charles of Bohemia as Roman Emperor.[47] Yet these and similar factors were accessory, Martellotti insisted. For, as investigations of Petrarch's library suggest, his preparation of biblical *vitae* for the *De Viris* was preceded by intensive studies of Augustine's *De Civitate Dei* and of Flavius Josephus' *Antiquitates Judaicae;*[48] from knowledge of the later Roman emperors acquired in the study of the *Historia Augusta* "the plan is born . . . to carry on the *De Viris* beyond Titus . . .";[49] and "it is from the reading of the *Com-*

---

[46] I here forgo discussing a further line of possible change—Petrarch's views of Alexander the Great. The subject is not vital for the present paper, and Petrarch's evaluation of Alexander in some of his latest works (especially in the *Invectiva Contra Eum Qui Maledixit Italiae*) approaches so closely the Roman bias of his Alexander censure in his earliest works (the *Africa* and the *De Viris*) that it is difficult to assess in a brief fashion the significance of the few more sympathetic words on Alexander in the two versions of the *Trionfo della Fama* in which, according to Martellotti ("Linee . . .," pp. 56–59), we might find traces of the trend recognizable in other of Petrarch's historical ideas.

[47] Martellotti, "Linee . . .," pp. 63, 67.

[48] *Ibid.*, pp. 76 f., 78.

[49] *Ibid.*, pp. 62, 80; "Il Petrarca e Cesare," p. 154.

mentarii [Caesaris] and from the opportunity to add it to the study of Suetonius and Lucanus that the breadth of the *De gestis Cesaris* takes its origin."[50] Basically, therefore, the apparent renewed affinity of Petrarch's views with certain medieval trends was an extension of his cultural interests, a fruit of his studies in his library ("*nasce dai suoi libri*"). "*Precursore della cultura moderna*," he returned to traditions preserved through the Middle Ages, "after having separated from them initially, with the intention to apply his historical method to the results, even though this was still done in a primitive and naïve fashion."[51]

The reconstruction of Petrarch's library and a careful study of the manuscript books owned and annotated by him are among the triumphs of recent critical scholarship, and any judgment on the nature and origin of Petrarch's attainments has to consider the solid bibliographical data which now throw light on his sources and, sometimes, his inspirations. Also, it is indispensable for us to know that the *rapprochement* with some aspects of the medieval outlook during the latter part of Petrarch's life occurred in association with the new methods created by the humanistic studies. Still, though Petrarch's biography of Caesar was written by a scholar who relied on sources not yet or little known to the Middle Ages, this in itself does not prove that the *cause* of his transition from sharp criticism of Caesar in the *Africa* to a new admiration of Caesar in the *De Gestis Caesaris* was the study of Caesar's *Commentarii*. Neither does it mean that Petrarch inserted the lives of biblical figures in his *De Viris* primarily because he had begun to study Augustine and Flavius Josephus, nor that he changed his plan of writing Roman history from Romulus to Titus because he had acquired a copy of the *Historia Augusta*.

Perhaps beneath the benefits derived from our present emphasis on Petrarch the bookman and erudite, there looms a certain danger that we may relapse into conceptions in which the history of Humanism appears as principally a recovery of the ancient authors and as a growth of philological erudition.

---

50 "Linee . . . ," pp. 79 f.; "Il Petrarca e Cesare," p. 152.
51 "Linee . . . ," pp. 79–80; "Il Petrarca e Cesare," p. 154.

One must not forget how diverse the reactions to every discovery of exceptional manuscripts and unknown pieces of ancient literature could be. When Petrarch, as its first reader after many centuries, became acquainted with a substantial part of Cicero's correspondence in 1345, he used his newly gained knowledge for reconsidering and severely censuring Cicero's way of life; he did not look upon the recovered source as a guide to a world congenial to himself.[52] A score of years later, on the other hand, he joyfully acclaimed the commentaries of Caesar as a mine of pure gold. Yet in the hands of civic-minded humanists of the Quattrocento, familiarity with Cicero's correspondence was to become the key to a new understanding of the Roman Republic and a rereading of ancient literature, no less original and even more destructive of the medieval outlook than Petrarch's use of Caesar's *Commentarii* had proved to be. One might perhaps object that the humanists of the Quattrocento evaluated Cicero's political anxieties and hatreds differently than Petrarch had done largely because they were familiar with other classical authors not yet known to Petrarch, especially Tacitus, who did not become accessible until about the time of Petrarch's death. But the scholars of the sixteenth and seventeenth centuries were to reread Tacitus in a fashion that made him appear a guide to despotic monarchy instead of a witness to Rome's fatal losses through the emperors' suppression of liberty—the Tacitus of many Quattrocento readers.[53]

In returning to Petrarch, we observe that it was not the lucky discovery of any manuscript that preceded the extension of his interest beyond Titus to the later emperors. Quite the contrary, it appears that only after his concept of the late Roman Empire had expanded to include the emperors from Trajan to Marcus Aurelius and even to Theodosius—the phase of his historical thinking known to us from the first draft of the *Trionfo della Fama* of shortly after 1350—did he become in-

---

[52] Cf. H. Baron, "Cicero and the Roman Civic Spirit in the Middle Ages and the Early Renaissance," *Bulletin of the John Rylands Library*, XXII (1938), 84–89; and *The Crisis of the Early Italian Renaissance*, rev. ed., pp. 121–23.

[53] For the Tacitus of the early Quattrocento humanists, cf. Baron, *op. cit.*, pp. 58 ff., 66 f., 70; for the Tacitus of sixteenth-century absolutism, Toffanin, *Machiavelli e il Tacitismo* (Padua, 1921).

terested in the *Historia Augusta* as a source of information and ordered a copy to be made from the treasures of the Verona Cathedral Library in 1356.[54] Similarly, it is probably wrong to assume that Petrarch lacked access to Caesar's *Commentarii* until the middle of the 1360's when he began to exploit them in every possible way and to draw from them the portrait of Caesar's greatness that characterizes all his last works. The curious fact is that Petrarch had included a long quotation from the *De Bello Gallico* in his *Rerum Memorandarum* as early as between 1343 and 1345, and although it has been suggested[55] that the quotation might have come to him indirectly through Suetonius, who cites the same paragraph, it is difficult to disagree with the results of Billanovich's attempt to prove that Petrarch most probably knew the *De Bello Gallico* when writing the *Rerum Memorandarum*. For, in the first place, in several minutiae the quotation in the *Rerum Memorandarum* does not follow Suetonius but seems to follow a manuscript of Caesar's genuine text. Furthermore, the well-known Troyes manuscript of Cicero, used by Petrarch early in his life, shows at one point an autograph marginal correction which also suggests that Petrarch had access to the text of the *De Bello Gallico*. Finally, Billanovich rightly wonders whether Petrarch, who grew up in contact with the best libraries in France where the *De Bello Gallico* aroused more interest than in other countries during the Middle Ages, should really not have known Caesar's work from his youth, or not have been able to obtain it if he had wished.[56]

The question to be asked, then, is why Petrarch, although he knew, or could easily have known, Caesar's *Commentarii* from his early years, did not care to use them until the last decade of his life, except for the one occasion on which Suetonius was his guide. It is at this point that Billanovich's argument does

---

[54] See Billanovich, "Nella Biblioteca del Petrarca," *Italia Medioevale e Umanistica*, III (1960), 40. It is probable that Petrarch, one or two years earlier, had begun to look for a copy of the book with the express purpose of obtaining a useful tool for the extension of the *De Viris* on which he was working; for this seems to be indicated by his statement in *Fam.* IX 15 (missive version; 1354 or 1355): "libro illo [the *Historia Augusta*, according to Foresti's persuasive hypothesis] valde egeo in virorum illustrium congerie." Cf. also Martellotti, "Linee . . . ," p. 60 n. 1.

[55] Bosco, "Il Petrarca e l'umanesimo filologico" (see note 14, above), pp. 84, 88–92.

[56] Billanovich, "Nella Biblioteca . . . ," pp. 41–45.

not seem persuasive, or at least sufficiently exhaustive. Petrarch, so he conjectures, may have been diffident about the value of the *Commentarii* because during most of his life he was confused about their authorship, variously attributed to Julius Celsus, Hirtius, or even Suetonius, but not to Caesar.[57] In view of Petrarch's well-known, indomitable curiosity and independence of judgment, this hardly satisfies. Such complete neglect of an accessible work for many decades rather warns us not to view Petrarch too one-sidedly as an erudite whose outlook depended chiefly on the material in his hands. He was a poet and historian who in the prime of life had produced a revolutionary and original view of ancient Rome and would enlarge or modify his new horizons at least as much according to the exigencies of his historical thinking, or according to some fresh experience in his ever-changing life, as in consequence of some further readings. The real question seems to be why, after all, the writer, who in his earlier years had rebuilt the memory of the Roman world by viewing it through the eyes of Livy, Lucanus, and Cicero, at the height of his life withdrew from Cicero the Roman statesman and citizen, and toward its end chose to view the course of Roman history and Caesar's impact on it in the light of Caesar's own writings. It seems to me that in Petrarch's literary works sufficient clues are available for a convincing answer to this question.

VI. Looking at the *Africa* carefully, we find that the same work which so bitterly censures Caesar for "turning his ever-victorious hands against the flesh and blood of his own commonwealth" (*Africa*, II 230 f.) includes a bitter disparagement of the republican institutions, which are presented not as a spur but as a fetter to outstanding men. Indeed, the greatness of Scipio Africanus Maior appears so incomparable in the epic because he achieved so much even though republican Rome begrudged him the independence and perpetuity of leadership which is a matter of course for every monarch. Had Scipio the Elder not been hampered by the termination of offices given him only for a limited period, and had he not

---

[57] *Ibid.*, pp. 41–42.

been obliged to share his power with other citizens, he would have gained so overwhelming a victory that no Scipio the Younger and no destruction of rival Carthage would have been needed after him.[58]

It is certain that Petrarch harbored this devastating criticism almost immediately after his return from his Roman coronation to Parma and the Vaucluse in May, 1341. For it is found not only in the *Africa*, but also in the second version of the *Vita Scipionis* written between 1341 and 1343, while in the first version of *ca.* 1339 the paragraph had not as yet appeared.[59] Moreover in the second version, Scipio's personal experience is made the measure for a judgment on Roman history in general: in order to realize the greatness of the Romans of the republican period (we read here), one must remember that after the days of the kings no leader of Rome was consul for more than a year, nor dictator for more than ten or twenty days; often "an evil and imprudent associate hurt a brave and eminent man." "What—may we believe—would those men have achieved, had they been permitted to wage their wars in the way of kings, without fear of successors or colleagues?" This, clearly, is the language of a writer in whom there was a deep-rooted lack of sympathy with civic life in both the contemporary Italian city-states and the ancient *Respublica Romana*.[60]

Such were the ferments that began to work in Petrarch after his disenchantment caused by the failure of Cola di Rienzo's efforts to revive the Roman Republic during the later 1340's. In the early 1350's, Caesar came to outshine Scipio in the poetic vision of the first draft of the *Trionfo della Fama*, and from about that time the tone of Petrarch's utterances on Caesar is transformed everywhere. Already in a letter of 1352 we find

---

[58] *Africa*, VIII 569–611.

[59] *La Vita di Scipione l'Africano*, ed. Martellotti (see note 13, above), pp. 130 ff., 210 ff.

[60] "Si ergo tot impedimentis obstantibus tot tam claros romanos duces novimus, quid illos futuros arbitramur, si more regis sine successoris aut college metu bella trahere licuisset?" Ed. Martellotti, pp. 211–12. More than one hundred and eighty years later, Francesco Guicciardini (*Dialogo del Reggimento di Firenze*, ed. Palmarocchi [Bari, 1912], p. 109) was impressed by the same passages in Livy that had fostered Petrarch's doubts —"Non avete voi letto in Livio che quelli consuli e senatori romani si lamentavono che per la brevità del consulato che durava uno anno, si perdevano molte occasioni?"— but the point to be learned, according to Guicciardini, was not the superiority of the rule of kings, but the need for the Florentine Republic to have an elected lifetime *gonfaloniere*.

Petrarch wondering whether one should not talk of "Caesar's monarchy" rather than of his "tyranny."[61] It is also unmistakable that these changes were related to the changing conditions of Petrarch's life. The year 1352 immediately preceded the period in which he chose the milieu of the north-Italian tyrant courts for his home for the rest of his life, disdaining a return to his ancestral city on the Arno, so importunately urged upon him by his Florentine friends. From 1353 to his death he lived, with few exceptions, as a counselor and associate of north-Italian princes.

In 1352 his plan to settle down in the Milan of the Visconti had not yet been made, but his connections with Italian courts were close. When late that year he wrote a letter (*Fam.* XIV 5) to the Doge and Council of Genoa, to urge them to conclude peace with Venice, he was, of course, dealing with the affairs of two Italian republics, and the letter reviewed the history of Genoa's republican liberty. It is all the more revealing about Petrarch's state of mind that the rather autocratic regime of the Genoese Doge, recently established, appeared to him as the haven in which the old republic had finally found a refuge after long and devastating civil wars. "Eventually, warned by these evils, you took refuge in the help provided by the rule of one just leader, which is the best condition for the commonwealth beyond any doubt," Petrarch concluded his survey of the history of the Republic.[62] So he was by then already well prepared to appraise Caesar's work with sympathy, and it is indeed during the years 1352–53 that Caesar's name begins to come to the fore in his letters. In 1352, Petrarch was exchanging letters with Niccolò Acciaiuoli, Grand Seneschal of the Kingdom of Naples, who had invited him to establish his residence and "new Parnassus" on the slopes of Mount Vesuvius in the south-Italian kingdom. In this correspondence, Caesar's, not Scipio's, harmonious junction of "strength of mind" and "eloquence" is—for the first time in

---

[61] Moreover, this occurs in a letter written in Cola di Rienzo's defense and addressed to the people of Rome. *Ep. Sine Nomine* 4. In P. Piur's edition (*Petrarcas 'Buch ohne Namen' und die päpstliche Kurie* [Halle/Saale, 1925]), pp. 90, 176.

[62] "Tandem malis admoniti, ad unius iusti ducis auxilium confugistis, qui optimus proculdubio reipublice status est." *Fam.* XIV 5, 29. (The quotation of the *Familiares*, here and subsequently, refers to the book, the number of the letter, and the numbered paragraphs; cf. p. 61, note 29, below.)

Petrarch's writings as far as I can find—used as a model, of which the patron is politely said to be a worthy imitator.[63]

Petrarch's relations to Charles IV of Bohemia, the German king, which began about the same time and resulted in a long correspondence calling upon Charles to revive Rome's political legacy in Cola di Rienzo's place, must also have influenced the balance between the *Respublica Romana* and the *Imperium Romanum* of the emperors in Petrarch's mind.[64] We have a striking hint to that effect from Petrarch himself, who in later years called his eagerness in asking Charles to re-establish the *Imperium* the resurgence of an inherited attitude. During his childhood in his parents' home, he said, he had been taught to respect the *Imperii Romani maiestas*.[65] It is all the more remarkable that this paternal legacy, as far as the postclassical, medieval Empire was concerned, remained dormant until Petrarch's world began spiritually and politically to change from the late 1340's or early 1350's onward. In an appeal to Charles in 1353 to come to Italy and restore the debased *Imperium* of Rome, Petrarch could already call Caesar a figure "to whom I often refer [*ipse quem sepe nomino Julius Cesar*]." In the letter, indeed, Caesar is presented as the model which Charles should follow in building up the Roman monarchy—all this on the basis of Suetonius and an occasional reference to Caesar found in Seneca, long before Petrarch began his serious study of Caesar's *Commentarii*.[66]

---

[63] *Fam.* XII 15, 4 (missive version): "Utriusque Cesaree laudis ornamenta mereberis ut sicut animi robore prestantissimum novimus, sic non modo militariter facundum sed etiam artificiosius eloquentem . . . agnoscamus. . . . Et licet ipse non sis Cesar, quis tamen prohibet Cesareum animum habere, Cesareos mores, Cesaream industriam imitari?" *Fam.* XII 2, 3 (also of 1352): "Nunc siquidem tempus est ut . . . ingentibus negotiis accingaris: nihil est actum, siquid Cesarei moris habes, cum et multa supersint. . . ."

[64] Cf. Piur's comment on Petrarch's first letter to Charles IV, *Fam.* X 1, 1351: with this return and appeal to the emperor "ordnet Petrarca sein politisches Denken, das in jüngeren Jahren wiederholt den Versuch gemacht hatte, die alten Geleise zu verlassen, wieder ein in die grossen Bahnen, die das Mittelalter ausgebildet hatte." (In K. Burdach's *Vom Mittelalter zur Reformation*, II, Pt. 2 [Berlin, 1928], 113.) Already in this first letter, there is a reference to Caesar as a model for Charles: "Scio tibi actus placere cesareos, nec immerito: Cesar es. Atqui primus ille opifex imperii tante celeritatis fuisse dicitur, ut ipse sepe adventus sui nuntios preveniret. Idem fac et quem titulis equasti, rebus equare satage." *Fam.* X 1, 11.

[65] *Fam.* XXIII 21, 2 (1364, as shown by Wilkins, *Later Years*, pp. 79–80) refers to "ille sacer animi calor, qui michi a parentibus relictus atque erga tuam [Charles IV is the addressee] semper ex quo michi primum notus es, erga vero romani imperii maiestatem ab infantia nutritus, in precordis meis vivit et in dies crescit."

[66] *Fam.* XVIII 1, 14 ff., 32, 45.

Petrarch's religious crisis of the 1340's, too, played a perceptible part in changing his initial attitude toward Caesar and the defenders of the cause of the *Respublica Romana*. When he had taken up this cause at the time of his early work on the *Africa*, adopting some of the arguments of Caesar's adversaries, he had passed over not only the political legacy of his Ghibelline forefathers, but also the teachings of Augustine. For the *De Civitate Dei* had tried to expose the vicious note of egoistic ambition and thirst for glory in those who resisted and killed Caesar. Petrarch expressly tells us that in studying Augustine's *De Civitate Dei* he became aware that Seneca and Cicero had been wrong in excusing and even praising Cato's suicide.[67] Petrarch's outright attacks on Caesar's murderers seem to begin with a paragraph which, in all probability, was inserted in the *Secretum* in 1353 or soon after. Here, Decimus Brutus and his allies are called "the participants in a perfidious conspiracy, whose covetousness could not be satisfied by the munificence of such a liberal giver" as was Caesar.[68] Much later, in a chapter of the *De Remediis*, written in 1366, we read that the correct verdict on Cato had already been passed by Augustine. Using him as a guide, Petrarch now finally endeavors to unmask Cato's false pride. In the last analysis, he asks, was not the cause of Cato's suicide envy of Caesar's glory? Was there really need for so much fear of Caesar, that "most clement and benevolent, not only of all tyrants, but

---

[67] *Variae* 33, in *Epistolae de Rebus Familiaribus et Variae*, ed. G. Fracassetti, III (Florence, 1863), 394 f.

[68] *Secretum*, ed. E. Carrara in *F. Petrarca: Prose*, p. 118. The assumption that the passage in question stems from 1353 or later, or was at least rephrased at that time, is derived from the observation that, since several other passages in the same section of the *Secretum* undoubtedly refer to that later period, this entire part of the text is probably an insertion. This will be discussed in the next chapter.

It is true that Petrarch, in referring to Caesar's murder, had already called him "a pure man" ten years earlier (in one of the *Miscellaneous Letters*—No. 4 according to Wilkins' *Petrarch's Correspondence*, pp. 10, 118, written about 1342). But there had been no word of disapproval of the conspiracy at that time; Petrarch had talked about the "consilium occidendi Julii Caesaris" as one "quo nullius unquam maius . . . agitatum est," and had called Marcus Junius Brutus a "vir acer [i.e., ardent] et strenuus." (In Fracassetti's edition of the *Familiares* and *Variae*, vol. III, Appendix, p. 531.)

About that time, more exactly in 1341, a *canzone* among the "*Rime Disperse*" had still called Cato, without any reserve, "quel si grande amico / di libertá, che piú di lei non visse." *Le Rime Sparse e i Trionfi*, ed. E. Chiòrboli (Bari, 1930), pp. 280, 282. It is by comparison with these earlier formulations that the profoundly changed tone in the *Secretum* passage is best recognized.

of all princes"? Was Cato spurred by the "vain" desire "to make his name famous through some great deed"?[69] The scene, then, had already been set for a sympathetic reception of Caesar's own version of his deeds. When Petrarch about the middle of the 1360's began to study the *Commentarii* with increasing care, he read them against the background of a long lost faith in the *Respublica Romana*. He not only found in them a world of new facts, but interpreted these facts in the light of an already changed conception of the Roman past. No doubt it is correct to emphasize—as students have constantly done since Gundolf's *Mantle of Caesar*—that Petrarch's *De Gestis Caesaris* succeeded in drawing a first objective balance sheet of the civil wars between Pompey and Caesar, showing with a truly psychological attitude that there were rights and wrongs on either side in each encounter. Still, when it comes to the historical perspective of the forces which rose against Caesar after his victory, the Petrarch of the *De Gestis* does not think in terms of two antagonistic worlds, of a clash between opposing ideas of citizenship and of the Roman state. He recognizes no other stimulus in Caesar's opponents but "*invidia*," the unwarranted envy that is bound to rise against any great historical figure. The error of Caesar's adversaries is seen, he says, when one remembers that a man who has achieved more than others may also claim more for himself.[70] True, Petrarch pictures Caesar for the first time, in the manner of the Renaissance, as a great personality and as a human model whose fame (in the words of Gundolf) "is no longer associated with a sacred office, or an allegorical significance, or a magical sound."[71] But an equally profound break with the

---

[69] "Quid tam horrificum vultus [so in *Opera*, Basel, 1554, p. 238; "vultum" in *Opera*, 1581] Caesaris habuit, ut esset morte etiam fugiendus, viri omnium non tyrannorum modo, sed principum clementissimi atque mitissimi." "C. enim Caesar, ut erat clemens, nihil aliud efficere volebat etiam in ipso belli civilis ardore, quam ut bene mereri de Repub. videretur." "Cato videtur causam quaesisse moriendi, . . . ut . . . suum nomen grandi aliquo facinore clarificaret." "En tibi alia praeter invidiam causa moriendi vanitas stulta . . . ?" *De Remediis*, Dial. II 118; *Opera* (Basel, 1581), pp. 207 f. For the date, cf. Heitmann, *Convivium* (1957), p. 19.

[70] See Petrarch's *Historia Julii Caesaris*, ed. C. E. C. Schneider (Leipzig, 1827), pp. 208 f., 328.

[71] "Mit dieser Biographie beginnt der eigentliche moderne Ruhm Caesars, der nicht mehr an einem heiligen Amt haftet oder an einem allegorischen Sinn oder einem magi-

medieval mode of thought had been effected by Petrarch's youthful rediscovery of pre-imperial Rome and of the human and national forces—the *virtutes Romanae*—which in the time of the *Respublica Romana* had made Rome great, but had afterwards declined.

In his relationship to Caesar and the *Respublica Romana*, Petrarch's development was so far from being just an expansion of his erudition that there was loss as well as gain. When Petrarch defended the cause of the *Respublica* and attacked Caesar's ruthless ambition in the founding of the imperial monarchy, he had by implication been forced not only to neglect Augustine's views but also to become skeptical about the medieval conception of a divinely appointed monarchy spanning the ancient and the medieval *Imperium Romanum*. At that time he had begun to speak of the end of Rome and her empire in the age of Titus. When, later in his life, he lost his faith in the *Respublica Romana* and viewed the Roman monarchy in a different light, his awareness of the distinction between the Rome of the ancient Roman people and the medieval *Sacrum Romanum Imperium* again dimmed. Although the *De Gestis* speaks of Caesar only as a personality, statesman, and general, and not as the founder or precursor of the Empire in which the Middle Ages had believed, in other writings of Petrarch's later years the renewed concept of the Empire as a half-political, half-religious structure in which antiquity and the present are joined is ever-present.

Not until all these successive factors are placed in focus, shall we be able to evaluate properly the causes and the consequences of Caesar's slow ascent from last to first place in Petrarch's outlook on history and politics.

VII. Whereas Petrarch's religious crisis after 1342 was merely one of several factors in the rehabilitation of Caesar, it appears as the crucial event in most other changes that made the intellectual horizon in Petrarch's later works differ from that in the works conceived before the *Secretum*. This applies to

---

schen Klang, sondern an der Kenntnis grosser Taten und der Betrachtung hohen Wesens." F. Gundolf, *Caesar. Geschichte seines Ruhms* (Berlin, 1924), p. 114; English trans. by J. W. Hartmann (London, n.d.), p. 132.

the gradual expansion of Petrarch's historical imagination to include some Old Testament figures. It is worthwhile to pay further attention to this process, because it has become more easily understandable, thanks to the steady advance of manuscript and chronological researches.

As we have mentioned, during the 1930's C. Calcaterra tried to trace some connection between the biblical interests of the "all-ages" version of the *De Viris* and the *Secretum* crisis. More recently, however, it has been suggested that here as in other areas we might better interpret the changes in Petrarch's outlook principally in terms of a growth in his erudition—more specifically, as a result of his study of Augustine's *De Civitate Dei*, which made it possible for him to synchronize some of the figures of the Old Testament with the legendary world of the Orient, and thus allowed him to give those figures a place in a historical picture.[72] But the fact is that in this area, too, the allegedly decisive stimulus for the enlargement of Petrarch's knowledge—Augustine's *De Civitate Dei*—was not new to him. *De Civitate* had been among the first volumes in his library and as early as about 1333 was listed among his favorite books. So we must keep our eyes open for other influences as well. What we find is that Calcaterra's hypothesis seems strengthened rather than weakened by the results of recent research.

In the first place, we now have an exhaustive testimony from Petrarch himself about the gradual growth of his biblical interests; it is contained in some recently discovered portions of the *De Otio Religioso*.[73] Reviewing the history of his occupation with the Bible, Petrarch relates there that not so very many years ago he would not have admonished even the monastic readers of *De Otio* to study the Scriptures constantly and avidly, as he now advises them to do.[74] Like others, he says, he had then forgone the wholesome nourishment of the Bible, repelled by the "simplicity" and "insignificance" of its outward appearance. Since he had grown up under teachers

---

[72] Cf. Martellotti, "Linee . . . ," pp. 78 f.

[73] Cf. the first complete text of *De Otio Religioso*, ed. G. Rotondi ("Studi e Testi," Vol. CXCV [Vatican City, 1958]), pp. 103–4.

[74] "Et sane quod nunc assero ante non multos annos forte vel tacite negassem." *Ibid.*, p. 103.

"qui psalterium daviticum . . . et omnem divine textum pagine non aliter quam aniles fabulas irriderent," his eyes did not begin to see the truth until lately. The decisive help came from Augustine's *Confessions*, and indirectly from the giver of the book containing this treasure—the Augustine friar, confessor of King Robert of Naples, Dionigi da San Sepolcro. *"Quiescat in secula sine fine felix, cuius manu ille michi primum liber oblatus est."* Wisdom and superior expression had both attracted him to Augustine, he relates. Slowly he tried to follow him, initially with relapses, *"revocantibus me studiis meis antiquis . . . et perdendi metu quod per omnem vitam, quamvis exiguum, non exiguo sudore paraveram"*; but gradually he found himself advancing more rapidly, until the task *"successit, agente Deo, felicius quam sperabam . . . et a semitis meis parumper abductus sum."* The reading of other Church Fathers—Ambrose, Jerome, Gregory, Johannes Chrysostomus, Lactantius—brought further help. "Thus, in the joyful company of the Holy Scriptures, I now move with awe in an area which I had previously despised, and everything, I find, is different from what I had presumed."[75]

There can be no doubt that this development took place before the early 1350's when Petrarch added the biblical *Vitae* to the original Roman plan of *De Viris*. The autobiographical account just cited seems to belong to the original (1347) draft of *De Otio*, since the basic design of the work is itself an outcome of the new relationship to the Scriptures. The *De Otio Religioso* is devised as a paraphrase of a biblical passage—David's *"vacate et videte"* (Ps. 45:11)—which is corroborated by many quotations from the Gospels, other Psalms, Job, Ecclesiastes, Ecclesiasticus, and several Church Fathers, especially Augustine, in addition to less frequent classical citations. In the quoted paragraph we have, then, Petrarch's own description of the period that followed the *Secretum* crisis of 1342. When he tells us that his progress had been slow and not without relapses, and that the full effects had not been seen until recently, we remember that the first major work after the *Secretum*, the *Rerum Memorandarum Libri* of 1343–45, had still been

---

[75] "Ita hoc pulcerrimo comitatu Scripturarum sacrarum fines quos ante despexeram venerabundus ingredior et invenio cunta se aliter habere quam credideram." *Ibid.*, p. 104.

a garner of merely classical memories, while many biblical and saintly examples appear in the *De Vita Solitaria* of 1346, a work written in such a spirit that the author could state in the concluding paragraph that, in writing this book, "I found it something dear to me, often to give a place in my humble, little book to the holy and glorious name of Christ, contrary to the use of the ancients, whom I am accustomed to follow in so many respects."[76]

We can, moreover, with the help of the precise chronological data available today, trace in detail how the changed values of the later 1340's persisted and became a dominant note in Petrarch's theory and practice during the early 1350's, at the same time that he was working on the biblical sections of the *De Viris*. In Petrarch's first *Ecloga*, written 1346–48 and sent to his brother Gherardo in a first draft during 1348 or 1349, a comparison is made between the poetry of Virgil and Homer and the poetry of David. The outcome shows Petrarch already full of praise and recognition of David's songs, but still inclined to seek his own place with the classical poets.[77] In 1353, in his *Invectivae Contra Medicum*, he finally was "swearing with sincerity" that he had not read the ancient poets for as long as seven years. Many of their verses, he said, were of course indelibly fixed in his memory. But he did not read them any more; rather, he was trying to improve his mind morally, writing useful things for posterity, "*et in sacris literis delector.*"[78] He made an identical claim when he composed a portion of his autobiographical letter *Posteritati* about 1353. He had shown talent, so runs this description of his development, in both moral philosophy and poetry, but had come to neglect the latter in the course of his life, "*sacris literis delectatus, in quibus sensi dulcedinem abditam, quam aliquando contempseram, poeticis literis non nisi ad ornatum reservatis.*"[79] We can even identify some of the external factors which determined this process. For in an insertion in the text of *De Otio*, about or not

---

[76] "Dulce autem michi fuit, preter morem veterum quos in multis sequi soleo, his qualibuscumque literulis meis sepe sacrum et gloriosum Cristi nomen inserere." *F. Petrarca: Prose*, pp. 588 ff.

[77] Cf. Martellotti's comment in *F. Petrarca: Rime, Trionfi*, pp. xv, 808.

[78] *F. Petrarca: Prose*, pp. 678–80. For the date, cf. *ibid.*, pp. 678, 1171 f.

[79] *Ibid.*, p. 6.

long after 1350, Petrarch added that his love and knowledge of the Psalter had eventually been enhanced by the "*oportuna necessitas*" regularly to participate in divine services—indubitably a reference to his obligations as a canon in Parma and Padua between 1348 and 1351.[80]

Having read Petrarch's own declarations, one finds it difficult to accept the theory that the major cause of the almost simultaneous appearance of biblical figures in the *De Viris* and in the first draft of the *Trionfo della Fama* can have been the advance of learning owed to a more intensive study of some books long in his possession, especially works of Augustine and Flavius Josephus. The actual sequence of the events must have been different: the student who had learned to read and admire the Scriptures, the writer who had begun to insert the name of Christ and episodes dealing with saints in his works, would have been dissatisfied with a book on famous men and with a pageant of glory without a place in them for the great figures of the Bible and for Christian emperors such as Theodosius and Charlemagne. Hence he would feel the need to acquire more information about these areas of the past because they had begun to mean more to him than previously; and consequently he would look for appropriate information in books in his possession, such as the *De Civitate Dei* and Josephus, and ask for others which were accessible, such as the *Historia Augusta*. We would, therefore, misrepresent his actual development if we drew the portrait of Petrarch as essentially that of a scholar who first directed all his interest to a limited

---

[80] The autobiographical note in *De Otio* on the gradual change of Petrarch's personal attitude toward the reading of the Bible, which runs from p. 103 line 18 to p. 105 line 11, ends with the passage: "Accessit oportuna necessitas divinas laudes atque officium quotidianum, quod male distuleram, celebrandi, quam ob causam psalterium ipsum daviticum sepe percurrere sum coactus. . . ." The first occasion on which Petrarch regularly participated in divine services in virtue of his ecclesiastical offices was offered by his canonry in Parma of which he took possession in December, 1347; he refers to his functions in the church in Parma in *Metr.* II 18. In 1351 he left Parma, to go first to Avignon-Vaucluse and in 1353 to Milan, never to return to Parma. He had no ecclesiastical position in Milan. In Padua he held another canonry, but remained there for longer periods only between 1349 and 1351, and from 1361 onward, a time when work on *De Otio Religioso* had already been finished. (Cf. Wilkins, "Petrarch's Ecclesiastical Career," in *Studies in the Life*, esp. pp. 13, 21-23.) Accordingly, Petrarch's professional familiarity with the Psalter, referred to in the quoted passage, was established some time in the period from 1348 to 1351, and the passage itself cannot be a part of the original draft of the work written in 1347 before his removal from Provence to Parma and Padua.

section of the history of Rome because he did not know enough about other periods, but later included something of the worlds of the Bible, the late *Imperium Romanum*, and the Middle Ages when the collecting, reading, and annotating of his manuscripts had given him sufficient knowledge of those other periods. This would obscure the powerful motive forces in an impassioned life, which from the days of early youth had drawn him in love or hatred into the political and religious struggles of his age, into an involvement from which all his political, religious, and ethical conceptions gradually emerged.

Moreover, an overstatement of the role of Petrarch's learning is liable to distort the general historical perspective of his work. It is, of course, important and correct to state[81] that the biblical and oriental *vitae* in the *De Viris* are different from all medieval biographies because they try to apply to Adam, Ninus, and Hercules the humanistic method worked out for Romulus and the Romans. But this does not necessarily mean that the creation of this group of *vitae* led to the main road of later Humanism, or even to the later major work of Petrarch himself. For humanistic attainments that could exert lasting influence a more profound divorce from medieval traditions was needed than resulted from an attempt to apply the humanistic method of selection and presentation to a pre-humanistic, legendary material. It certainly was not from mere personal whim that when Francesco da Carrara, during Petrarch's last years, wished to translate the idea of the *De Viris* into an actual hall of fame decorated with portraits, as well as brief comments by Petrarch, he insisted on a return to Petrarch's original Roman plan.[82] And, indeed, mythical biographies like the ones mentioned, or those of Noah, Abraham, and Moses, composed in terms of their "*gloria*" and "*virtus*," would hardly have led to that world of new tastes and historical insights for which Humanism, precisely through the work of Petrarch, came to stand. On the other hand, if Petrarch, when adding the *De Gestis Caesaris* to his

---

[81] As Martellotti does, "Linee . . . ," pp. 78–79.

[82] As is well known, Petrarch himself has told us that it was Francesco who insisted on the return to the Roman plan. Cf. Wilkins, *Later Years*, p. 286.

De Viris in his old age, had really still wished to continue in the strongly Christian direction of the 1340's and early 1350's, he would in his *De Gestis* have presented the ascendancy of the founder of the Empire as the crowning triumph of a divine plan for human history, as virtually every medieval writer had done. Instead, the *De Gestis* abandoned every reminiscence of the medieval Caesar legend and of the medieval concept of the Empire. By concentrating on Caesar's personality, and by rediscovering the nature of Roman politics during the civil wars, Petrarch's biography became a true steppingstone to Renaissance historiography.

Some similar comment is needed to characterize the nature of the entire crisis that occurred midway in Petrarch's life. His protestations of a change of spirit in his studies were not repeated in later years; neither the Psalter nor any other piece of the Scriptures actually became part of his humanistic program of studies. The extensive admixture of biblical and spiritual figures in the *De Vita Solitaria* and in the second version of the *De Viris* was not in fact the beginning of a lasting fusion of classical and Christian subject matter. The final phase of Petrarch's development reflected even in this area the rhythm established by Martellotti along other lines: the ultimate balance gave more weight and influence to the values of Petrarch's early years than any contemporary reader of the *Secretum*, the *De Otio*, or the 1351–53 version of the *De Viris* could have foreseen.

VIII. One phase of this development of Petrarch's about which, perhaps, too little has yet been said is found in the ideas and values of his youth. There have lately been doubts regarding the correctness of Petrarch's own contention that his youth had been characterized by a determined classicism and that he had not seen the positive side of biblical and patristic studies until the crisis of the 1340's. To be sure, investigations into the composition of the *Familiares*, as we have noted, have confirmed rather than refuted the validity of the perspective from which Petrarch viewed his youth in retrospect; the modern criticism of the *Familiares* has helped to remove from their first books all traces of Petrarch's later stoicism, as well as the heavy emphasis on his alleged conversion on Mont Ventoux by Augustine's *Confessions*.[83] The reconstruction of Petrarch's library in recent years, however, has seemed to some to raise uneasy questions. Among his early manuscript acquisitions more items of a religious nature have been identified than one would have expected, one of them a major work of biblical instruction: Augustine's extensive *Enarrationes in Psalmos*, purchased in 1337 in Rome and densely covered with Petrarch's marginal annotations. Billanovich, therefore, when he discovered and made available some of these notes, suggested that we may have "to abandon, or at least modify, the conventional picture as outlined by Petrarch himself," the assumption, that is, that "he could not bring himself to study the Fathers until the time of his final maturity"; we rather should recognize that Petrarch developed *"un gusto per i testi sacri"* at a very early date.[84]

This argument would be persuasive if it could be shown that Petrarch spent considerable time and energy on the study of books like the *Enarrationes* before the time of the *Secretum*, but there is actually no indication that more than a few entries of the heavy marginal annotations were made before the period, after the *Secretum*, when Petrarch was preparing his *Psalmi Poenitentiales*.[85] On the other hand, we have available an authentic early testimony by Petrarch himself in an autographic list of books which, as B. L. Ullman demonstrated many years ago, was most probably jotted down in 1333 and represents a record not of the nonreligious items on his shelf, as had been thought in Nolhac's days, but of his favorite books—*"Libri mei peculiares. Ad reliquos non transfuga, sed explorator transire soleo,"* as the superscription reads.[86] In this listing of the central part of Petrarch's intellectual armory in about his thirtieth year, there appear only classical authors with the exception of four works, all by Augustine: *De Civitate Dei, Confessiones, De Orando Deo,* and *Soliloquia*.[87]

---

[83] See pp. 19 f. and 22 f., above.

[84] Billanovich, "Nella Biblioteca . . . ," pp. 15–16.

[85] Cf. Billanovich's communications, *ibid.*, pp. 9 f., 14 n. 1.

[86] "My specially prized books. To the others I usually resort not as a deserter but as a scout," in Ullman's translation. B. L. Ullman, "Petrarch's Favorite Books," *Transactions of the American Philological Association,* vol. LIV (1923); adapted and reprinted in Ullman's *Studies in the Italian Renaissance* (Rome, 1955), pp. 117–37, esp. 118, 134.

[87] *Ibid.*, pp. 122–23.

When this invaluable document is added to our other knowledge, the trends of Petrarch's mind during the pre-*Secretum* period become perfectly clear. The core of his studies at that time was the poetry, literature, and history of ancient Rome, a fare unmodified by any "favored" studies of religious or medieval writings, with the one exception of Augustine. Those *Epistolae Metricae* and *Familiares* of the 1330's whose authenticity has stood up to critical examination fully confirm the sway of his classicist obsession. Augustine, indubitably, exerted some counteracting influence, especially after Petrarch in 1333 had received from Dionigi da San Sepolcro the pocket-sized copy of the *Confessiones* that he could carry with him on his travels. Augustine's stimulation, however, was an exception in the full sense of the word: not an organic part of Petrarch's other studies, but a message from a different realm of the spirit that, except for certain episodes, remained in abeyance until the time of the *Secretum*. Today, we are not only aware that we must not overrate the role of the Mont Ventoux experience of 1336 by viewing it through the eyes of the later Petrarch, but we are further warned by the discovery that in the very year of the ascent, according to his correspondence, he had to defend himself against accusations that he was rendering lip service to Augustine's teachings.[88] One year later, he paid his first visit to Rome, which was followed by a period in the Vaucluse in which the *Africa* and the *De Viris* were conceived and partially written; and, finally, in 1341 came the climax, his coronation on the Roman Capitol. The interests that totally dominated Petrarch's mind during those years were a new view of the *Respublica Romana* as reflected in the plans underlying the *Africa* and the *De Viris*, and (as we know from that unique document, his coronation oration) a bold assertion of the love of glory and the right of passion— a world of ideas in complete contrast to the mixed Augustinian and stoic teachings found in the *Secretum* and in most of his later writings.

Against this background of Petrarch's youth, the key role of the *Secretum* crisis of 1342–43 with its sequels reaching into the early 1350's, far from being a matter of mere hypothesis,

---

[88] *Fam.* II 9, December, 1336.

stands out clearly. In every case to which we have referred, a daring, fresh approach, a turning away from medieval conventions, formed the beginning. But from the time of the *Secretum*, or from the mid-forties at least, those early tendencies became restrained and for a while were overshadowed by attitudes more reconcilable with the traditions of Petrarch's century. Eventually, however, the seminal ideas of Petrarch's youth reasserted themselves in certain ways or forms, especially after 1353 when Petrarch finally exchanged his home in southern France for a new home in the nascent world of Renaissance Italy.

When this precise scheme and rhythm of Petrarch's development is visualized,[89] it seems perplexing that, while such a picture is emerging from the sources, a fundamental and widely read book on Petrarch, like that by Umberto Bosco, should at the same time present him as a man *"senza storia,"* and should be acclaimed by literary students for its denial of any evolution in Petrarch's thought.[90] Perhaps the situation becomes less puzzling when we consider that our answers may rightfully differ if they respond to different aspects of Petrarch's lifework—the lifework of a genius who was three things in one: a great poet, a pioneering scholar, and an original thinker.

Petrarch's lyrical poetry arose from a psychological state of sadness and despair which frequently returned, probably with few changes, throughout his life. And since the poet Petrarch was a child of the late Middle Ages who was perhaps the first to understand the fascination of a new world of values, but was not yet able to bring himself to have a consistent faith in it, there could, indeed, result that melancholic sense of the eternal instability of all things and of man himself that colors his lyric poetry. The danger for us lies in trying to extend a characterization which may be appropriate on its particular

---

[89] Guido Martellotti, to whom more is owed for the beginnings of an evolutional picture of Petrarch's thought than to any other single scholar, has in his "Introduzione" to *F. Petrarca: Prose* surveyed some of the major elements. This sketch, brief as it is, clearly points in the same direction as our present essay.

[90] See pp. 11–12, above. Bosco's *Petrarca* has been republished virtually unchanged, except for new biographical and bibliographical appendices, in 1960 and once more, with only a few bibliographical additions, in 1965.

level—Petrarch's poetry—into a catchall for the study of Petrarch's mind.

In studying the growth of Petrarch's learning and classical erudition, no one has yet allowed himself to be confused by the concept of the writer as one "without a history" and to be diverted from reconstructing the steady advance of classical scholarship as a new discipline in Petrarch's hands. When, instead of Petrarch the classical scholar, we deal with Petrarch the political writer, the historical thinker, the teacher of a new cultural program, or the humanistic "moral philosopher," we would do well to reflect that here again we are proceeding on different levels, and that we need not feel constrained by views which have shown their usefulness in the appraisal of Petrarch's poetry. It has been the intention of the present chapter to demonstrate that there exists no valid reason for letting Petrarch remain a stepchild in the adoption of the genetic methods that have proven successful elsewhere in the study of Humanism. As a fruit of the extensive work of preparation done in recent years, an evolutionary reinterpretation of Petrarch's mind within the framework of his life is in our reach—even though, given his unique procrastination in the publication of his writings and the countless fluctuations of his thought in a century of transition, Petrarch will always set the student of the Renaissance one of his most trying tasks.

2 PETRARCH'S *SECRETUM:* WAS IT REVISED—AND WHY?

I. For none of Petrarch's works are we in greater need of conclusive criteria to distinguish between the first conception and later alterations than for the *Secretum.* This dialogue was intended by its author to testify to his state of mind at a specific turning point in his development—the time after the completion of the first draft of the *Africa,* and after his return from his Roman coronation and from Italy. Finding himself once more in the world of his youth in the Vaucluse and Avignon, Petrarch in his small book expressed remorse for much of the life he had led during the last agitated years, just as he felt Augustine had expressed remorse for his former life in his *Confessions.* In reviewing the inner history of this past period, Petrarch vowed to repress the passions which had torn him away from contemplation and, perhaps, religious devotion. The discourse, which he thus imagined himself to have had with Augustine in a vision or dream, was, as the Proem says, committed to paper in order to remind him in later years of his struggles and thoughts at that moment of crisis; unlike his literary works, the book was not meant to be read by alien eyes or to increase its author's fame.[1]

In such an autobiographical document any subsequent, unnoticed insertion or modification must seriously mislead our interpretation, and there is every reason to believe that

First published in *Bibliothèque d'Humanisme et Renaissance,* XXV (1963), 489–530, under the longer title "Petrarch's *Secretum:* Was It Revised—and Why? The Draft of 1342–43 and the Later Changes."

[1] "Non quem [libellum] annumerari aliis operibus meis velim, aut unde gloriam petam (maiora quedam mens agitat) sed ut dulcedinem, quam semel ex collocutione percepi, quotiens libuerit ex lectione percipiam. Tuque, ideo, libelle, conventus hominum fugiens, mecum mansisse contentus eris, . . . ut unumquodque in abdito dictum meministi, in abdito memorabis." Ed. E. Carrara in the volume *Francesco Petrarca: Prose,* a cura di G. Martellotti *et al., La Letteratura Italiana: Storia e Testi,* vol. VII (Milan: Riccardo Ricciardi, 1955), p. 26. This edition will be used throughout this study. Quotations from the *Secretum* in English follow, though not without frequent alterations, *Petrarch's Secret or the Soul's Conflict with Passion, Translated from the Latin* by William H. Draper (London, 1911).

51

Petrarch in later life dealt with the text of this volume of "confessions" in the same way that he dealt with the manuscripts of his other works, that is, keeping them in his desk for a long time and altering a passage here and a passage there as the years passed by.

There can be no doubt about when the original draft was composed. Apart from unmistakable allusions to the coronation of April 1341 and to Petrarch's past study of Greek with Barlaam, who had left Avignon in October (probably early October) 1342, we are told in the third and last book that Petrarch had been nourishing his love for Laura *"in sextum decimum annum."*[2] Since he had first seen and fallen in love with Laura on April 6, 1327, we may surely be more definite in our dating than the vague "1342–43" usually given for the *Secretum* and regard it as almost certain that the dialogue was composed between October 1342 and March of the following year.

We also have fairly exact information about the date of the transcription of the text on which we must primarily rely. When, after Petrarch's death, Fra Tedaldo della Casa, at the request of the Florentine circle of humanists, copied some of Petrarch's major works, including the *Secretum*, from manuscripts in Petrarch's library in Padua, he found that Petrarch had written the year 1358 at the head of his own copy and had promised, here as well as in the title line, that he would write, as a counterpart to the three books *"De secreto conflictu curarum mearum,"* three other books *"de secreta pace animi"* if anywhere he found peace (*"si pax sit usquam"*).[3] In other words, it was only in 1358 that Petrarch had the final copy made, and since even at that time he considered the possibility of resuming the work, the conflicts and anxieties underlying the *Secretum* had probably remained vital issues until not long before 1358. It would be strange if they had not left their mark on the text

---

[2] Ed. Carrara, p. 136; the allusions to Petrarch's study with Barlaam and to the coronation on the Capitol are on pp. 98 and 158.

[3] "Scripsi Padue ab exemplari de manu dicti domini Francisci [Petrarche]," says Ms. Laur. XXVI sin. 9 in Tedaldo's hand. Title: "De secreto conflictu curarum mearum liber primus incipit, facturus totidem libros de secreta pace animi si pax erit." Special note: "Fac de secreta pace animi totidem si pax sit usquam 1358." Cf. Sabbadini "Note filologiche . . ." (see next note), p. 27.

during the fifteen years which separate the first draft and the final copy.

To reveal such changes is nevertheless not easy. An inquiry into the state of an author's soul and mind such as the *Secretum* represents, where much remains indistinct about the external conditions of life, provides poor material for a critic seeking to discover and date insertions by examining the author's knowledge of contemporaneous biographical or literary events. This method has not been left untried for the *Secretum;* the first—and still indispensable—textual study, a paper by Remigio Sabbadini published in 1917, followed chiefly this line of inquiry.[4] But the results almost without exception were disappointing, and they may teach us to beware of the pitfalls in any method which relies primarily on the identification of apparent allusions to external conditions.

At first sight, Sabbadini's most definitive finding seems to be that Petrarch alludes to a well-known occurrence of 1353. When interrogated by Augustine, in the second dialogue, about the causes of his despondency—his *accidia*—Petrarch refers with tears in his eyes to the blows of fortune, because "on a single day Fortune, with a vicious blow, knocked me, my family and home, and all my hopes and resources down";[5] and Augustine tries to comfort him with the thought that he may in a way be proud that his "small hut [*tuguriolum*]" has shared the lot of so many royal castles which in the course of history have been destroyed by fire.[6] Petrarch's tiny house in the Vaucluse had been broken into and partly burned by burglars on Christmas night 1353, soon after his final return to Italy. So Sabbadini argued that this was the event to which the "*conflagrasse*" of Petrarch's "*tuguriolum*" referred. Here, Sabbadini claimed, we have final evidence that Petrarch revised his work during the 1350's in Milan.[7] Since then, how-

---

[4] R. Sabbadini, "Note filologiche sul *Secretum* del Petrarca," *Rivista di filologia e di Istruzione Classica*, XLV (1917), 24–37.

[5] "Fortuna . . . uno die me spesque et opes meas omnes et genus et domum impulsu stravit impio."

[6] ". . . ut non pudeat tuguriolum tuum cum tot regiis edibus conflagrasse." Ed. Carrara, pp. 118 ff.

[7] Sabbadini, pp. 26 f.

ever, E. H. R. Tatham[8] and E. H. Wilkins[9] have asked how, after all, the partial burning of Petrarch's abandoned "hut" in the Vaucluse could have robbed him of "*spesque et opes meas omnes et genus et domum,*" and today it appears incredible that anyone should have overlooked that the word "*tuguriolum*" must have been used in a merely metaphorical sense, standing for the insignificance of Petrarch's lost ancestral inheritance and family connection in comparison to the historic ruin of royal houses and riches.

Sabbadini's second and related argument has, as far as I am aware, never been contradicted; yet it seems to be based on a similar misapprehension. In the third dialogue, Augustine is made to quote a paragraph from the *Tusculans* which compares the brevity of human life to the life span of certain small animals which, according to Aristotle, complete the cycle of youth, adulthood, and old age during a single summer day. Petrarch's Augustine, citing Cicero from the *Tusculans* on the matter, adds that Cicero had related the story "either in these or at least in similar words, for at the moment there is no copy of that book at hand."[10] It is obvious, commented Sabbadini, "that when the quoted phrase was put into the text the poet was absent from his library in the Vaucluse"; and this appeared to Sabbadini to be evidence that he had come across a change made when Petrarch was away from the Vaucluse.[11]

I am doubtful of this interpretation because it would compel us to accept two scarcely admissible implications. In the first place, if the phrase really meant that Petrarch was unable to consult the *Tusculans* when writing the paragraph in question, how is it possible to explain that he did not look up the exact text while making his last revision and preparing the final manuscript with his library at hand? Second, how can we forget that the remark about the lack of a Ciceronian text is made in the *Secretum* discussion not by Petrarch but by Augustine—the same Augustine whom we find throughout the book

---

[8] E. H. R. Tatham, *Francesco Petrarca, The First Modern Man of Letters* (London, 1926), II, 260.

[9] E. H. Wilkins, *Petrarch's Eight Years in Milan* (Cambridge, Mass., 1958), p. 234.

[10] ". . . aut his verbis aut profecto similibus, neque enim libri nunc illius copia est." Ed. Carrara, p. 210.

[11] Sabbadini, p. 26.

constantly citing the *Tusculans*, often in exact, lengthy quotations. If Petrarch at this one point makes Augustine doubt the accuracy of his own memory, it must be meant to serve as a warning that on this special occasion he is paraphrasing the Ciceronian text somewhat freely—which is precisely what a comparison between the Petrarchan and the Ciceronian wording brings out.[12] Petrarch, in other words, thought it desirable to change the phrasing and the focus of this specific quotation, and Augustine's assertion that he was not vouching for the accuracy of the quotation is nothing but a literary device used by the author as an excuse for taking so much liberty. We would, therefore, make a serious error if we removed the words of Augustine from their literary context, speculating that they allowed us a glimpse at conditions in Petrarch's own life.

We are equally frustrated when we follow Sabbadini's attempts to detect insertions through a search for sources used in the *Secretum* but unfamiliar to Petrarch until some time after the first draft of the *Secretum* had been written. Since we know from indications in Petrarch's correspondence that he did not read Terence *in extenso* until relatively late, and since Sabbadini's investigation seemed to bear out that this did not occur earlier than 1345–46, references to Terence encountered in the *Secretum*, according to Sabbadini, may be supposed to have been inserted, except in cases where they can be traced to some intermediary source. Two of Petrarch's three Terence quotations seem to be direct, and so Sabbadini believed that he had discovered two insertions in the 1342–43 text. But this conclusion, too, turned out to be a deception

---

[12] *Secretum*, ed. Carrara, p. 210:
" 'Apud Hypanim' inquit 'fluvium, qui ab Europe parte in Pontum influit, bestiolas quasdam nasci scribit Aristotiles, que unum diem vivant; harum que oriente sole moritur, iuvenis moritur; que vero sub meridie, iam etate provectior, et que sole occidente senex abit, eoque magis si solstitiali die. Confer universam etatem nostram cum eternitate, in eadem propemodum brevitate reperiemur ac ille.' "

Cicero, *Tusc.* I, 39, 94 (*Scripta Omnia*, ed. C. F. W. Mueller, vol. IV 1 [Lipsiae, 1904], p. 315):
"Apud Hypanim fluvium, qui ab Europae parte in Pontum influit, Aristoteles ait bestiolas quasdam nasci, quae unum diem vivant. Ex his igitur hora octava quae mortua est, provecta aetate mortua est; quae vero occidente sole, decrepita, eo magis, si etiam solstitiali die. Confer nostram longissimam aetatem cum aeternitate; in eadem propemodum brevitate, qua illae bestiolae, reperiemur."

when Arnaldo Foresti's revision of the chronology of Petrarch's letters revealed that Petrarch had known the comedies of Terence not only from 1345–46 onward, but as early as August 1342 and, consequently, in time for the first draft of the *Secretum*.[13]

Of all of Sabbadini's ingeniously established relationships between a few *Secretum* passages and certain known events in Petrarch's life, only one can today still serve as the basis for a valid hypothesis. This is the observation that a reference to some lines of the comic poet Atilius, which are encountered early in the third dialogue[14] and are clearly borrowed from Cicero's *Epistolae ad Atticum*, must be later than 1345 because Petrarch did not read this corpus of Ciceronian letters before 1345 when (as is well known) he found a manuscript in the Cathedral library of Verona. Of course, even this conclusion is not absolutely certain because it depends on how sure we feel that Petrarch, who for a long time had been in close contact with Veronese humanists, cannot have received from them some foretaste of the Ciceronian manuscript. If we exclude this possibility, we may believe that Sabbadini's analysis has succeeded in establishing the presence of one insertion in the text.

His efforts have not remained entirely without sequel. Since in a few places the *Secretum* alludes to Petrarch's own writings, later students have submitted these passages to the same sort of inquiry; but the risk inherent in casual identifications has again imperiled the results. Of the three instances in which our text might refer to works possibly composed after 1342, the reference found in Enrico Carrara's edition of the *Secretum* on page 174, line 12, has been unquestionably misinterpreted. According to Carrara's comment, Petrarch there means his *Epistola Metrica I 14, Ad seipsum*, an autobiographical piece probably written during the Black Death in 1348.[15] This *Metrica*, however, does not mention the failure of Petrarch's life in the Vaucluse to relieve him from his passion of love,

---

[13] Sabbadini, p. 37. A. Foresti, "Quando il Petrarca conobbe Terenzio e Plauto," in Foresti's *Aneddoti della vita di Francesco Petrarca* (Brescia, 1928), pp. 132 ff., esp. p. 137.
[14] Ed. Carrara, p. 142.
[15] Cf. for this date, Wilkins, "On Petrarch's *Ad Seipsum* and *I' Vo Pensando*," *Speculum*, XXXII (1957), 84–87.

which is the point in question in the passage. The work that Petrarch undoubtedly has in mind is *Metr.* I 6; it does include the beautiful image, praised by Augustine, of Petrarch in the Vaucluse, his mind at peace, yet suddenly made restless by the thought of Laura. This poem is older than the first draft of the *Secretum:* it was sent to Bishop Giacomo Colonna as early as 1338.

As for the time of origin of the shortly preceding allusion to Petrarch's *Psalmi Poenitentiales,* I personally have no doubt that these psalms were written in 1347,[16] and in such a case we would, indeed, be faced with the use of a later work. But since it is not generally accepted that the penitential psalms were composed in 1347 rather than 1342,[17] this conclusion cannot be said to be fully assured. We are left with only one incontestable identification: a reference to Petrarch's praise of Italy in *Metr.* III 25, a poem whose date, 1349, is today no longer in doubt.[18]

The result, therefore, is the discovery of a single irrefutable insertion; moreover, we know nothing about its date except that the reference cannot have been made before 1349. Even if we were to add to this finding the two other possible instances —the borrowing from Cicero's *Epistolae ad Atticum* known to Petrarch after 1345 and the reference to 1347 probably implied in the citation of the *Psalmi Poenitentiales*—we would still be far from a starting point from which to explore the nature and circumstances of Petrarch's revision. As far as this broader task is concerned, there seems no denying that until now all inquiries into the text and the composition of the *Secretum* have led to a dead end. Though it has remained the prevailing assumption that the *Secretum* was *"ritoccato tra il 1353 e il 1358"* (as defined not very long ago by Enrico Carrara),[19] this claim

---

[16] As Martellotti has shown to be most probable; see in *Studi Petrarcheschi,* VI (1956), 248 f., and in the Ricciardi volume *Francesco Petrarca: Rime, Trionfi e Poesie Latine* (Milan, 1951), p. 866. Cf. also *La Rassegna della Letteratura Italiana,* LX (1956), 560. According to M. Casali, the date would be a little later, 1348; cf. *Humanitas,* X (1955), 696–704, and *La Rassegna* LIX (1955), 565. The reference in the *Secretum* to the *Psalmi Poenitentiales* is found on pp. 172–73 of Carrara's edition.

[17] Wilkins, *Eight Years,* p. xviii, and *Life of Petrarch* (Chicago, 1961), pp. 37–38, accepts 1342, the date proposed by a number of earlier scholars and especially by Foresti, *Aneddoti,* pp. 106–10.

[18] Ed. Carrara, pp. 172–73. For the date of *Metr.* III 25 see p. 90 below.

[19] In the Ricciardi volume of Petrarch's *Prose,* p. 1162.

has no foundation except the erroneous identification of the *"conflagrasse"* of Petrarch's *"tuguriolum"* with the burning of his "hut" in the Vaucluse during Christmas, 1353. Thus, when E. H. Wilkins in 1958 finally disproved this identity, he could only conclude that although "several passages" of the *Secretum*—which he did not name—continued to look like interpolations, there were in his judgment "none that are definitely assignable to the period of Petrarch's residence in Milan," that is, to the period 1353–58.[20]

But have we no alternative to the treacherous method of trying to identify occasional allusions to Petrarch's life or studies? Is it not possible, even probable, that if any serious later changes were made in a work of literature and auto-biography like the *Secretum*, breaks in the argument or even outright contradictions would indicate the places where inter-ference with the text had occurred? A systematic search for violations of this sort might, after all, disclose gaps in Pe-trarch's apparently smooth train of thought.

The observations which follow are intended to show that by carefully studying the reasoning of the *Secretum* dialogue we can, indeed, detect a number of such inconsistencies and thus create the precondition for a new approach.[21]

II. It is only fair to state that Sabbadini was not unaware of the opportunities offered by this method. He did note that

---

[20] Wilkins, *Eight Years*, p. 234.

[21] No doubt there is a certain hazard in such an investigation before the long-promised, critical edition of the *Secretum*, based on systematic examination of all extant manu-scripts, has been published in the *Edizione Nazionale* of Petrarch's works, especially since the original prospective editor, Enrico Carrara, who died in 1958, promised, when publishing Tedaldo della Casa's transcript in 1955, that "l'edizione critica, attraverso l'esame di tutti i codici, ci permetterà di distinguere anche nel testo del *Secretum* varianti d'autore e di precisare meglio che non si possa alla lettura i diversi stadi della composizione" (p. 1163). I have nonetheless decided not to delay the pub-lication of the following investigations any longer, chiefly because in the absence of such a study we are constantly in danger of misinterpreting Petrarch's state of mind in 1342–43 by relying on later changes and insertions in the *Secretum* text; and it is my conviction that this is being done in publication after publication as the years go by. It must also be considered that no scholar seems yet to have found any early manu-scripts preceding the text represented by Tedaldo's copy; and consequently we can hardly expect to be given variants that on their own authority could decide the prob-lems of the genesis and structure of the *Secretum*. I therefore dare to hope that if and when more variants become available, they will prove compatible with and comple-mentary to the findings at which we arrive through a historical and literary criticism of Tedaldo's text.

Augustine, in discussing Petrarch's *accidia*, is made to scold
him with the words *"in medios urbium tumultus, urgente cupiditate, relapsus es,"* and that this phrase implies that Petrarch,
in opposition to other parts of the *Secretum*, was "away from
the Vaucluse" (in *"lontananza da Valchiusa"*)—a fact which,
Sabbadini argued, is in *"contradizione con l'anno 1342–43."*[22]
But Sabbadini did not follow up the apparent contradiction;
and no later student resumed work on the problem. This may
have been due partly to the fact that the progressive exploration of external evidence had shaken the conviction still
shared by Sabbadini that during 1342–43 Petrarch spent most
of his time in the Vaucluse. When Arnaldo Foresti proved
that *Fam.* IV 15 and *Metr.* II 3, two letters in which Petrarch
laments about the noise in Avignon, belong to the summer of
1342,[23] the idea that Petrarch's "confessions" were conceived
in the *"solitudo"* of the Vaucluse became suspect to a number
of scholars. Before long it was argued that Petrarch probably
composed the *Secretum* while living in Avignon. We find in
Foresti's own studies a tendency to see Petrarch's situation in
1342–43 in this light,[24] while Tatham ventured to say in 1926
that Petrarch "seems scarcely to have been at Vaucluse at all
in the years 1342 and 1343," and that the *Secretum* "was certainly written in Avignon."[25] Nothing characterizes the
change of opinion better than the comments of E. H. Wilkins
on the years 1342 and 1343 in his successive publications. In
his *Petrarch's Eight Years in Milan*, which appeared in 1958,
Wilkins still maintained that "in the spring of 1342 Petrarch
returned to Vaucluse, where he remained—except for visits
to Avignon—until the autumn of 1343." But in his *Life of
Petrarch*, published in 1961, we read that "much as Petrarch
loved Vaucluse . . . , and much as he hated Avignon, the city
held him most of the time from the summer of 1342 until the
following spring"; and in an article on Petrarch's *accidia* in
1962, Wilkins concludes that "the *Secretum* was written in

---

[22] Sabbadini, pp. 25–26.
[23] Foresti, *Aneddoti*, pp. 132–35.
[24] Cf. note 23, above, and note 30, below.
[25] Tatham, II, 209.

1343, probably in Avignon."²⁶ Given this view of Petrarch's life, the argument that indications of *"lontananza da Valchiusa"* denote a *"contraddizione con l'anno 1342-43"* naturally loses its cogency.

But can we go so far as to say that in 1342-43 Petrarch spent so much of his time as a city dweller in Avignon that the *Secretum* must have been written away from the Vaucluse? What we actually know about his whereabouts is limited to the few facts that, after a happy sojourn—or several sojourns—of unknown duration in the Vaucluse during the spring of 1342, he spent approximately the months of August and September in Avignon, where he then learned a little Greek from Barlaam,²⁷ and that he was again in Avignon, probably for a long stay, after Cola di Rienzo arrived there in January 1343. Whether he stayed on through the spring and summer of 1343, not returning to the Vaucluse even temporarily, we do not know, nor can we more than conjecture where he had spent October to December 1342. We can safely conclude, however, that he must have been in Avignon from the middle of January 1343 onward, not only in order to meet Cola, but especially to engage in an upsetting lawsuit at the

---

²⁶ *Eight Years*, p. xviii; *Life of Petrarch*, p. 33; *Speculum* XXXVII (1962), 589, n. 1. It may be noted that the decision in favor of 1343 instead of 1342 (not based on strong evidence, but "believed" to be correct also by Tatham, II, 242) would take us back to a position held by a number of scholars before Sabbadini; cf. E. Carlini Minguzzi, *Studio sul Secretum di Francesco Petrarca* (Bologna, 1906), pp. 11-13. The reasoning of those earlier students is no longer of much practical value today. In the first place, it was based on information regarding Petrarch's whereabouts during 1342 and 1343 which subsequently was decisively corrected through Foresti's revision of the chronology of Petrarch's letters. Second, one of the major arguments in favor of the year 1343, initially relied upon, has with good reason quietly receded into the background: an alleged reference in the *Secretum* to the birth of Petrarch's illegitimate daughter, Francesca (born at some unknown date in 1343). The actual meaning of the passage, found in the discussion of Petrarch's "luxuria," is only that he had lately relapsed into what he called "libidines corporeae" and thus become estranged from his religious feelings ("et nunc meo pudore in antiquas miserias relapsus, quid me iterum perdiderit cum amarissimo gustu mentis experior," p. 100); there is nothing to indicate that a child had already been born, or that the cause of Petrarch's "misery" was anything but his "shame" for once more having been unable to live without sexual intercourse. The relationship of which Francesca was the issue may well have taken place in 1342 and, consequently, can have preceded the *Secretum* even if this work was written during the latter part of 1342.

²⁷ Petrarch may have gone to Avignon a little earlier—there is no definite evidence—but he cannot have stayed with Barlaam for any length of time. Wilkins, *Life*, p. 34, assumes that "beginning perhaps in August, Petrarch studied Greek privately with Barlaam. . . ." *Fam.* IV 15, the letter which tells us that Petrarch suffered from Avignon's heat and noise that summer, also was written in August.

Curia, by which he hoped to be confirmed in a previous appointment to the priorate of Migliarino near Pisa but, instead, found himself frustrated when the cause was decided in favor of a rival claimant on February 28—a decision made final on November 8.[28] Since the rival had registered his claims as early as October 1342, we cannot exclude the possibility that Petrarch had gone to Avignon for the defense of his cause much earlier than January. But no document tells us that he did, or that he was supposed to be present at that stage of the proceedings. Unless we have good reason, however, to believe that Petrarch cannot have spent an extensive period in Vaucluse between October and late December 1342, why should we conclude that he was in Avignon for most of 1342–43, not excepting the period when he composed the *Secretum?*

Moreover, we have a letter by Petrarch—*Fam.* VII 3—dated January 14, 1343, which implies a situation inconsistent with the assumption that Petrarch did not return to the Vaucluse between his stay at Avignon while studying with Barlaam (in August–September 1342) and his stay at Avignon because of the Migliarino litigation. The letter reports to his intimate friend, Ludwig van Kempen ("Socrates"), a dream of the preceding night, wherein he and Socrates had found a rich treasure of coins in the grounds owned by Petrarch in the Vaucluse. The seignorial lord of the region had claimed the treasure for himself, and in the ensuing legal struggle Petrarch had sadly lost his old happiness and inner peace, being forced, in order to uphold his cause, to move to the noisy and restless city—"*iam ab otio ruris ad urbana negotia.*"[29] If one reads between the lines of this parable, one learns two things: that Petrarch must have gone to Avignon for the defense of his cause by January 14 (this was already seen by Foresti, who first drew attention to the letter),[30] and that at this time his stay at Avignon had probably not yet been of long duration,

---

[28] On the Migliarino affair cf. N. Sapegno, *Il Trecento*, pp. 176 f.; Wilkins, *Studies in the Life and Works of Petrarch* (Cambridge, Mass., 1955), pp. 9 f.

[29] *Fam.* VII 3, 5. Quotations from the *Epistolae familiares* refer to the book, the number of the letter, and the numbered paragraphs in Vittorio Rossi's critical edition of the *Familiares* in the *Edizione nazionale delle opere di Francesco Petrarca*, vols. X–XIII (Florence, 1933–42).

[30] Foresti, *Aneddoti*, p. 150.

but had been preceded not much earlier by *otium ruris* in the Vaucluse; for Petrarch would hardly have related that in his parable-dream he "had been transferred *iam ab otio ruris ad urbana negotia*" for his litigation, had he been living in Avignon continuously since the preceding summer.

Since the parabolic meaning of Petrarch's communication to his friend may be open to different interpretations, we cannot call his closely preceding stay in the Vaucluse an established fact. Still, the theory that Petrarch was in the Vaucluse between October and December and there wrote the core of the work which, as it seems, was composed considerably earlier than April 6,[31] appears in this framework to be a better informed guess than the assumption, unsupported by external evidence, that "the *Secretum* was written in 1343, presumably in Avignon."

In any case we need to clarify the circumstances in which the *Secretum* was conceived by scrutinizing the text itself. Despite the perspicacity applied by scholars to the epistolary and other background sources, we must ultimately resort to the approach suggested by Sabbadini's query whether Petrarch's work does not contain embarrassing, but possibly revealing contradictions.

III. I do not find that any student of the *Secretum* has yet been sufficiently aware that the Proem—which is not one of those prologues that might have been added later, but an integral part of the work without which the subsequent dialogue would not be understandable—seems to place the location unequivocally in the Vaucluse. When Petrarch after long introspection finds himself in a daydream in the presence of Lady Truth, he wonders whether she has entered with a companion—a device used to introduce Augustine, the chief speaker. As Petrarch puts it, he was looking around "*an quisquam secum* [*cum Veritate*] *afforet, an prorsus incomitata mee solitudinis abdita penetrasset.*"[32] *Mee solitudinis abdita*—these are key words for his lonely refuge in the Vaucluse, where he

---

[31] Otherwise Petrarch could not have called his love for Laura a passion that had lasted "in sextum decimum annum." Cf. p. 52 above.

[32] Ed. Carrara, p. 24. Cf. also the quotation in note 1, above.

liked to go because no one unwanted would "penetrate" there. Unless one believes that Petrarch could have expressed himself in these terms while thinking of his residence in noisy, crowded Avignon, the *Secretum* must have been conceived as a dialogue with Augustine in the solitude of the Vaucluse.

We can find more indications of this fact. Both Augustine's reasoning and Petrarch's defense are in places clearly based on the supposition that Petrarch is a hermit in the Vaucluse. When Augustine, in the second dialogue, accuses Petrarch of being ambitious, Petrarch retorts that this vice is foreign to a man who has fled the cities ("*Nichil ergo michi profuit urbes fugisse?*"). Was it not proof enough, "that I have scorned public affairs and the ways of the crowd, have gone to live in the recesses of the woods and in the silence of the fields, and have made it very clear that I hate empty honors"?[33] Now it is true that the sentence "*Nichil ergo michi profuit urbes fugisse*" is followed by the words "*dum licuit*," which leaves the possibility that Petrarch's flight from the cities was at the time of his writing an event of the past. But the phrase "so long as it was granted to me" may well have been inserted at a later time, for it has no impact on the argument, since Augustine, in refuting Petrarch's defense, takes it for granted that Petrarch *is*—not, *had been*—pursuing his studies in country solitude. "And as for your boast that you have fled the towns and have longed for the woods," he says, "although you did abandon the road trodden by the crowd, yet your country life is only another way of catering to your ambition. For your objective remains glory, "to which *otium*, solitude, a carefree attitude toward human affairs, and your studies always draw you."[34]

Moreover, the rural situation presupposed in the conversation remains unchanged when Petrarch's life is examined for the next vice, gluttony. Augustine has no fear for Petrarch at

---

[33] Cf. ed. Carrara, p. 94.

[34] "Et quod fuga urbium silvarumque cupidine gloriaris, non excusationem sed culpe mutationem arguit. Multis namque viis ad unum terminum pervenitur; et tu, michi crede, licet calcatam vulgo deserueris viam, tamen ad eandem, quam sprevisse te dicis, ambitionem obliquo calle contendis; ad quam otium, solitudo, incuriositas tanta rerum humanarum, atque ista tua te perducunt studia." Ed. Carrara, p. 96.

this point, even though he occasionally shares a more luxurious meal with his friends to please them. "For as soon as
the countryside has regained its denizen, having snatched him
away from the cities, any [such] temptation . . . forthwith
disappears; and I have noticed, and take pleasure in acknowl-
edging, that when you are alone you live in such frugality
and temperance that you surpass what could be expected of
your years and age."[35] Surely, nowhere in all these passages
does Petrarch appear as a captive of Avignon, or as one who,
having lost his former rural happiness, is now imprisoned by
city life. If these passages were written in Avignon, they must
have been written by an author whose mind was shaped by
his rural solitude and who moved freely to and fro between
the city and the Vaucluse.

When we turn from these paragraphs to the pages of the
Secretum which examine Petrarch's *avaritia* and *accidia* we
must indeed feel puzzled and confused by the contrast. We
have already examined the passage culled by Sabbadini from
the *avaritia* discussion; but one must read the entire page in
context to realize how greatly it differs from the tenor of other
portions of the work. "*Meministi quanta cum voluptate reposto
quondam rure vagabaris,*" thus Augustine paints Petrarch's
rural happiness as a past paradise; then you walked with a
free mind over the hills and through the meadows of the
valley, "*nunquam otiosus, mente aliquid altum semper agitans, et,
solis Musis comitantibus, nusquam solus.*" Like the old man in
Virgil (*Georgics* IV 130 ff.) who, coming home in the evening,
happily spreads out on his simple table the plain fare which
he had gathered for himself, "you would come back at sunset
to your humble shelter; and, contented with your good things,
did you not find yourself the richest and happiest of mortals?"
Whereupon Petrarch cries: "Woe is me! I recall it all now, and
the remembrance of that time makes me sigh with regret."[36]
Then Augustine scolds him: you alone have brought about

---

[35] "Quotiens enim urbibus ereptum rus suum recuperavit incolam, omnes repente
diffugiunt insidie talium voluptatum. Quibus amotis, ita te viventem fateor animadver-
ti ut et proprios et comunes annos supergressa sobrietate ac modestia delectarer."
Ed. Carrara, p. 96.

[36] ". . . nunquid non tibi omnium mortalium longe ditissimus et plane felicissimus
videbaris?" "Hei michi! nunc recolo, atque illius temporis commemoratione suspiro."

the change in your life. "Since you first began to scorn the fruits of your own trees and to find despicable the plain clothing and food of country people, egged on by cupidity, you have once more plunged into the midst of the tumultuous life of the cities."[37] Perhaps God, seeing your sins, will allow "that there, where you passed your childhood under a harsh master, . . . you will end your miserable old age."[38]

A counterpart to this paragraph is the description of Petrarch's relationship to Avignon in the discussion of his *accidia*. Had the cause of his suffering from *accidia* perhaps been a *"latens molestia"*? Augustine had asked, and Petrarch (in the passage already mentioned) had referred to the loss of his family and family property, continuing as follows: "Who could find words to describe the daily disgust of my life, the view of this most dejected and disorderly of cities, narrow and dark sink of the earth, where all the filth of the world is collected?"[39] "What brush could depict the nauseating spectacle: streets full of disease and infection, dirty pigs and snarling dogs," the noise of vehicles, the pandemonium of members of all nations, of poverty and wealth, everything inimical to the work of the poet who needs the solitude of lonely woods. Augustine rejoins that if Petrarch suffers so grievously from the *"tumultus urbium"* he might console himself with the thought "that, since you have been reduced to this frustration by your own doing, you can also escape by your own free will . . . ,"[40] or else he could become accustomed to the noise of the crowd by *"consuetudo longior."* Petrarch replies with a denial that he could easily leave the cities behind. "Although much of what you said provokes me, and especially your opinion that to leave the cities would be easy for me and only a matter of my own will," still I will

---

[37] "Ex quo primum cepisti ramorum tuorum bachas fastidire, amictusque simplicior et agrestium hominum sorduit convictus, in medios urbium tumultus, urgente cupiditate, relapsus es."

[38] Ed. Carrara, p. 86.

[39] ". . . mestissimam turbulentissimamque urbem terrarum omnium, angustissimam atque ultimam sentinam et totius orbis sordibus exundantem."

[40] ". . . quod tua sponte in hos incideris anfractus, tuaque sponte, si omnino velle ceperis, possis emergere."

give up the fight before, as has happened at other times, I lose the day.[41]

We could refer to yet another part of the work in which the conversation is said to take place "*in hac ipsa civitate,*" that is, in Avignon. It occurs in a paragraph in the discussion of Petrarch's *amor* for Laura[42] where Augustine uses these words when advising Petrarch to leave Provence in order to escape the former scenes of his love. But the portion of the text in which the phrase appears is suspect for valid reasons, as will be seen later; this reference to Avignon as the place of the conversation is, therefore, best excluded from the present sifting of the evidence. Yet, even without it the result of our comparisons is conclusive: while Petrarch in some portions of the *Secretum* appears as a solitary whose mind is shaped by his life in the Vaucluse, in the two sections on *avaritia* and *accidia* that happy country life is described as something of the past and Petrarch appears as a city dweller—indeed, as a captive of the cities, from which he finds it difficult, if not impossible, to escape.

So deep a contradiction cannot be adequately explained by the assumption that Petrarch's references to city life reflect the relatively brief span of time he may have spent at Avignon in 1342–43. This, it is true, is the explanation given by E. Carrara in his edition of the *Secretum* in discussing the paragraph which speaks of Petrarch's "relapse" into the "*urbium tumultus*" and of his concern that he might be going to spend his old age in the hated city. A similar assertion had already been put forth by Foresti.[43] Yet no one seems ever to have questioned whether in the winter of 1342–43 Petrarch could really have talked of his peaceful life in the Vaucluse as something long passed, describing it in a reminiscent mood: "*Meministi . . . , quondam rure vagabaris?*" "*Nunc recolo, atque illius temporis commemoratione suspiro.*" To be sure, had Petrarch never returned to the Vaucluse after his journey to Naples, Rome, and Parma (extending from early 1341 to early spring 1342),

---

[41] "Quanquam multa me vellicent, atque illud in primis quod urbes relinquere quasi rem facilem mei censes arbitrii, tamen, quia in multis me ratione superasti, volo et hic, prius quem deiciar, arma deponere." Ed. Carrara, pp. 120, 126 f.

[42] Ed. Carrara, p. 170.

[43] Cf. ed. Carrara, pp. 86–87, n. 3; Foresti, *Aneddoti*, pp. 93 f.

his preceding happy and productive sojourn in the Vaucluse in 1338–39 might have appeared to him in 1342–43 as a "*quondam*" paradise, but the revised chronology of his letters and sonnets has shown that during the spring of 1342 he did take up his former country existence in the familiar surroundings. One of the most serene eulogies of his Alpine solitude is *Fam.* VI 3, dated May 30, 1342,[44] a letter which shows Petrarch at home in the Vaucluse and as profoundly secluded as he had been in any previous year. Here he tells a friend in Rome mock-seriously that whenever he chooses to make a boat trip down the Tiber, across the Mediterranean, and up the Rhone and Sorgue he will find his Petrarch on the Sorgue's right bank: a man without want, and not intent on great gifts of Fortuna; "*a mane ad vesperam solivagum . . . ruricolam*"; a lover of the meadows and hills, "*execrantem curas curie, tumultus urbium vitantem, . . . totis diebus ac noctibus otiosum, gloriantem musarum consortio, cantibus volucrum et nimpharum murmure, paucis servis sed multis comitatum libris; et nunc domi esse, nunc ire, nunc . . . in gramine lassatum caput et fessa membra proicere; et que non ultima solatii pars est, neminem accedere nisi perraro.*"[45] Accompanying this letter was the only slightly earlier Sonnet 114, "*De l'empia Babilonia,*" where evil "*Babilonia,*" that is, Avignon, is contrasted with the happy Sorgue valley, to which "*son fuggito io per allungar la vita.*" And from another letter and poem we know that in the early spring (March or April) he had found it easy to escape at will from the Curia and Avignon, making plans to stay with Philippe of Cabassoles at Cavaillon (near the Vaucluse) and finally deciding to proceed to Laura's birthplace in the country and, eventually, to the Vaucluse.[46]

Thus, no more than about half a year before the composition of the *Secretum*, probably from April to July 1342—for there is no reason to think that he went back to Avignon for his studies with Barlaam before August[47]—Petrarch had been leading precisely the sort of happy country existence in the

---

[44] Proved by Foresti, *Aneddoti*, pp. 86–87.

[45] *Fam.* VI 3, 66–70.

[46] Sonnet 113 and *Ep. Sin. Nom.* I. Cf. Foresti, "Da Valchiusa in sull' aprirsi della primavera 1342," in *Aneddoti*, pp. 85–91.

[47] See note 27, above.

Vaucluse which the *avaritia* and *accidia* discussions tell us he had led *"quondam"* in the past and before he began to disdain rural dress and food, as he was now doing when he felt it difficult "to leave the cities." Can the paragraph containing these statements really have been written under the conditions of the year 1342–43?

The psychological improbability that in 1342–43 Petrarch would have described his life in the Vaucluse as a past paradise can be demonstrated in another way. If one searches his itinerary in detail, one finds that even his *solitudo* of 1338–39 had been merely episodic, preceded and followed by extended activity in Avignon. To be sure, in 1338–39 he had at times been so deeply withdrawn and sensitive to any contact with life in Avignon that once when he had gone to the city to meet one of his best friends he had fled by night in a morbid state, returning to the Vaucluse even before having seen him.[48] Nevertheless, Petrarch must have spent a considerable part of the autumn of 1339 and the following winter in Avignon, since at that time he made the acquaintance of a number of important men whom he can only have met in the city.[49] Provided that *Metr.* III 3 was written in 1338–39, as is most probable, Petrarch was already in those years using his small house on the Sorgue for slipping out of town when his activities in Avignon left him free.[50] All these details taken together make it increasingly difficult to believe that in 1342–43, after spending a few troubled weeks or months in Avignon, Petrarch could have felt that his way of life and the habits of his former years had been substantially affected, or even changed forever.

These observations serve to recall the important fact that

---

[48] *Variae* 13, to Guglielmo da Pastrengo, 1338–39.

[49] Tatham, II, 85–86, 92.

[50] Cf. *Metr.* III 3: "Hic unus cum pace dies exactus aventi / vix totus, tot me laqueis tot Curia curis / implicat." Ed. E. Bianchi in *Francesco Petrarca: Rime, Trionfi e Poesie Latine*, a cura di F. Neri *et al.*, *La Letteratura Italiana: Storia e Testi*, vol. VI (Milan: Riccardo Ricciardi, 1951), p. 784. A letter, *Fam.* V 1, in which Petrarch reports that, having received the crushing news of King Robert's death one morning in Avignon, he fled before nightfall to the Vaucluse, to surrender himself in solitude to his grief ("Hec . . . tibi flens ad fontem Sorgie dictabam, notum procellarum animi mei portum, quo heri ad vesperam solus fugi, cum mane me Rodani ad ripam rumor mestissimus invenisset"), falls in the spring of either 1342 or 1343. Cf. for this date Wilkins, *Studies in the Life*, pp. 216–18.

during all those early years the Vaucluse and Avignon—and, therefore, *solitudo* and city existence—were for Petrarch not really alternatives between which he had to choose. On the contrary, until 1346–47, when he received a well-endowed canonry in Parma with the prospect of further prebends and left the service of Cardinal Giovanni Colonna, his life was tied to Avignon in such a way that, alone or with friends, he could from time to time spend a few days or a number of months in the Vaucluse on his creative work and for the sake of his peace of mind. As late as 1346–47 he was still journeying the few miles to and fro between the Vaucluse and Avignon, as we learn from some of his letters. On New Year's Day 1347, he and Socrates, apparently just for a few, happy vacation days, "on a sudden impulse took refuge here from the noisy and disorderly capital (like shipwrecked sailors seeking shore), motivated by a longing for retirement and leisure." And in August–September, when sending Cola di Rienzo *Eclogue* V, composed in the Vaucluse, he told him in an accompanying letter "I have left Avignon for Vaucluse only recently. . . . It is my accustomed haven from the storms of the Curia . . . in whose service I am growing old. . . . The place is 15 miles distant from the most turbulent of cities. . . . Though it is so near, it is so dissimilar that in passing from one to the other I seem to have journeyed from the extreme West to the extreme East. They have nothing in common but the sky."[51]

His almost simultaneous existence in these two contrasting worlds did not prevent Petrarch from hating the one passionately, whereas his mind was so profoundly shaped by the other that in the same years, 1346–47, he composed the two most genuine expressions of his love of Vaucluse solitude—the *De Vita Solitaria* and the *De Otio Religioso*. Yet, since his life constantly fluctuated between the city on the Rhone and his haven on the Sorgue during the entire period he spent in Provence from 1338 to 1347, we have no way of knowing whether the works conceived during those years were, indeed, composed completely in his solitude and not partly in

---

51 *Fam.* VI 9, Jan. 2, 1347; *Variae* 42, Aug.-Sept., 1347. (The translated passage from *Variae* 42 follows Tatham, II, 406.)

Avignon. In any case, however, even though the text of the *Secretum* may have been written in more than one place, in 1342–43 its author could not possibly have envisaged his life as a process leading from a free and simple existence in nature to captivity in the noise and greed of the *urbes*—the view presupposed in the *Secretum* discussions on Petrarch's *avaritia* and *accidia*. So we must ask whether the text of these two sections was possibly modified later at a time when the alternative between *solitudo* and a final domicile in urban surroundings had become a reality.

It seems to me that a careful search of the *avaritia* and *accidia* paragraphs reveals a definite answer.

IV. In both paragraphs, the accusation that Petrarch has become a captive of the cities is intertwined with the reproach that he has "relapsed" into city life largely on account of his *avaritia*. For, as Augustine charges, it is Petrarch's cupidity that has alienated him from his simple life in solitude; and in the course of the conversation on the causes of his *accidia*, Petrarch himself considers dissatisfaction with his relative poverty one of the major factors responsible for his gloom. Since Petrarch's material and professional aspirations changed as the years passed, the conversations on his "avarice" may reveal connections between passages of the *Secretum* and the external conditions of his life.

In the very first lines of Augustine's reproof in the *avaritia* section that overzealous solicitude has destroyed Petrarch's peace of mind, we find a veiled and puzzling allusion. Anticipating an excuse before Petrarch can make it, Augustine interrupts himself: "You will answer, I believe, that you are motivated by affection for your friends, and so you will invent a beautiful name for your error. But how great is your folly if, in order to be a good friend to someone else, you declare war and enmity against yourself!"[52] These are very specific references which must relate to some definite episode in Petrarch's life. That the description does not fit the conditions of Petrarch's litigation for the Migliarino priorate in 1342 is

---

[52] "Respondebis, ut arbitror, amicorum te caritate compelli, et pulcrum errori nomen invenies. Atqui dementia quanta est, ut alteri sis amicus, tibi ipsi bellum et inimicitias indicere!" Ed. Carrara, p. 82.

obvious; and it is just as obvious that in his later life there occurred a well-known situation which accurately fits the account in the *Secretum*. In 1351–52, when he stayed in Avignon for the last time—and for longer periods than in the winter of 1342–43—he was accused of having given himself endless worries at the Curia by his avarice and ambition, just as he is reprimanded by Augustine in the *Secretum;* and just as implied in the *Secretum*, he defended himself then by attributing his restless bustle—with some exaggeration, but not without truth—to his endeavors on behalf of friends.[53] The "friends" were his son Giovanni, whom he successfully helped obtain a canonry, and more especially a certain Don Ubertino, a protégé of one of Petrarch's most intimate Florentine friends, Francesco Nelli. To intervene in favor of Don Ubertino, says Petrarch in his correspondence with Nelli, he toiled in the offices of Avignon as he had never done for himself; Nelli would have pitied him had he seen him, a lover of freedom and solitude, stuck in the papal palace amid the crowds there. Along with the personal affairs requiring his attention in Avignon, these conditions, he confessed, had made him utterly restless and distressed. "I am worn out, I am tormented, . . . I am wasting my time, but not to fail my friends . . . is worth that much."[54] It is only the knowledge of these events of 1351–52 that allows us to understand the enigmatic intrusion into the conversation about Petrarch's *avaritia* of the assertion that he had toiled largely *"amicorum caritate."*

In examining the section on *accidia*, we find a strikingly similar turn of dialogue at the point where Petrarch sees a major cause of his *accidia* in the frequent malevolence of Fortuna from which he had suffered. Augustine, who considers this complaint an indication of Petrarch's latent avarice, charges that the root of the evil is Petrarch's ambition for a *"primus locus"* in life when he should be seeking *"mediocritas."*

---

[53] See, for instance, Sapegno, *Il Trecento*, pp. 184 f.; for the charge of avarice brought against him by his enemies in 1352 cf. *Fam.* XIV 4, and Wilkins, *Studies in the Life*, p. 24.

[54] "'Quid facis in curia?' langueo crucior affligor indignor et, qua nulla iactura gravior, . . . tempus perdo. . . . Sed tanti est amicorum votis ac precibus non deesse." *Fam.* IX 5, 45 (Dec., 1351). Cf. also the description in Wilkins, *Life of Petrarch*, pp. 112 f., and *Studies in the Life*, pp. 85 f., 103, 127.

"But it is precisely this that throws you headlong into this distress: the very fact that everyone is oblivious of his lot and strives for the highest place. . . . If men were only aware of the misery of high status, they would tremble at the thought of it, instead of desiring it." No one should know this better than Petrarch, "whom experience has long persuaded that all the fortune of very high status is nothing but toil, trouble, and misery."[55] Petrarch roundly denies the charge. "That I have never aspired to first place [*summum nempe nunquam me locum exoptasse*], Lady Truth, here, who watches all of us and knows all my thoughts, is my witness." She knows that he has always held to the conviction that "the tranquillity and serenity of mind" for which he longs is alien to the "*supremum fortune culmen*"; "and, therefore, I have abhorred a life full of anxieties and cares and have prudently preferred a mediocre state." As proof he refers to the fact that he had been criticized for "indolence and lack of energy [*secordiam atque segnitiem vocant*]" because he had not striven for more.[56]

If there were really no truth behind Augustine's accusation, why such a dispute in a book of "confessions" in which the Church Father is the representative of Petrarch's own conscience and a teacher who is to uncover those secret trends of Petrarch's mind which he tries to hide from himself? Clearly, the presence of these charges in the *Secretum* means that Petrarch had at least harbored desires, or entertained hopes, for a higher position in life than was compatible with the "*mediocritas*" he professed. We must probably also consider it a fact that his normal reluctance to aspire to the higher curial offices open to a man with his personal connections and gifts had been criticized as "*secordia atque segnities*".

To comment thus on the meaning of the paragraph is to recognize that in all likelihood it cannot have been written in 1342–43. Apart from being *capellanus* of Cardinal Colonna, Petrarch had by then just begun, in the manner of the time, to accumulate a few clerical prebends: a canonry at Lombez in

---

[55] "Sed hoc est quod vos in has precipitat erumnas: proprie quilibet sortis oblitus supremum mente locum agitat. . . . Quod si summi status miserias agnoscerent homines, quem exoptant perhorrescerent." Especially Petrarch should know, "cui longa experientia persuasum est omnem status altissimi laboriosam atque solicitam et prorsus miserabilem esse fortunam."

[56] Ed. Carrara, pp. 112–14.

1335 and a canonry at Pisa in 1342; besides these, if he had been successful he would have added—or would have replaced some of them with—the priorate of Migliarino. At this time, when his clerical career was still so modest, what point would there have been in discussing whether Petrarch was free from the sin of aspiring to the highest places? Nor does one see how and why the opposite criticism—that he had not stirred himself enough to obtain greater prizes—could have been leveled against him at that stage.

As for his claim in the same paragraph that he had always striven for "*aurea mediocritas*" in the Horatian sense but "to my grief have, indeed, never seen *mediocritas* become my lot,"[57] his actual reactions during the period preceding 1342–43 reveal that he had thought of himself as rather a recluse, happy and proud in his poverty. In a description of his life in the Vaucluse, contained in *Metr.* I 6, he explains his state of mind in 1338 as follows: "the first thing is that the association which fits my wishes best is the bond with poverty—a golden poverty, not something sordid, nor a poverty that is a sulky guest. If only Fortuna lets me keep my small estate, my tiny house, and my sweet books, she may retain everything else. . . . I do not care for landed wealth, nor for my father's fortune, heavy burden that it is for someone striving for higher things . . . ; provided that my leisure, not poisoned by ambition, remains undisturbed."[58] That this was still Petrarch's style of living and thinking after his journey to Italy we know from the above-cited picture of his regained solitude in May 1342, where his Roman friend is told he would find Petrarch on the right bank of the Sorgue, "in want of nothing, and not expecting anything too eagerly from Fortuna's hands."[59] When the mirage of the Migliarino priorate arose four months

---

57 ". . . hanc profecto mediocritatem nunquam michi contigisse doleo." Ed. Carrara, p. 114.

58 "Hoc primum placitis mecum concordat egestas / aurea federibus, non sordida nec gravis hospes. / Si libet, exigui fines michi servet agelli / angustamque domum et dulces Fortuna libellos; / cetera secum habeat vel, si libet, omnia nullo / auferat hinc strepitu; sua sunt. Non rura requiro, / divitiasque patris, pondus grave celsa petenti / vinclaque dura animi et cuntorum alimenta malorum; / Cireas non tangat opes nec nostra lacessat / otia, sollicito non ambitiosa paratu." *Metr.* I 6, in *Francesco Petrarca: Rime, Trionfi e Poesie Latine*, pp. 726-28.

59 ". . . nullius egentem rei, nil magnopere de fortune manibus expectantem." See p. 67 above.

later, he became, to be sure, untrue to his former self and did hope for some larger gift from Fortuna. But even this not unusual priorate was nothing one might have considered a *"primus"* or *"supremus locus"*, whereas, on the other hand, Petrarch could never have been less blamed for professional *"secordia et segnities"* than during his all too eager litigation for Migliarino in 1342–43.

Whereas from the perspective of 1342–43 these aspects of the paragraph on *accidia* are as little intelligible as were the passages on *avaritia*, we can find circumstances in Petrarch's later life that correspond closely to Augustine's reproaches. Again it is his experience during his last stay in Avignon, in 1351–52, that accurately fits the account in the *Secretum*. The "avarice" with which he was charged at that time included suspected aspirations for a high curial office even though nothing came of them; and afterwards Petrarch defended himself with precisely those arguments in favor of an unburdened, lower station that he puts into the mouth of Augustine in the two paragraphs of the *Secretum*.[60]

One office offered to him was that of papal secretary—a proposal already made and declined for the first time in 1347. But in 1351–52 Petrarch's reaction was no longer entirely negative, for he did work out and present a draft of a chancery document, which, however, merely proved to everyone that he was not the right man for bureaucratic work.[61] And why in 1351, on learning that he was wanted at the papal court, had Petrarch moved back from Italy to Avignon at all, although several Italian friends had tried to dissuade him?[62]

---

[60] *Fam.* XVI 3, 4: "Nunquam tantum habere continget quin multis et michi ipsi, si avaritie credidero, pauperrimus ac mendicus videar; luxuria et avaritia et ambitio nullis finibus sunt contente; falsis vero opinionibus omnia plena sunt, quibus nisi resistitur, urgent usque ad extrema miseriarum; . . . quibus qui se ferendum dedit, ubi voluerit non subsistet." Cf. these convictions of Petrarch in March, 1353, with Augustine's teaching in the *Secretum:* "Quid ergo te crucias? Si ad naturam tuam te metiris, iam pridem dives eras; si ad populi plausum, dives esse nunquam poteris, semperque aliud restabit, quod sequens per cupiditatum abrupta rapiaris." "Sufficiebant tua quidem usibus necessariis, si tu ipse tibi suffecisses; nunc autem ipse quam pateris indigentiam peperisti. Cumulationem enim opum necessitatem ac solicitudinem cumulare, iam totiens disputatum est." Ed. Carrara, pp. 86, 88.

[61] P. Piur, *Petrarcas 'Buch ohne Namen' und die päpstliche Kurie* (Halle/Saale, 1925), p. 118. For the date concerning the position of secretary, cf. also Wilkins, *Studies in the Life*, p. 102.

[62] See Wilkins, *Studies in the Life*, p. 76.

If his reaction to the offer of a position as papal secretary was half-hearted, had even higher aspirations perhaps urged him to cross the Alps? His letters are ambiguous on this point, but it has always been suspected that he may have been hoping for as much as a cardinalate. E. H. Wilkins, in the latest re-examination of this affair, has concluded that the conflicting evidence presumably reflects a real struggle in Petrarch's mind, and that, if he ever did wrestle with such desires, he must have done so between 1350 and 1352.[63] In any event, such rumors were circulating, and Petrarch was painfully aware of them. On the other hand, he was at that time re-proached by friends for his lack of response to the offer of a papal secretaryship—a burdensome, but esteemed and richly paid office—with the same arguments against which he defends himself before Augustine in the *Secretum.* "You and all my friends *to whom I appear too indolent* [*quibus segnior appareo*] should know," so he wrote to Nelli in March 1353, "that I have vowed to keep my aspirations within the bounds of moderation."[64]

Thus the complex and apparently confusing situation pre-supposed in the *accidia* section of the *Secretum*—Petrarch aspiring for a *"primus locus"* in spite of all his denials, and at the same time reproached for not aspiring enough—actually existed in 1351–53, the very time when he also exerted himself strongly in the interest of friends, in the manner reflected in the *avaritia* section of the *Secretum.*

After having detected events of the early 1350's behind the reproof of Petrarch's aspiration for a *"primus locus"*, one wonders whether the passages professing *"mediocritas"* of fortune as his ideal may not equally point to conditions of his later years. In the sentences immediately following the dis-cussion of *"primus locus"* we find first two extensive quotations from Horace's *Carmina,* cited as illustrations of Horatian *aurea mediocritas.*[65] Although arguments based on the dates of Petrarch's first familiarity with certain ancient authors are

---

[63] *Ibid.,* pp. 76 ff., esp. p. 80.

[64] *Fam.* XVI 3, 3. We know of similar reproaches in later years, but these fall after 1358; cf. "amicis licet indignantibus" in *Fam.* XX 14, 17, 1359, and "Indignantibus dominis et amicis" in *Var.* 15, 1371.

[65] Ed. Carrara, p. 114.

75

dangerous, as we have seen, it is a fact that Horace's *Carmina* (Odes) were not well known during the Middle Ages, and that Petrarch did not read them thoroughly and use them widely until 1350–51.[66]

The quotations are followed by the assertion, already mentioned, that Petrarch had always striven in vain for "*mediocritas,*" and that no one in his generation "*modestiora concupiverit, nemo difficilius ad concupita provectus est.*"[67] Not only would it be difficult before the Migliarino affair of 1342–43[68] to find a situation in which Petrarch had thought himself too poor and had vainly striven to increase his income, but in this case, too, the attitudes and evaluations found in the *Secretum* reappear in his later writings. After he had settled in Parma and there, in 1346 and 1348, had received his richer prebends, he was anxious, as one learns from his poems and correspondence, to build up a comfortable *Horatian mediocritas.*[69] In 1352–53, it is true, his hopes for Parma failed because of the growing enmity of Bishop Ugolino dei Rossi of Parma; his dream of several years for a life of *mediocritas* on Italian soil was for a while, early in 1353, replaced by the resigned decision to spend the remainder of his life under more modest conditions in the Vaucluse.[70] But after this interlude and his final return to northern Italy in mid-1353, he obtained permanently, at first in Visconti Milan, the rather affluent *mediocritas* echoed in many of his later letters.[71] Whatever doubt may remain about the origin of single phrases and words, it is indubitable, therefore, that the ideal of an affluent *mediocritas* as proposed in the *accidia* paragraph corresponds with Petrarch's experience and way of thinking during the late 1340's and early 1350's far better than with the attitude characteristic of him in the late 1330's and early 1340's.

---

[66] G. Billanovich, *Petrarca Letterato*, vol. I: *Lo scrittoio del Petrarca* (Rome, 1947), p. 49; Wilkins, *The Making of the 'Canzoniere' and Other Petrarchan Studies* (Rome, 1951), p. 313.

[67] Ed. Carrara, p. 114.

[68] Cf. pp. 60 f., 74 above.

[69] Cf. esp. *Fam.* VIII 3 of 1349 and also Baron, "Franciscan Poverty and Civic Wealth" (see note 71, below), pp. 8 f.

[70] For the reconstruction of this aspect of his last stay in Avignon and the Vaucluse in 1352–53, see Foresti, "Il sogno di Valchiusa," in *Aneddoti*, pp. 270–87.

[71] Cf. H. Baron, "Franciscan Poverty and Civic Wealth as Factors in the Rise of Humanistic Thought," *Speculum*, XIII (1938), 10 f., and also p. 80, below.

V. Precisely when can the textual changes have been made? Although some suspected passages, as demonstrated, refer to Petrarch's sojourn in Provence during 1351–53, the pervasive mood of the *avaritia* and *accidia* discussions—a melancholy regret for a lost happiness in the Vaucluse and for Petrarch's present captivity in the *"tumultus urbium"*—cannot possibly be explained by the assumption that the extant text of the two paragraphs was phrased during Petrarch's last residence in Provence. Even then life in Avignon was not totally severed from life in the Vaucluse, for the autumn-winter of 1351–52 and the autumn of 1352, both chiefly spent in Avignon, were preceded, divided, and followed by three of Petrarch's happiest stays in the Vaucluse.[72] So in light of our knowledge that the two sections on *avaritia* and *accidia* include varied experiences of the early 1350's, but that the work of revision may have been done or continued at any time until the final copying in 1358, let us re-examine the descriptions in the *Secretum* of changes in Petrarch's life since the happy days of his past *"solitudo"*.

In the paragraph on *avaritia*, Augustine tells Petrarch (as we already know): you plunged yourself into endless worries and unhappiness "since you first began to scorn the fruits of your own trees and to find despicable the plain clothing and food of country people."[73] We have observed that this statement does not fit the situation in the winter of 1342–43, when Petrarch temporarily left the Vaucluse for Avignon to support his litigation and certainly not because he was dissatisfied with the coarseness of simple country life or because he had any intention of starting a more luxurious existence away from his Alpine retreat. But do we know of any situation in Petrarch's later life to which these particulars would apply?

In *Fam.* XIII 8 we are given a detailed picture of Petrarch's sojourn in the Vaucluse during the summer of 1352. One of its highlights is the description of the strenuous, but human and kindly life of the old peasant couple who took care of Petrarch's personal needs and small estate. Petrarch stays with them, reports the letter, dressing almost like a peasant him-

---

72 Cf. Wilkins, *Studies in the Life*, pp. 89–92.
73 Ed. Carrara, p. 86. Full quotation p. 65, above.

self, and sharing their coarse bread. "What shall I say about my clothes and shoes? Everything is changed; you would call me a peasant or a shepherd." "Eventually I so trained my palate and my stomach that I am now often satisfied with my herdsman's bread and often even take delight in it."[74] His relish in imparting this as a piece of news suggests that these were fresh experiences to him in the summer of 1352 (or, possibly, the preceding year) and not mere reiterations of something he had already known during his stays in the Vaucluse during the 1330's and 1340's.

When, one year later, Petrarch moved to Milan, he started a new way of life in an urban and refined milieu, living henceforth in a comfortable house well staffed with servants. We learn from his correspondence that during his early years in Milan he began to pay greater attention to clothes, and that he felt this to be a change from his former style in the Vaucluse—a change which made him uneasy about himself. In 1359, recalling his letter of 1352, he remarked that what he had once reported about his love of plain country dress in the Vaucluse should not be understood as a reflection of his innate modesty; it had been, rather, the effect of his rural environment. After moving to Milan, he said, his tastes had changed —*"prope alius rure michi videor, alius in urbibus"*—and only recently, very gradually, had he begun to return to greater simplicity.[75] The parallel with the situation alluded to by Augustine in the *avaritia* paragraph could not be more precise. At least this part of the *Secretum* text can hardly have been written at any time other than after Petrarch had left the Vaucluse and moved to Milan.

We find another parallel in the paragraph on *accidia*. As we have noted, Augustine answers Petrarch's outburst against

---

[74] "Quid de vestibus, quid de calceis loquar? mutata sunt omnia. . . . Agricolam me seu pastorem diceris." "Iam vero gulam ventremque sic institui ut sepe bubulci mei panis et michi sufficiat, sepe etiam delectet." *Fam.* XIII 8, 8 and 10. Cf. also Wilkins' summary of this letter in *Life of Petrarch*, p. 107.

[75] "De vestibus et reliquo apparatu olim ex me, dum in transalpino Elicone agerem, audisti. Ne falsam tamen opinionem plene frugalitatis indueris, cogita ruris incolam et rusticane faventem continentie, dum id scriberem, me fuisse. . . . Quid intendam, vides, nam et ego . . . prope alius rure michi videor, alius in urbibus. . . . Vel victor itaque vel invictus ad reliqua, in hac parte belli hereo . . . , et in eo plus michi negotii est quod ad comunem et modestum, ne dicam philosophicum, vestis modum vixdum inclinare animum incipio." *Fam.* XXI 13, 8-12.

the *"tumultus urbium"* with "you should be greatly comforted when you remember that since you have been reduced to this frustration by your own doing you can also escape by your own free will if only you begin to will"; to which Petrarch replies: "much of what you said provokes me, and especially your opinion that to leave the cities [*relinquere urbes*] would be easy for me and only a matter of my own will."[76] From our observations on his situation in 1342–43, we have concluded that it would have been most improbable for Petrarch to talk of "leaving the cities" and to fear that he could not forsake city life were these passages actually written then, that is, at a time when he had gone from the Vaucluse to Avignon on private business for a number of weeks or months and had no reason to doubt he would be back in solitude before long. On the other hand, in view of our discovery that the chapter on *avaritia*, which is so closely related to that on *accidia*, includes at least one insertion from the time when Petrarch had left the Vaucluse forever and was living in Milan, a satisfying explanation suggests itself in the theory that the *accidia* chapter, too, was emended from the perspective of Petrarch's later life in northern Italy.

One would, of course, wish to be sure that during his first years in Milan Petrarch actually experienced a mood in which despair over having robbed himself of the chance to retreat again to the Vaucluse can have colored the last revision of his work. This is precisely what is borne out by his correspondence from Milan. His inner equilibrium in Milan was achieved only after two or three years during which he often lamented his separation from his "transalpine Helicon" in words almost identical with those of Augustine in the *Secretum*. In September 1353, four months after his arrival in northern Italy, he despairingly told Francesco Nelli that many undesirable occupations had taken the place of the "leisure and sweetness of my beloved solitude." "I had been happy too long and too completely!" Either God, or fate, or the wantonness of his mind (so he now brooded) had caused him to become untrue to his former intentions—perhaps because, contrary to what he had believed, he had not been free enough of

---

[76] Ed. Carrara, p. 126. Full quotation pp. 65 f. above.

"passiones" to live in solitude forever.[77] Early the next year he sighed once more: "I do not know whether my own fault or Fortuna has begrudged me my sweet hiding-place." Petrarch was now truly in a situation where he looked back longingly from city life to his lost *"solitudo"* in the Vaucluse. "Since my youth," he said, "I have been such a great lover of solitude and the woods, and now that I have grown older I must labor in the cities and among the crowd, and I feel ill at ease." Nothing, he added, was left to him but "to think, in chains, of liberty; in the cities, of the country; in labor, of quietude; and—reversing a dictum of my beloved Scipio Africanus [i.e., *'in otio de negotiis cogitare'*]—*'in negotiis de otio cogitare'.*"[78]

Not before about 1358 was his inner peace restored. At that time his letters report that he had truly reached the "golden mean" and overcome greed in spite of increasing wealth,[79] and that he was also beginning to find peace of mind in the city. Although he still sighed, he said, for the *"vera solitudo"* and for the coarse dress and rustic house of the friend to whom he was writing, he had now mastered the art "of being at rest in the center of the storm" and of "achieving solitude and leisure in the midst of city life [*in mediis urbibus ipse mihi solitudinem atque otium conflare didicerim*]."[80] At that time Petrarch could believe that the "struggles of his soul" reflected in the *Secretum* had come to an end. In such circumstances he at last made the final copy of his work and added to the title, *De secreto conflictu curarum mearum,* the cautiously hopeful note that he would write a continuation *"de secreta pace animi,"*

---

[77] *Fam.* XVI 14, 14–15 (missive version).

[78] "Ita ego a prima etate tantus amator solitudinis ac silvarum, iam senior in urbibus et odiosa frequentia laboro, et male michi est." ". . . ut intelligas . . . me tamen de libertate vel in vinculis, si sors cogat, de rure in urbibus, in laboribus de quiete, postremo, ut tritum illud Africani mei dictum vertam, in negotiis de otio cogitare." *Fam.* XVII 10, 26–28, Jan. 1, 1354. Ed. Rossi, p. 263.

[79] Cf. "Franciscan Poverty and Civic Wealth," *Speculum,* XIII (1938), 10 n. 4.

[80] *Fam.* XX 10, 2 and 4 ("Reliquum est ut plebeie toge tue . . . invideam, et rustico lare tuo quod uti prohibeor suspirem"); probably 1358, cf. Wilkins, *Eight Years,* p. 160.
Variae 52, *Epistolae De Rebus Familiaribus et Variae,* ed. I. Fracassetti, III (Florence, 1863), 443 f.; between 1357 and 1360 because written in Milan, but not in 1356 or 1361 according to Wilkins, *Eight Years,* p. 214, while in 1354 and 1355 Petrarch's mood had been completely different as we know from his other letters.

"si pax sit usquam."[81] His feeling that he was at long last reaching shore was enhanced by the contrast of the years just preceding, when the last of the ideas and motives were formed which had merged in his report on his past struggles.

That Petrarch's final manuscript was transcribed in 1358 is, therefore, hardly accidental but reflects the fact that the concluding work on the *Secretum* had been done not very long before, and that the author now considered his book to have reached its ultimate phase. We do not know—at least not at present—how many parts of the text contain his late changes, but in the sections on *avaritia* and *accidia*, at any rate, self-condemnation for having forever forfeited rural simplicity and solitude expresses the growing pains of the period during which the hermit of the Vaucluse gradually became a denizen and courtier of the north-Italian cities.

This much can definitely be stated, even though we may not always be able to prove with finality that individual passages or words referring to Petrarch's last stay in Provence must have been formulated after his move to Milan; it is, for instance, not impossible that the veiled references to Petrarch's helping his friends and to his striving for a *"primus locus"* were entered in Avignon shortly after the events had occurred. But, as we have seen, it seems more plausible to think of them as part of the revision which, demonstrably, was made in Milan. In any event, the changes are not simply insertions that can be neatly cut out of the text, but represent such a skillful fusion of successive experiences in Petrarch's life that the result is a tightly knit picture of Petrarch's life in Avignon which is fully true neither of 1342 nor of 1352.[82]

---

[81] See note 3, above.

[82] A characteristic example is Petrarch's ideal in the *Secretum* of affluent "mediocritas," to which we have referred (pp. 73 and 75 f. above). That it was not the ideal formulated and positively accepted by Petrarch in 1342–43 is evident from the fact that Petrarch's letters in that period emphasized his pride in his "paupertas" rather than his longing for "mediocritas" (p. 73, above). On the other hand, when Petrarch attained considerable affluence during the late forties and mid-fifties and made "mediocritas" his standard, as we know from his correspondence (pp. 75 f. above), he could no longer feel that "mediocritas" had unjustly escaped him. So, in his revisions he rationalized his past efforts to gain the Migliarino prebend by defending himself before Augustine with a charming picture of Horatian "mediocritas" and the contention that this was the fair and well-considered goal he had set for his life. Actually, Petrarch in 1342–43 could not yet have argued along these lines, and in the fifties could no longer complain about his poverty. The paragraph in the *Secretum* presents the situation of 1342–43 in the light of the matured experience of Petrarch's later life.

But the artistic unity of the final product does not make it less imperative for us to discern the various elements which went successively into its making. It might be well to keep in mind the trap by which students were caught when reading in the *Metr.* I 6 of Petrarch's brave journeys to all parts of the Mediterranean, to the Pyrenees, and to the coast of Britain to escape his memory of Laura. This poetic narrative tempted readers to believe that after his first return from Rome, in 1337, Petrarch continued his journey northward to the Atlantic and the English Channel,[83] until eventually it was realized that the poet's powerful imagination had transformed and blended various recollections of his southern journey of 1337 and his preceding northern journey of 1333 to Paris, the Netherlands, and the Rhine. In a similar way, the student of the *Secretum* must be aware that the sections on *avaritia* and *accidia* present us with a portrait of Petrarch in which his artistic imagination and desire to dramatize cause us to ascribe ideas born of various situations of his later years to one moment of his early life. At least in those two sections, the text of the *Secretum* must be judged a complex of elements which stem from the experiences he had had in the Vaucluse and Avignon in 1342–43, from the Vaucluse and Avignon in 1351–52, and from the first year or years that followed Petrarch's dissociation from Provence in June 1353.

VI. Do we find any comparable organization or reorganization of the text in other parts of the *Secretum?*

When we first proposed to examine the passages which Petrarch seems to have written in Avignon rather than in his *solitudo* in the Vaucluse, we found it advisable to omit from our discussion a page of the third dialogue in which Augustine counsels Petrarch to rid himself of his love for Laura by fleeing from "*hac ipsa civitate,*" clearly Avignon.[84] The passage was not indispensable for the question then under discussion, because the city is there not contrasted to the country: Petrarch should flee both Avignon and the Vaucluse. But since Petrarch's growing antipathy to Avignon and the papacy

---

[83] Cf. Tatham, I, 349–56.
[84] Ed. Carrara, p. 170. See p. 66, above.

makes any reference to Avignon a likely spot for alterations, we must now investigate whether the conversation on Petrarch's life in Avignon in connection with his love for Laura —the discussion of his *amor*—may not be another area where later changes were made.

Let us first examine the context of the episode in which Augustine advises Petrarch to flee Provence. Augustine begins by calling *amor* and *gloria* the worst "chains," because Petrarch loves these passions, whereas he fears most of the others. Petrarch's reaction proves him right, for Petrarch cries: with your warnings against my love you want to rob me of the most beautiful of my concerns (*"speciosissimas curas"*), my most noble sentiments; *"atqui nichil unquam rectius arbitratus sum, nichilque unquam rectius arbitrabor."*[85] Indeed, whatever Augustine proposes for curing this "disease" proves it to be too strong, and when he finally judges that the only hope left is to dislodge one love through another, Petrarch replies that he is so firmly wedded to this love that his eyes will never be pleased by any other woman; if this means he is incurable and damned, then *"actum est; perii."*[86]

It is at this point that Augustine recommends the alternative that Petrarch seek forgetfulness by leaving Avignon and the Vaucluse where everything reminds him of Laura; he should travel abroad—advice accepted by Petrarch after a few pages but not without a request for any other helpful remedies which Augustine may know.[87] Whereupon Augustine refers to Cicero's saying in the *Tusculans* that three things are capable of turning the mind away from a consuming love: *"satietas, pudor, cogitatio."* To talk of "satiety," however, he adds, would be vain in your case since you think it impossible that your love could ever diminish (*"quoniam impossibile iudicabis tibi, ut res se habet, satietatem amoris ullam posse contingere"*), and even if you should admit that it could happen in the future, "would claim that your burning passion is still as far as possible from satiety—as I agree it is."[88] In the remainder of the conversation, therefore, only "shame" and

---

[85] Ed. Carrara, p. 132.   [86] Ed. Carrara, p. 164.   [87] Ed. Carrara, p. 174.

[88] ". . . ab ardentissimo tamen desiderio tuo quam longissime hanc [satietatem] abesse contendes, egoque ipse consentiam." Ed. Carrara, p. 176.

philosophy are discussed as potential remedies, until Petrarch begins to feel that these two have alleviated the evil even though it has not been healed.[89]

This, then, is the gist of the discussion of Petrarch's *amor;* but does the paragraph in which he is advised to flee from Provence[90] form a logical and integral part of the argument? The paragraph, as we have just seen, is immediately preceded by Petrarch's protestation that Augustine's efforts will remain futile because his burning passion lies too deep. It is followed by Augustine's assent that this passion will not grow weaker in the foreseeable future. The introductory as well as the concluding portions, therefore, show Augustine in the position of a teacher who points to helpful remedies which the disciple cannot yet use, or only partially, because his emotions still resist too much. If the intermediate portion containing Augustine's quickly accepted advice for Petrarch to travel abroad were not part of the original text but an insertion from later years, one might expect to find there a changed state of mind—a diminution of Petrarch's passion.

If with this anticipation we examine the travel paragraph, we do, indeed, observe a subtle difference in the relationship between the two speakers: Petrarch here believes that he has advanced further on the road to liberation than his partner is ready to concede. For, whereas Augustine, following Seneca, gives advice for lovers in various conditions, saying that *"peregrinationes"* will not help one who takes his passion with him on his journey, but can heal a mind already prepared or help to preserve regained health (*"sanumque custodiunt"*), Petrarch declares himself interested precisely in the latter possibility, which, consequently, is made the subject of the conversation. Augustine, the voice of Petrarch's conscience, seems to express in this conversation both Petrarch's hopes and doubts. In advising Petrarch not to stay on "even if you were healed," the teacher does not suppress the remark that this is "a state from which you are still very far"; but his subsequent counsels are addressed not to one still far from "health" but to a lover who is well advanced toward his

---

[89] Ed. Carrara, p. 188.

[90] In Carrara's edition, pp. 164–74.

liberation. *"Neque enim convenit vinculis egressum,"* he says, *"circum carceris fores oberrare,"* while the keeper of the prison (*"carceris dominus"*) might scheme to catch him again. "A tiny draught of water has done harm to many who were regaining their health. ... Sometimes the smallest cause plunges a convalescent mind back into utmost misery. ... A slight turn of an eye rekindles dormant love."[91] When he wrote these lines Petrarch must have envisaged a time when his love was slowly turning into a sweet though still stirring memory of the past—a state of mind different from the tormenting passion he described when writing the introduction and the concluding portion of the section.

To be sure, unless supported by other evidence, this does not necessarily mean that the advice of *peregrinationes* was written later than the preceding and following parts; Petrarch could conceivably have shifted the focus of his argument, wondering, in view of his present incurable state, what might be done at a time when his ardor had died down. But from the outset, the more probable explanation is that a change of focus betrays a change in the author, or, more precisely, that the paragraph which proposes a remedy for one who is "healed" or near to health was written at another time than the paragraphs in which Petrarch's passion appears uncontrollable. There are facts that point in this direction.

One of them is especially revealing to a reader who is aware of the tension in the *Secretum* between the *solitudo* of the Vaucluse and the *tumultus urbium*. To be sure, nostalgic longing for a lost happiness in the Vaucluse had been foreign to Petrarch's feelings before the 1350's, but even in 1342–43 the solitude of the Vaucluse appeared to him as a haven, and throughout the *Secretum* separation from the Vaucluse is considered a desertion responsible for many of Petrarch's guilty passions. The one thing not to be expected from Augustine in the *Secretum* is, therefore, the reproach that Petrarch was in error to live in his *solitudo*, let alone the counsel that he should quit the Vaucluse altogether. Yet this is what we read in the paragraph advising Petrarch to go abroad on *peregrinationes*.

---

[91] "Nocuit multis ad sanitatem redeuntibus parcissimus haustus aque. ... Quam minima sunt interdum que animum emergentem in summas miserias reimpellunt! ... Levis oculorum flexus amorem dormitantem excitat." Ed. Carrara, p. 170.

Not only does Augustine warn him against continuing his life in solitude as long as his passion prevents his peace of mind—*"donec sentias morbi tui nullas superesse reliquias"*—but even his past flight into the stillness of the Vaucluse is branded a mistake. Had not Petrarch himself often lamented in his poems that on his lonely walks he would suddenly be seized by the thought of Laura? "What remedy were you likely to find," says Augustine, "in a place so lonely and remote? Let me confess that often when you retreated there by yourself, sighing and turning longing eyes back to the city, I laughed heartily and said to myself: What a blind fool love has made of this unhappy man! It has led him to quite forget the verse every schoolboy knows . . .: 'Lover! whoe'er you be, dwell not alone; / In solitude you're sure to be undone. / You're safer in a crowd; the word is true, / Lone woods are not the place for such as you' [Ovid, *De Remed. Amoris,* 579–80]. . . . Since you not only know all the adverse testimony of the ancients, but have yourself experienced the evils of solitude, it astonishes me that you should commit such a blunder as to seek it."[92] Is the assumption that Petrarch could have condemned his flight into the solitude of the Vaucluse while at the same time praising it above everything else in the same piece of writing not far less believable than the alternative that the few pages of unexpected condemnation were added later when the context of the entire work was less immediate in his memory?

It is true that these arguments—like all conclusions drawn from apparent inconsistencies in an author's position—still demand confirmation by evidence outside the literary document under discussion, because one cannot exclude the possibility that the lack of consistency is due simply to a momentary lapse of the author. Such evidence, however, does exist. The paragraph advising Petrarch to flee both the Vaucluse and Avignon conflicts not only with other parts of the *Secretum* but also with the external circumstances of Petrarch's life during the years 1342 and 1343. Augustine's advice is not of a vague and general kind, such as might be given at any time,

---

[92] "Ego quidem eo magis in sectanda solitudine errorem tuum admiratus sum, quod et autoritates veterum adversus id noveras, et novas addideras." Ed. Carrara, p. 174.

but is accompanied by two important specifications. One is that Petrarch should leave Provence as "one who will not come back (*irrediturus*),"[93] for otherwise the longing to return would always keep his passion alive. Second, his destination should be Italy, because he would nowhere be happier than in his beloved fatherland; his flight should mark the end of his exile. "*Nimis diu iam et a patria et a te ipso exulasti. Tempus est revertendi.*"[94]

To assume that Petrarch wrote these passages, and thus considered a permanent return to Italy, during the winter of 1342-43 would conflict with all available information—information which is not only complete but which forces the conclusion that this plan could not have been formed until more than a year later. In fact, it did not yet exist when, in September 1343, several months after writing the *Secretum*, Petrarch departed for Italy on a diplomatic mission for the Pope and Cardinal Colonna to the court of Naples. That he then still considered his home to be in Provence and expected his trip to Italy to last only a few months we know for certain from the letter which he sent from Naples on December 1, 1343, toward the end of his mission, to Cardinal Colonna in Avignon. "Unless you hear to the contrary," he wrote the Cardinal, "you may be sure that within three days—even if my object [at the court of Naples] is unaccomplished—I shall have taken wing first into Cisalpine, then into Transalpine Gaul, and towards yourself."[95] Only after this letter written on the eve of his return did he suddenly interrupt his homeward journey at Parma, just as he had done in 1341, thus breaking his freely given promise to the Cardinal.

As an explanation of this abrupt change, Arnaldo Foresti has proposed the interesting hypothesis that when Petrarch wrote to the Cardinal from Naples on December 1, 1343, he did not yet know that on November 8 a papal board in Avignon had finally dashed his hopes for the Migliarino prebend; the sad news from Provence must have reached him shortly before or after his arrival at Parma. So his decision not to continue his journey back to Avignon was in part caused by

---

[93] Ed. Carrara, p. 166.   [94] Ed. Carrara, p. 172.
[95] *Fam.* V 6, 6; the translation primarily follows Tatham, II, 332.

his reluctance to return to the papal circle after this bitter disappointment.[96]

Although we should not forget that Petrarch was in every situation of his life a man of many motives, we may, I think, regard it as virtually certain that the news from Avignon was one of the preconditions for his change of mind: it was not until that moment that he began to cherish the idea of permanent repatriation. None of his intimate friends in Avignon was expecting this outcome of his Neapolitan mission. But by the time that Socrates at some unknown date in 1344 bade him return, so many deeper motivations—including those we know from the *Secretum* episode—had crystallized in Petrarch's mind that he was absolutely firm in his refusal, even apart from the impact of the Migliarino affair. He had begun to look upon Azzo da Correggio as a lord and friend with whom he wished to live out his days, and the life of Italy had cast its spell upon him. "Though a tired wanderer, it will be happiness for me to put my foot on Italian soil and look up at the pure, serene sky and the stars of our country. And when, after a long, laborious life, my last day dawns, it will be sweet solace in death . . . to find my rest in the earth of Italy. . . ." "This is the life congenial to me, and after experiencing all this I will never return to the Curia and its world of envy and ambition." True, his love for Laura had even now not wholly ceased to disturb his peace of mind; and Socrates was dealing badly with him by trying to overwhelm him with sweet recollections of his past life. "Precisely these memories caused me to take flight some time ago, because this was my last hope in defeat." Renewed energy had now replaced his languor: "*stat iuncta labori gloria languentem spernens operosa soporem.*"[97]

This was Petrarch's state of mind at Parma in 1344, as we

---

[96] Foresti, *Aneddoti*, pp. 150–51.

[97]   "Gratius iste quidem, quamquam iam fessus eundi,
Pes Italam calcabit humum, purumque serenum
Laetius his oculis, et sydera nostra videbo.
Post ubi longaevo finem factura labori
Affuerit suprema dies, solamen et ipsum
Mortis erit, ...
.   .   .   .   post proelia tanta
Fortunae, Ausonia saltem tellure recondi
Dulce mihi, et patriis longum requiescere saxis;
Seraque quum fragilem tumulum convulserit aetas,

learn from his answer to Socrates in *Metr*. III 27. Not until that time, in any case not before Petrarch had settled in Parma early that year, can Augustine's advice have been couched in the words we find in the version of the *Secretum* handed down to us. Most probably, however, this part of the text was written at a still later date, if only because Petrarch can hardly have had the manuscript of the *Secretum* with him on a journey planned as a brief diplomatic mission; presumably he did not see his work again until he returned subsequently to the Vaucluse in the autumn of 1345. The years which followed (1346 and 1347) were those in which the *De Vita Solitaria* and the *De Otio Religioso* were written during stays in the Vaucluse —one of the most peaceful stretches of Petrarch's life, when he was most unlikely to ascribe to Augustine the advice that he should leave his solitude and return to Italy. Not until the last months of 1347 did he once more leave Provence for the peninsula, and this time frankly for an extended or perhaps even permanent separation. Since, on the other hand, the *Secretum* paragraph under discussion continually speaks of Laura in such a way that it must have been written before her death on April 6, 1348, the autumn of 1347 appears to be the most probable moment for Augustine's advice. At that time, Petrarch was about to undertake a journey to Italy which was much more in keeping than the conditions of 1342–43 with the situation presupposed in the *Secretum*. For he had left the

---

Lenius Hesperia cinis hic agitabitur aura."

"Haec mihi vita placet, non ambitionis in aulam,
Individiaeque sacram, post tot documenta reverti."

". . . . . Tu calcar amoris
Incutis absenti, quo frena morantia rumpam,
Dum meminisse iubes, quod ut obliviscerer, omni
Exhortandus eram studio: tu dulce caducum,
Ingeris expertae formaeque fugacis honorem,
Et veterum mihi multa novas monimenta dierum.
Haec tamen ipsa olim (quae spes erat ultima victo)
Causa fuere fugae; iamque haec puerilia retro
Linquimus . . . ."

". . . . . Sed quis locus absque periclo?
Quae magna cum laude quies? Stat iuncta labori
Gloria languentem spernens operosa soporem,
Despiciensque minas . . . ."

Metr. III 27, in *Francisci Petrarchae Poemata Minora*, ed. Domenico de' Rossetti, vol. II (Milan, 1831), pp. 142, 136, 140.

service of Cardinal Colonna and crossed the Alps without the obligation to return. Moreover, the events connected with Cola di Rienzo's Roman uprising that year had brought to a climax Petrarch's desire to be again an Italian in Italy.

Closer examination shows, however, that, in part at least, the text of the *peregrinationes* paragraph is of an even later date than 1347. When counseling Petrarch to return to his native land, Augustine quotes *Metr.* III 25,[98] which is a fervid eulogy of Italy from the period of Petrarch's return. This poem was not written until 1349 when Petrarch, because of his rift with Ugolino dei Rossi, Bishop of Parma, had begun to look elsewhere, and had established a second foothold in northern Italy at Padua.[99] More was inserted at that time than the sentence containing this quotation. Augustine continues with the curious comment that he does not wish to tie Petrarch down to one locality on the peninsula: *"Ad unum vero eius angulum te arctare noluerim. I modo felix, quocunque te fert animus."*[100] Before early 1349 a return to Italy had meant returning to the house which Petrarch had owned in Parma since 1344. So the advice that Petrarch should not tie himself to one "corner" of the peninsula is also likely not to have been written before 1349. This advice in turn is followed by the quotation from the *Psalmi Poenitentiales* already mentioned. We would again arrive at about the same period if this work were written in 1347 or 1348, as I see no reason to doubt.[101]

It appears, therefore, that the pages with which we are dealing were originally inserted not before 1347 and not after April 6, 1348, and were further expanded in or after 1349. We can probably be even more precise. With regard to the quotation of *Metr.* III 25, one must, of course, admit that a reference to a poem written in 1349 in itself only tells us that 1349 is a *terminus a quo.* But there is another way to arrive at the conclusion that it was exactly in 1347 and 1349 that Petrarch once again put his hand to the text of the *Secretum.* In Frate Tedaldo della Casa's transcription of the manuscript of 1358

---

[98] See p. 57 above.
[99] That this, and not 1347, is the date of *Metr.* III 25, has been definitely proved by P. Sambin, *Archivio Veneto,* XLVI–XLVII (1950), 36–39.
[100] Ed. Carrara, p. 172.   [101] See p. 57 above.

we find an enigmatic entry. On the last page of the transcript, next to the scribe's closing line *"Explicit liber tertius . . . Et sic liber de secreto conflictu continet 3 libros"*, is the marginal note *"Modo 3. 1353. 1349. 1347."* As Sabbadini suggested, *"Modo 3"* must mean "only three books," that is, the promised *"de secreta pace animi totidem"*[102] did not exist. But what about the three years *"1353. 1349. 1347"*? Sabbadini conjectured that Petrarch "with these three years may have indicated three periods of revision of the dialogue."[103] As we concluded from our observations on the *avaritia* and *accidia* sections, the crucial and final insertions there must have been made soon after Petrarch's move to Milan which occurred late in June 1353. So the second half of 1353 may easily have been the time of these changes, and 1353 therefore one of the years in which Petrarch revised his work. In our analysis of the *amor* section we now seem to have encountered insertions pointing to the other two years—1349 and 1347—which were listed by the author in looking back upon the genesis of his work. We have, therefore, added reason for believing that the revision of the *peregrinationes* paragraph did occur in the very years 1347 and 1349.

In any case, we have found that in some parts at least the *Secretum* was decisively reworked under the impact of the change which came about in Petrarch's life when, temporarily in 1347 and finally in 1353, he left the places where he had conceived his work and returned to Italy. The significance of this conclusion for the genetic reconstruction of Petrarch's outlook on life is evident.

E. H. Wilkins suggested in one of his last publications that Petrarch's *accidia* and the deep emotions aroused at the time of the *Secretum* by his *avaritia*, his love for Laura, and his desire for glory may not have had a strong effect on his life

---

[102] See p. 52 above.

[103] Sabbadini, p. 27. In the years preceding Sabbadini's paper, E. Carlini Minguzzi, *Studio sul Secretum* (1906), pp. 45, 127, had considered the note to mean that the third dialogue was revised in 1347, the second in 1349, and the first in 1353—an utterly improbable explanation for the mysterious figures. Still earlier, there had been an even more absurd interpretation, namely, that the three books were composed ("expliciti") in that strange, inverse order—an assumption made by L. Mehus in his *Vita Ambrosii Traversarii* (Florence, 1759), p. 237, and still regarded in G. Voigt's *Die Wiederbelebung des klassischen Alterthums* (3d ed., Berlin, 1893, I, 132, 134) as a reason for denying the existence of inner unity and order in Petrarch's work.

far beyond the period when the first draft of the *Secretum* was written. "Those experiences, intense though they were in and about 1343, had ceased to be characteristic of him before many years had passed"; the reasons for his *accidia* "had become largely inoperative . . . within a few years after 1343."[104] It is quite true that this appears to be the situation as long as the changes which left their mark on the *Secretum* go unnoticed. In light of these changes, however, it is impossible to overlook that both his *avaritia*, which to Petrarch in the *Secretum* seems to be one of the principal roots of his *accidia*, and his love remained strong forces in his life and recurrent incentives for his secret struggles. Their impact on the text of his work can be traced until the 1350's, when the long history of the *Secretum* came to an end.

VII. Petrarch's skilful interweaving of earlier and later strands of the text into a coherent and fluid dialogue rarely allows us to detect the seams; we must usually be satisfied with recognizing that the ideas underlying a certain section belong to a period of his life different from that of the first draft. But in the case of the *peregrinationes* paragraph our answer to the question whether the entire paragraph was inserted in and after 1347 can be more confident.

In theory, to be sure, it is quite possible that advice to seek psychological relief through *peregrinationes* was already contained in the first draft but was subsequently so thoroughly transformed that in the present phrasing all crucial sentences contain elements that must have originated after 1342–43. Nevertheless, one cannot deny that if the entire paragraph on *peregrinationes* were eliminated we would obtain a more logical transition from the sentence preceding the advice to go abroad to the sentence which follows it. The present text, indeed, fails to show any inner connection between the recommendation of peregrinations and Augustine's subsequent counsel. In the last passage on peregrinations, Augustine, having warned Petrarch against further solitude at this stage, praises *Metr.* I 6 because the poem had honestly conceded that even

---

[104] Wilkins, "On Petrarch's *Accidia* and His Adamantine Chains," *Speculum*, XXXVII (1962), 589–94, esp. 592 f., 594.

within his solitude Petrarch was perturbed by the thought of Laura. To this praise Petrarch replies, concluding the paragraph: "I never would have thought that my verses could be so harmonious as to be worthy of your commendation. They will be all the dearer to me now that I know it. If, however, you have another remedy, please do not withhold it from one who needs it."[105]

This desire for further suggestions, despite the fact that Augustine with his counsel to go abroad had succeeded in giving effective advice (*"Recte tu quidem,"* Petrarch had previously admitted, accepting Augustine's counsel), is an astonishingly lame transition to the subsequent debate. If the paragraph on peregrinations were removed, Petrarch's request and its urgency would have much greater meaning. The sentence preceding the *peregrinationes* discussion had ended with Petrarch's confession that he was unable to take Augustine's first advice: to drive away the memory of one love by trying to fall in love with another. If "in order to be cured of this love I must love another woman, you make impossible terms for me. In that case all is over; I am lost."[106] The next logical question would be: or can you help me with any other counsel? If the *peregrinationes* paragraph were omitted, the text would then, indeed, go on: "If, however, you have another remedy, please do not withhold it from one who needs it [*siquid autem alterius remedii habes, oro ne subtrahas egenti*]." It is highly probable that this coherent sequence had formed the original text.

Regardless of where we place the boundary lines of the insertion, what is the particular significance of the discovery that the advice to flee the Vaucluse and Avignon and end Petrarch's exile from Italian soil was not part of the first draft but must have originated around and after 1347?

This finding, in the first place, helps us to recognize further the original conciseness and artistic unity of a work that has often been blamed for being diffuse and contradictory in spite

---

[105] "Nunc amare carmen illud incipio. Siquid autem alterius remedii habes, oro ne subtrahas egenti." Ed. Carrara, p. 174. That the poem in question is *Metr.* I 6, not Petrarch's *Ad seipsum*, was noted pp. 56 f., above.

[106] ". . . si aliam amare iubes, ut sic ab amore liberer, impossibilem michi conditionem obicis. Actum est; perii." Ed. Carrara, p. 164.

of its great literary qualities. In the original form of the *Secretum*, as we have seen, a more modest role had been played by the eventually overlong sections on *avaritia* and *accidia;* everything pointing to a nostalgically conceived contrast between past solitude and present bondage to city life, and every passage expressing strong concern for the material basis of Petrarch's happiness must have been added or at least expanded. In the equally long paragraph on Petrarch's *amor,* everything connected with Augustine's advice to shun the solitude of the Vaucluse and return to Italy forever is a subsequent addition that has weakened the original conciseness of the argument.

Second, we can discern that the alterations in the *peregrinationes* paragraph are not simple insertions referring to some later events and aspirations. At the end of 1347, just as in late 1343, Petrarch did not journey to Italy in order to escape his love. He first intended to join Cola di Rienzo in the Roman uprising, and after his bitter disappointment with the Roman tribune decided to live in northern Italy, now that he was entirely free after the termination of his service with Cardinal Colonna. On the other hand, in 1344 he had already discovered in Parma that a sojourn in Italy could help him to overcome his broodings and his passion, so that he dreaded a return to Provence. Eventually, therefore, in revising the *Secretum*—presumably not before 1347 and in part not until 1349—he used successive experiences for rounding out and dramatizing the dialogue; he turned it into a composite picture of all the motivations that at one time or another had driven him away from Provence, making it appear as if all this had taken place at the time of his first writing. We observed exactly the same method in the elaboration of the *avaritia* and *accidia* sections where Petrarch fuses events of his last stay in Avignon in 1351–53 with the perspective gained during his subsequent Milanese period in order to develop the original, briefer discussions into a richly motivated, variegated narrative. It is important to be clearly aware of this subtle and complex method of revision.

In the third place, it is now evident why the phrase *"in hac ipsa civitate,"* employed by Augustine in his advice to Petrarch not to remain *"in his locis"* (that is, Avignon and its environs), must be omitted from discussions concerning the place where the body of the *Secretum* was written. Appearing, as it does, in a paragraph which quotes writings not composed before 1347–49 and which recounts plans that Petrarch cannot have made before 1344, this reference to Avignon may not have occurred at all in the draft of 1342–43.

VIII. A knowledge of the genesis of the *Secretum* is indispensable not only for a better understanding of its original structure and of the gradual development of Petrarch's thinking, but also with a view to some of the practical implications in using this work as a historical source.

Our inquiry has shown that we can more or less distinctly define certain disturbed areas in the text of the *Secretum* in which the author retouched or replaced and generously supplemented the first version of his work. In the second dialogue, as we have seen, such areas include the entire paragraph on *avaritia*[107] and almost the entire second half of the *accidia* discussion—that is, wherever Petrarch in analyzing his *accidia* searches for the roots of this evil in the blows of fortune[108]— while in the *amor* discussion in the third dialogue we encountered extensive changes in the paragraph which advises Petrarch to flee from the scenes of his love and return to his Italian *patria*.[109] The fact that we recognize these disturbed areas in the text—and any others which future research may identify—can be essential for an evaluation of specific information found in the *Secretum*. We may, of course, assume that, apart from the general changes in attitude which guided his revisions, Petrarch in these sections altered many minor details, for instance, by adding or modifying classical and other *exempla*, or by citing work in which he was engaged or opinions which he had formed or changed in the course of his studies. Among the especially significant alterations are those to which we find parallels in his other writings. For embarrassment is frequently created by the fact that ideas which are likely to belong to later periods of Petrarch's life because they appear in his later works are also found in the *Secretum*,

---

[107] Ed. Carrara, pp. 82–94.
[108] Ed. Carrara, pp. 112–28. [109] Ed. Carrara, pp. 164–74.

that is, in a work attributed to 1342–43. In these situations the puzzle will often be solved by the discovery that such an idea occurs in one of the disturbed areas of the text—in a place, that is, where various changes and insertions were made at a time that can be roughly ascertained. In such a context, the appearance in the *Secretum* of a theme also found elsewhere in Petrarch's works, instead of plunging us into chronological difficulties, may corroborate a conclusion drawn from other evidence. A small group of pertinent examples from the *accidia* section will serve to illustrate the great potential role of the "disturbed areas" in the *Secretum* text.

The first example concerns a problem that has turned up in recent discussions about the date and genesis of the *De Remediis Utriusque Fortunae*. As far as we know from other sources, Petrarch began to plan the *De Remediis* about 1347, and the bulk of the work was done between 1354 and 1357.[110] Yet, at two points in the *Secretum* section on *accidia* we already seem to move in the atmosphere of the *De Remediis*. In the first of these places, Augustine advises Petrarch to store in his memory suitable passages from writings on man's conduct so "that, no matter when or where some urgent case of illness occurs, like an experienced physician you have the remedy, so to speak, already written in your head. For, among the maladies of the soul, just as among those of the body, there are some in which delay is fatal; if you defer the remedy, you take away all hope of cure. Who is not aware, for instance, that certain impulses of the soul are so swift and strong that unless reason checks the passion from which they arise they overwhelm and destroy the soul and body and the whole man, so that a tardy remedy is a useless one."[111] Carrara, in his edition of the *Secretum*, notes that this is *in nuce* the task of the *De Remediis*. That the latter work was indeed in Petrarch's mind when he worked on these pages becomes clear a little later when, while asking whether Fortuna does or does not, after all, really exist, he adds the promise: "*Ego autem quid sentiam, aliud forte tempus ac locus alter fuerit dicendi*"[112]

---

[110] K. Heitmann, "La genesi del *De Remediis Utriusque Fortunae* del Petrarca," *Convivium*, XXV (1957), 9–30; and Wilkins, see note 114, below.

[111] Cf. ed. Carrara, p. 122.   [112] Ed. Carrara, p. 128.

—which is, of course, the *De Remediis*, where the theme of the existence of Fortuna is treated.

It is unnecessary to emphasize how much our understanding of Petrarch's entire development depends on whether or not his outlook and work plans anticipated the *De Remediis* as early as 1342–43. K. Heitmann, in his article "*La genesi del 'De Remediis*',"[113] was quite aware of the probability that the passage on the existence of Fortuna did not belong to the original draft of the *Secretum*, but was inserted during the 1350's. Still, as he stated, since the successive chronological layers of the text have not been clearly distinguished, "one cannot exclude the possibility that the cited passage already belonged to the initial text of 1342–43." Consequently Heitmann summarized the known data on the genesis of the *De Remediis* as "*concepito prima del 1347 (possibilmente anche prima del 1342–43). . . .*" In light of our knowledge that the intimations of the *De Remediis* occur in one of those "disturbed areas" of the *Secretum* which are full of traces of the early 1350's, we may free ourselves of any lingering doubt and forget the strange and confusing assumption that, writing in 1342–43, Petrarch already carried in his mind the ideas of a work of his old age.

Incidentally, the cautious phrasing of the insertion "*ego autem quid sentiam, aliud forte tempus ac locus alter fuerit dicendi*" suggests that at the time it was written composition of the *De Remediis* had either not yet begun or, in any case, was not yet far advanced. Since it is established that work on the *De Remediis* began in 1354,[114] we have here an indirect confirmation of our hypothesis that the revision of the *accidia* paragraph occurred soon after Petrarch's move to Milan, and probably as early as the second half of 1353.[115]

A page or two before these traces of the *De Remediis* we find in the same part of the *accidia* discussion a reference to Caesar and his murderers. Even men who are most highly placed must live for others, says Augustine; so, in a sense, Julius Caesar lived for those who murdered him, that is, "for D. Brutus, T. Cimber, and the other participants in a perfidious conspiracy, whose covetousness could not be satisfied by the

---

[113] Heitmann, *La genesi*, pp. 9–30, esp. p. 10.
[114] Wilkins, *Eight Years*, pp. 69–71, 235 f.   [115] See pp. 81, 82, 91 above.

munificence of such a liberal giver."[116] This is a strong condemnation of the motives of those who claimed to liberate Rome from its tyrant. It is as difficult to attribute such an attitude to Petrarch in 1342–43 as it is to imagine him conceiving the idea of the *De Remediis* at that early date. During his younger years, Petrarch had taken a passionate stand against Caesar in his *Africa*. In 1341, in one of his *canzoni*, he called Cato "*quel si grande amico di libertá, che piú di lei non visse*," and in a letter of about 1342 he described Marcus Junius Brutus as a "*vir acer* [i.e., ardent] *et strenuus.*" To judge from the sources outside the *Secretum*, a change in his attitude did not occur until the early 1350's when, in Petrarch's letters to Emperor Charles IV, Caesar gradually became something like a patron saint "to whom I often refer," as Petrarch said in 1353, whereas by 1366, when the *De Remediis* was finished, Cato had become a vainglorious, evil-minded enemy of one of "the most clement and benevolent princes."[117]

Were it not for the *accidia* passage of the *Secretum*, this would be an utterly lucid and logical development, with the fundamental change occurring from the late 1340's to the early 1350's. The evidence is, indeed, strong enough to make it quite unbelievable that as early as the beginning of the 1340's Petrarch could have talked of the "*perfida coniuratio*" against Caesar, contrasting the "*cupiditas*" of the conspirators with his munificence. Nevertheless, no certain reconstruction of this aspect of Petrarch's development could be made were it not that the problematic *Secretum* passage occurs within an area of the text which abounds in insertions and changes from the very period suggested by our other sources—the early 1350's.

In the same context, Petrarch names as one of the causes of his *accidia* his sufferings caused by the hated city life of Avignon. "*Quis vite mee tedia et quotidianum fastidium sufficienter exprimat, mestissimam turbulentissimamque urbem terrarum omnium, angustissimam atque ultimam sentinam et totius orbis sordibus exundantem? Quis verbis equet que passim nauseam con-*

---

[116] "Vivebat . . . D. Bruto, T. Cimbro ceterisque perfide coniurationis auctoribus, quorum cupiditates explere non valuit tanti munificentia largitoris." Ed. Carrara, p. 118.

[117] See the discussion of this development in the preceding study, pp. 35–40 above.

*citant: graveolentes semitas, permixtas rabidis canibus obscenas
sues . . .; tam diversas hominum species. . . ."*[118] Petrarch does
not say here in so many words that he is surrounded by these
torments at the moment of his writing; he tries to identify
the causes that used to bring on his attacks of *accidia*. Given
the constant alternation of his residence between the Vaucluse
and nearby Avignon, it would not be impossible that he wrote
this page while seated in his study in the Vaucluse.

But while we must be careful not to overestimate the significance of the passage for determining where the first draft
of the *Secretum* was written, the phrase arouses our interest
by the tone of its attack on Avignon. Following the quoted
portion, the passage ends with a citation of the verse *"Silva
placet Musis, urbs est inimica poetis"* from Petrarch's *Metr.* II 3,
a poem probably written in the summer of 1342. There we find
a similar, bitter reproof of the life in Avignon; yet there is a
basic difference. The complaint in the poem is one that also
occurs in other poems and letters of the late 1330's and early
1340's. The noise of Avignon, we are told, kills every contem-
plative and creative mood; people from all nations converge
at the papal seat and make Avignon the noisiest and most un-
pleasant of all cities. *Metr.* II 3 describes with despair the often
farcical street scenes forced upon the onlooker's attention.[119]
There is, however, no counterpart in the poem, nor in any of
the contemporaneous letters, to the violent disgust—the very
heart of the *Secretum* passage—voiced against Avignon as the
stinking dregs of all the world (*"angustissimam atque ultimam
sentinam et totius orbis sordibus exundantem"*) and its streets as
"graveolentes semitas, permixtas rabidis canibus obscenas sues."
Outside the *Secretum*, it is, in fact, not until the early 1350's,
when Petrarch composed his *Espitolae Sine Nomine* and other
of his most bitter attacks against the Curia, that he uses the
motif of impure Avignon, a place of moral contagion and
pestilence, reeking with evil smells.[120]

---

[118] Ed. Carrara, p. 120. A translation p. 65 above.

[119] *Metr.* II 3, verses 11–51.

[120] Cf. *Fam.* XIII 8, 16, 1352: ". . . odorque pravissimus toti mundo pestifer; quid
mirum si vicinitate nimia unius parvi ruris innocuam polluit puritatem!" *Sine Nomine*
15, *ca.* 1353: "Non populum sed rotatum uento puluerem putes, neque magis ciuitatis
infande uicos quam ciues ipsos fedos ac lubricos fateare" (ed. in P. Piur's *Petrarcas 'Buch
ohne Namen' und die päpstliche Kurie* [Halle/Saale, 1925], p. 216).

So for a third time we have found a passage in which the tone and phrasing contradict what we should expect for the early 1340's on the basis of other sources, whereas it corresponds with what we know of Petrarch's thinking and writing in the early 1350's. Since the passage appears in a portion of the text which shows several other changes made during the early 1350's, there can be little doubt that we must regard the portrait of Avignon in the *accidia* section as having been written or essentially retouched during Petrarch's last stay in Avignon, or soon afterwards in Milan.

These are in all likelihood not the only passages which careful comparison with other works by Petrarch would reveal as inconsistent with his outlook during the early 1340's, but in harmony with later phases of his life. For instance, the long page on the need to control anger (*ira*), found between the passages just discussed,[121] has very much the same tone as the *De Remediis* and seems quite superfluous to the original scheme of the work because *ira* had already been dealt with in its proper place in the context of Petrarch's character portrait.[122] Since at that point Petrarch had been found relatively free from this vice, there was particularly little reason for a return to it in the debates on *accidia*. Very probably, therefore, it was the later philosopher of the *De Remediis* who found it desirable to deal in greater detail with the relationship between *ira* and reason.

But we make no pretense of providing an exhaustive analysis of the entire text, not even within the three extensive sections in which we have encountered so many marks of later years. Although a book of personal confessions, the *Secretum* is much too elaborate and finished a work of art for us to hope ever to divide its text neatly into successive layers. Not only is it impossible, but fortunately there is no desperate need for it thanks to the wealth of other literary and epistolary sources from which the growth of Petrarch's thought can be observed. The best view of the possible historical uses of the *Secretum* can perhaps be gained by considering this work together with Petrarch's closely preceding major opus, the *Africa*. Both works were conceived relatively early, were revised in tone

---

[121] Pp. 122–24 in Carrara's edition.   [122] Ed. Carrara, pp. 96–98.

and details in periods when Petrarch's attitude toward life had changed, and so carefully integrated afterwards that no effort to separate the layers can ever be fully successful. In each case, the essential thing is to advance as far as is necessary to judge the tendency of later changes and to become sufficiently equipped for dealing with the vexing questions which arise wherever information taken from these works seems to contradict that from other sources.

The study of the *Africa* has over the years yielded many helpful insights into the nature and structure of the places where the text of the epic has been tampered with. The observations made in the present chapter prove that we can succeed equally well with regard to the *Secretum*. Here, too, the fundamental point is the recognition that there exist definable areas where the text is extensively disturbed, and that attention paid to the occurrence of a suspicious-looking passage in such an area can often spare us the perplexity bound to arise as long as we consider the *Secretum* to be all of a piece and a document that gives evidence of Petrarch's thought merely for the year 1342–43.

3 CHRONOLOGY AND HISTORICAL CERTAINTY: The Dates of Bruni's *Laudatio* and *Dialogi*

I. The past ten years have seen wide assent accorded to the conclusion that it was the defense and survival of the Florentine Republic in the wars against Giangaleazzo Visconti that finally determined the emergence in Quattrocento Florence of a politically minded, community-conscious Humanism, which we call "Civic Humanism". Unless all signs are misleading, however, we have by now reached the point where scholars would like to take another hard look at the basis and prerequisite of this assumption—the recent revision of the dates of many works of Florentine literature of about 1400, and especially of Leonardo Bruni's early humanistic writings.

If critical re-examination of the revised chronology is to produce lasting results, our questions must be put into focus from those vantage points which have by now become accessible, more than a decade after the ground was broken. We should not wait to see how arguments first set forth in 1955[1] will stand up under today's questioning but should rather try to revaluate, reorder, and reduce to essentials the fundamental data. But before considering any details, we must recall the reasons why students should have ventured to ascribe the role of a historic turning point—psychologically, intellectually, and politically—to the concluding phase of the Milanese-Florentine struggle: the last years of Giangaleazzo's life, and most of all the climactic spring and summer of 1402.

The rise in early-Quattrocento Florence of a type of Humanism different in vital respects from everything seen in the Trecento is a phenomenon that would have to be taken into consideration even if the Visconti wars were of less importance for the changes in political and cultural outlook than is at present usually assumed. Even in that case it would remain true that Florentine humanists, during the early fifteenth

---

[1] Primarily in my *Humanistic and Political Literature in Florence and Venice*, as well as in chapters 10 and 11 and some notes and appendices of the first edition of *The Crisis of the Early Italian Renaissance*.

century, produced a code of civic values not found among men who were essentially courtiers or *literati*, unattached to the life of an active, political citizenry. And it would still remain a fact that nearly all Florentine humanists adhered to a view of the historical past—Roman as well as Florentine—which did not develop outside Florence except under Florentine influence; just as among Florentine humanists there sprang up at an earlier date than in other humanistic circles a critique of classicism, defending the Moderns against excessive adoration of Antiquity and especially intended to vindicate the vernacular, the language of modern Florence and Italy.

Nevertheless, the phenomenon of civic Humanism would be much less transparent in its motivations, and its development would look quite different, if the belief that the wars against Giangaleazzo were a strong molding influence had to be dismissed. In the picture of the period which I attempted to draw in 1955, Florentine Quattrocento Humanism is not viewed as a mere gradual transformation of fourteenth-century movements, whether Petrarchan Humanism or Florentine Trecento life and thought. Just as Florentine art during the first generation of the Quattrocento experienced a profound metamorphosis in style, technique, and motivation, so a comparable transformation is seen to have occurred in the political thought and Humanism of that generation. There emerged in a brief span of years a new style in political thinking, a new perspective in historiography, new techniques in historical criticism, and changed ideals of human and civic conduct. In short, we assume in this view that Florentine Humanism after 1400 was marked by a rapid affirmation of new values and a fresh, realistic perceptiveness that in many respects meant the transition from medievalism to a more modern pattern of thinking.

We could hardly believe in the possibility of such a sudden change were there no explanation to fall back upon save growing humanistic intimacy with the literature of antiquity. When we look for other factors, we find no major social, constitutional, or economic transformations in Florence or Italy. But, owing to the successful resistance to Giangaleazzo, there did occur in the international status of the Florentine city-state a profound change whose emotional effects and actual impact on the political structure of Italy went far toward causing an upheaval in the world of the Trecento. In consequence of the steady expansion of the Milanese territory, the Republic of Florence was, by the time of Giangaleazzo's death in September 1402, the only state still fighting on against the otherwise established domination of the entire region between the Alps in the north, the Venetian island state in the east, and the Papal State in the south by the strongest tyranny in Renaissance Italy. Until not many years before, Florence had considered itself, and acted in its foreign relations, as one of the many members of the Guelph camp led by the papacy. Now, for the first time, it acted independently as a great power and as the only great Italian republic (for Venice, protected by its island position, was not yet participating in the struggle for the Italian mainland). Thus, in the year 1402, the political fate of the peninsula and the future of republican freedom in Italy seemed to depend on the Florentine citizens who decided to keep up their lonely resistance.

Once attention is focused on this complete and abrupt change in Florence's international position and stature, many features of Florentine thought and ideals during the early Quattrocento seem to fall into place. From the very first decade of the century, Florentine humanists began to be convinced that Rome had flowered when it was the free *Respublica Romana*, and that it had decayed under imperial monarchy. This view of Rome's history had not been elaborated to any extent by Florentine humanists during the Trecento. To the generation which saw the Giangaleazzo wars it quickly became so persuasive as to sap the traditional tendency to look upon the monarchy of the Roman emperors as the chrysalis of the divinely guided Universal Empire of Christian times. From then on, Florentine citizens dared to compare themselves with those of the republics of Rome and Athens, to view Florence's position among the Italian states as analogous to those held by Rome in Italy and Athens in Greece, and to draw a parallel between the growth of their own culture and language and that of the culture and languages of the ancient city-state republics.[2]

---

[2] This is the picture of Florentine early Quattrocento thought first proposed in the 1955 edition of *Crisis* and epitomized in the "Epilogue" of the revised edition of 1966.

It is impossible to believe that all these profound changes in thought, evaluation, and self-awareness could have occurred so rapidly unless impelled by something other than the gradual extension of the humanistic knowledge of classical authors. And since no cause but the resistance to the deadly threat of the Visconti is discernible, one would expect the political events of the year 1402 to play the role of a dividing line in Florentine literature; one would assume that the works characterized by a new outlook on politics and history were naturally composed not before but after—and not long after—the experience of 1402.

When, during the 1930's, the conception of a "Civic Humanism" was first being tested in various fields, the historical evidence was still far from sufficiently sifted and weighed. In most cases, the dating of the Florentine writings of the period had been left to neo-Latin scholars or to students of Italian literature. The findings of these scholars seemed to give little encouragement to the assumption that the year 1402 marked a critical turning point. Some of the relevant writings were thought to have preceded the decisive events of the war; others, according to the accepted view, had originated under conditions in which the influence of the wars was little felt. The possibility of conceiving Florentine Humanism as a strongly politically oriented movement from its inception depended clearly on the possibility of altering the dates of many of those works—on historical criticism of the sources of information no less than on a new historical interpretation and reconstruction. When, therefore, my *Crisis of the Early Italian Renaissance* appeared in 1955, analysis and narrative were accompanied by an effort to revise the chronology of practically all the important pieces of Florentine literature in the period of the transition—the burden of *Humanistic and Political Literature in Florence and Venice at the Beginning of the Quattrocento.*[3]

The critical exploration of Bruni's works was merely a part of this general revision. To see the full meaning of their re-dating, one must view them in the context of what it has been possible to establish about the dates and motivations of the

---

[3] And also of some pages of *Crisis;* see note 1, p. 102, above.

works of other writers of the period. There were four major groups of Florentine writings that had to be restudied.

In the first group was the *Paradiso degli Alberti*, a novel which describes conversations allegedly held by Florentine humanists and citizens in 1389. It assigns to their discussions some aspects of the republican interpretation of Roman and Florentine history characteristic of Florentine writers during the Quattrocento. Study of the *Paradiso* in 1955 revealed that some of the information from classical authors used in the alleged debates of 1389 actually did not become accessible until after 1400. In the second group—war pamphlets of publicists—two rejoinders to Milanese propaganda by the citizen Cino Rinuccini and the humanist-chancellor Salutati could be proved (as, indeed, their text implies) to have been written while the fight was on; they were not mere literary exercises done after the wars were over, as the traditional chronology had it.[4] Their changed dates also show that Rinuccini, a

---

[4] This is true even of Salutati's pamphlet, although its composition was interrupted and it was neither finished nor allowed to circulate until after the war. The fact that the groundwork for Salutati's answer had been laid soon after the beginning of hostilities in 1397 is proved in particular by his assertion in the pamphlet that certain vital political events, which occurred after 1398, would never occur. This has been strangely overlooked by B. L. Ullman in an attempt to revive the opinion that the pamphlet was *in toto* written after the war because a letter of Salutati of 1403 on the release of his work fails to state that Salutati had known, and begun to answer, Loschi's attack years before. (See Ullman's *The Humanism of Coluccio Salutati* [Padua, 1963], pp. 33 f.) Ullman, in other words, arrives at his astonishing assertion by refusing (without an explanation) to undertake a structural analysis of Salutati's work; by basing all his conclusions on that most notoriously deceptive of arguments, *ex silentio;* and by thoroughly misinterpreting the meaning of Salutati's letter, as I have pointed out in some detail in the revised edition of the *Crisis*, pp. 484 ff.

Despite the fallacy of his objections to the new chronology, it may be well, however, to state that even if Ullman's case were better than it is, the oddly incoherent *Invectiva* of Salutati, which is remarkable by its very failure to let itself be influenced by the lessons of the Giangaleazzo wars, is not a source whose dating is of prime importance for a chronology determined by the sequence of changes of ideas under the impact of the Florentine confrontation with Milan. Insofar as Salutati's humanistic work plays any role at all in the chronology of change about 1400, the only vital point is the (fully demonstrable) fact that his critical reconstruction of Florence's foundation by veterans of Sulla, which was eventually incorporated in his *Invectiva*, had not yet existed in 1398; that is, not before the final Florentine encounter with Milan (see *Humanistic and Political Literature*, pp. 22 f.).

Equally important is the establishment of another date. Vital for the validity of the chronology, as far as the writing of the publicists during the war is concerned, is our transfer of the exchange between Loschi and Rinuccini, which had been placed after the war by literary students, to the first phase of the combat in 1397. On this date depend the conclusions that the start of a republican reinterpretation of history, owed to Rinuccini, occurred under the impact of the events of the war, and that the reaction of this citizen who was not a humanist preceded any of the new ideas of Quattrocento Humanism.

non-humanist citizen, was the first to stress the role of republican liberty in history, whereas among the humanists comparable observations had to wait for Bruni. In examining the third group—Florentine historical interpretations of the wars with Giangaleazzo—precedence was again found in a Volgare writer, Gregorio Dati. His *"Istoria* of Florence 1380–1406" proved to have been written early enough after the Florentine trial to be a witness to the full, immediate impact of the Florentine-Milanese struggle. As our next chapter will show, this result of the re-examination of Dati's work can now be buttressed by new findings.

It is with the knowledge of the proven relatedness of this entire literature to the political experience of the Giangaleazzo era that we must approach Bruni's early works—the fourth group of Florentine writings around 1400. At the center is the *Laudatio Florentinae Urbis.* Here we encounter the claims that Florence had saved liberty in Italy, had become the heir to the republicanism founded by the *Respublica Romana*, and was in humanistic studies and vernacular literature providing a focus for Italy as Athens had provided a focus for the culture of Greece. Confronted with these claims and the tone of Florentine confidence pervading the work, no reader would think of any other date for its composition but the years immediately following the Florentine survival, were it not for one puzzling and confusing fact: the *Laudatio* is discussed in detail in the other major work of Bruni's youth, the *Dialogi,* a composition, according to its opening pages, of the summer of 1401. Given this cross-reference by the author himself, scholars, in spite of the internal evidence, had long wavered over the date of the *Laudatio* when, in 1955, the old puzzle seemed at last to be solved—here, too, in favor of the assumption of the decisive impact of the Florentine-Milanese struggle, and of a post-1402 origin.

The significance of the *Laudatio* chronology for the entire history of Humanism and political thought in Florence must by now be evident. Unless a post-1402 date can be established in this case, it would not help us to know that the new Florentine ideas are elsewhere found only after 1402. If they existed anywhere before 1402, they could not have been a consequence of 1402. The answer to the crucial question—whether we are allowed to look upon the nascent Quattrocento ideas as a response to the actual events of Florentine life—depends, therefore, largely on the date of the *Laudatio*, or, because of the citation of the *Laudatio* in the *Dialogi*, on the solution of the chronological puzzle of both works. No student or historian of the Renaissance can ignore this problem of historical criticism. The new chronology, with its special emphasis on Bruni's two works, and the historical interpretation of fifteenth-century Florentine Humanism as "Civic Humanism" are allied in the sense that if one is harmed, the other, too, must suffer.

This reciprocity explains why the chronology of Bruni's humanistic beginnings has had changing fortunes in recent years. Whereas in 1955 no serious student seemed to doubt the finality of the chronological revisions then first proposed,[5] doubts were eventually raised by those who, for one reason or another, found themselves unwilling to accept the view that a type of Humanism developed in Florence that was profoundly transformed by the conditions of Florentine life.

Three schools of scholarship, in particular, have of late emerged which are inherently critical of a historical interpretation based on the concept of civic Humanism. First there are those who do not believe that a genuine desire for republican freedom was still a factor in the Quattrocento. Quite understandably, these students are inclined to question a chronology suggesting that Humanism in early Quattrocento Florence was molded by republican sentiment sparked by a war for independence. Similarly incredulous are those who, with certain modifications, cling to the traditional concept of

---

5 Except for the objections raised by M. Seidlmayer in *Göttingische Gelehrte Anzeigen*, 1956 (pp. 35–63)—mere speculations and insinuations, lacking any factual basis, but contending that the entire new chronology was "ein methodisch gefährlicher Weg," a "*circulus vitiosus*": "die Gian Galeazzo These wird für die Datierungen richtungweisend und diese wiederum müssen jene erhärten und erklären." As for the dates of the *Paradiso*, the *Laudatio* and *Dialogus II*, although "bei den ausserordentlich komplizierten und langwierigen Erörterungen Barons" it was impossible "diese kritische Reserve an Hand von Beispielen näher zu begründen," and although "auch keine einfache Ablehnung der von Baron vorgelegten Datierungen ausgesprochen werden soll," "muss es ebenso offen gesagt werden, dass wir . . . nicht imstande sind, ernstliche Fragezeichen [though not explained or named] hinder den Ergebnissen des Verfassers zu unterdrücken" (esp. pp. 60 f.). These helpless efforts to undermine confidence in the new chronology could not be taken seriously and, according to my knowledge, were hardly paid attention to until their recent republication in Seidlmayer's *Wege und Wandlungen des Humanismus* (Göttingen, 1965).

Humanism as primarily a new philology or a new development in rhetorical aspirations—viewpoints from which the Humanism of the Quattrocento may appear less unlike that of the Trecento. Followers of this philological-rhetorical school find it *a priori* unlikely that the social and political environment should have caused such profound and sudden changes in the nature of Humanism as the picture of the period suggested by the new chronology would imply. If humanists praised liberty—so we are told—they did so in the uncommitted manner of "rhetoricians", just as they praised monarchy on other occasions; they did not do it because their convictions had changed under the impact of events, such as those of the Giangaleazzo wars.

Obviously, students influenced by these two tendencies—distrust of Quattrocento republicanism, and a recrudescence of the emphasis on humanistic rhetoric and philology—can easily cooperate, and the reluctance of both groups to believe that fundamental changes occurred around 1400 is strengthened by a third new trend: the relatively negative evaluation of the Quattrocento now found in various schools of economic history. First came the widely accepted theory of a general European economic stagnation and regression after the middle of the fourteenth century, which darkened the picture of the Quattrocento. Then, more recently, economic historians, especially in Italy, began to regard the world of the thirteenth- and early fourteenth-century Italian communes with their highly developed commercial elite as having produced the real "Renaissance," and fifteenth-century Humanism and politics merely as its late and already declining phase—a view leading to further skepticism toward any approach in which the intellectual and political struggles of about 1400 appear as significant causes in the transition of Renaissance Italy, and Florence in particular, to a more modern pattern of life and thought.

There is no doubt that the new assumptions, combining with one another, have brought about a changed climate of opinion in which, only a decade after their initial formulation, the theses of 1955 face a much harsher test than could have been foreseen when these current trends in scholarship had not yet emerged. As stated in the introduction to my present book, I think, under the circumstances, a serious effort should be made to expand the chronological study of the crucial documents, and especially of Bruni's early works, beyond the results reached in *Humanistic and Political Literature* to the point where the dates of their composition can be proved without any reference to the interpretation of Florentine Humanism of which my theory of their genesis was originally a part. To put it more succinctly, the interpretative reasoning in favor of the new chronology given in the *Crisis* with the help of such textual and manuscript observations as were available through *Humanistic and Political Literature* must now be paralleled by a purely technical line of reasoning that can stand on its own. I want to state clearly, however, that I do not regard any part of the interpretative reasoning of the *Crisis* in favor of the new chronology as faulty or out of date. It is still true that, as far as the *Laudatio* is concerned, full understanding of its purpose and origin demands a knowledge of the nature of the Florentine-Visconti struggle, as well as of the rhetorical objectives of the work, which in some cases determine inclusion or exclusion of references to events of the war. By the same token, an exhaustive view of the nature and relationship of the two "*dialogi*" requires the awareness, developed in the *Crisis*, that each dialogue reflects a different attitude of the author toward his Florentine environment, as well as toward the Ciceronian work (the *De Oratore*) that served as a literary model in both dialogues, though to a very different extent. This, however, does not mean that it is not also possible to date either work without recourse to these or any other interpretative considerations.

The pages which follow will be a complement to, not a replacement of, the earlier line of thought also because in 1955 I found it indispensable to set forth the complete findings of long years of investigation; a full account had to be given of all the routes that had been traveled, including those that had led to less than final conviction. Moreover, I had for every work of Bruni to establish not only whether it was written after the dividing line of 1402, but also whether it originated in 1403, or 1404, or even later, and in which month, and at what place—all of which must be known for Bruni's biography and for the full story of the genesis of fifteenth-century Florentine Humanism. Today, when several antagonistic interpretations of Florence's Humanism and politics are contesting, the all-decisive question which must be answered by everyone—whatever theory he may hold—comes to the simple alternative: were the *Laudatio* and the *Dialogi* composed before or after the experience of 1402? Within these narrower boundaries, the validity of the new Bruni chronology can be demonstrated quite differently from the more inclusive argument of 1955. Based in part on fresh observations in the analysis of the texts, the reasoning with respect to this more pointed question can, indeed, be greatly simplified and more sharply focused upon the degree of cogency attained by the inherent logic of the argument.

Truly effective historical criticism has usually gone beyond the mere accumulation of "plausible" or "probable" inferences. It has sought to establish self-evident certainty for one or a few crucial data, or to single out a number of mutually supporting findings of such certainty that the opposite becomes incredible. If evidence of this sort can be found, it is no longer the *quantity* of observations which is needed to turn the balance; it even may be best to ignore some merely "plausible" lines of reasoning, in order to forge a chain in which all the links are of equal strength. What counts in such a context is the place and function of every piece of proof and, consequently, the particular order—the intrinsic logic—of the argument.

I do not think that the logic of the reasoning which proves the post-1402 origin of the *Laudatio* and of some related writings of Bruni's was brought out clearly enough in 1955; nor could this have been done at the time, for the reasons already pointed out. Yet when it comes to the final test for the new chronology, the very method of our procedure—the question of what forms of conclusive critical demonstration are applicable to the case—will account for the result as much as the soundness of any single finding.

II. The chronological bewilderment encountered in the study of Bruni's *Laudatio* and *Dialogi* is of a kind not unknown to students of the literature of the Italian Renaissance. The history of Bruni's literary production seems to begin with an absurdity: the *Laudatio*, a work which to all appearances talks of the era of Giangaleazzo as a period already past and mentions the Milanese occupation of Bologna, Florence's last ally (in June 1402), is cited in the *Dialogi*, a work composed in the summer of 1401 according to indications at the opening of the first dialogue. We know two other, more famous incidents in Italian Renaissance literature where an author's reference to what appears to be a later, not yet written, work has challenged the ingenuity of critical readers: the reference in Dante's *De Monarchia* to the *"Paradiso"* of the *Divine Comedy* (his last work) and the mention in Machiavelli's *Prince* of a work which must be the later published *Discourses*.

In each of these perplexing cases we must choose between two potential explanations: either the later work named in the cross-reference already existed in an earlier version which was different from the published version that we have, or else the cross-reference in the earlier work is an interpolation or, in any case, was written later than its presumed date. If we had very early manuscripts, there would probably be no difficulties at all, but since prepublication texts have rarely survived, the occurrence of no less than three such provocative instances in the history of Renaissance political thought warns us that the student, thus challenged, cannot forgo critical reasoning in the hope of finding documents in the future. He has to try to solve the puzzles that need to be solved.

Modern criticism of the *Laudatio-Dialogi* problem began eighty years ago with the hypothesis that the *Laudatio*, when summarized in the *Dialogi*, did not as yet include the passages referring to the events of 1402 and that, therefore, the composition of the *Laudatio* took place in two stages, one before 1402 and the other after—even though no concrete evidence pointing in this direction could be produced when this conjecture was made in 1889. However, the hypothesis was not really farfetched; a scholar at that stage might well feel himself in a prison with only two doors; having assured himself that his key did not fit the one exit, he could hope that it would open the other. Since G. Kirner, the author of those earliest critical efforts, realized his inability to get around the apparent fact that the *Laudatio* had been praised and summarized in a work of 1401, he was entitled to propose as a working hypothesis the only possible alternative—the assumption of a gradual genesis of the *Laudatio* itself. It must be emphasized, however, that, as the years passed, nothing was found that might be considered even the slightest indication of interpolations having been made. On the contrary, it is possible to make a number of observations that seem to run counter to any theory of a successive composition of the *Laudatio*.[6]

To begin with, the eulogy imitates a Greek work—the *Panathenaicus* of Aelius Aristides—which celebrates Athens as the savior of the cities of Greece from the despotism of the King of Persia. Bruni would hardly have chosen this model as his guide before the time when Florence, after its lonely resistance to Giangaleazzo, could in similar terms be celebrated as the savior of the cities of Italy. It is very unlikely that any version of the *Laudatio* was written until the events of 1402 had allowed Bruni to see Florence through Aristides' eyes.

Second, the arrangement of the section in which the major references to the struggle with Giangaleazzo occur suggests that the author must have known of Florence's triumph from the moment he planned his chapter. The chapter in question is that on the "*res foris gestae*" and is designed to eulogize Florence's deeds against other states; it was already part of the text when the *Laudatio* was summarized in the *Dialogi*. In analyzing the chapter, we find that, in addition to the description of the wars with Giangaleazzo, it includes only two other examples of Florentine military deeds, both from the middle of the thirteenth century. Would any eulogy of Florence be imaginable in which the most recent "great deed" of the city mentioned lies a century and a half in the past? Moreover, in the introductory survey of his work, the author states expressly that in the "*res foris gestae*" chapter the past and the present are equally intended to make his point: the city's greatness would become clear "from . . . her deeds in both our own age and earlier periods." Thus it is certain that praise of the wars with Giangaleazzo was a part of Bruni's

---

[6] For details on Kirner and on the objections to his thesis, cf. the chapter "Two Versions of the *Laudatio*? A Blind Alley" in *Humanistic and Political Literature*, esp. pp. 75 ff. His *Della 'Laudatio Urbis Florentinae' di Leonardo Bruni* appeared in 1889.

text from the beginning. How could he possibly have offered such praise in 1400 when it looked as if the struggle with Giangaleazzo would end in one of the worst humiliations in Florence's history?

Finally, it is impossible to reconcile our information concerning the first reception of the *Laudatio* with the two-version hypothesis. A letter by Bruni of 1403 or 1404 seems to say that Salutati on that occasion was to be shown a manuscript of the *Laudatio* for the first time.[7] If the two-version hypothesis were correct, he ought to have known the work, except for the post-1402 insertions, since 1401. Moreover, since the discussion in the *Dialogi* presumes that the *Laudatio* had already brought Bruni honor, how can we speculate about interpolations in a circulated work as long as there is no trace of manuscripts descended from the texts of the alleged first version?

To point out the high degree of persuasiveness carried by all these observations is not to forget our postulate that the chronology of the *Laudatio* and the *Dialogi* should avoid the danger of mere "probability." The two-version hypothesis, if it is to be conclusively refuted, must be given a *coup de grâce* on safer grounds. These grounds will gradually emerge in the course of our discussions. Until then we should keep in mind that the two-version hypothesis for the *Laudatio* riddle still retains a glimmer of life, even though it is a rather feeble one, to judge from what we have seen. Its feebleness explains why scholars never cared much for it and why about ten years later a totally different attempt was made to harmonize the interpretation of the *Laudatio* with the apparent testimony of the *Dialogi*.

This second hypothesis now seems to have been a counsel of despair. Is it not suspicious, it was asked in 1901 by a student of Italian literature, F. P. Luiso,[8] that, when we forget about the general tenor of the *Laudatio*, we find only a single ap-

---

[7] "*Seems* to say" because Bruni does not expressly say "for the first time"; but this appears to be implied in his way of expression. See *Humanistic and Political Literature*, pp. 72 f., 81 f.

[8] In "Commento a una lettera di L. Bruni e cronologia di alcune sue opere," *Raccolta di studii critici dedicata ad Alessandro D'Ancona* (Florence, 1901), pp. 85–95. For what follows, cf. the chapter "The Alleged Pre-1402 Origin of the *Laudatio*. A Refutation," *Humanistic and Political Literature*, pp. 82 ff.

parent occurrence from the year 1402, namely, the occupation of Bologna, clearly cited, whereas even the death of Giangaleazzo Visconti is nowhere referred to? The events of the war which are mentioned, with the single exception of the subjection of Bologna, all took place in 1400 or the preceding years. Are we not, therefore, mistaken in considering that the *Laudatio* was necessarily composed after 1402? Might it not be that what seems an exception—the Bologna incident—is actually a reference to an event of the time around 1400, the years so well represented in Bruni's account? According to what Bruni, many years later, narrated in his *Historiae Florentini Populi*, there had been rumors in 1399, soon proved false, that the people of Bologna, tempted by the offers which Giangaleazzo was then extending to many cities, "had entered into friendship with him and in some manner let drop its old alliance with Florence."⁹ If this was the incident Bruni had in mind, exaggerating it for rhetorical purposes, the entire *Laudatio* could have been written in the second half of 1400 or during the first few months of the next year.

Seldom has a weaker case been presented by a responsible scholar. If Bruni's words in the *Laudatio* really did suggest anything comparable to the suspicion of secret negotiations mentioned in the *Historiae*, we might have reason to consider the possible identity of the Bologna episodes referred to in the two works, but the *Laudatio* says that in the case in question Giangaleazzo "had . . . *occupied* Bologna." Bologna was occupied by Milanese troops in June 1402; in 1399 it was not even rumored that this had happened. A year or two after 1399, therefore, when it was clear that Bologna had not seen a single Milanese soldier within its walls, Bruni could not possibly have spoken of an "occupation," whatever the degree of willful rhetorical distortion of which a suspicious reader might deem him capable.

Let us, however, assume for the sake of argument that Bruni did the unbelievable and that, late in 1400 or early in 1401, he did wish to inflate the rumor of 1399 into an "occupa-

---

⁹ "Per haec ipsa tempora, Bononienses, Galeatii legationibus deliniti, in eius amicitiam concessisse putabantur, ac veterem Florentinorum societatem quodammodo antiquasse." *Historiarum Florentini Populi Libri XII*, ed. E. Santini (*Rerum Italicarum Scriptores*, XIX, pars 3), p. 276.

tion" of Bologna. Could he have written the passage in the
Laudatio at that time? The passage states that, at the height
of Giangaleazzo's formidable power, all city-states in northern Italy, Tuscany, and the Flaminia (that is, roughly,
Emilia and Romagna), from one sea to the other, "were
under his rule and obeyed his order. In Tuscany he held Pisa,
Siena, Perugia, and Assisi in his grip, and eventually he had
even occupied Bologna."¹⁰ This is a list of Giangaleazzo's
conquests that proceeds chronologically. Pisa accepted his
lordship early in 1399, Siena during the summer; Perugia
recognized him as *signore* at the beginning of 1400, Assisi received Milanese troops in May. Conjecturing with Luiso
that the passage was written during the autumn–winter of
1400–1401, that is, after Perugia and Assisi had become
Milanese, and that Bologna was included on account of an
event that had taken place in 1399, it is evident that Bruni
could not in that case have placed Bologna at the end of his
list; he would have mentioned it along with Pisa and Siena,
which lost their independence in 1399, before listing the fall
of Perugia and Assisi in 1400. Under no condition could he
have stated that Bologna had been the last of Giangaleazzo's
conquests; yet this is what his words, "and *eventually* he had
even occupied Bologna [*tandem etiam Bononiam occuparat*],"
expressly say. Here we have left the realm of speculation and
conjecture and are confronted with a definite fact: the passage
as it stands *cannot have been written before June 1402.*

Although this statement would be valid without any further
proof, the sentence yields equally incontestable evidence by
its grammatical structure, namely, by its use of the past
tense. Bruni unquestionably describes Giangaleazzo's empire
as a thing of the past: all those lands "were [*not* are] under
his rule and obeyed [*not* obey] his order"; "he *held* in his
grip [*tenebat*]" Pisa and other city-states until "eventually he
had even occupied [*occuparat*]" Bologna, that is, he no longer
held and occupied those places. Needless to say, had Bruni been
writing in 1400 or 1401, he could not have phrased these pas-

---

¹⁰ "Potentiam habebat maximam atque formidandam: omnes Gallie cisalpine tractus,
omnes ferme civitates que ab Alpibus ad Etruriam atque Flaminiam inter dua maria
continentur, in eius potestate erant dictoque parebant; in Etruria vero Pisas, Senas,
Perusiam, Assisium tenebat, tandem etiam Bononiam occuparat." See the edition of
the *Laudatio*, p. 257, below.

sages in the past tense because at that time Giangaleazzo's control of Pisa, Siena, Perugia, Assisi (and later Bologna as well), was a grim reality—a deadly menace to Florence's future existence. The mere fact, therefore, that all this is reported in the past tense rules out any speculation that the sentence was composed during Giangaleazzo's lifetime, even as a working hypothesis.

It would be equally impermissible for a critic to speculate, with Luiso, about the reasons why the *Laudatio* does not tell us explicitly about the death of Giangaleazzo. In a *history* of the wars with Giangaleazzo it would, no doubt, be puzzling if the death of the archenemy were not told in sufficient detail; but the description of wars given in the *Laudatio* is nothing but an illustration of some "great deeds" of the Florentines in their relations with other states—the *res foris gestae* section—and one could think of many reasons why the author should not have wished or cared to repeat what every reader knew a year or two after Giangaleazzo's death, namely, that the Duke had died of the plague. Once more, if we want to rise above mere speculation, we must not inquire into the motivation, which we cannot know, of Bruni's failure to do a thing he was under no compulsion to do, but must ask whether what Bruni wrote can have been written under the historical conditions of the period before Giangaleazzo's death. What Bruni could not foresee in Giangaleazzo's lifetime was that Florence would survive in a lonely fight; nor could he, at that time, view Giangaleazzo's menace to Florence as already past. One must also remember that in 1400–1401 Milan had either occupied or caused to defect from the Florentine alliance every single north- and central-Italian city with the exception of Bologna, whereas on the morrow after the triumph of 1402 Florence could feel that it had defended a common cause until the moment when the subjects of Giangaleazzo's empire could again become independent. All this must be borne in mind when one reads Bruni's portrait of Giangaleazzo and of Giangaleazzo's relationship to Florence:

> Can . . . anybody be found who would deny that all Italy would have fallen into the power of Giangaleazzo, had not this one commonwealth withstood his might with

its energy and wisdom? For who in all Italy was then comparable to that enemy . . . [*Quis enim erat in tota Italia qui . . . cum illo hoste comparari potuisset*]? Or who would have endured to the end the onset of a foe whose very name brought terror to every mortal?

The Milanese Duke, Bruni goes on to say, could have been a happy and eminently able prince, had he repressed his vicious desire to sow discord among the Italian states in order to rule over the divided. But Florence remained mindful of her traditional mission to preserve the freedom of Italy; she resisted, and saved all. As Bruni had claimed earlier in the eulogy:

> What greater thing could this commonwealth accomplish . . . , than by her own efforts and resources to liberate the whole of Italy from the threat of servitude [*quam universa Italia suo labore suisque facultatibus a servitutis periculo liberata*]? In consequence of which feat she receives congratulations, praises, and thanks from all nations every day.
>
> Only a very short time ago, this city fought the most powerful and resourceful enemy through many years with such energy that all the world was filled with admiration [*Nuperrime vero adversus potentissimum et opulentissimum hostem ita summa vi per multos annos contendit ut omnium mentes in admirationem converteret*]. For, the same Duke who, on account of his resources and power, was a source of fear to transalpine nations as well as to all Italy [*cuius opes et potentiam et transalpine gentes et reliqua omnis formidabat Italia*], puffed up in his hopes, vainglorious in victory, racing along like a tempest, occupying everything with amazing success, found himself confronted by this one commonwealth, which not only repulsed the invader and checked the course of his victories, but even overthrew him after a long war [*verum etiam post longum bellum affligeret*].[11]

Here as elsewhere, there may be certain hyperbolical contentions that do not correspond to the actual course of events—Florence did not "overthrow Giangaleazzo after a long war"; it was the plague that caused his eclipse and the dissolution of his state. Yet, unmistakable in spite of all rhetorical distortions is Bruni's confrontation of a past dominated by

---

[11] See the full text pp. 256–58 and 238, below.

the Lord of Milan with a present in which his figure has disappeared. There is a recurrent assumption that Florence, not long ago (*nuperrime*), survived the fiercest onslaught in a defense of all Italy, and that, accordingly, now that the peninsula has become free again, all Italy feels grateful to the Florentine people. It is impossible that these ideas could have been expressed in 1400 or 1401, when the last free states in central Italy were falling under Milanese domination, without a miraculous presentiment of what would happen in 1402. Like the statement on the Milanese "occupation" of Bologna following the seizure of Perugia and Assisi, these are passages capable of one and only one chronological interpretation. We are accustomed to say that we cannot reach mathematical certainty on problems of historical criticism, but the self-evidence of these various observations on the *Laudatio* is just as incontestable. There can be no disputing that what we read in the *Laudatio* concerning Bologna and the already bygone relationship between Florence and Giangaleazzo cannot have been written before June and September 1402, respectively.

The one scruple that remains is how it can have happened that observations which appear self-evident were not only missed in 1901 by an earnest scholar, but were also subsequently overlooked for more than half a century. One explanation is that, once it had become clear that the two-version hypothesis of Kirner could not be buttressed by any concrete evidence, Luiso's effort to move the date of the *Laudatio* back to 1400 held an uncommon appeal. Since nobody, after the abandonment of the two-version hypothesis, had yet found a way to reconcile the date of the *Laudatio* with that of the *Dialogi*, the turn to the apparent only alternative—that the contemporary political picture drawn in the *Laudatio* had been wrongly identified with the time after 1402—can be well understood. It then seemed to be the only possible solution. Moreover, the reasoning that the omission in the *Laudatio* of certain important events of the year 1402, including Giangaleazzo's death, constitutes a "fact", whereas the different moods of an author writing in 1400 or after September 1402 are "intangibles," suited the positivistic assumptions that prevailed among literary students about 1900.

Last, but not least, it must be noted that the originator of the shift of the *Laudatio* to the pre-1402 period was a student of literature, who considered too few of the historical implications of his theory. He failed to note the chronological sequence of Giangaleazzo's conquests in Bruni's report, as well as the incongruity of the political perspective of this report with the pre-1402 situation—the very points that a student of history is apt to make. Luiso may have noticed the fatal lacunae of his conjectures belatedly, for he never followed up the brief article in which he had proposed them with the planned final book, a reorganization of the chronology of Bruni's *Epistolario* and of his related literary works, even though the book was set up in print and circulated among friends in two or three sets of proofs.[12] As a consequence of the incomplete and frustrating state in which Luiso had left his studies, his working hypothesis for the *Laudatio*, which ought to have been carefully examined and quickly refuted, remained untested and unchallenged until 1955. The factor which finally changed the situation was the discovery that the *Dialogi* offered an escape from the apparent dilemma.

Before dealing with this next phase of the problem, however, we should briefly consider the consequences of our establishment of the post-1402 origin of the *Laudatio* for the biographical reconstruction of Bruni's intellectual development. It happens only too often that apparently definitive critical findings give rise to new problems at other points. It is, therefore, important to recognize that the removal of the *Laudatio* to its correct chronological place in 1403 or 1404 (I here leave untouched the question of the precise date and refer the readers to the studies published in 1955) gives the very opposite results: Bruni's early biography and intellectual development are not exposed to any new uncertainties, but become far more intelligible than before.

This is true, in the first place, of the growth of Bruni's philology, especially in Greek studies. One of his undated early letters[13] refers to both the publication of the *Laudatio*,

---

[12] See *Crisis*, 1st ed., pp. 521 f.

[13] *Epistola I 8.* On the establishment of the date of this letter, as well as the consequences for Bruni's development as a scholar, cf. *Humanistic and Political Literature*, pp. 114 ff.

which he had just finished, and the beginning of his work on the Latin version of Plato's *Phaedo*, his first translation from the Greek. Attribution of the *Laudatio* to the autumn–winter of 1400–1401 would force us to assume that Bruni was at that early date already a skilled translator from the Greek ("skilled," because the letter discusses intricate questions of Plato's Greek style). Yet, at that time he had completed little more than two years of Greek under Chrysoloras' guidance. With the change of the date of the *Laudatio* to post-1402, all this information is transferred from 1400–1401 to 1403 or 1404. We thus obtain a reasonable span of time for the gradual emergence of Bruni's capabilities as a scholar, and especially as a student of Greek.[14]

A similarly important correction becomes possible for our picture of the formation of Bruni's ties with Florence—from the time when he was a newcomer to Florence and a student in Salutati's group to the phase of his life during which he set down in the *Laudatio* most of the motifs of his later historical, political, and patriotic ideas. In 1401, when he sent the conversations described in the *Dialogi* to a friend in Padua, Pier Paolo Vergerio, Bruni had still been far from considering himself on the way to becoming a Florentine. He had no share in that happiness that springs from having a *"patria clara ac nobilis,"* he wrote Vergerio in the Proem; for, alas, his native Arezzo had been humiliated and reduced by fate to near-nothingness. His consolation was that he was privileged to live in a city that was not only flowering in population, architectural beauty, and every other aspect of city life, but had preserved some seeds of the almost extinct *"humanitas"* and *"optimae artes,"* "which grow here daily and before long will surely bring forth much light."[15] Thus Florence was to

---

[14] See "Bruni's Development as a Translator from the Greek," in *Humanistic and Political Literature*, pp. 114 ff.

[15] "Vetus est cuiusdam sapientis sententia felici homini hoc vel in primis adesse oportere, ut patria sibi clara ac nobilis esset. Nos vero, Petre, etsi hac parte felicitatis expertes sumus, quod patria nostra crebris fortunae ictibus diruta est et paene ad nihilum redacta; tamen hoc solatio utimur, quod in ea civitate vivimus, quae ceteris longe antecellere ac praestare videtur. Nam cum frequentia populi, splendore aedificiorum, magnitudine rerum gerendarum civitas haec florentissima est, tum etiam optimarum artium totiusque humanitatis, quae iam penitus extincta videbantur, hic semina quaedam remanserunt, quae quidem in diem crescunt, brevi tempore, ut credimus, lumen non parvum elatura." *Prosatori Latini del Quattrocento* ("La Letteratura Italiana. Storia e Testi," vol. XIII [Milan, 1952]), ed. E. Garin, p. 44.

Bruni at that time an admired center of intellectual stimulation, as Paris has often been for foreign intellectuals settling down on the banks of the Seine to study and write.

By the time Bruni wrote his *Laudatio* two or three years later, he had come in close, personal touch with the political traditions and the contemporary political life of Florence. That this is not mere speculation we learn from his own evaluation of the *Laudatio* found in the *Dialogi*. For, in the second dialogue, Salutati is represented as depicting Bruni as a patriotically motivated defender of the legacy left by Dante, Petrarch, and Boccaccio, while the other members of the circle are made to acknowledge the contribution of Bruni's *Laudatio* to Florentine historical consciousness: they praise his criticism of the overthrow of the Roman Republic by the Roman emperors, and his establishment of a historical link between Florentine Guelphism and the struggle for liberty of the last Roman republicans. For all this, his friends are made to say in *Dialogus II* with a view to the *Laudatio*, Florence should be thankful to Bruni.[16]

These changes in Bruni's contacts with Florence during the years from 1401 to 1403/1404 fit excellently our other evidence for the gradual growth of his ties with the city and of his increasingly intimate relationship with Salutati. In drawing his own portrait in the first dialogue, Bruni, in 1401, had pictured himself as one of the followers of the new philology advocated by Niccolò Niccoli; but, evidently, he still felt himself somewhat of a stranger to the traditions represented by Salutati. For otherwise he would not have made Salutati say that "Leonardo so fully agrees with Niccolò in every opinion that I believe he would rather go astray with him than follow the truth with me." After the composition of the *Laudatio*, the correspondence between Salutati and Bruni reveals that these relations had changed. In 1405 or 1406 Salutati told Bruni that he felt him to be "more than half of my mind, my own self through and through." This is in fact the relationship between the two men which seems to prevail in the second dialogue. It is to Bruni that Salutati is there

---

[16] Cf. ed. Garin, pp. 76 ff.

made to entrust the verdict on Niccoli's attack upon the three great Florentines of the Trecento.[17]

But with these observations we have returned to the perplexing problem of chronology posed by the *Dialogi*. Since it is certain that the *Laudatio* was written after 1402, and since this work is nevertheless discussed in the opening scene of *Dialogus II*, there are potentially only two explanations: either the reference to the *Laudatio* in the *Dialogi* was written after 1403, the earliest date of the *Laudatio*, or else the date 1401 alluded to at the beginning of the *Dialogi* was wrongly suggested by the author.

III. Actually, given the specific circumstances, there is no such alternative; for there can be no doubt about the correctness of the date of 1401 suggested in *Dialogus I*.

Admittedly, we must not accept the author's word without examination when he tells us that his work was written shortly after Easter in the seventh year following the death of a Florentine dear to Salutati's circle, Luigi Marsili (who died in August 1394).[18] For, of course, we cannot exclude the possibility that Bruni changed the number of years which had elapsed since Marsili's death in order to attribute the conversation to a specific moment. Also, a writer may make an unintentional slip in estimating the time since a certain event. But we can find two confirmations, independent of each other, of the date as Bruni gives it.[19]

One lies in the fact that Vergerio in Padua, to whom the work is dedicated, had left Salutati's group and Florence permanently in the spring of 1400. Bruni's *Prooemium* is a warm, personal letter to this former companion, whose departure is still daily felt with distress. As the letter says, the purpose of the small work was to give Vergerio a report on one of the first holiday gatherings of the group after he had left. Easter 1401 is under these conditions a rather late date,

---

[17] On the changes in the relationship between Bruni and Salutati, *Crisis*, 1st ed., pp. 211–14; rev. ed., pp. 234–41.

[18] ". . . Ludovicum theologum . . . , qui abhinc annis septem mortuus est." Ed. Garin, p. 50.

[19] *Humanistic and Political Literature*, pp. 156 ff.

but since Vergerio had still been in Florence on Easter 1400, the following Easter is the one suggested. The second piece of evidence lies in the absence from the *Dialogi* of a figure who would surely be found in a depiction of Salutati's circle in the year 1402 or later. By the spring of 1402, young Poggio Bracciolini had succeeded Vergerio in the friendship of Salutati, Bruni, and Niccoli and had become one of the pillars of Salutati's group. He had not yet played such a role and could, therefore, well be omitted on Easter 1401, when he was nothing but a twenty-one-year-old student who had been a copyist in the service of Salutati for only a few weeks, if at all.

Thus, from whatever angle one approaches the date when Bruni sent his work in its original form to Vergerio, one arrives at the early part of 1401; and, consequently, no doubt is left about the direction in which the solution of the riddle of the *Dialogi* must be sought: the cross-reference to the *Laudatio* must have been an addition to the initial text for Vergerio.

Did this addition comprise only the few paragraphs in which the *Laudatio* is reviewed and praised? One must, of course, seriously consider this possibility, but, on the other hand, it is a basic rule of historical criticism that the hypothesis of an interpolation must never be considered unless we have apparent indications of it—such as we have in Machiavelli's *Prince*, where, only a few lines from the famous cross-reference to the *Discourses*, a subsequently written preface was added to the text. In the case of Bruni's *Dialogi*, no external evidence of later interference with the text has ever been discovered. And, probably, it cannot be discovered; for, since the discussion of the *Laudatio* occurs on the introductory page of *Dialogus II* and not within the context of the debate itself, we have no opportunity to investigate the possible coherence or interruption of the text.

In this situation, there is only one sound procedure: to consider such a hypothesis as a last resort, after all other potential explanations have been tried. If these, too, should remain inconclusive, we would, of course, have to admit that an insertion in a text of 1401 could not be totally excluded. But by examining all other possible lines of inquiry, we certainly will not arrive at a draw. Since 1955 we have known a great number of facts which suggest that *Dialogus II* had not yet been conceived when the *Prooemium* and *Dialogus I* were sent to Vergerio. How certain are these facts and the conclusions that can be drawn from them? Are they capable of putting an end to any apprehension that merely the reference to the *Laudatio* might have been inserted in a text otherwise composed in 1401?

1. Precedence must be given to an observation without which there would be no opening for further inquiries: the concluding pages of *Dialogus I* fail to prepare for a second meeting; its final scene brings the discussion to an end with no indication that the participants intend to continue it on the following day.

It is true that this is not as readily seen as stated here. On the surface, the language of the last sentences of the first dialogue is equivocal, and this explains why scholars, although deeply vexed by the chronological riddle of the *Laudatio* and the *Dialogi*, failed for so long to wonder about the absence of the needed bridge between the two dialogues. To look at the precise wording of the first dialogue: shortly before the end, in response to Niccoli's attack on the three great Florentines of the Trecento, Salutati remarks that their defense could not be undertaken in a hurry and that, therefore, he preferred "to postpone this defense until a more suitable time."[20] What is this "more suitable time"? The reference may be a hint at a second part to follow, but may just as well be an excuse for the failure of the work to embark upon a criticism of Niccoli's bold theses; the order and construction of the debate leave room for either interpretation. This is so because a passage near the end harks back to the beginning of the dialogue, which had opened with Salutati's exhortation to his younger friends to train themselves by frequent "disputations." Following his refusal to answer Niccoli toward the end, Salutati is made to avow that he for one will always remain an admirer of those great Three and, also, that he will never change his lifelong opinion that "*exercitatio*" through

---

[20] "Itaque ego istam defensionem aliud in tempus magis commodum differam." Ed. Garin, p. 74.

frequent "*disputatio*" is the best intellectual training.[21] With this return to the beginning of the debate, the conversation is rounded out in form and content and could easily stand by itself without any sequel. There is nothing to make it improbable that Salutati's "at a more suitable time" means "outside the frame of the present work."

Is this interpretation not only possible, but also necessary? The answer depends on Bruni's handling of a technical matter. If Salutati's cryptic words should refer to a planned reunion of the members of his circle on the next day, there would have to be during the first conversation some move or provision that would cause the group to reassemble. The gathering had originally come to pass by chance. The members had not made any advance appointment for the Easter holidays, in which case it might be possible to assume that they had planned to spend more than one day together. Rather, as Bruni describes it in detail, the meeting had taken place without any preparation. Bruni and Niccoli, during a holiday walk, decided to pay a visit to Salutati and on their way met Roberto de' Rossi, who joined them. When all were seated in Salutati's house, silence prevailed for a while. For Salutati wondered whether his visitors had come with any special purpose in mind, whereas the guests, who had dropped in so casually, waited courteously for the old man to bring up a subject.[22] In other words, we are most definitely introduced to a situation in which the end of the visit is of necessity the end of the emerging debate unless the participants agree upon a second meeting—in this case, in Rossi's country house, where the group will reappear without any new motivation in *Dialogus II:* "on the next day, when all of us who had been together the previous day had reassembled . . . [*Postridie vero, cum omnes qui pridie fueramus in unum convenissemus . . .*]." Yet the members had separated the day before without making any arrangement for a reunion. Following Salutati's reaffirmation of confidence in training by "*disputatio*," the first meeting had wound up with nothing but the remark "After these words from him, we rose [*Haec cum dixisset, surreximus*]."[23]

---

[21] Ed. Garin, pp. 74 f.   [22] Ed. Garin, p. 46.   [23] Ed. Garin, pp. 76 and 74.

The possibility must be considered, of course, that the absence of the crucial provision from the first dialogue is simply due to lack of literary skill in the author, but this is not only quite improbable in view of the masterly construction of the opening of the dialogue; it can be finally dismissed when we take into account that in this work Cicero is often used as a closely followed guide. Now Cicero, in his dialogues, had been careful to provide suitable links between successive gatherings, whenever they were needed for continuing and completing a discussion. The host, in such cases, would ask his guests to stay overnight, or invite them for a second meeting or meal; or all those present would together fix another day, hour, or place for their reunion. That Bruni knew and liked these Ciceronian devices is seen at the end of *Dialogus II* where, with slight modifications, they are used as a means to illustrate the friendly social relations within the circle: an invitation extended for dinner the next evening by Rossi to all those present, followed by Salutati's disclosure that he himself had already invited the other three; and, eventually, an agreement that Salutati should come to see Rossi together with his guests. To be sure, this demonstration of Bruni's literary competence is found in the second dialogue, not in the first; but if both dialogues had been written simultaneously, Bruni would have shown his skill at the very time when he composed *Dialogus I.*

Theoretically, of course, a capable writer could in a convincing manner have brought the participants together on the second day as well as on the first even though their reunion had not been prepared. But then he would have had to make all the members of the group meet once more by chance, or would have had to tell some other ingeniously excogitated story. This would have been a questionable undertaking especially because interruption of the conversations by a new, fully elaborated background story had no counterpart in form and language in Cicero's dialogues, where at most a few of the participants depart or join the circle during continuing debates. Given the fact that the apparatus of stage-setting and articulation of the exchange was in this first revival of the classical form of the dialogue borrowed from Ciceronian models, these difficulties help to explain why Bruni did not make any attempt to work out a reasonably motivated beginning for the second meeting.

It is assuredly not want of practice in the Ciceronian technique that can account for Bruni's failure to employ in advance the devices needed for a resumption of the debate; on closer view, one discovers that he had not forgotten his Cicero, but at the end of the first dialogue makes use of Cicero's phraseology wherever it expresses what he wishes to say. Compare the following details.

The concluding sentence, "*Haec cum [Colucius] dixisset, surreximus*," is itself of Ciceronian origin and reveals the kind of situation Bruni had in mind when writing the last page of *Dialogus I*. With only slight differences, the sentence repeats the formula that Cicero used at the end of conversations when no reunion was to follow. "*Quod cum ille dixisset, . . . in oppidum . . . perreximus omnes*," are the concluding words of Cicero's *De finibus bonorum et malorum;* and Bruni's last word ("*surreximus*") is the very same that also ends the final sentence of *De divinatione:* "*Quae cum essent dicta, surreximus.*" Thus we are able to recognize that Bruni, in concluding *Dialogus I*, looked to Cicero for help in terminating a debate, and not in carrying it over from one gathering or reunion to another.

To sum up, Bruni, at the end of *Dialogus I*, does not do the obvious thing that any reasonably able writer would do—and which Cicero had taught him how to do—in order to make it possible to continue the conversation; instead, he borrows from Cicero the very phrases that are used at the ends of familiar Ciceronian works. Does not this alone make the assumption impossible that the two dialogues were planned and written as one work?

But we need not rely on this one line of observation. Several other approaches, of equal conclusiveness, open up when we proceed from the formal problems of literary construction to a confrontation between what the author says about his work in the *Prooemium* and what really happens in each dialogue.

2. The first point in question is Bruni's statement in the *Prooemium* that the debates described in his work take place

"in Salutati's house": "*cum est apud Colucium disputatum.*"[24] This is indeed the scene of *Dialogus I*, but the same description does not at all fit the gathering depicted in *Dialogus II*, where the scene is a "*porticus*" on the suburban "*villa*" of Rossi.

There can be no question that "*apud Colucium*" means "in the house of Salutati," and not merely in Salutati's presence— a phrase possibly applicable to either dialogue. The word *apud*, when used to express nearness to a person, usually connotes *before* (Lat. *coram*) *an authority* which is expected to hand down a decision: before a judge, a magistrate, a public council, a teacher. Bruni, on the contrary, is thinking of the phrases used by Cicero in descriptions of cultured circles, where every member participates in the debate on an equal footing and no one is the judge and master *before whom* (*apud quem*) the others appear for a decision. Niccoli's recantation in *Dialogus II* is not judged by Salutati sitting as an authority, even though Bruni once jokingly remarks that Niccoli would have to justify himself "*Colucio auditore et censore.*"[25] Rather, it is one of the younger members of the group, Pietro di ser Mino, who finally says that, since Niccoli had accepted his fellows as his judges, he for one absolved him on the grounds of his second speech.[26] And it is Rossi who adds the verdict that Niccoli's speech had restored him to the good graces of their circle.[27]

Rossi's mode of expression follows Ciceronian precedents exactly,[28] and so does the phrase of the preface in which Bruni talks about the disputation "*apud Colucium*"; for these words are taken from a dialogue by Cicero widely used by Salutati during those years, the *De natura deorum*. There, in an entirely parallel situation (a visit of a group of friends on a holiday, paid to one member of the group) Bruni had read the phrase "*apud C. Cottam familiarem meum . . . disputatum est*" (IV. VI. 15), which he used for his own "*cum est apud Colucium disputa-*

---

[24] Ed. Garin, p. 44.   [25] Ed. Garin, p. 82.

[26] "Quamobrem, si nobis iudicibus usus es, quandoquidem sedere ad causam audienda[m] iussi sumus, ego te mea sententia absolvo." Ed. Garin, p. 96.

[27] "Nox ista, te, Nicolae, nobis reddidit: nam eiusmodi a te heri dicebantur, quae a nostro coetu planissime abhorrebant." *Ibid.*

[28] "Nox ista te . . . nobis reddidit," etc., *Dialogi*, p. 96; "Nox te nobis . . . expolivit hominemque reddidit," etc., *De oratore* II 40.

tum." Nobody, of course, has ever doubted that "*apud C. Cottam*" in Cicero's usage denotes "in the house of Cotta," and nobody, therefore, can doubt that "*apud Colucium,*" in the usage of Bruni's *Prooemium,* means "in the house of Salutati." Moreover, the connotation of "Salutati's house" has counterparts in kindred phrases of the first dialogue describing the initial encounter of the friends in the streets of Florence: Bruni and Niccoli are said to have made up their minds "*ut ad Colucium Salutatum iremus,*" and afterwards they meet Roberto de' Rossi "*qui . . . ipse etiam una nobiscum ad Colucium secutus est.*"[29] There cannot be the slightest doubt that Bruni would have characterized the conversation described in the second dialogue as occurring "*apud Robertum Russum,*" and not "*apud Colucium.*"

3. Having referred, in the *Prooemium,* to "Salutati's house" as the place of the conversation, Bruni goes on to define what to him appears to be a basic feature of his work. He had wanted to confront, he says, Salutati in his dignified earnestness and Niccoli as an "opponent . . . who is most passionate in goading others." He (Bruni) "had tried, above all, to keep faithfully the manner of each unchanged. You [Vergerio] will judge how well I have succeeded."[30]

It is again very hard to believe that Bruni could have written this characterization with a view to *Dialogus II.* In *Dialogus I,* we do find throughout a confrontation between a dignified Salutati and an impetuous Niccoli. But in the second dialogue, Salutati and Niccoli nowhere confront each other, since after the discussion of the *Laudatio* in the introductory scene Salutati declines to answer Niccoli and Niccoli becomes the only major speaker until, after his recantation, he is readmitted into the good graces of the group, not by Salutati but, as we have seen, by other members of the circle.

Also, in this recantation Niccoli no longer speaks as one "who is most passionate in goading others." In his apology

---

[29] Ed. Garin, p. 46.

[30] "Scis enim Colucio neminem fere graviorem esse; Nicolaus vero, qui illi adversabatur, . . . in lacessendo acerrimum. . . . Maxime conati sumus, ut morem utriusque diligentissime servaremus. Quantum vero in ea re profecerimus, tuum erit iudicium." Ed. Garin, pp. 44 f.

he is made to point to his conduct in his youth, when he memorized Dante and traveled to Padua in order to obtain the text of the unpublished *Africa* after Petrarch's death.[31] In actual fact Niccoli had come to renounce those acts and he would not have boasted of them after forming his mature program of the new critical studies. In the remainder of his speech, too, Niccoli does not speak as he would have spoken in the presence of friends in 1401; he voices all the ideas on Dante and Petrarch that were to be defended by Bruni himself in later years.[32] In other words, the Niccoli of *Dialogus II* is Bruni's mouthpiece: he says what, in Bruni's opinion, he ought to have said, or what Bruni suggests as a better solution than that espoused in Niccoli's classicistic radicalism. Nowhere in the second dialogue does Niccoli talk in the characteristic vein described in other sources and known to Vergerio from his visit to Florence; his function in the discussions has become different from what the *Prooemium* had promised.

Something similar may be said of Salutati as presented in *Dialogus II*. During Vergerio's stay in Florence, the historical Salutati had in his *De Tyranno* defended Dante's condemnation of Brutus and Cassius and Dante's praise of Caesar; in *Dialogus II*, however, Salutati, like Niccoli, is made to soften the extremism of these views. There is no reason to think that he ever did so in reality.[33]

In short, the fact that Niccoli's and Salutati's conduct in *Dialogus II* does not correspond to the behavior and thought of the men whom Vergerio had known in 1400 is another strong reason for doubt that *Dialogus II* accompanied *Dialogus I* in 1401. How could Bruni otherwise in a personal letter to Vergerio—for this is what the *Prooemium* is—have dared to ask to be judged by the success of his effort "to faithfully keep the manner of each [Niccoli as well as Salutati] unchanged"?

4. Bruni's *Prooemium* contains a third sign pointing in the same direction: it calls the work sent to Vergerio "the

---

31 Ed. Garin, pp. 82 ff.

32 Cf. *Crisis*, 1st ed., pp. 203, 206, 399; rev. ed., p. 514.

33 *Crisis*, 1st ed., p. 215; rev. ed., pp. 242 f.

disputation described for you *in this book* [*Nos autem disputationem illam in hoc libro descriptam misimus . . .*]." If there had been two dialogues in 1401, the characterization in the preface should have read, according to classical usage, "two disputations" described in "two books." Now, one observes that Bruni in the titles and prefaces of all his other writings rigorously adhered to this ancient mode of carefully naming the exact number of "books," or similar units, of which a work is composed. Just as the titles of Cicero's works varied between *De oratore libri III* and *Brutus sive de claris oratoribus liber*, or between *Tusculanarum disputationum libri quinque* and *Laelius sive de amicitia dialogus*, so Bruni called one of his own writings *Commentaria Tria de Primo Bello Punico*, but spoke of his *Commentarium Rerum Graecarum* in a case where there was no subdivision.[34]

I have been able to find only one apparent exception in Bruni's usage, and this exception finally proves the rule— namely, the dedication-preface to Bruni's translation and annotation of the Pseudo-Aristotelian *Economics* of 1420–21. In Bruni's revision this work is composed of two books, whereas the dedication-letter to Cosimo de' Medici calls it, in the singular, a "*libellus*." On closer examination[35] this turned out to be not a deviation from Bruni's custom, but valuable evidence that Bruni in the case of the *Economics* did exactly what we suspect him to have done in the case of the *Dialogi*. At the time when, in his letter to Cosimo, he spoke of the *Economics* as a "*libellus*" he actually sent him only the translated *first* book with its accompanying commentary, whereas the Latin text and annotation of the *second* book were worked out and added at a time when the dedication-letter could no longer be changed. When, on the strength of these observations, the extant manuscripts of Bruni's *Economics* were carefully searched, it turned out that a considerable group (a little less than 10 per cent of the manuscripts)[36] contains in

---

[34] These and other examples in *Crisis*, 1st ed., pp. 195 f.

[35] See the chapter "The Genesis of Bruni's Annotated Latin Version of the (Pseudo-) Aristotelian *Economics* (1420–21)" in *Humanistic and Political Literature*, pp. 166 ff.; as well as the corroboration by J. Soudek in *Scriptorium*, XII (1958), 260 ff. (cf. *Crisis*, rev. ed., pp. 509 f.)

[36] According to J. Soudek, "Leonardo Bruni and His Public," *Studies in Medieval and Renaissance History*, V (1968), pp. 55–59.

fact only the dedication-letter together with Bruni's transla-tion—often also his annotation—of the first "*libellus*". Subse-quently, after the publication of the second book, Bruni did refer in his correspondence to the "*libellos quosdam*" of his work on the *Economics*.

No more striking test case could be imagined for the sound-ness of the hypothesis that in 1401 nothing existed but the dedication to Vergerio and *Dialogus I*.

5. There remains one apparent cause for doubt: ever since the fifteenth century Bruni's work has been called "*Dialogi*" in the plural. If this had been the author's title from the beginning, how could the work at any time have been com-posed of one dialogue? Investigation of this problem, how-ever, leads to a clear *nihil obstat*.[37]

As has been known since 1955, the titles of the manuscripts, as well as the references to the work by contemporaries, reveal that the title-forms *Dialogorum Libri Duo* or, more simply, *Dialogi* are not found until about the year of Bruni's death. At that time, some forty years after the letter to Vergerio, such titles were coined by Bruni's obituarists in circumstances which can be traced in detail.[38] As for the manuscripts, only in those of the second half of the fifteenth century do we find the plural title adopted. During Bruni's lifetime, the manu-scripts either had no title at all or used such forms as *Dialogus* (sometimes divided into two *libri*), *Collatio*, or *Liber*, in most cases followed by a few words characterizing the contents (on the three great Florentines of the Trecento, on the com-parison of the modern, that is, Florentine, and ancient writers, and so on)—a Babel of variations which indicates that Bruni initially must have left this work without a formal author's title. Even if the form of a *Dialogus* divided into two *libri*, a phrasing and arrangement known to some of Bruni's closest friends, had originated with the author (it might be the title adopted after the composition of the second dialogue), this would only lend added strength to the two crucial inferences

---

37 Cf. for what follows the chapter "The Title of the *Dialogi*" in *Humanistic and Political Literature*, pp. 145 ff.; also, *Crisis*, 1st ed., pp. 193 ff.

38 *Humanistic and Political Literature*, pp. 148 ff., discusses the procedure and the motiva-tion of the obituarists.

which can be drawn from the testimony of the manuscripts and contemporary reports: that there must have been something irregular in the genesis of this *opus*, because a title intended from the very first to head two dialogues would not have been phrased in the singular according to Bruni's usage; and that his work, as far as the history of the title is concerned, was indeed a *Dialogus* before it became the *Dialogi*.

One would wish to add further confirmation by discovering some indisputable traces of the one-dialogue manuscript sent to Vergerio in 1401, especially since in the case of the *Economics* a group of manuscripts derived from the one-book version for Cosimo has been identified. In the case of the *Dialogi*, some one-dialogue manuscripts (containing the *Prooemium* and *Dialogus I*) do exist, and one can add to the small group of surviving copies indications of the use of one-dialogue manuscripts found in early citations of the title—for instance *"De utilitate disputationis"* or something similar, a wording that does not fit the second dialogue. By this device we are, in fact, able to trace the circulation of one-dialogue manuscripts back to Constance in the 1410's, when, during the Church Council, Vergerio stayed there for two years as a curial secretary and, later, as an official in the imperial chancery.[39] But, unfortunately, the search comes to a halt at that point. We have no means of proving that the appearance of some early one-dialogue manuscripts in Constance is not due simply to the arbitrary copying of only the first part of a two-dialogue manuscript, at a time when Vergerio was living in the town;[40] and the situation becomes even more confusing because the two one-dialogue manuscripts written in Constance are so corrupt that it is not easy to believe them to be direct copies from Vergerio's original, whereas the two copies with the best, and indeed a superior, text bear no mark of Constance origin, but are most likely to have been written in Italy, possibly in Florence.[41]

---

[39] For all these details, cf. the chapter "One-dialogue Manuscripts of the *Dialogi*" in *Humanistic and Political Literature*, pp. 129–45.

[40] *Ibid.*, pp. 139 f.

[41] The two excellent texts which do not point to Constance are Cod. Riccardianus 976, described in *Humanistic and Political Literature*, pp. 131 f., and Ms. 2 Qq C 79 of the Biblioteca Comunale of Palermo. In 1958, Prof. Paul O. Kristeller kindly brought

Since groups of "incomplete" manuscripts of other works by Bruni are known only in the case of the *Economics* and there indicate initially separate publication of the first book, the parallel situation in the transmission of the *Dialogi* is so striking that it should certainly not go unmentioned. Conceivably, future findings of manuscripts may lead us here to yet another conclusive line of demonstration. Nevertheless, since the present state of our manuscript knowledge is far from enlightening about the origin of the one-dialogue texts, it will be wise not to dilute the persuasiveness of our results by the inclusion of arguments which rest on a debatable basis.

If we ignore this portion of the evidence, how valid is the testimony of the remaining facts? Do the five lines of investigation which we have traced indeed add up to incontrovertible proof?

The kind of certainty established by our study of the *Dialogi* is different from that found in dating the *Laudatio*. In the case of the *Laudatio*, no one can question that the reference to an "occupation" of Bologna which followed the submission of Perugia and Assisi in 1400 cannot mean anything but the event of June 1402; nor can anyone deny that various reflections in the *Laudatio* regarding Giangaleazzo and Florence's triumph must have been written after Giangaleazzo's disappearance from the Italian scene. Obviously, we cannot claim so much for the outcome of any of our five approaches to the *Dialogi*. Not that our evidence is merely "plausible" or "probable". Observations such as the one that the author's own dedication-letter describes the work in terms that apply only to its first half or that the two successive conversations are not connected by any literary provision in the text, alter

---

to my attention, and sent me a description of, the latter humanist miscellany, which is particularly rich in (often rare) Latin translations of Greek authors and includes a copy (no. 18) of Bruni's dedication letter and first dialogue from about the middle of the Quattrocento. Thanks to Prof. Giorgio Santangelo and Dott. Emma Alaimo, Direttrice of the Biblioteca Comunale, I obtained a microfilm of the Bruni text. The superscription is "*Dialogus Leonardi Colucii et aliorum*" and the subscription "*Leonardi Aretini dialogi liber explicit. Valeas.*" These phrasings imply that the scribe copied a manuscript which included only *Dialogue I*. Here, too, the work lacks a specific title, except for the single term "*dialogus*" (turned into a "*liber dialogi*" by the scribe at the end). Collation shows that this text, like that in the Biblioteca Riccardiana manuscript, is among the best that have yet become known.

the very starting-point for critical appraisal. These findings shift the burden of proof to the shoulders of those who, in the teeth of so much contrary evidence, would cling to the traditional belief in the unity of the work. In order to deny the successive composition of the two dialogues, they would have to conceive of some other theory that could explain these three things: how it could happen that the author's description of his work contradicts its present contents; why the participants in the conversation reappear on the second day without the slightest motivation for a reunion; and why the work did not receive the plural title of *"Dialogi"* until many years later. Unless all these perplexing riddles can be solved in some other fashion, our findings prove that when the first half of the work was written, the second did not yet exist.

The only reason why this demonstration is not on a par with the evidence obtainable for the chronology of the *Laudatio* is the remote possibility that, in describing the scene of his work, the author may not have been as attentive as usual, perhaps because his mind was so exclusively fixed upon the initial part of the discussions that he forgot about the rest; or that because of an unaccountable lapse he failed to provide for an indispensable transition and used a typical concluding phrase of Ciceronian dialogues when he ought to have used a Ciceronian device for continuing a debate. The chance of an author like Bruni making even a single mistake of this kind is slight, and he would certainly not make several, all of the same type. When in a case like that of the *Dialogi* no fewer than five separate lines of evidence can be used for mutual corroboration, there will be no danger of being deceived by a possible slip on the part of the author. For all practical purposes, therefore, the chronology we have established for the *Dialogi* is no less compelling than the self-evidence of the date of the *Laudatio*.

This outcome of our investigation should dissipate the last lingering doubts regarding the relationship of Bruni's two works. In theory, the reader will remember,[42] the enigma of the citation of the *Laudatio* in the *Dialogi* might be soluble by the conjecture of insertion in either work of all the pas-

---

[42] See above, pp. 112–14 and 124.

sages that must have been written after 1402. Since there is no trace of such insertions, however, this was never more than a mere hypothesis based on the hope that it might yield some future results unless another and conclusive explanation was found. This explanation has now been finally given through the proof that *Dialogus II* as a whole, including the challenging cross-reference, originated at a later time than *Dialogus I;* and, thus, any possible hypothesis of insertions is finally put to rest.

As far as Leonardo Bruni's early writings are concerned, therefore, no reasonable doubt remains that could militate against the chronological assumptions on which our concept of the genesis of civic Humanism is built.

4 A CRUCIAL DATE IN THE HISTORY OF FLORENTINE HISTORIOGRAPHY:
The Composition of Dati's *Istoria di Firenze* in 1409

I. Next to the *Laudatio* and the *Dialogi*, the foremost role in any reconstruction of the intellectual situation in Florence around 1400 is played by Gregorio Dati's *Istoria*, according to its preface "the history of the long war, the greatest in our day in Italy, between the tyrant of Lombardy, Duke of Milan, and the magnificent Commune of Florence."[1] Together with Bruni's panegyric, it is in Dati's analysis of the war that the historical realism and some of the politico-historical ideas which were to dominate the Florentine Renaissance appear for the first time.[2] If the *Istoria* had been written not immediately after the duel with Giangaleazzo Visconti, as we assume today, but at some later time in Dati's long life (he died in 1435), our estimate of the impact of the Visconti wars on the rise of Florentine Quattrocento ideas would need serious modification. Moreover, since Dati was not a humanist, current assumptions concerning the origin of his work during the opening decade of the Quattrocento seem to support, and are indeed a major testimony to, the thesis that some of the key political and historical ideas of Quattrocento Florence were first expressed by Volgare writers, before they were developed and perfected by Latin humanists. Finally, the determination of the time when the *Istoria* was composed is basic for the appraisal of Dati's originality as a politico-historical writer. For only if Dati conceived his political realism at the presumed early date, would he stand out as a

---

[1] ". . . la storia della lunga e grandissima guerra di Italia che fu a questi nostri dì tra il tiranno di Lombardia, duca di Milano e il magnifico Comune di Firenze." L' *"Istoria di Firenze" dal 1380 al 1405*, ed. L. Pratesi (Norcia, 1904), p. 11; in the edition by G. Manni (Florence, 1735), pp. 1 f. The latter must be consulted together with Pratesi's edition, as will be seen later.

[2] The crucial place of Dati's work has been pointed out in my *Crisis of the Early Italian Renaissance* variously, especially in the sections "A Volgare Writer on the Road to Pragmatic History," "Harbingers of the Political Art of the Quattrocento" in Dati, and "Dati's Account of the Florentine Wars for Liberty," *Crisis*, rev. ed., pp. 168–88.

thinker on politics who was in many respects ahead of most of his contemporaries.[3]

That the political situation which followed the Florentine triumph over Giangaleazzo (in 1402) and the capture of Pisa (in 1406) had not yet changed when Dati's work was written seems to emerge from its concluding pages.[4] It was on the basis of their testimony that I ventured in 1955 to assign the date 1407/08 to the work; like other scholars, I have been using this date ever since.[5] At the end of the *Istoria*, the question is asked whether Florence, after its tremendous exertions in the war, had preserved its old and essential financial power; Dati's answer is affirmative and includes a most confident prognosis for the years ahead. He admits that Florence has contracted crushing debts, but these have been outweighed, he says, by the economic advances forced upon its citizens by the necessities of the past war. Also, victory has produced a sizable increase in value of all Florentine landed estates resulting from the belief that after the breakdown and dissolution of the Visconti empire the threat of new wars has disappeared. "Now that the tyrant of Lombardy is dead and his people are undone forever, and Pisa is in the possession of Florence, the Florentines feel assured that they cannot [again] be involved in war." In such a world, Florence is bound to be richer than ever before as long as there is no new expense for war—as long as the Florentines, "now that others can no longer undertake war against them, . . . do not seek to undertake war against others." "I pray to God that He may give them the wisdom to restrain, control, and carefully direct their actions, not to waste their resources, and not to undertake anything against others that would displease God."[6]

---

[3] These three appraisals form the basis of the chapter on Dati in the *Crisis;* cf. rev. ed., pp. 167 ff., and also pp. 77 f., 157, 448.

[4] That is, really the concluding pages of the eighth book (ed. Pratesi, pp. 138–40), which are followed by still another, ninth, book; but this book, whether or not a later addition, is not a part of the history of the wars between Florence and Giangaleazzo, but an appended survey of all existing Florentine offices and public institutions.

[5] H. Baron, *Humanistic and Political Literature,* pp. 66–68; cf. *Crisis,* rev. ed., pp. 171, 500.

[6] ". . . il tiranno di Lombardia . . . , ora che egli è morto e disfatti in perpetuo i suoi e Pisa è de' Fiorentini, e' sono sicuri di non potere avere guerra." ". . . poi che a loro non può esser fatto guerra che non la cerchino fare ad altri." ". . . priego Iddio che conceda loro sapersi temperare e reggere e regolare, e in non fare spesa, nè impresa eglino contro ad altri che dispiacessono a Dio." Ed. Pratesi, p. 139.

This is a description of the climate of opinion following Giangaleazzo's death and Pisa's fall, at a moment when, in Dati's judgment, no new menace had as yet shipwrecked a possible program of peace, nor had Florence as yet entered any other war. These clearly defined experiences of the post-Giangaleazzo period should help us to determine the span of time during which the *Istoria* must have been written. We have proof here that, when Dati ended his report of the past wars, he did not yet know the full development of the rapidly approaching attempts of another powerful monarchical state —this time Naples under King Ladislaus—to conquer large parts of the peninsula. It was in 1408 that Ladislaus of Naples occupied almost the entire Papal State, including Perugia and Assisi in Umbria; and it was in June 1409 that he captured Cortona, southern bastion of Tuscany—a threat met by the formation of a broad anti-Neapolitan alliance between Florence, Siena, Bologna, and other Italian and even European powers, including France. Florence joined the coalition, but there was strong opposition to this new involvement; and although the Republic had her *condottieri* participate in the war, Florentine cooperation was soon ended when Ladislaus in 1411, to split his adversaries, ceded Cortona to Florence in exchange for a money payment. But since Neapolitan expansion continued nevertheless, war broke out again in 1413— this time a full-fledged war, which had reached a climax by 1414 when Ladislaus suddenly died. "Dati, therefore, must have worked out his narrative," so I concluded twelve years ago, "at some time between 1406 and 1413; one should suppose, before the disquieting events of 1409."[7]

One wonders whether this conclusion has retained its full force. Chronological criteria derived from the examination of an author's outlook may be essentially right, yet in need of the correctives that come from application to the sometimes uneven course of actual historical developments. In the case of Dati's concluding plea not to disturb the peace established by the disintegration of Giangaleazzo's empire and the loss of Pisa's independence, one aspect of the political situation in Florence does complicate the situation. Although under the

[7] *Humanistic and Political Literature*, p. 67.

impact of the Neapolitan invasion from the south—with Ladislaus' troops gradually surrounding Tuscany in the east and northeast, and with Florence, allied to Siena and Bologna, again becoming a partner in a war—military action had undoubtedly replaced peace during extensive portions of the years 1409–14, the longing to preserve the post-Giangaleazzo tranquillity remained so strong that it survived, represented by an active antiwar party. Up to the death of Ladislaus in 1414, the members of this group worked feverishly for reconciliation with the King, refusing to believe that a deadly encirclement by foes, such as had occurred in the years before Giangaleazzo's death, could ever be repeated after the apparently permanent dissolution of the Visconti empire and the winning of access to the sea by the acquisition of the Pisan coast. In 1411, in spite of Florence's new policy of alliance, fervent hope for peace was still so widely spread that a new city council—the Council of the 200—was created expressly to satisfy the desire for a further controlling organ capable of vetoing any unnecessary warlike action by the government; and even as late as 1414 a Florentine ambassador to the King transgressed his commission in an attempt to bring about a compromise such as the peace party was envisaging. Could not a critic from this camp, who opposed any policy of new involvement, even at that late date have phrased Dati's verdict that any further military action was unnecessary? After Ladislaus' death, when the pendulum swung back to the north and Filippo Maria Visconti started the slow work of rebuilding his father's state, without yet openly transgressing the ancient borders of Lombardy, the same opinion might well have been held until 1423, when Filippo Maria opened a drive from the Romagna to the south, and for roughly two decades Florence was back in the kind of struggle against Milan that had seemed a thing of the past in the years immediately following 1406.

One might rightly say, to be sure, that to conclude on this basis that Dati's warning could have been written at any time until 1422 would stretch caution too far as long as we have no information, or any reason to think, that Dati was a member of the persistent antiwar party. Moreover, in order to defend such a hypothesis, one would have to conveniently overlook the tenor of the end of the *Istoria*, which seems to be that Florence had not yet become involved in a new war such as the one that started at the time of the Neapolitan occupation of Cortona in 1409 and was waged with even greater force in 1413 and 1414. Nevertheless, once suspicion has been aroused by the existence for so many years of a peace group, it will be difficult to silence doubts unless it can be shown that knowledge of the contemporary scene, in the *Istoria*, does not extend to political events that must still have been unknown to an author writing before the outbreak of the war with Ladislaus. In 1955 my only observation on this score was that Dati had failed to mention in his appended *Liber IX*—a minute description of all Florentine offices, as already mentioned— the two city councils established in 1411, the Councils of the 131 and of the 200. But their omission cannot be worked into a wholly conclusive argument, because the absence of the acts that instituted these councils from the official collection of Florentine laws published in 1414 suggests that during the first years of their operation they were not yet regarded as necessarily permanent. Although this should not have prevented Dati from considering them in a detailed tableau of all extant offices, there is no final answer to those who might prefer to be skeptical. But one can point to some less controversial passages.[8]

II. A statement that betrays the time during which the author was working appears in his narration of the reoccupation of Bologna for the Church in September 1403, a year after Giangaleazzo's death. Here Dati mentions that after the papal triumph at Bologna *"messer* Baldassare cardinal Coscia re-

---

[8] This is owing to the initiative of Professor Anthony Molho of Brown University, who, after a study in Italy of the manuscripts which contain the text of the *Istoria*, freely and generously discussed with me his findings on Dati's work, playing initially the *advocatus diaboli* for any suspicion of a later date. On the pages which follow I will present the conclusions at which I eventually arrived, largely as a result of the provocative discussions in which the two of us repeatedly engaged, finally seeing eye to eye regarding most of the basic questions. This does not mean that Mr. Molho necessarily agrees with every phase of my reasoning, and I alone must be blamed if there should be any mistake among the points here made. But it ought to be emphasized that this study of Dati would not have been written without Mr. Molho's intervention, and the reader should look upon the major results as the offspring of an exceptionally fruitful scholarly exchange, for which I wish to express profound thanks to Mr. Molho.

mained there as papal legate and, until this day, has been *signore* of that city and of other territories in the neighborhood."⁹ Cardinal Balthasar Cossa became Pope John XXIII on May 17, 1410. It is highly improbable that a historian reporting the events of 1403 after Cossa had become pope would have referred to him as "cardinal" without mentioning that he had meanwhile become known under his papal name; it is absolutely impossible that a historian, after Cossa had been elevated to the papal see, could have made the statement that "cardinal Cossa, until this day, has been *signore,*" that is, the papal governor, of Bologna and the surrounding papal territories. This part of Dati's history at least must have been written before May 1410. If in some other part of the work we should find a similar *terminus ad quem,* we could assume that the validity of the chronological evidence just given is not limited to the chapter in which it occurs.

The reference to the Bologna episode of 1403 is found in the sixth book of Dati's *Istoria.* At the end of the fourth we read the following reflections of the author. After the Church had been split between two popes, it was in the nature of things that the government of the temporal order of the world would follow the example of the spiritual order; the Empire, too, eventually saw two rulers. "The Lord, therefore," adds Dati, "may provide that unification in the government of the spiritual order come about; and then the flesh will follow [the example of] the spirit." In other words, the Empire, with God's help, will again have one emperor if and when the Church is again unified under one pope.¹⁰

We must here consider that the Church, whose schism had begun in 1378, remained under two allegiances until June 26, 1409, when Alexander V, the predecessor of John XXIII, was elected by the Council of Pisa to replace the rival popes in Avignon and Rome. Admittedly, his election did not at once

⁹ Bologna "fue restituita a santa Chiesa, e rimasevi legato messer Baldassarre cardinale Coscia, che insino a oggi è signore di quella [città] e di più altre terre vicine." Ed. Pratesi, p. 81.

¹⁰ ". . . quello che seguitò nella Magna tra i detti due imperadori e chi ottenne, perchè nè il primo nè il secondo accettò e prese la corona." "Dappoi che il capo dello Spirituale era diviso in due parti, cioè il papa, pare che sia seguito, come debbe, che il capo del Temporale seguiti quello dello Spirituale e sia diviso l'imperio tanto che Iddio provegga che il capo Spirituale s'unisca e la carne seguiterà lo spirito." Ed. Pratesi, p. 64.

end the schism, since henceforth, until the Constance Council, there were three popes, none of whom lost his pontificate before May 1415. Whether, however, a writer felt after June 1409 that the schism had legally ended with the election at Pisa of one universal pope, or whether he felt that there were now three instead of two papal rivals, in neither case could he still regard the Church and the Empire after June 1409 as being caught in an essentially parallel calamity, two rival emperors having followed the example of two competing popes. To go on thinking in these terms was further made impossible by the fact that very shortly after 1409 there were no longer two rivals on the imperial throne, because on May 18, 1410, King Rupert died, and from September onward Sigismund, the newly elected king, was in the eyes of all Christianity—soon assembled at Constance for the Council—the only aspirant for the imperial crown, while Wenceslaus, though alive until 1419, had sunk into total oblivion as far as claims to the imperial dignity were concerned. To put it differently: it is impossible that Dati's reflections regarding the parallel conditions prevailing in the Church and the Empire can have been written very long after the middle of 1410 (the death of Rupert); and it is extremely unlikely that they were written later than the middle of 1409 (the time of the election of Alexander V).

Summing up, we can say that not only does each of the various available testimonies appear to be conclusive in itself, but together they make the years 1409–10 a watershed beyond which we no longer find the world reflected in the *Istoria*. To repeat: in June of 1409 Cortona was menaced and occupied by Ladislaus, a defiant threat to the peace of Tuscany answered by Florence's cooperation in the building of an anti-Neapolitan coalition; during the same month the Council of Pisa put or tried to put an end to the division of the Church under two rival popes. In May 1410 the rivalry between the two emperors, Wenceslaus and Rupert, ended with Rupert's untimely death; simultaneously, the papal legate, Balthasar Cossa, who had been a familiar figure to the Florentines and their close ally in the neighboring territory of Bologna, ceased to be Cardinal Cossa and became pope. Nothing of this had yet happened when Dati laid down his pen.

III. Was the *Istoria* written long, or not so long, before these events occurred? Only a look at the concrete details of Dati's life about that time and during the preceding years will make an answer possible.

We find some vital information about the vicissitudes of Dati's life in his *Libro Segreto*. A typical Florentine business diary, it is not concerned with entries about his writing and his studies, but, in addition to births, marriages, and deaths in his family, it gives a precise account of his political career, his business ventures, his travels, and his financial conditions. We learn from these records that 1403 and 1404 had been years of great prosperity for Dati, but that in 1405 some vital enterprise of his in Spain began to fail because he had been unable to supply what his representative had promised to the King of Castile. The subsequent years, 1407 and 1408, were among the most trying and depressing of his life, when, in order to maintain his business credit and his "*onore*" as a citizen, he desperately strove, and finally managed, to pay off his debts, trying to keep up his courage for the hard time to come after this period of financial bleeding. Eventually, after serving for the fourth time as a consul of his guild, he decided to travel to Spain, in order to see whether anything could be done on the spot to save a portion of his fortune there. On November 12, 1408, he left Florence and traveled by land via southern France and Valencia to Murcia, a province of Castile, in southern Spain, where he arrived on the last day of November. There he stayed, trying every possible means and waiting long months for his business associates to obtain some relief for him, until, disappointed in his hopes, he started on his return journey in May 1410, almost a year after the crucial events of June 1409. He first stopped in Valencia, where the war of Florence with Ladislaus and his ally, Genoa, prevented him from continuing his journey to Italy until February 1411. At that time he finally found an opportunity to obtain passage by sea from Barcelona to Florence, where he arrived on March 15.[11]

The gist of this information is that during the critical time

---

[11] Gregorio Dati, *Il Libro Segreto*, ed. C. Gargiolli (Bologna, 1869), pp. 58 f., 80 f., 87–90.

for the composition of his history—that is, during the one or two years preceding the middle of 1409—Dati first spent a period at home in Florence, completely filled with frantic business activity, litigations, court proceedings, attempts to salvage his standing as a citizen (his "*onore*"), and finally with service for his guild in high office; and that in a subsequent period, after being on the road most of November 1408, he stayed for a long time in Murcia in Spain, where he waited for an opportunity that failed to arrive, until he departed a year and a half later "without having gained anything but much trouble and grief." Since the *Istoria*, for the reasons already established, must have been written during one or the other of these two periods of Dati's life, it is difficult, in choosing from these alternatives, to think that it originated at any time other than during his protracted stay at Murcia, or, rather, during its first six months, namely, prior to the various political changes that took place from the middle of 1409 onward.[12]

Is it, however, at all believable that Dati's history of the Florentine wars was written while its author was away from Florence?

As soon as one examines the *Istoria* with such a question in mind, one becomes aware of features apparently not yet noticed by any of its readers. According to the *Proemio* and to the indications throughout the work, the dialogue form reflects—or is supposed to reflect—a situation in which the author was met daily after lunch by an interrogating audience, whose successive queries he answered. Was this presupposed audience made up of Florentine fellow citizens? The main speaker and respondent in the dialogue, that is, the author, talks about the actions and fortunes of "the Florentines," just

---

[12] At first sight, the second period might seem to include Dati's stay at Valencia on his return journey, from May 1410 to February 1411—a hypothesis that looks attractive because nine months of waiting for passage ought to have given him ample opportunity for literary leisure. But the fact that by May 1410 Dati must have known about the events connected with the fall of Cortona and the election of the Pisan pope in June 1409 excludes so late a date; and the circumstance that his forced stop at Valencia was caused by Florence's new involvement in war, as he himself reports in his *Libro Segreto* (". . . e soprastetti a Valenza per li pericoli del camino per mare e per terra, ch'era guerra tra noi e 'l re e' genovesi"), makes it impossible that he could at that time have written a book ending with the hope that Florence would not become involved in another war after the end of the struggle with Giangaleazzo.

as the interrogators inquire about "the Florentines," the deeds and institutions "of that city [*di quella città*].¹³ He explains the geography of Tuscany, as a Florentine would do for people who have no intimate knowledge of it. This is especially striking where he introduces Montepulciano, the local town on the border of the Florentine territory, well known to every Florentine, as lying between the bigger and, to strangers, more familiar centers: "In Tuscany, between Arezzo and Cortona and Perugia and Siena, there is a large territory. Though it is not an episcopal see, it is situated in a place that can be well defended, and its location is in a very fertile region. Its name is Montepulciano."¹⁴ Once one has become aware of these characteristics of the descriptive language of Dati's dialogue, one finds it more difficult to assume that passages such as these should have been written by a Florentine writing in Florence than that they come from the pen of an author who had a non-Florentine audience in mind. These doubts regarding the composition of the book in Florence should be weighed together with the fact that the long waiting period at Murcia, unlike Dati's last Florentine years, offered him an opportunity for regular exchanges with non-Florentines, meetings that could inspire him to explain and extol the role of his native city during the past wars, perhaps first in oral conversations and, afterwards, in a book.

Admittedly, there may be certain inaccuracies in our attempts to determine the precise days or months when the *Istoria* was composed during Dati's stay at Murcia. As we have argued, the *Istoria* must have been written during the first half of 1409 (provided that we discard the initial few weeks of Dati's stay in December, 1408, as the least likely time). We might, nevertheless, be wrong by a month or two in regard not only to the beginning, but also to the end of this period, because the news of Ladislaus' attack on Cortona and of the election of a pope at Pisa expected to unify the

---

¹³ The interrogator asks: "poichè io ho inteso de' grandi e magnifici fatti di fuori e della ricchezza e bellezza e gran signoria di quella [ed. Manni: questa] città, ti priego . . . che tu . . . dicami del modo del regimento de' Fiorentini e gli ufici loro." Ed. Pratesi, pp. 139 f.

¹⁴ "In Toscana, tra Arezzo e Cortona e Perugia e Siena, sta una grossa terra benchè non sia città di vescovado, posta in luogo forte e in paese molto abondevole, la quale si chiama Montepulciano." Ed. Pratesi, p. 28.

Church (events which both occurred in June 1409) must have needed some time to travel to Spain. It is, therefore, not impossible that Dati was still ignorant of those developments as late as July or even August. And there is, evidently, a possibility that he wrote his concluding remarks shortly *after* hearing of the fate of Cortona and the conclusion of an anti-Neapolitan league, when he did not yet know the details and, therefore, expressed his fears with the sigh: may God grant us not to get involved in wars again! But any such slight, marginal uncertainties do not affect our basic results. These remain: in the first place, that the composition of Dati's work in 1409 and, consequently, still under the immediate impact of the wars with Giangaleazzo and Pisa has now been conclusively proven; and, second, that we are in a position to visualize the unusual circumstances that caused the emergence of an analytical work on history and politics without equal or parallel among the Volgare writings of Dati's generation.

IV. One question remains: though we have established the early date of Dati's work, can we also be reasonably sure that the text as we read it does not include any major alterations from later times?

Like the editors of the two extant editions of the *Istoria*, we are dependent on a text based on a few, undistinguished manuscripts which show traces of interference.[15] As I pointed out in 1955, however, these intrusions are found principally in the ninth book, the survey of all extant Florentine offices and institutions. It is not surprising that this list was kept up to date, possibly by the author and certainly by later users; we even find some references to institutions not created before the times of Lorenzo de' Medici and Savonarola.[16] But this does not mean that comparably great changes must have occurred in the eight books of analysis of the wars with Giangaleazzo. Originally a mere conjecture, this inference, too, has now been fully confirmed. For, the fact that the above-noted references to pre-1409 conditions were not changed subsequently when they became outdated is tantamount to proof that the

---

[15] Mr. Molho's recent examination of Italian library holdings, he allows me to report, have not brought to light any new authoritative manuscripts.
[16] *Humanistic and Political Literature*, pp. 63 f.

text did not later undergo any systematic revision. Surely, in that case an author as profoundly interested as Dati in everything connected with Guelphism and the papacy would not have left the passages referring to "cardinal" Cossa and to the existence of two popes and two emperors unchanged.

Lack of such a revision is also suggested by the outcome of the recent careful re-examination of the text to which we have referred,[17] because, except in Book IX, textual alterations were found only in a very few places where Dati's work was able to serve as a kind of *cicerone* or guide and, just as in Book IX, required being kept up to date. In 1955 I noted that in the latter book the post of *Capitano di Cortona* is listed, even though Cortona was not acquired by Florence until 1411.[18] Similarly, in the sixth book, a description of the ceremony in which the subject communes annually paid homage to Florence on the festive day of S. Giovanni mentions Cortona together with the other cities of the territory.[19] For without its insertion—whether Dati or a later reader made it—the list of homages given in the text would have been outdated after 1411. Again, in the eighth book, in a chapter which describes the artistic decoration of a few selected Florentine churches and oratories, the case of Or San Michele is of interest because on Dati's departure for Spain only the first few marble statues for the exterior had been placed in their niches. It was during the following decade that the remaining niches were filled not only with other marbles, but, from about 1415, in some instances with bronzes. Large bronze statues which rivaled those of antiquity were objects of special curiosity that contributed to Florence's fame; they could therefore not be omitted from Dati's list once they had made their appearance on the walls of Or San Michele. In a relatively early manuscript, used for Manni's edition, we read that one of the statues in the niches "is of bronze and of wonderful beauty," whereas from a later manuscript, printed by Pratesi, we learn that "*two* of them are of bronze and of wonderful beauty."[20]

---

[17] See note 8, above.

[18] *Humanistic and Political Literature*, p. 64.

[19] Ed. Pratesi, p. 93.

[20] ". . . e quale è di bronzo di maravigliosa bellezza," ed. Manni, p. 109; "e due n'è di bronzo di maravigliosa bellezza," ed. Pratesi, p. 117.

Here we have a chance to observe how the text of such guide-like chapters was gradually brought up to date. On the other hand, the very fact that interpolations of this sort have been encountered only in paragraphs that give lists or catalogues, bears out the conclusion that, whatever changes were made, were made for practical purposes; they do not affect the political and historical substance of the work.

To sum up: the chronology proposed in 1955 needs to be changed but little. Instead of 1407/08, the *Istoria* was composed during the first half of 1409, and one should add that there was little difference in the political climate and in the author's views between the year 1408 and the time in which he was at work in 1409. The real value of the present findings and reasonings lies in the fact that the thesis that the *Istoria* was not a later creation, but a product of the first few years of the century, has become a certainty, and that the historical situation in whose context the genesis of Dati's work can be understood has at last been identified.

The recognition that the *Istoria* reflects the thought and emotions of the Florentines on the morrow of their triumph over Giangaleazzo and their Pisan neighbor must, after all, remain one of the guideposts in any study of the emergence of the politico-historical ideas of the Renaissance.

5 IMITATION, RHETORIC, AND QUATTROCENTO THOUGHT IN BRUNI'S *LAUDATIO*

After the *Dialogi*, the *Laudatio Florentinae Urbis* is the single most important piece of writing from Bruni's youth. Rivaled only by Dati's *Istoria*, the *Laudatio* represents our major document of the Florentine reaction to the threat of subjection to Milan; moreover it is also the most interesting source for the history of the period in which fifteenth-century rhetoric, classicism, and the new Greek studies came to the fore.

In the latter respect, the work offers opportunities for fresh observation—beginning with the consequences of the emerging influence of Greek literature, an element for which the period has not yet been systematically explored. The *Laudatio* was the first Florentine work, and perhaps even the first work in Humanism as a whole, to profit substantially from the knowledge of Greek. This role should be carefully appraised, or the picture of the intellectual forces in the background of Bruni's early Humanism remains incomplete.

The crucial task is to observe the point at which imitation of Greek models was transformed into creative emulation reflecting Florentine conditions. At the same time one must try to integrate the results with all the other elements that have previously been recognized or can now be recognized as making the *Laudatio* distinct from the traditions of the Trecento and representative of the transition of Florentine thought about 1400.[1]

I. If Bruni's panegyric is as significant as it appears at present, why (it will be asked) did it arouse so little interest until very recent times? Bruni and his contemporaries would have

---

[1] In the course of my discussion I shall, by necessity, have to epitomize some of the observations already made in the chapter on "Promise and Tradition in Bruni's *Laudatio* of the City of Florence" in *The Crisis of the Early Italian Renaissance*. Wherever feasible, I have tried to avoid repetitions of that (easily accessible) analysis, but without summarizing a few of my former results I would have found it impossible to give the new, often complementary observations their due place.

been surprised by the long oblivion it was to suffer; for it was precisely the *Laudatio* which first established Bruni's fame among humanists, within and outside his adopted *patria*, Florence. The pride he took in this early achievement of his Humanism is keenly expressed in the passages of *Dialogus II* where the members of Salutati's circle are made to praise it for creating a new historical perspective of the past and for the honor it has done to Florence. Even late in life—in 1440— when Bruni looked upon the *Laudatio* as the work of a beginner, he insisted that "in my discussions very much will be found that a fair and careful reader . . . should not despise."[2]

A few years earlier, the panegyric had been sent by its author, now chancellor of Florence, to the Fathers at Basel to support a recommendation that Florence be made the seat of the Council[3]—a change of place which finally came to pass in 1439. In 1436, a counterpanegyric in praise of Milan, by Pier Candido Decembrio, paid Bruni's youthful writing the honor of close imitation, while Enea Silvio Piccolomini used it in 1438 as a guide and model for a literary portrait of the city of Basel. Even Thomas Chaundler, author of the eulogy of an English city, the episcopal town of Wells, followed it in some significant details twenty or thirty years later.[4] But though the power of the *Laudatio* to impress readers thus still proved strong around the middle of the century, its fame declined during the second half; and when after 1500 the printing presses of Basel produced the editions of many works of

---

[2] Bruni, indeed, there made the point that the first-fruits of able authors, even though immature, always retain a value of their own: "Fuit enim ea Laudatio michi tanquam puerilis ludus, ac exercitatio ad dicendum. Recti vero judicis est cum aliorum multorum, tum etiam temporis considerationem habere. Neque enim Ciceronis oratio, quam dixit adolescens pro P. Quintio, eandem meretur laudem, quam oratio post ab eodem dicta pro A. Cluentio. Laudamus tamen utranque, alteram ut adolescentis optimae spei, alteram ut perfecti jam oratoris. Demosthenis quoque orationes illae, quas adolescens scripsit in tutores suos, non ejusdem sunt virtutis, qua est illa subtilis de immunitate ad Leptilem, aut illa praestantissima pro Ctesiphonte, aut illa grandis et plena, in qua falsae legationis Aeschinem accusavit. Equidem pari quoque adolescentia Laudationem illam scripsi, sed tamen in ea ipsa juvenili Laudatione permulta reperientur a me tractata fuisse, quae lector aequus et diligens, ut leniter dixerim, non aspernetur." *Ep. VIII 4*, 1440, ed. L. Mehus, vol. II, p. 111.

[3] See the full reconstruction of this episode, with the help of new documentary material, by Eugenio Garin in *Storia di Milano*, ed. Fondazione Treccani degli Alfieri, VI (Milan, 1955), 581 f.

[4] For the various imitations of the *Laudatio*, see *Crisis*, rev. ed., pp. 209 ff.

fifteenth-century literature that were to be read for the next
few centuries, Bruni's *Laudatio* was not among them.

Why this quick change of fortune? In a way, the very vir-
tues of the *Laudatio* condemned it to a short life. It had been
written at the moment when Italian Humanism, especially
in its Florentine cast, was beginning to establish a changed
relationship to history and politics but no lasting achievement
of the new historiography and political philosophy had yet
been attained. In such circumstances, the guidance offered by
a portrait of Athens found in a work of Greek rhetoric—the
Panathenaicus, written about 100 B.C., of the sophist Aelius
Aristides—was able to give Bruni a tremendous head start in
the presentation of many aspects of Florence and its history.
But when by the second half of the century, largely as a result
of his own work, a higher type of historical and political
analysis had emerged, and when every Italian state possessed
its full-blown humanistic history, few readers remained satisfied with the short-cut approach of the *Laudatio* which at the
advent of Quattrocento thought had been so provocative.
Bruni himself had in 1440 defended his early work by pointing
out the difference between *history* and a *panegyric:* the latter,
in order to impress its readers effectively, must at times go
"beyond the truth [*supra veritatem*]."[5] The rhetorical simpli-
fication and exaggeration which Bruni had in mind, and
which are, indeed, obvious in the *Laudatio*, were necessarily
bound to lose their fascination once readers had become
familiar with the same new views in the more sober and objective setting of truly historical presentations.

Consider some of the striking features of the work. At the
center of the historical reasoning of the *Laudatio* is the two-
fold thesis—basic for the work according to Bruni's own appraisal in *Dialogus II* and according to the reaction of his
contemporaries—that Florence, more than any other Italian
state, could claim to be the heir of ancient Rome and that the
secret of Rome's greatness had been republican freedom, which
was bequeathed to the colony on the Arno because it was
founded before the despotism of the emperors had destroyed

---

[5] Bruni, *Ep. VIII 4;* see note 2, above. As pointed out in *Crisis* (rev. ed., p. 508 n. 14),
Bruni, an admirer of Polybius, undoubtedly took his inspiration from Polybius X
21. 8, where a similar distinction is made between ἐγκώμιον and ἱστορία.

Roman civic freedom. In the rhetorical framework of the *Laudatio* the historical perspective is presented as a black-and-white picture and put forth with naïve partisanship. Since it could be said that any territory disputed by Florence in the course of her history had once been the property of her founder, Rome, Florence could always claim that she was asking only for what was just and hers by the right of inheritance.[6] As for the condemnation of the imperial monarchy which followed the republican era—a problem of appraisal that soon became central to historical reflection in fifteenth-century Florence—the only reason given in the *Laudatio*, other than the evil doings of such emperors as Caligula and Nero, is the contention found in Tacitus, first observed and emphasized by Bruni, that under the emperors Rome's cultural vitality had waned.[7] When later in the fifteenth century readers had been given a penetrating analysis in Bruni's *Historiae Florentini Populi* of the psychological consequences of shifting all power to the one city of Rome, and, in Rome, to one man, there was little on this score that the *Laudatio* could still offer. It had just as little to offer a reader looking for the facts of Florentine history. Once he had learned from Bruni's *Historiae* that in 1254 the Florentine citizen army had succeeded in conquering the almost impregnable mountain city of Volterra, not by breaking down the walls, but by entering through the open gates together with the Volterra citizens who had fled back to their city after defeat in the open country, he would no longer be interested in the *Laudatio*'s rhetorical picture of rocks and arrows raining down from the walls upon the brave Florentine assailants.[8] And there were those many wearisome

---

[6] *Laudatio*, p. 244, below.

[7] *Laudatio*, p. 247, below. Cf. *Crisis*, rev. ed., pp. 58 ff., on the role of the rediscovery of Tacitus for Bruni.

[8] Compare *Laudatio*, p. 255, below, with the mature and balanced report—in which each individual fact, no longer rhetorically overdrawn, has fallen into place—found in Bruni's *Historiae* (*Rerum Italicarum Scriptores*, XIX, pars 3, pp. 29-30): "Volaterrani magna multitudine ab oppido irruentes, repentino impetu Florentinos invasere. Adiuvabat terrorem natura ipsa loci. Declivis enim praecepsque ab oppido descensus est, facilisque telorum de superiori parte coniectus, ut primo statim impetu coacti sint Florentini pedem referre. Sed conscia virtutis mens, insignisque victoriarum memoria, adversissimis etiam locis superare hostem in animum induxit. Itaque sese invicem cohortati, facto globo, sursum versus signa intulerunt. Volaterrani, utpote qui neque duce certo, neque ordine ullo, sed ut quemque tulerat casus in hostem descenderant, ubi contra quam rati fuerant dirigi in se aciem ac signa inferri viderunt, parumper tolerantes praelium, referre primo pedem, mox effuso protinus cursu ad oppidum re-

pages of the *Laudatio*[9] in which, in compliance with the prescriptions of ancient rhetoric, it was contended that the eulogized city was unequaled, even though other cities were in one respect or another able to compete; for here, in Florence, without exception, every imaginable kind of *virtus* flourished. In a way, then, we may say that the *Laudatio* became outdated so soon because, within the span of only one or two generations, many of its new ideas were brought to a level of maturity far above that reached in it.

II. But why had Bruni's early work abounded in new and often seminal ideas? No doubt the changes in the political climate brought about by Florence's trial and survival in the wars with Giangaleazzo were opening up new vistas, as every deeply stirring experience is likely to do; but this is only half the story. New kinds of historical and political analysis, as well as of literary presentation of cultural achievement, would not have developed so rapidly had certain writings of antiquity, created under similar conditions, not offered invaluable help. Was the imitation of a product of Greek rhetoric, however, not bound to be a drawback rather than a spur, especially since Bruni had chosen to follow the work of a late Greek orator? This, evidently, is a basic question which students of the *Laudatio* must face and try to answer concretely by retracing the steps of its young humanist author.

For a long time after the revival of modern scholarly interest in the *Laudatio* during the 1880's, Bruni's literary relationship to Aelius Aristides was usually condemned as an all too submissive dependence upon a model alien to the needs of a fifteenth-century writer. But now that the date of the *Laudatio* has been shifted to the morrow of Florence's survival in the Milanese wars, the underlying reasons for Bruni's choice of Aristides as a guide have become more readily understandable.

---

fugere: quos insecuti victores usque ad portas, ceciderunt terga. In ipsis vero portarum angustiis maxime tumultuatum est, conantibus aliis super alios irrumpere. Tantaque fuit trepidatio, ut desertam omni praesidio portam mixti simul victi victoresque intrarent." The first to draw attention to the difference in the two reports was E. T. Klette, *Beiträge zur Geschichte . . . der italienischen Gelehrtenrenaissance*, II (Greifswald, 1889), 33 f.

9 *Laudatio*, p. 263, below.

Aristides, in his *Panathenaicus*,[10] had tried to impress upon his audience that during the Persian wars Athens had saved civic freedom in Greece from the despotism threatening from abroad; Athens had emerged after war and victory as the potential leader of the Greek city-states, eventually gaining a position of political hegemony and becoming the focus of all Greek culture. Had Florence not also been the protagonist and savior of many other cities in a struggle for freedom against despotism from abroad? Would Florence, as a consequence, not also gain leadership among the other city-republics and become the focus of culture in Italy? Since no one writing shortly after 1400 had our knowledge of the future cultural predominance of Florence, we would not expect a work of 1403 to picture Florence as Italy's cultural center. Yet the *Laudatio* does just this.[11] Undoubtedly, the young Aretine newcomer to the Florentine world would not have gained his precocious insight, long before we find comparable claims in any other source, had his model not provided a suggestive pattern. The imitation of a Greek work had the effect of opening Bruni's eyes to parallels between old Athens and new Florence at an amazingly early time.[12] Was the price he paid for following a product of late classical rhetoric too high?

The nature of the *Laudatio*'s relationship to the *Panathenaicus* emerges clearly from Bruni's description of Florence's geographical position in its surrounding countryside—a high point of the author's literary art. It is the impact of reality that has molded this picture; and throughout we find a clarity that reflects the sensibility of a fifteenth-century author. Bruni, at this point, had a special reason for wishing to re-create reality as intensely as he had experienced it. Here he referred for the first time in his eulogy to Florence's triumph in the

---

[10] Printed, together with a Latin translation, in *Aelii Aristidis Adrianensis Opera Omnia Graece et Latine*, ed. S. Jebb, I (Oxford, 1722), 91–197.

[11] *Laudatio*, p. 263, below.

[12] Bruni himself described this relationship in later years (in *Ep. VIII 4*, 1440): "Non enim temere neque leviter id opus aggressi sumus, neque vagi aut incerti per semitas nobis incognitas peregrinantium more nostro ipsi arbitratu processimus, sed ducem itineris, totiusque laudandi progressus certum indubitatumque habuimus Aristidem celebrem apud Graecos Oratorem eloquentissimum hominem, cujus extat oratio pulcherrima de *Laudibus Athenarum*. Illius sermo tanquam magister michi fuit: conatus vero imitandi tanquam ludus, exercitatioque adolescentiae." (Ed. Mehus, vol. II, p. 111.)

past war;[13] his object was to impress the reader with the beauty and majesty of the city so as to awe him and make him concede that they matched the role attributed to it by the panegyric in the realms of history, politics, and culture. As the moon by the stars, says Bruni, so the mighty city is surrounded by outlying towns; and then he uses a second simile: the city in its landscape, as spread before the eyes of a spectator who watches it from a near mountain top, resembles a round shield, with the Palazzo Vecchio rising, like a mighty castle, as a boss in the center, surrounded by many concentric rings. First, there is the inner city, then the city walls, the suburbs, the country houses, the rural towns, and, finally, the enclosing mountain ranges—all merged in one broad panorama in which the world of the walled city and the scenery of the open country are viewed as the consecutive parts of an immense buckler.[14]

Although this is in every way the picture of the actual landscape of Florence, not of a city in the clouds, reality is here strikingly molded by eyes of the Quattrocento: we find at work the same sensibility which is familiar to us from panoramic drawings of Florence by Quattrocento artists—the same love of geometric regularity and proportion which was to express itself throughout the Renaissance in so many diagrams of "ideal cities". The *Laudatio*, however, in this respect as in others, precedes all comparable examples by at least a generation. Thus, when reading the work, we should ask ourselves to what extent this precedence was due to the aid of the Greek model.

Both of Bruni's similes—that of the moon and the stars, and that of the buckler—had been used by Aristides in his panegyric of Athens. But there they had not served the purpose of illuminating the impression which a visitor would have of Athens. Aristides had talked of the stars surrounding the moon in order to give a better mental picture of how the Cyclades and other Aegean islands were geographically situated around Attica, the heart of Greece;[15] and the simile of the

---

[13] *Laudatio*, p. 238, below.
[14] For the two similes, see *Laudatio*, p. 240, below.
[15] Aelius Aristides, ed. Jebb, I, 96.

rings around the center of a buckler had been used to illustrate the theory of a unique geographical position on the globe. Greece, so Aristides had pointed out, was surrounded on all sides by barbarism while, within Greece, Attica formed the innermost circle, at the heart of which lay Athens, with the Acropolis at its center, predestined to be the focal point of all Greek culture, because it was farthest removed from barbarian darkness.[16] This, obviously, is something utterly different from what Bruni was to make of it; an imaginary, mathematical relationship between the regions of the globe was assumed to give support to the rhetorical claim that Athens, culturally as well as geographically, was the center of the world. To Aristides, the simile of rings geometrically surrounding a central point did not serve—as they did to Bruni—to illuminate the experience of an actual landscape whose structure and aesthetic values were to be described.

Now, it is true that Bruni would not have had those metaphors available for his description of Florence's scenic position had he not found them in his ancient model.[17] But this must not cause us to exaggerate his dependence. It would not even be enough to say that he did not imitate blindly because he adapted his model to Tuscan conditions. The workings of Bruni's mind were different from what the term "imitation" primarily implies. What he gained from Aristides was not so much the ability itself to convey the visible impression of a city lying in its surrounding countryside. Rather, he found in the Greek work conceptual patterns which he could use to impose a rational order upon his observations of the world in which he lived. He thus achieved a concrete grasp of reality

---

[16] Attica "longissime distat a barbaris; quantumque ab iis est loci intervallo remota, tantundem et moribus discrepat. . . . Tanquam ad umbilicum clypei, ob omni extremitate tendit Graecia, eamque variis cingit orbibus partim marinis, partim terrenis. . . . Unde factum est ut et sinceris incorruptisque semper usa sit moribus, et accuratum purumque ac suave dicendi genus, quod omnes imitarentur Graeci, introduxerit." "Sicut enim in orbibus clypei in se invicem incurrentibus, quintus umbilicum implet, qui est omnium pulcerrimus: sic et Graecia est in medio totius terrae, Atticamque in sui medio complectitur, in qua deinde media jacet Urbs, et in huius medio Arx." Aelius Aristides, ed. Jebb, I, 98 f.

[17] As E. Garin, "La Cité idéale de la Renaissance italienne" (in *Les Utopies à la Renaissance, Colloque international 1961* [Brussels, 1963], p. 22), observes, the impression must have been especially strong because Plato, in the sixth book of his *Leges*, 778 c, also describes the layout of a city in concentric circles around the market place and public buildings in the center.

and a visual clarity to which we find no counterpart in his Greek *cicerone*, but which, without the help of Greek abstraction, would have had to wait until a much later phase of the Renaissance. Such inspiration from Greek attitudes is certainly not found everywhere in the *Laudatio*. At some points, imitation becomes nothing more than the rather mechanical reproduction of certain rhetorical devices of antiquity. But elsewhere the Greek model served to introduce patterns of thought that accelerated, or even made possible, the intellectual mastery of the humanist's own world. The recognition of this aspect of "imitation" during the early Quattrocento is one of the lessons we can learn from the study of the *Laudatio*.[18]

III. The places in the *Laudatio* where Aristides' eulogy of Athens helped Bruni to discover similar, but not identical, conditions in Florence and Italy include everything connected with Florence's history, cultural primacy, and constitutional life. To begin with Bruni's statement of the foundation of Florence, we find the *Laudatio* transforming Aristides' theses on the beginnings of Athens into something basically new in comparison with what the Middle Ages as well as Antiquity had proposed for the origin of cities.

It requires some detailed examination to realize that not only the authors of *laudes* of medieval cities but also the scholars of the Italian Trecento had done little to prepare the way for the new approach of the *Laudatio* to the problem of Florence's origin. Until the time of Dante, a constant objective of chronicle-writing even in Italy had been to ascribe the foundation of every city to a hero of medieval legends—the biblical Noah, who was said to have traveled to Europe; the Trojans, alleged forebears of many knightly families; or Caesar, founder of the providential Universal Empire. When, during the decades immediately preceding Petrarch, classical authors, especially Livy, began to be read more systematically, critical minds were able to see the fallacy of these contentions, because no acceptable authority could be adduced

---

[18] Cf. Bruni's *De Militia*, ed. in C. C. Bayley, *War and Society in Renaissance Florence* (Toronto, 1961), pp. 370–78, and Bayley's analysis of this aspect of Bruni's work, pp. 319–23.

for them. From the start of the Trecento, therefore, a skeptical attitude toward the medieval legends began to develop. But this does not mean that the historical approach found in the *Laudatio* was thereby prepared.

This becomes very clear from an examination of the most advanced and, until recently, hardly accessible representative of historical criticism early in the century, Benzo d'Alessandria, whose *Chronicon* (composed *ca.* 1310–20) includes a survey of the histories of the founding of many Italian cities, in particular those in northern Italy, and often deals with the medieval fables in a critical fashion.[19] To this early Lombard scholar, who in the Cathedral library of Verona became more fully acquainted with classical writers than anyone else before Petrarch, Livy as well as the pagan and Christian historians of late antiquity—such as Justinus (the abbreviator of Trogus Pompeius), Orosius, and Eusebius—seemed basically distinct from the medieval propagators of legends. They were the *"scriptores autentici"* and *"certi,"* in contrast to the unreliable chroniclers who came later. With the help of this criterion, he eliminated the more fantastic aspects of the medieval stories. In the case of Milan, the whole web of legends which had been spun around the figure of Noah was dissolved; for no "authentic" author gave a hint of Noah's coming to the West. As Benzo concludes: *"Deus novit, ego ignoro"* why the writers of later centuries (*"scriptores novissimi"*) had made those allegations. There was, after all, the testimony in Livy's history that Milan had been founded by a leader of the invading Gauls, Bellovesus, at the time of the Roman King Tarquinius the Elder—the testimony of *"omnium scriptorum et historiographorum maximo, in cuius narracione omnis tacet oblocutor et gaudet elocutor."*[20]

No less significant was Benzo's restraint whenever such clear evidence was not forthcoming. With respect to Genoa, for instance, he cut through the tangle of medieval hagiography,

---

[19] The text of Benzo's descriptions of the cities of northern Italy has only recently been printed *in extenso* in J. R. Berrigan's "Benzo d'Alessandria and the Cities of Northern Italy," *Studies in Medieval and Renaissance History*, IV (1967), 125–92. On Benzo and his work, cf. L. A. Ferrai in *Bullettino dell'Istituto Storico Italiano*, VII (1889), 97 ff., and R. Sabbadini, *Le Scoperte dei Codici Latini e Greci ne' secoli XIV e XV: Nuove Ricerche* (Florence, 1914), pp. 128 ff.

[20] Benzo, ed. Berrigan, pp. 142 f., 144.

which in Jacopo da Voragine's *Aurea Legenda* had enveloped
the beginnings of Genoese history. But he found himself unable to discover anything about the *real* city-founder from
"reliable" authors ("*in certo auctore non legi*"), and what he
found "*in quadam cronica*" of the Middle Ages he merely listed;
he did not consider it reliable. Benzo always returned to such
formulas in comparable situations. He did so with special
clarity in the cases of Pavia and Tortona. "I have not found
anything authentic and certain," he stated here, listing the
information encountered in medieval chronicles together with
a note expressing his reservations, such as "if one could have
confidence in such assertions," or "how much one may rely
on them I do not know."[21]

These were great strides forward, but Benzo's *Chronicon* also
reveals a less positive aspect of Trecento thought—one which
must be remembered for a fair perspective of the *Laudatio*.
Not only did the outcome of Benzo's efforts too often remain
a mere "*ignoramus*"; even where he succeeded in establishing
"authentic" information, as in the case of Milan, he had no
real use for his findings, since he was not searching for a new
interpretation of history to which they might be applied.
This lack of any new historical vision is characteristic of
Trecento Humanism, and remained so even after Petrarch,
until the advent of the development of thought of which the
Laudatio is the first representative.

In the second half of the Trecento, around 1380, for instance,
Benvenuto Rambaldi da Imola, commentator of the *Divina
Commedia* and a humanistic scholar of Bologna, showed a
skeptical attitude toward history strongly recalling that of
Benzo early in the century. Rambaldi, too, was unable to
advance from critical skepticism to a new historical outlook.
Although he said he was aware of the ludicrous side of ascrib-
ing the founding of countless cities to one man, Caesar, we
look in vain for any alternative theory. In the case of Florence,
after excluding Caesar, he simply states that this insight does
not help us to establish the true founder. "When, how, or by
whom" the founding of Florence took place, "I confess I

---

21 "Nil autenticum sive certum inveni."—"... si fides dari possit assertis."—"...
quibus quante fuerit fidei ignoro." From the chapters on Pavia and Tortona, *ibid.*, pp.
165, 166, 183. For Benzo's doubts regarding Genoa's origin, *ibid.*, p. 187.

know not."[22] When an answer to these questions—through the theory of the founding of Florence by veterans of Sulla—was found by Salutati, the latter, too, failed to make any significant use of his discovery. He used it only to argue that what had always been assumed—that Florence had been founded by Rome—was now confirmed by authentic, ancient sources.[23]

Against this background one realizes that Bruni in his *Laudatio* injected a new historical meaning into the findings of Salutati and other Trecento scholars when he observed that the original Florentines, as settlers from Sulla's army, had been Romans of the *republican* period and, consequently, had transmitted to Florence the Roman republican tradition. This emphasis, in turn, led him gradually to a revision of the histories of Rome and Florence until, by the time of his *Historiae Florentini Populi*, his view of the course of history had basically changed. In other words, the revolutionary element in the changing pattern of historical thought about 1400 was not the new critical reading of the historical sources. Humanistic criticism had been developing as early as pre-Petrarchan times; but when Trecento thought gave way to that of the Quattrocento, such criticism was neither the sole nor the decisive factor. Although the changes in outlook and perceptiveness at that time would not have been possible without the help obtained from the growing objectivity of the historical criticism of the Trecento humanists, the profundity of the transition about 1400 was due to the emergence of a new historical vision—primarily of the Roman Republic, which had been forgotten during the Middle Ages, and of the role of the Roman emperors, who had been viewed chiefly as mediators or representatives of the divinely ordained, universal *Sacrum Imperium*.

Why did Bruni succeed in initiating new and original historical conceptions, whereas the fourteenth-century scholars, including even Salutati, had failed? One cause, and probably the basic one, was the incentive of the political threat to the republican city-state of Florence by the ever-expanding mon-

---

[22] On Benvenuto Rambaldi da Imola, see *Crisis*, rev. ed., pp. 63, 153 f.
[23] *Ibid.*, p. 159.

archy of the Visconti during Giangaleazzo's last years. In fact, ever since we have known that Bruni's Florentine eulogy was composed after 1402, the *Laudatio* has served as the most important testimony to the political motivation of the intellectual changes that occurred at the threshold of the Quattrocento.

Yet, though the motivation was fundamentally political, the rapidity and extent of the intellectual transformation once more depended on the spur of the simultaneous emergence of Greek studies. The way in which the *Laudatio* presents the idea of the Florentine mission inherited from the *Respublica Romana* makes this dependence perfectly clear. In Aristides' panorama of Greece, Athenian hegemony in politics and culture had been justified not only as a consequence of Athens' defense of liberty against Persian despotism but also as a natural result of the early history of Athens and Attica, which had been different from that of other parts of Greece, as Aristides boldly maintained. Athens' original citizens had been indigenous, grown on the soil of Attica, whereas all other Greek populations, including the Athenian metics who lacked full citizen rights, were later immigrants.[24] This claim of autochthony complemented Aristides' speculation that Attica was the heart of Greece because it was geographically farther removed than any other Greek region from the surrounding barbarian world. Bruni did not try to imitate Aristides by claiming that the Florentines, too, were nearer to being indigenous than the citizens of other Italian cities. But adherence to Aristides' speech as a blueprint compelled him to find some analogy for Florence—some force that, from the city's origin, had propelled it toward greatness in the same way that the origin of Athens was thought to have produced Athenian preeminence. Thus the idea of a special psychological and ideological legacy that the *Respublica Romana* had bequeathed to Florence at its founding was substituted for Aristides' claim of the autochthony of the inhabitants of Attica. Again, a piece of abstract reasoning—Aristides' application to Athens of the Greek commonplace that autochthony is superior to immigration—was replaced by an attempt

---

[24] Aelius Aristides, ed. Jebb, I, 102 f.

to reconstruct concretely the nature and meaning of Florentine conditions.

The results, here as elsewhere in the *Laudatio*, it is true, were still far removed from the mature political thought and historiography to which Florentine Humanism of the Quattrocento would shortly attain, yet they represent the first and decisive step along the road from Trecento medievalism to the Renaissance. This historical position of the *Laudatio* is unmistakable as soon as its politico-historical ideas are placed in the context of the subsequent development of Florentine thought, beginning with Bruni's own later writings.

IV. We have already recalled the framework of Bruni's view of the founding of Florence: the changed accent placed on the republican period in Roman history. Here the panegyric allows us to observe both the relative crudity and formative effect of the first phase of the new historical approach. Undoubtedly, the elaborate analysis in Bruni's *Historiae* of the psychological perversion and physical extermination of active, upright citizens under a despotic monarchy was on an incomparably higher level than the tale of the horrors of Caligula and Nero found in the *Laudatio*. Nevertheless, the brief reference in the latter work to Tacitus' dictum on the disappearance of great intellects in Rome under the rule of the emperors[25] produced the ferment for the rise of a school of historiography critical of Caesar and Universal Monarchy—the school that was to reach its climax in Machiavelli.

A very similar relationship of promise and fulfilment exists between the *Laudatio* and the *Historiae* with regard to Bruni's rediscovery of the ancient precedents and sources of Florentine republican liberty. In the *Laudatio*, we find the young historian still spinning a thin thread. It is drawn out from the republican interpretation given to Salutati's finding that Florence was founded by veterans of Sulla's army and from the idea that the spirit then implanted in the Florentines, together with their Roman blood, had predestined Florence to become the foremost Guelph city, forever antagonistic to Empire and Monarchy. By the time of the *Historiae*, yet an-

---

[25] As mentioned p. 154, above.

other fountainhead of Florentine republicanism had come to light: pre-Roman Tuscany—ancient Etruria. "Colony of the Romans, commingled with the old inhabitants of Tuscan origin," Florence was eventually called by Bruni in 1428.[26] In the more psychological approach of the later Bruni to the problem of Republic or Monarchy, the claim that the *libertas* which had made the Etruscan city-republics great was revived in the history of Florence became the guiding idea of his philosophy of history. The rise of Rome to supremacy, he argued in the *Historiae* and later, was bound to destroy the freedom and energies of Etruria and the other city-state republics in Italy; but after the fall of Rome's Universal Empire civic freedom and vitality could rise again in independent city-states, especially in Tuscany, thanks to its pre-Roman legacy, and most of all in Florence, where the Tuscan inheritance was strengthened by the legacy of Rome's own republican past.[27]

Thus, in Bruni's final view of history, the idea that Florence was the favorite daughter of the *Respublica Romana* has become a single strand in a rich fabric, all parts of which are clearly interrelated and derived from a common source. The conviction that civic *virtus* is dependent upon the freedom which allows citizens to participate directly in the affairs of their city-state was the last ripe fruit of Florence's fight for survival against the Visconti efforts to build another empire in Italy; and the belief that the greatest value of the small republican state since pre-Roman times had lain in its ability to generate *virtus* would live on until Machiavelli and Guicciardini.

V. As for the remaining themes in the *Laudatio*—Florence's role in humanistic culture and Volgare literature, and the ethos and working of the Florentine constitution[28]—the immediate impact of the Giangaleazzo wars was, by necessity, less powerful. Yet, in the atmosphere of the postwar years, the *Laudatio* even here established "firsts" in several respects,

---

[26] In the *Oratio Funebris* on Nanni degli Strozzi; see *Crisis*, rev. ed., p. 415.

[27] *Crisis*, rev. ed., pp. 64 ff., 74, 417 f.

[28] *Laudatio*, pp. 258 ff., below.

standing at the very start of a number of well-known Florentine developments.

Indirectly, of course, Florence's political triumph in 1402 greatly contributed to its eventual rise to cultural leadership; but nobody could foresee these long-range consequences at the time when the *Laudatio* was written. It was not until 1428 that Bruni fully expressed his awareness of the unique place which Florence had come to occupy in the history of Renaissance Humanism. At that time he stated in his obituary eulogy of Nanni degli Strozzi, actually a second *Laudatio* of Florence, that it was in the Florentine commonwealth that the *litterae politioresque disciplinae*—"the *studia humanitatis* themselves, surely the most excellent of studies"—and even the knowledge of Greek letters had been brought back to life after more than seven hundred years. "Such studies," he said, "took root in Italy after originating from our city."[29] So much, of course, could not be asserted before nearly three decades of the Quattrocento had witnessed Florence's stupendous cultural ascendancy; but it is all the more remarkable that the *Laudatio* had nonetheless already stated that the *artes liberales* were flowering in Florence, just as they had flowered "among every leading people."[30]

To make such a claim for Florence with a view to the new humanistic studies was in 1403 much more daring than is easily realized. Not very long before, Benvenuto Rambaldi da Imola had taken it for granted that Bologna, seat of the old, renowned university, was "mother and nurse of all studies and sciences in Italy," "*humanitatis piissima nutrix*"; and at about the same time as the *Laudatio*, a north-Italian humanist and admirer of Giangaleazzo, Giovanni Conversino da Ravenna, was honestly convinced that just as the new studies

---

[29] *Crisis*, rev. ed., p. 417.

[30] ". . . que in omni principe populo semper floruerunt." Cf. *Crisis*, rev. ed., p. 146, and *Laudatio*, p. 263, below. That Bruni in the *Laudatio* talks of "artes liberales," instead of "studia humanitatis," is of little significance, because he and Salutati were already using the term "studia humanitatis" in their correspondence—Bruni to Salutati, Sept. 13, 1405, on the "florentinae urbis habitatores," "si praesertim studiis dediti sint humanitatis" (*Archivum Romanicum*, XV [1931], 322); Salutati to Bruni, Nov. 6, 1405, "hanc urbem studiorum humanitatis esse domicilium" (Salutati, *Epistolario*, vol. IV, p. 119)—and the term also appears in the *Prooemium* to *Dialogus I* in 1401 ("civitas haec florentissima est, tum etiam optimarum artium totiusque humanitatis," ed. Garin, p. 44), as well as later in *Dialogus II* (Petrarch "studia humanitatis, quae iam extincta erant, reparavit," ed. Garin, p. 94).

had flourished in tyrant states during the Trecento, they could be expected to flourish only there in the years ahead, whereas in city-republics, of which he mentioned Venice and Florence, they had never flowered and would never do so.[31] In the middle and latter half of the fourteenth century, indeed, nascent Humanism in northern Italy had generally lived in association with the tyrant courts, which offered lucrative employment in the chanceries, and even closer ties with the court through positions for humanists as educators of young princes. There was at that time still little of a humanistic movement in the Florentine Republic, nor could Florence yet boast of any outstanding humanists except for the impressive figure of Salutati, venerated master of the small, recently formed circle to which Bruni belonged. It is against this background that one must appraise the young Bruni's astonishing confidence— perhaps, after all, not so much an anticipation of things only dimly visible at that time, as an invaluable testimony to the faith in the new studies that sustained Salutati's and Niccoli's group. As mentioned earlier,[32] already in the preface to *Dialogus I,* that is to say, in 1401, when Bruni still felt himself to be a stranger from Arezzo in Florence, he had rejoiced that good fortune had allowed him to live in a city where one could find the almost extinct *"humanitas"* and *"optimae artes,"* "which grow here daily and before long will surely bring forth much light." What the *Laudatio* adds to this earlier utterance is the political and patriotic emphasis: intellectual pursuits, which flourish in "every leading people," now do so in Florence.

To a degree, Bruni was again led to claim so much at this point because he was following Aristides as a guide; he had to furnish a Florentine counterpart to the claim that Athens had been "the nursery" of Greek culture.[33] But he would certainly not have made his counterclaim that the Florentines were a "leading people" had it not been for the political

---

[31] Benvenuto Rambaldi da Imola, *Comentum super Dantis Aldigherij Comoediam,* ad *Purg.* cant. XIV; ed. J. P. Lacaita, vol. III (Florence, 1887), p. 390. For Conversino, see *Crisis,* rev. ed., pp. 137 ff.

[32] See above, p. 121.

[33] ". . . exemplum . . . aut fundamentum . . . omnium studiorum, vitaeque generum, ac totius denique Graeciae seminarii"; . . . καὶ, τὸ σύμπαν εἰπεῖν, τοῦ τῶν Ἑλλήνων σπέρματος." Aelius Aristides, ed. Jebb, I, 126.

experience of 1402. Although the precedent provided by Aristides helped him in posing his question, the answer was his own and was based on the actuality of Florentine life. This included Florence's already established primacy in Volgare literature. He praised the city for having set up a standard for vernacular speech and for the glory of being able to call the greatest writers in Volgare her own.[34] Niccoli, the militant classicist, would not have dreamed of such a boast, and even Poggio would not have made such a claim when expressing pride in the studies of Salutati's circle. But for Bruni it is characteristic that he referred to the glories of the Florentine Volgare, because this foreshadows the man who by the 1430's was to set forth the first mature defense of the Volgare—maintaining that "every language has its own perfection"[35]—and who was to write the first full-blown humanistic biographies in the native language, the *Vite di Dante e di Petrarca*. Thus, once again we observe the pattern of Bruni's civic Humanism already forming in the *Laudatio*.

The discussion of the institutions and political offices of Florence represents another area in which the effects of the Giangaleazzo wars are not evident on the surface. If the *Laudatio*, nevertheless, has something very new to say about the Florentine constitution, the novelty of Bruni's presentation here, too, stems from his efforts to match his Greek model in the use of theoretical abstraction and yet remain true to the reality of Florentine life. Instead of giving a summary of all the contemporary offices and boards of the Republic, he sought to explain the purpose and function of every agency which he described and to characterize the general direction of Florentine legislation. About a decade after the *Laudatio* was written, Bruni remarked that the important point in a discussion of public offices was not to note the bare fact that a certain office had been established in a certain year, but rather to "understand and explain *why* it had been instituted. For it is by knowing the *cause* that we gain knowledge of a thing."[36] In the *Laudatio*, Bruni had already tried to show that the consistent motivation of all basic Florentine laws

[34] *Laudatio*, p. 263, below; cf. *Crisis*, rev. ed., p. 337.
[35] *Crisis*, rev. ed., pp. 338 ff.   [36] *Ibid.*, p. 207.

was to prevent the misuse of a powerful office for tyrannical ends and to protect the equality of the citizens before the law by restraining the strong and aiding the weak.[37] It is true that Bruni's examination was restricted to the highest offices and the city councils, with the result that only a surface layer of the institutions was analyzed. But to be fair we must compare Bruni's work with medieval city *laudes*, a comparison which shows that their authors had never attempted to analyze and characterize city constitutions at all.[38] Even during the Quattrocento, the very writings composed in opposition to or under the influence of Bruni's work would not contain anything comparable to Bruni's all too brief appraisal.[39]

Bruni's guide had at the point in question again maintained that Athenian excellence was due to adherence to a general principle and theory: the constitution of Athens, according to Aristides, was a perfect blend of the three possible forms of government. Bruni, instead, tells us that he intends to trace "the many ways in which [in Florence] care is taken" to prevent those placed in power "from imagining that not custodianship of the citizens, but a tyrannical position, had been given to them."[40] To this end, as the *Laudatio* states, high offices are always filled with a number of people, not with one man, and all appointments are for a very brief period. In addition, each of the four quarters of the city is represented in each set of *Signori*. The latter must, by law, consult counsellors, and city councils must approve every law, with the result that "nothing can be resolved by the caprice of any single man against the judgment of so many."[41] Other regulations, according to the *Laudatio*, are meant to reduce the influence of the great, thus bringing about equality before the law.[42]

These political ideals and pretensions sprang neither from mere rhetoric nor from mere imitation of Bruni's literary model; the living source for the newcomer from the Tuscan region-state to Florence was undoubtedly Salutati. In his

---

[37] *Laudatio*, pp. 259, 262, below.
[38] *Crisis*, rev. ed., p. 198.
[39] *Ibid.*, pp. 209 ff.
[40] *Laudatio*, p. 259, below.
[41] "Nichil ex unius aut alterius libidine contra tot hominum sententiam possit constitui." *Laudatio*, p. 260, below.
[42] *Laudatio*, p. 262, below.

diplomatic exchange with other city-state republics, the latter had on suitable occasions long voiced the same Florentine convictions. In letters to Bologna and Siena from as early as the beginning of the 1390's, which have recently been brought to light,[43] Salutati had called Florence the freest city in Italy and even in the world, because the men in power there would not dare to commit arbitrary acts against either citizens or foreigners. In Florence, thousands of citizens share in the administration of their state, and since offices are held only for a limited time, the *populus Florentinus* has never had to submit to the rule of a restricted few.[44]

What had thus in political correspondence occasionally been said in praise of Florence, in the *Laudatio* became a yardstick for a sustained effort to interpret the spirit of the Florentine laws. At the same time, the effect of the contact with Greek ideas is unmistakable in the pleasure with which the coherence and rational perfection of Florence's constitution is perceived and pointed out. In each single case, Bruni declares (even though he does not show it in detail), the excellence of Florence is derived from the "inner order, neatness, and workman-like construction [*ordo rerum, . . . elegantia, . . . concinnitas*]" with which all Florentine laws carry out those basic principles. In Florence's constitution, as in the harmony produced by harpstrings, "nothing is ill-proportioned, nothing improper, nothing incongruous, nothing left vague; everything occupies its proper place which is not only clearly defined but also in the right relation to all others."[45]

In these sentences we find once more the attitude which makes the description of Florence's geographical position in the Tuscan landscape so remarkable: the love of geometric proportion, the nascent Quattrocento sense for the beauty of clarity and good planning. Moreover, it is for the first time in Florentine literature that we are clearly told about the Florentine design to maintain civic freedom through the

---

[43] By P. Herde in *Archiv für Kulturgeschichte*, XLVII (1965), 182 f.

[44] ". . . nec credimus aliquam in Italia civitatem vel per universum mundi spacium reperiri, que magis libera sit et tuta et ubi minus liceat per potentiam contra cives aut extraneos aliquid attentari." "Milia sunt hominum, qui nostram rem publicam administrant, qui communitatis intra limitata tempora magistratibus nobis consulunt nosque regunt, nec solet populus Florentinus subesse paucis. . . ." Ed. Herde, pp. 182 f.

[45] *Laudatio*, p. 259, below.

workings of a constitution which shrewdly prevents the misuse for tyrannical ends of any single office in the state.

On the other hand, just as the *Laudatio* draws only a rudimentary picture of the Florentine Quattrocento view of Roman and Florentine history, so its perspective of the Florentine constitution illuminates merely one of the elements which in later years were to form the mature idea of the Florentine constitution—even in Bruni's own later writings. When, during the 1420's, he was again to define the nature of Florentine liberty, he found—in accord with his historical views—the decisive influence on the *virtus* of Florentine citizens to lie in a political system which, in principle, gave every citizen the opportunity to participate actively in the state. "For where men are given the hope of attaining honor in the state, they take courage and raise themselves to a higher plane; where they are deprived of that hope, they grow idle and lose their strength."[46] This view of the *libertas Florentina* focuses on an aspect of Florentine life on which, as late as the time of Savonarola, actual citizenship and, eventually, some of the guiding ideas of Machiavelli were built.

But the other principle of Florentine constitutional life— that to which attention had been drawn in the *Laudatio*—also held its own. For the conviction that checks and balances had been implanted in Florence's institutions in order to prevent misuse of constitutional power for tyrannical ends continued throughout the Renaissance, as did the belief that civic *virtus* depends on free access for every full-fledged citizen to the councils and offices of the Republic.

Thus, even in the area of constitutional thought the *Laudatio* proves to be an indispensable source for any effort to reconstruct the genesis and gradual evolution of the ideas of the Florentine Renaissance.

---

[46] *Crisis*, rev. ed., p. 419.

6 EARLY RENAISSANCE VENETIAN
CHRONICLES: Their History and a Manuscript
in the Newberry Library

I. The Venetian chronicles of the early Renaissance were not literary works like the chronicles of the Villani and their successors in Florence, which were copied and printed basically unchanged during the fifteenth and sixteenth centuries. The Venetian chronicle, rather, was a product of aristocratic life, without exact parallel in the historiography of other states. Chronicle-writing in the patrician families in Venice sprang from the practical needs of a political elite; it did not develop from an intellectual interest, nor was it undertaken to provide reading matter for a general audience. Each of the ruling families required handy information on Venice's politics in recent years, as well as in the days of their ancestors—not the kind of information that could be gained from works of literary historiography, but the particular knowledge which a patrician, who usually was also a great merchant, wanted to keep alive for himself and his descendants.

The widespread custom of chronicle-writing did not mean that every Venetian noble family produced great historical writers; but there emerged a pattern of average usefulness, which was closely followed by countless memorialists. While more or less fully transcribing one eminent predecessor for one period and another predecessor for another, the author of such a chronicle could give his account a personal touch by his selections, omissions, condensations, and occasional additions. When it approached the time of his own adult life, his narrative would gradually come to use a greater variety of sources, until finally his own experience began to determine the tone and range. We find, therefore, as we trace the long succession of annals from generation to generation, that the contributions of the earlier writers are neither fully displaced

This study first appeared, under the title of "A Forgotten Chronicle of Early Fifteenth-century Venice: The Copy in Newberry Manuscript f 87.1," in *Essays in History and Literature, Presented by Fellows of The Newberry Library to Stanley Pargellis* (Chicago, 1965), pp. 19–36.

nor preserved in their original state; they are transformed in successive adaptations and continue, in this disguise, to influence the views of later writers. At the same time new experiences and opinions are continually integrated into the thinning older body of information. At least until the first half of the sixteenth century, the uniqueness of this Venetian literary genre lies in the constant reproduction of the old in spite of gradual innovation.

Formally, these characteristics of the Venetian early Renaissance chronicles are similar to, if not identical with, a well-known pattern of medieval chronicle-writing. Monastic and clerical writers had generally been accustomed to starting their narratives with only slightly adapted transcripts of earlier accounts of past periods; to these they added their own narratives, as they approached their lifetime and the events of which they had direct knowledge. This had been the typical form of the "world chronicle" from the eleventh to the thirteenth century; and that the type remained in use when the chroniclers were laymen during the later Middle Ages can best be illustrated with the example of the "London Chronicles" from the fourteenth to the sixteenth century.[1]

The striking medieval feature of this genre of historiographical writing is a lack of individuality; so strong is the predominance of a typical outlook and form of presentation that the work of preceding authors can be incorporated in a later chronicle more or less intact, without a jarring note between the earlier and the newly written portions. In Florence, even Giovanni Villani's early-Trecento chronicle exhibits so unmistakable a tone of its own that the individual unity of his work overshadows his extensive reliance, in the early sections, on the accounts of predecessors. After the coming of Humanism—in Florence, from Leonardo Bruni onward—we would certainly no longer expect that our analyses of chronicle texts might end with the identification of more or less unchanged earlier works incorporated in the later narratives— the very condition continually encountered in a study of the

---

[1] They have been described by C. L. Kingsford in terms very similar to what has just been said about the character of Venetian chronicle-writing. Cf. Kingsford's *English Historical Literature in the Fifteenth Century* (Oxford, 1913), pp. 107 ff., and his introduction to the edition of the *Chronicles of London* (Oxford, 1905), p. xxiii.

Venetian fourteenth- and fifteenth-century writings. This difference reflects the much slower pace in the reception of Humanism and the Renaissance in Venice than in Florence. On the other hand, one should also look below the surface of Venetian traditionalism. There is little doubt that diversity of politico-economic interests and sensibilities is wider and more sharply expressed among these merchant-statesmen of Venice than in any group of medieval chroniclers, notwithstanding the similarity of the literary form. On the pages which follow, we are repeatedly confronted—sometimes embarrassed—by the constant differences in evaluation and emphasis among the Venetian reports, despite their relatedness. Final statements on all these aspects of Venetian fifteenth-century historiography, however, will have to wait until the time when exhaustive analysis and evaluation of the surviving texts have provided a generally acceptable basis.

This task of critical research has until now remained a *desideratum*, even though a reliable picture of the long process of preservation and change of information in the existing chronicle manuscripts would be invaluable for a full understanding of Venetian attitudes and opinions. The reason why the preparation of such a picture seems so difficult is partly technical: it is almost impossible to establish a line of growth in the enormous mass of extant manuscripts before major portions of the chronicle succession have been made accessible in print for comparison and consultation. But scholars have been slow in editing these texts (except the earliest, from the beginning of the fourteenth century or before) chiefly because, until many more individual manuscripts have been examined, it is most difficult to distinguish, even in the known major chronicles, between sections in which older information is recopied or condensed and those parts where the author's original contribution comes into its own. In the present state of knowledge, therefore, all reconstructions of the historical development must be accepted with a grain of salt.

It is only with such strong reservations firmly in mind that we can regard the following outline as a likely picture of the succession of Venetian Renaissance chronicles.[2] Although the

---

[2] This history can be reconstructed from the available monographs: M. F. Thiriet, "Les Chroniques Vénitiennes de la Marcienne et leur importance pour l'histoire de la

number of surviving manuscripts of histories of Venice, or periods of Venetian history, is legion—more than two hundred handwritten volumes have been counted in Venetian libraries, more than one hundred in the Österreichische Nationalbibliothek in Vienna (which includes a major Venetian eighteenth-century collection, that of the Doge Marco Foscarini), and dozens in France and England[3]—only a handful go back as far as the first half or the middle of the fifteenth century; and later copies can rarely serve as substitutes for older manuscripts because transcriptions were prone to distortion of the text once interest, language, script, and orthography had substantially changed. There exists, to be sure, one (rather tardy) synthesis of the information given in the early chronicles that can be consulted in print—the *Vite dei Dogi* by Marino Sanudo the Younger, composed between 1490 and 1530, and through the medium of this late narrative students have in fact always known and indirectly read a number of the older chronicles, which Sanudo reproduced by shortening and adjusting or paraphrasing their content. From this late synthesis, however, it is often not easy to work one's way back to the original Quattrocento sources.

In writing about the late fourteenth and early fifteenth centuries, Sanudo exploited especially two substantial works of that period in which some basic historiographical concerns of the Renaissance had come to the fore for the first time—an eager interest in economic and statistical facts, in the financial resources of states, and in the vicissitudes of the Venetian empire in the Levant as well as in northern Italy. One of these early accounts is a chronicle by Antonio Morosini, which, after 1403, broadens into an almost daily journal that reflects the author's widening interests, extending far beyond Venice. Until its end in 1433 this chronicle remains our most

Romanie Gréco-Vénitienne," *Mélanges d'Archéologie et d'Histoire* (*École Française de Rome*), LXVI (1954), 241–92; F. Lane, *Andrea Barbarigo, Merchant of Venice* (Baltimore, 1944), Appendix "Chronicles in Manuscript," pp. 150–52; and the studies by M. Zannoni cited in note 9 below. Still useful among earlier publications are R. Fulin, "Saggio del catalogo dei codici di Emmanuele A. Cicogna," *Archivio Veneto*, IV (1872), 337–78; V. Lazzarini, "Marino Faliero. Fonti—Bibliografia," *Nuovo Archivio Veneto*, XIII (1897), 5–20, republished in Lazzarini's *Marino Faliero* (Florence, 1963), pp. 95–107; H. Kretschmayr, *Geschichte von Venedig*, II (1920), 535–47.

3 Thiriet, "Les Chroniques Vénitiennes de la Marcienne . . . ," pp. 243–45.

valuable report.[4] Sanudo does not refer to Morosini and may never have read him directly; his constant reference is to a later chronicle by Pietro Dolfin, who lived from 1433 to 1503 and composed his work shortly before Sanudo began to write the later portions of his *Vite*. But Pietro Dolfin had reproduced Morosini's work so literally for the late fourteenth and early fifteenth centuries that, as a modern student has said, Sanudo "through Dolfin's text actually received his inspiration from Antonio Morosini."[5] Here, then, the body of our historical information stems from a largely unprinted source from the first decades of the fifteenth century, adopted and adjusted by a late fifteenth-century chronicler, and, after 1500, cast by Sanudo into the form in which it is still read today.

This pattern is closely paralleled in the other line of fifteenth-century annals leading to Sanudo. In this instance, the core of our information derives from an anonymous near-contemporary of Antonio Morosini, whose work has been preserved in a manuscript of the Biblioteca Marciana, Cod. Marc. It., VII. 2034.[6] Like other chroniclers, the anonymous writer of "2034" is seldom original in the earlier parts of his narrative and even for later periods seems to have drawn heavily upon Antonio Morosini's slightly earlier account.[7] But the nearer he approaches his own time, the more independent information he has to offer, and for the years 1433–43, after the end of Morosini's chronicle, he provides our best information, just as Morosini is our richest source for the preceding period. The influence of the "2034" chronicler on Sanudo is similar to that of Morosini in both extent and mode of transmission. The situation is more complicated, however,

---

[4] On Morosini, cf. R. Cessi, *Enciclopedia Italiana*, XXIII (1934), 869; G. Lefèvre-Pontalis in vol. IV of his edition, from Morosini's chronicle, of "Extraits Relatifs à l'Histoire de France" (Société de l'Histoire de France; Paris, 1912), esp. pp. 38, 120 f., 134, 172; Thiriet, *op. cit.*, pp. 272–79.

[5] Lefèvre-Pontalis, *op. cit.*, p. 183, who also comments on Sanudo's relationship to Morosini. Cf. also Fulin, *op. cit.*, pp. 347–48, and (on Sanudo's use of Pietro Dolfin) the note by Lino Lazzarini in V. Lazzarini, *Marino Faliero*, p. 102 n. 4. I have been unable to see R. Cessi's introduction to Pietro Dolfin's *Annalium venetorum pars quarta* (fasc. 1 published by the Istituto Veneto di Scienze, Lettere ed Arti in 1943).

[6] On the manuscript Marc. It., VII. 2034, cf. Zannoni, "Le fonti . . . di Giorgio Dolfin" (see note 9, below), esp. pp. 524–38; V. Lazzarini, *loc. cit.*, p. 13 (in *Marino Faliero*, p. 102), with list of manuscripts related to "2034"; Thiriet, *op. cit.*, esp. p. 253; Lane, *op. cit.*, p. 151.

[7] Lane, p. 151.

for there can be no doubt that the chronicle preserved in "2034" was consulted by Sanudo both directly[8] and by way of an intermediary, the chronicle of Pietro Dolfin's father, Giorgio (Zorzi) Dolfin, who had lived and carried his account to 1458.[9] Just as Sanudo's reading of Pietro Dolfin's chronicle actually put him in debt to Antonio Morosini, so his continual reliance on Giorgio Dolfin's work made him, without his knowing it, an equally heavy debtor to the pre-Dolfin author of the chronicle in "2034."[10]

As for Giorgio Dolfin, one historian of Venice has gone so far as to remark that the elder Dolfin's use of the material contained in the manuscript Marc. It., VII. 2034 is so inclusive "that it would seem superfluous to study the anonymous author of the '2034' directly."[11] This statement no doubt exaggerates the closeness of the two chronicles and distorts their respective significance. As recent students have established, the anonymous chronicle is different in method, scope, and attitude from Giorgio Dolfin's work. Its unknown author is a counterpart to his semi-contemporary Antonio Morosini especially in paying attention to economic and commercial events and to everything connected with the voyages of the Venetian ships.[12] In Giorgio Dolfin, on the other hand, this interest is largely replaced by emphasis on happenings related to the building up of the Venetian region-state on the Italian mainland.[13] Indeed, the more Dolfin, after the 1360's, ap-

---

[8] Cf. G. Monticolo's references in the apparatus of his edition of Sanudo's *Vite dei Dogi*, in *Rerum Italicarum Scriptores*, tomo XXII, parte IV (1900), pp. 185 ff., and *passim*.

[9] On Giorgio Dolfin, cf. Maria Zannoni, *Giorgio Dolfin cronista veneziano del sec. XV* (Padua, 1942 [Extract from Accademia di Scienze, Lettere ed Arti in Padova, *Memorie*, LVIII, 1941-42]); M. Zannoni, "Le fonti della cronaca veneziana di Giorgio Dolfin," *Istituto Veneto di Scienze, Lettere ed Arti, Atti*, CI, parte II (Classe di Scienze morali e lettere) (1942), pp. 515-46; Thiriet, *op. cit.*, pp. 286-90.

[10] For Sanudo's reliance on Giorgio Dolfin, cf. Monticolo in his cited edition of Sanudo's *Vite, passim*. There is a further channel by which the information contained in the "2034" chronicle might conceivably have reached both Giorgio Dolfin and Sanudo—the so-called *Cronaca Zancaruolo*, which has been preserved only in a sixteenth-century manuscript, but which according to one hypothesis was composed early enough to have transmitted material from "2034" to Giorgio Dolfin and to Sanudo. However, since the date and place of the Zancaruolo chronicle are not conclusively known, while there are sound reasons for doubting an early fifteenth-century origin of Zancaruolo's work (see below, note 42), we may omit Zancaruolo from our present outline of the established picture.

[11] Kretschmayr, *op. cit.*, II, 542.

[12] Thiriet, *op. cit.*, p. 253.   [13] *Ibid.*, pp. 287 f., 290.

proaches his own time, the more he displays his personal range of interests. This is especially so between 1443 and 1458, that is, from the end of the anonymous chronicle, when he no longer had a crutch to lean on, to the year of his death.[14] But we find loss as well as gain when we proceed from the pre-Dolfin "2034" to Giorgio Dolfin; while new objectives and subjects come to the fore, much of the wealth of information found in the older chronicle is shortened, paraphrased, omitted, or replaced in Dolfin's account.

To summarize, according to our present knowledge there existed, during the first half of the fifteenth century, three major chronicles distinct in many respects. As for their relations to each other, while Morosini stands apart (though consulted by the two others), Giorgio Dolfin rests squarely on the foundations laid by the "2034"; his work appears to be the successor and continuator of the chronicle preserved in the "2034" manuscript.

As further texts of the fifteenth century come to light, how do they fit into this apparently neat and simple picture?

II. Manuscript f 87.1 of the Newberry Library contains a Venetian chronicle of the mid-fifteenth century which, if the following observations are not too wide of the mark, may add some unexpected touches to the history of Venetian chronicle-writing.

Manuscript "87.1" (as we shall call it) was written in Venice, presumably about the year 1450.[15] It remained there until the early nineteenth century, at which time it formed part of a patrician collection, the library of Lorenzo Antonio da Ponte, whose engraved book plate bearing the number CCXIV. C is pasted on the inner front cover. In 1821 Da Ponte's library was sold to the book dealer Adolfo Cesare,[16] through whom "87.1" must have come into the collection of Sir Thomas Phillips in Cheltenham, England, where it was numbered

---

[14] Zannoni, "Le fonti . . . ," pp. 531, 537.

[15] The script appears to belong to the second third of the century and can hardly be much later; the *terminus post quem* is January 1434, when the text suddenly breaks off.

[16] E. A. Cicogna, *Saggio di bibliografia veneziana* (Venice, 1847), p. 75.

Manuscript 7503.[17] It was eventually acquired by the Newberry Library from the New York firm of H. P. Kraus in
November 1957.

The Da Ponte–Newberry manuscript opens with three introductory pieces: a legendary account of the deeds of Attila,
especially his raids in northern Italy, which led to the establishment of the refuge in the lagoons that was to become
Venice;[18] a summary of the major vicissitudes of Italy after
Attila, roughly from 428 to 1125;[19] and a survey of Venetian
institutions and offices.[20] Then follows the chronicle itself,
which is not a diary kept currently, but an account of events
written in retrospect.[21] The text begins on a general note:
"*E le degna chosa in tute le opere dar laude al sumo creator. . . .*
Segondo chel se troua nele instorie antige scrito, la zita de ueniexia
aue principio dapoi la destruzion de troia" (fol. 14r–v), and it
ends in the midst of a sentence telling of the arrival in Venice,
January 15, 1434 (1433 according to the Venetian year), of
two ambassadors from Pope Eugenius IV—the Archbishop
of Taranto and the Bishop of Corinth—"*i qual son do sapientis-*
simi homini, e foi fato grando [. . .]" (fol. 217v).[22]

Even in truncated form, a text from the middle of the fifteenth century can make some contribution to the vexed

[17] C. Castellani, *Elenco dei manoscritti veneti della collezione Phillips,* 2d ed. (Venice, 1890),
p. 34, lists "7503—Cronica veneta(?). *Bibl. Da Ponte.*"
[18] Fol. 1r–4v. *Inc.*: "Qui uederemo chome atilla flazelum dei pagam crudelisisimo . . .
Da puo la passion del nostro signor miser iesu cristo fo li suo apostoli gram tenpo
dispersi . . ." *Ex.*: ". . . per deffar la crestianitade e diistruzer la fede di iesu cristo."
[19] Fol. 4v–11v. *Inc.*: "Questo sie quanto che segui da poi la morte de atilla flazelom
dei . . ." *Ex.*: ". . . che quatro enrigi auea tegnudo lo imperio uno drieto laltro."
[20] Fol. 11v–14r. *Inc.*: "Qui sera notado tute le dignitade, Rizimenti e dofizij che da la
Ilustrissima signoria . . ." *Ex.*: ". . . e de far far le cherche e de schuoder el dazio
dele carne e dele pelle."
[21] It contains cross-references not only to preceding but also to following sections, for
instance the note (fol. 171v) "quel che segui vederemo avantj"; or (fol. 174r) "con
molte cosse secrete che avantj le dechiaremo."
[22] "Adi quindexe zener zonse a veniexia do seleni anbasadori de papa eugenio quarto
che fo larziueschouo da taranto el ueschouo de chorneto iqual son de sapientissimi
homini e foi fato grando [. . .]." Subsequently, on pp. 218–30 (the last leaves, which
were originally blank), a hand of the late fifteenth century has entered information
about more than seventy families entitled to sit in the council of the Republic. There
are also two Italian documents in the same hand, relating to the cession of Crete to
Venice by the Marquis Boniface of Montferrat, King of Salonica, in 1204 (fol. 226r–
230v). Apparently the same later hand has also entered some extensive marginal additions in the first half of the chronicle, and from the time of this continuator, or even
from the sixteenth century, stem marginal water-color designs of the arms of each
Doge.

questions of Venetian historiography. It should be once more recalled, however, that no effort to determine the place of an individual manuscript of Venetian fifteenth-century chronicles can hope to reach more than tentative results as long as complete printed editions of Morosini, the "2034," and Giorgio Dolfin are unavailable. Although enough extracts have been published to allow us to identify some of the relations which exist between these chronicles and particular manuscripts, we are, on the basis of the few published fragments, quite often unable to ascertain whether a passage in Giorgio Dolfin, or in another chronicle, is the author's own property or merely a borrowing from some earlier work. This want of finality characterizes all the existing theories on the relations of the Venetian chronicles to each other. On the other hand, in such a situation observations based on even a single early manuscript might lead to the detection of gaps or misrepresentations in the accepted picture.

It is not difficult for a reader of the Da Ponte–Newberry manuscript "87.1" to see that this text, although it must have originated by the middle of the fifteenth century, is not identical with any of the three chronicles which are now known to have been written successively during the first half of the century. There is no recognizable relationship of "87.1" to Antonio Morosini. Paragraphs from Morosini available in print span the long period from shortly after 1400 to 1433; one can compare them with the text of "87.1" for 1403,[23] 1410,[24] 1417,[25] and 1430-33,[26] including the end of Morosini's chronicle in November 1433.[27] Nowhere is there the slightest similarity.

Nor is "87.1" a copy of Giorgio Dolfin's chronicle. This can best be seen where Dolfin refers in a personal manner to contemporary happenings or conditions. At one point, the story that the bodies of certain saints found their final resting place in 1095 in the church of St. Nicolò di Lido is given in Dolfin's chronicle along with a report of the display of those relics

---

[23] Lefèvre-Pontalis, *op. cit.*, pp. 206 f.

[24] Fulin, *op. cit.*, p. 350.   [25] Thiriet, *op. cit.*, p. 275.

[26] Lefèvre-Pontalis, *op. cit.*, pp. 222–27.

[27] Thiriet, *op. cit.*, p. 273; Lefèvre-Pontalis, *op. cit.*, pp. 208 f.

during the year of jubilee 1450.[28] "87.1" lacks Dolfin's statement about the 1450 events and merely says (in a passage related to but not identical with Dolfin's) that the "*chorpi santi*"
were placed in "*san Nicholo de lido*" in 1095 (fol. 24v). A number of pages earlier, Dolfin had compared another event of
early times with conditions in his own day. In rather close
conformity with "2034"[29] he there reports the damage in-
flicted upon the campanile of St. Angelo in Venice by an earthquake during the year 1093. He comments that the tower had
remained in a damaged state to the year of his writing, 1455
("*a questo tempo MCCCCLV*"), adding some further news on
later renovations.[30] The same earthquake is described in
"87.1," fol. 24v, but without mention of Giorgio Dolfin's
remark "*rimasto fino a questo tempo*" or of his information on
renovations during the 1450's. Instead, save for details, the
phrasing is that found in "2034."

Can "87.1" be a replica, or a near-replica of "2034"? In some
places it would so appear. As G. Monticolo in his comments
in the critical apparatus accompanying Sanudo's *Vite dei Dogi*
reports,[31] the chronicle "2034" contains an extensive account
of Venetian actions in Palestine during the year 1124, whereas
Giorgio Dolfin merely epitomizes that report. "87.1," in narrating the events of the same year (fol. 27v), does not epitomize the original report; except for details, the narratives in
"2034" and "87.1" are identical. But this correspondence is
not found everywhere. Maria Zannoni, in her study of the
sources of Giorgio Dolfin, reprints three reports on Cyprus
on the eve of the Chioggia war, waged between Venice and
Genoa from 1378 to 1380. The three accounts are taken respectively from "2034," Giorgio Dolfin, and a manuscript (Marc.
It., VII. 760) in which Marino Sanudo transcribed some
source material on the Chioggia war in his own hand. One
learns from this confrontation that, while Dolfin's chronicle
and Sanudo's manuscript represent a basically identical ver-

---

[28] Zannoni, "Le fonti . . . ," p. 521 n. 5, last quotation from Giorgio Dolfin's chronicle.

[29] Cf. Monticolo, *op. cit.*, note 156/9 on p. 157.

[30] Zannoni, "Le fonti . . . ," p. 521; Monticolo, *op. cit.*, note 156/9 on p. 157.

[31] In note 5 on pp. 186–87.

sion,[32] the text in "2034" is different and longer. Where does "87.1" stand? What follows is the opening of the report in all four manuscripts:

"2034"	Giorgio Dolfin	"760"	"87.1"
Fol. 238r: Siando stadi ly Venyziany puocho tenpo in reposo anzy *se puo dir* liy jera anchora in uera. Da nuouo lo ochorse in questo mylessymo soradito el prjnzjpio de la uera de Zenouexi che commenzia ad questo modo. E lo fo prima per la inchoronazion delo re Perin de Zepro fiol delo re Piero.	Fol. 121: E siando stadi Venetiani e Zenoexi pocho tempo in paxe da nuouo loccorse in questo milleximo che per la incoronation del re Perin de Cypro fiol del re Piero . . .	Fol. 53r–v: Siando stadi li Venetiani e Zenoexi puocho in paxe locorse in questo milesimo ch el principio la uera e fo prima per la incoronation del Re Perin de Cypro fio de lo re Piero . . .	Fol. 77v: Siando stadi i Veniziani e zenouexi *se puo dir* puocho in paxe da nuouo lo chorse in questo milleximo sora dito chel principio la uera. E fo prima per la incoronation del Re perin Re de zepro fio delo re piero . . .

There can be no doubt that "87.1" here concurs on the whole with Dolfin's chronicle and Sanudo's manuscript, differing much as these texts do from the account in "2034." But the words *se puo dir*, which I have italicized, are like a fossil shell, indicating the origin of "87.1" by its preservation of a fragment of the text of "2034." It is, of course, impossible that the same words which stand in "2034" can have been accidentally used by "87.1" in precisely the same place. One conclusion alone is possible: "87.1" must have descended from "2034." And since "87.1" in so many details coincides with Dolfin, differing from "2034," the chronicle preserved in "87.1" in the quoted section functions as a link between the narrative in "2034" and that in Dolfin; or, to put it in another way, in this paragraph Dolfin appears to have copied and slightly modified not "2034" but "87.1."

This may sound like a bold hypothesis, but other observations support it. When Maria Zannoni, a little later in her investigation, compares the "2034," Dolfin, and Sanudo versions of another episode of the Chioggia war, "2034" again turns out to differ considerably from Dolfin and Sanudo. And when here, too, we examine the text of "87.1," this proves

---

32 Zannoni, "Le fonti . . . ," p. 534. She conjectures, pp. 533 and 536, that Sanudo's manuscript is a copy of Dolfin's text, but to this thesis we will return later.

to be largely identical with Dolfin and Sanudo, but once again at certain points preserves some vestiges of the "2034" text. For it has kept intact two "2034" phrases—"*et a questa palada lo uene . . . et retornar a Malamocho*" and "*et vegniando la gramde moltitudine . . . che jera fato suxo lo lido*"—which in Dolfin and Sanudo are substantially changed.[33] So the suspicion grows stronger that a text of the type of "87.1" was an intermediary between "2034" and Giorgio Dolfin; that Dolfin, in his narrative of the Chioggia war at least, employed and modified the *Cronaca Pre-Dolfina* (if we may coin this term) in the version of "87.1" and not in that of "2034."

There is further support for the conclusion that the chronicle of "87.1" is a late phase of the *Cronaca Pre-Dolfina*. In the "2034" manuscript, according to Maria Zannoni, the entry about the decision of September 1422 to rebuild a ruined wing of the Palazzo Ducale is supplemented by a marginal note in red ink which gives the name of the architect and the amount decided upon as his remuneration: "*et fo fatto sora la dita fabrica Ser Nicolo Barbaro di Santa Giustina con salario de ducati X d oro al mexe.*" In "87.1," we find this marginal supplement, in almost the same words, as an integral part of the text itself.[34] Evidently, at this point, "87.1" represents a revised form of the chronicle known from "2034."

On a closer view one can discern the chronological relation of the two versions still more clearly. For since the architectural reconstruction of the ducal palace—a fresh start in Venetian art—was not commissioned until 1423/24 and not completed until 1438/39, it seems certain that the author of "2034" did not add his red-inked, marginal supplement before 1423/24; and since the new edifice, when finished, was a landmark of the city and among the monuments of which Venice was proud, it is very likely, to say the least, that he would have added more than a reference to the appointment

---

[33] Zannoni, "Le fonti . . . ," pp. 535 f.; "87.1," fol. 87r. To be precise, the second phrase appears in its changed form in Dolfin only, not in Sanudo, because Sanudo's text had been interrupted a few lines earlier.

[34] "El palazo nuouo de veniexia quela parte chexe verso la giexia de miser san marcho fo prexo chel se fesse del mille e quatro zentro e uinci do e foxe pagado laspexa per ihofiziali dal sal *e fo fato per sora stante sier nicholo barbaro chon ducati diexe doro al mexe* e sta fabricado e fato nobelissimo chome anchuo di el sta e fo de grande honor de ueniexia." ("87.1," fol. 116v.) The marginal note in "2034" is reproduced by Zannoni, p. 524 n. 1, last entry.

of an architect had he written after 1438/39, when the new monument to civic pride was standing. In the revised form of the text in "87.1" we find, indeed, an expression of this pride added to the mention of the architect—the new edifice now "*sta fabricado e fato nobilissimo . . . e fo de grande honor de ueniexia*"[35]—proof that this passage of "87.1" originated after 1438/39.

Furthermore, we have an indication that the quoted sentence in "87.1" was written, not immediately on the completion of the building in 1438/39, but later. For the author of "87.1" further adds to the statement that the new edifice had been "*fabricado e fato nobilissimo*" the words "such as it stands until this day [*chome anchuo di el sta*]"—an expression hardly imaginable before a number of years had passed. How many years? Two facts may guide us. First (as will be seen later) we have reason to think that the chronicle version represented by "87.1," which in this manuscript breaks off in January 1434, actually spanned one more decade, until 1444 (1443/44 according to the Venetian year);[36] and since this is a chronicle with cross-references to the later parts, not an annalistic compilation, its entire later section was probably written after 1443/44. Second, since according to our previous observations a manuscript of the "87.1" text was used by Giorgio Dolfin, and since Dolfin's chronicle repeatedly refers to the 1450's as the time of its composition and was completed by 1458 (the year of Giorgio's death), we shall not be far from the truth if we conclude that the account of early fifteenth-century events given in "87.1" was written after 1444 and before the 1450's.

Although one cannot claim finality for any theory so long as the major chronicles of the period are not available for comparison in printed, let alone critical, editions, the upshot of our observations seems to be that, although only a few years intervened between the completion (in or after 1443) of the "2034" chronicle and the composition (during the 1450's)

---

[35] See the preceding note. For the dates of the reconstruction of the ducal palace, cf. M. Ongaro, *Venezia: Il Palazzo ducale* ("Piccolo Cicerone moderno," no. 6; *ca.* 1913), p. 12; E. Bassi, *Il Palazzo ducale nella storia e nell'arte di Venezia* (Milan, 1960), pp. 27 ff.

[36] See pp. 189 and 190, below.

of Giorgio Dolfin's work, Dolfin's dependence on "2034" was not always direct, but occurred, at least in part, through the mediation of a hitherto overlooked link in the chronicle chain. Or, seen from another angle, we seem to have found that the *Cronaca Pre-Dolfina*, first written in the form of "2034," was between 1443/44 and the 1450's revised and circulated in a changed, second version represented by "87.1."

III If this theory is correct, we may have to revise some of the present assumptions about Giorgio Dolfin's place in Venetian historiography.

Had Dolfin known the *Cronaca Pre-Dolfina* merely in the version handed down in "2034," we would be justified in regarding him as original wherever he departs from "2034" in his views or phrasing, as Maria Zannoni does in her careful study. But if we have to assume that Giorgio Dolfin knew also the differing form of the *Pre-Dolfina* represented by "87.1," we must ask how many of the apparently original features of his chronicle may have been adopted from the latter. A comparison of "87.1" with those few paragraphs of Dolfin's chronicle available in print yields some remarkable results.

To begin with, we are told by Maria Zannoni that Giorgio Dolfin in describing the later part of the Chioggia war "reproduces three letters in Latin sent by the [Venetian] *signoria* to their captain, Giovanni Barbarigo. No trace of these is found in '2034'. . . ." As a consequence, to the question "From what source has Dolfin taken these letters?" Maria Zannoni replies that "certainly he took them from the records of the chancery of the Doge or, even more probably, from the archives of the Barbarigo family."[37] But there was no need for Giorgio Dolfin to resort to any archives: the three Latin letters are found *in extenso* in the account of the same episode in "87.1" (fol. 83r–v). Dolfin's full relationship to his sources, it is true, may be more complicated than this example suggests; for when, a little later, he adds two more such letters,[38] we can again locate one in "87.1," but not the other (fol. 90r). He may have obtained the fifth letter from yet

37 Zannoni, "Le fonti . . . ," pp. 534 f., 537.
38 *Ibid.*, p. 536.

another chronicle source.[39] In any case, the proposition that
Dolfin must have studied in archives appears disproved.
In an earlier section of Dolfin's chronicle we come across another interesting example. The passage in question refers to
architectural work on the Church of S. Marco in 1073. Monticolo, in the apparatus of his edition of Sanudo's *Vite*,[40] points
out the striking difference between the accounts in "2034"
and in Giorgio Dolfin's chronicle, both of which he reproduces. The text of "2034" merely states

> chomo in tenpo di questo doxie per soa devozion et di
> Venyziany ly fexe lavorar et premzipiar la gliexia de misièr
> sam Marcho de muxaicho chomo la xé al prexente, et fo
> premzipiada a laxorar la dita hovra del MLXIII [*sic*].

Giorgio Dolfin, on the other hand, presents the following
more extensive report:

> ne li anni del signor Yesu Cristo MLXXIII al ditto doxe
> universalmente Venetiani termenò de honorar quel glorioso
> corpo dil nostro protector et defensor misièr san Marcho
> evangelista et di rinovarli da nuovo et fabrichar la sua
> chiexia in altra maniera de quello la era a quel tempo et fo
> comenzada a fabrichar questo nobile edificio come al pre-
> xente la se comprende nobile et excellente, richa et tri-
> umphante, lavorata di musaico, la qual de prima |era pichola
> cosa a rispecto di questa.

The corresponding text in "87.1" (fol. 23v) reads as follows:

> La gliexia de miser san marcho euangelista nel mille e
> setanta tre, el sopra dito doxe, e uniuersamente tuti iueniza-
> ni delibero de honorarle areuerentia de quel glorioso santo
> protetor e defensor de quela magnifica zita e fexela chon
> menzar afabrichar nel muodo che la sta al presente per che
> per auanti non ne iera cha una pichola chosa.

Quite evidently, this information and its phrasing are considerably nearer to Dolfin's report than is the text of "2034."
Once more we are compelled to judge that Dolfin could have

---

[39] The manuscript of Marino Sanudo, Cod. Marc. It., VII. 760, to which we have referred, contains the fourth and fifth, but not the first three letters; whereas a Venetian
chronicle in the Biblioteca Civica of Padua—C. M. 548—reproduces the first three
letters. Maria Zannoni gives this information elsewhere, pp. 543–44.

[40] Monticolo, *op. cit.*, pp. 153 f.

taken most of his apparently original information and phrasing from a manuscript of the "87.1" type.

Another basic divergence between Giorgio Dolfin's account and that given in "2034," this time about fifteenth-century events, has been described by Maria Zannoni. The two chronicles express different attitudes toward the *cause célèbre* of the *condottiere* Carmagnola, who, after a long career in the service of the Republic, was tried for treachery and executed by the Venetian government in 1431. Whereas the narrative in "2034" is full of animosity against Carmagnola, accusing him of malicious passivity and errors, of "*superbia*" and ingratitude, Giorgio Dolfin exhibits a calm objectivity. He does not make Carmagnola the scapegoat of the Venetian defeats, but declares at the critical juncture that another Venetian *condottiere*, Nicolò Trevisan, made serious blunders, so that Carmagnola was unable to help. Moreover, Dolfin simply states that the Venetian government was forced to proceed against Carmagnola when it discovered that he had eventually acted against the good of the Republic. "Dolfin's narration is less impassioned than that in '2034'; his judgment is just and impartial, and possibly not free from a certain pity for so great a personality."[41]

So far Maria Zannoni. But is the good judgment and objectivity that she applauds to be credited to Giorgio Dolfin? When we compare "87.1" with Dolfin's account as summarized in Maria Zannoni's study, we find that "87.1" shows the same wish not to blame Carmagnola for the errors of other generals. If Venice suffered defeat, we read in "87.1," "*questo intrauene per che el dito sier Nicholo [Trevisan] non iera homo da tanto governo,*" making it impossible for Carmagnola to do the right thing (fol. 202v). On the occasion of Carmagnola's condemnation there is no vituperation of the fallen general, but merely the factual report that the Venetian *Signoria*, seeing "*quel che lauea adoperado chontra . . . Veniexia chontra dio e raxioni e chontra il suo sacramento*" in spite of all the honors and gifts he had received, had him tried and executed under the columns of the piazza (fol. 208r). Here the divergence of "87.1" from "2034" amounts to more than merely technical

---

41 Zannoni, *op. cit.*, p. 545.

changes, additions, and abbreviations. The same reserve and historical objectivity for which Giorgio Dolfin has been esteemed must have characterized the anonymous writer of "87.1."[42]

IV. Is it correct to think of the Da Ponte–Newberry manuscript, as we have done, in terms of a chronicle fairly well known in its own time and even later? The answer is that information available in printed catalogues and summaries of manuscripts makes it perfectly sure that there existed a considerable group of texts with the same *incipits* and *explicits* as "87.1," and probably identical in content.

This group includes two manuscripts of the fifteenth century. Since "87.1" by all appearances is not an author's autograph, but an (incomplete) fair copy made either by a contemporary or by the author himself, the survival of a few other contemporary—possibly more complete—manuscripts is precisely what one would expect. Among the texts listed in printed catalogues, the most interesting seems to be Cod. Marc. It., VII. 46. For this manuscript, which opens with the same introductory piece on *"Attila, Flagellum Dei"* as

---

[42] At this point it should be briefly stated why it is improbable that the anonymous of "87.1" has anything to do with the unknown author of the so-called *Cronaca Zancaruolo*, despite the fact that a number of paragraphs of Dolfin's chronicle that are more or less identical with Zancaruolo's narrative reappear, with only slight differences, in "87.1." Although the *Cronaca Zancaruolo* is known to us only from early sixteenth-century manuscripts, it has recently been claimed (especially by Thiriet, p. 288), that its parallels with Dolfin's chronicle prove that Zancaruolo's work preceded Dolfin's and was one of its sources. As Maria Zannoni (pp. 539 and 543) has rightly pointed out, such parallels might just as well indicate the opposite relationship—a borrowing by Zancaruolo from Dolfin. To Maria Zannoni's arguments that the latter was the true relationship we can now add an evaluation of the fact that some of the phrases common to Dolfin and Zancaruolo are also found in "87.1." Starting from these coincidences, the following reasoning seems in order. If in places where all three chronicles are roughly identical, Dolfin uses certain key words which literally appear in "87.1" as well, but not in Zancaruolo, then either Dolfin or "87.1" must in these passages have borrowed from the other, or rather—since we have established that "87.1" preceded Dolfin—the latter must have drawn upon "87.1" and not upon Zancaruolo. Zancaruolo in his turn would seem to have copied the passages which he shares with the two other chroniclers from Dolfin. This is the situation in a paragraph, intervening between the first and the second of the aforementioned Latin letters to Barbarigo, where the three chronicles basically agree, but some significant words—"intendandose" and "in questo caxo"—are exactly alike in "87.1" and Dolfin, while lacking in Zancaruolo. (Cf. Zannoni, p. 542, for Dolfin and Zancaruolo, and see the corresponding paragraph in "87.1" on fol. 83v.) Hence closer scrutiny of "87.1" may help to solve the Zancaruolo riddle: it probably will support the theory that Zancaruolo's chronicle is not an early fifteenth-century work but rather a later compilation, partly derived from Giorgio Dolfin.

"87.1," and has the same *incipit*, runs on to 1444.[43] Thus it goes even farther than the Cod. no. 205 of the Bibliothèque de la Ville de Metz, the second listed fifteenth-century manuscript which carries the Attila piece and *incipit*, but stops in 1441.[44]

So far as printed information tells us, the other texts are younger, none being much earlier than the year 1500, a fact which emphasizes the value of each of the few extant fifteenth-century manuscripts. As a number of the younger copies prove, a type of chronicle with all or most of the features characteristic of the Da Ponte–Newberry volume was circulating in Venice during the later Renaissance. The most interesting of these copies, listed in Marco Foscarini's eighteenth-century synopsis of Venetian literature, *Della Letteratura Veneziana*,[45] appears to have been an exact counterpart of "87.1," and might have been a transcription of it. This copy was a manuscript, preserved during the eighteenth century in S. Giorgio Maggiore in Venice, which not only started with the same Attila introduction as "87.1," but also ended with exactly the same words in the same unfinished sentence.[46]

Whether this double, or more probably this descendant, of "87.1" still exists, I am unable to say; but we can point to a number of extant sixteenth-century manuscripts which, beyond doubt, contain in their body as well as in the introductory section at least large parts of the text of "87.1." Two of them, Brit. Mus., Add. Mss. 16565 and Newberry Ms. Case F 35993.212, stem from the beginning of the sixteenth century and seem to agree with "87.1" in their entire contents—in the prelude on Attila, in the introductory summary of the Venetian public offices, and in the chronicle proper.[47] In both

---

[43] Thiriet, *op. cit.*, p. 256; G. Mazzatinti, *Inventari dei manoscritti delle biblioteche d'Italia*, LXXXI (Florence, 1956), p. 15. *Inc.*: "Laus deo, come Atila flagelum dei naque . . . Da poi la passione del nostro signore misier Jesu Christo li soi apostoli forno dispersi longamente per el mondo."

[44] A. Prost, "Les Chroniques Vénitiennes," *Revue des Questions Historiques*, XXXI (1882), 539, 547. *Inc.*: "Noi vederemo come Atilla flagelum dei paganu crudelissino naque . . ."

[45] First ed. (Padua, 1752), p. 150 n. 133; 2d ed. (Venice, 1854), p. 164 n. 3.

[46] "Nui vederemo come . . ." ". . . Do sapientissimi omeni e foi fatto grande . . ." Foscarini, *loc. cit.*

[47] Manuscript Brit. Mus., Add. 16565 is described by C. Foligno, *Nuovo Archivio Veneto*, N.S. X (1905), 121–22. The *incipits* of its four sections, to be compared with

manuscripts, however, the chronicle is even less complete than in "87.1." The British Museum manuscript breaks off in October 1405;[48] the Newberry manuscript, about 1415, begins to shorten or leave out all more substantial entries.[49] No such curtailment occurs in two sixteenth-century manuscripts, Cod. Marc. It., Z. 20 and Brit. Mus., Add. Mss. 27430, which run beyond the chronological limits of "87.1"—the Cod. Marcianus to late 1434 and the British Museum manuscript all the way to 1444. These two texts are, however, adapted to the taste of the second half of the sixteenth century in language and orthography. Characteristically, moreover, they have replaced the survey of Venice's public offices by a "*serie delle Famiglie Veneziane.*"[50] There are undoubtedly more specimens

---

those of "87.1" in notes 18–20, above, are: "+oi vedremo como Atilla . . ." / "[Q]uesto si é quello che seguì da puo la morte di Atilla . . ." / "[Q]uivi serà notado tute le dignitade . . ." / "[E] l'è degna chossa in tute le opere . . . Segondo che'l se trova nele istorie . . ." In the Newberry manuscript Ms. Case F 35993.212 (former Phillips manuscript 5203), first half of sixteenth century according to the script, the *incipits* and *explicits* are: *Inc.* (fol. 1r): "Nui vederemo como Attila flagellum Dei pagan crudelissimo . . . Dapoi la passion . . ." *Ex.* (fol. 6r): ". . . per desfar la christianitade e destruzer la fede de iesu christo." / *Inc.* (fol. 6v): "Questo si e quello che seguí dapoi la morte de Atila flagellum Dei . . ." *Ex.* (fol. 16v): ". . . che quatro henrigi hauea tegnudo lo imperio uno driedo l'altro." / *Inc.* (fol. 16v): "Qui sara nottado tutte le dignitade Rezimenti et officij . . ." *Ex.* (fol. 21v): ". . . e de suoder el Datio de le carne e delle pelle." / *Inc.* (fol. 21v): "E le degna cosa in tutte le opere dar laude . . . Segondo ch'el se trouaua nelle historie antige scritte . . ."

[48] Manuscript Brit. Mus., Add. 16565, *explicit* (according to Foligno): ". . . per le qual parolle lo dito signor [Francesco da Carrara] respose come homo sinalmorado." Cf. "87.1," fol. 121r: ". . . per le qual parole lo dito signor respoxe chome homo sina morado."

[49] Two extensive sections in "87.1," fol. 146v–148r and 148r–149v, both referring to 1416, are omitted in Ms. Case F 35993.212, fol. 223v and 224v, and subsequently this manuscript copies only sporadic extracts from "87.1," eventually mixing these with other information. On fol. 225v, the account jumps from the year 1418 to 1420, on the next page from 1421 to 1424, and so on. This fragmentary narrative continues to the year 1483.

[50] Manuscript Marc. It., Z 20 (dated 1568) is described in C. Frati and A. Segarizzi, *Catalogo dei codici Marciani*, I (1909), p. 19; Manuscript Brit. Mus., Add. 27430 in Foligno, *op. cit.*, p. 126. (The survey of patrician families is here described as "Origine delle casate veneziane, ordinate alfabeticamente.") A somewhat earlier manuscript in the Österreichische Nationalbibliothek in Vienna is mutilated in the beginning, but should not be entirely passed over here, since it bears further testimony to the circulation of the chronicle around 1500. This manuscript, originally cod. Fosc. CCLIV and now manuscript 6208* of the Austrian National Library, an anonymous *Cronaca Veneta* which runs to 1437, is according to T. Gar's description (*Archivio Stor. Ital.*, V [1843], 302) "from the end of the 15th or the beginning of the 16th century," "not by one hand," and opens with the sentence "D'Ongaria era questa donna; era unica fiola; la fortuna permise che questo Attila Flagellum Dei fu nudrigado et venne grande et fortissimo, et sozedette al reame d'Ongaria . . ." Although this is not the *incipit* of any of the sections of "87.1," it is the same text, lacking presumably its first leaf, because the quoted sentence is literally found in "87.1," fol. 2r, i.e., not very far down

190

of our chronicle among sixteenth- and seventeenth-century uncatalogued or insufficiently catalogued manuscripts, for at least four others—Paris 337 and 1192, and Marc. It., VII. 31 and VII. 45—begin with the familiar *incipit* of the Attila prologue.[51] Obviously, later Venetian readers were acquainted with the "87.1" chronicle. One wonders, therefore, whether its influence also reached Marino Sanudo's *Vite dei Dogi*, the final basin where so many of the earlier streams of Venetian historiography eventually merged. The *Vite*, in addition to using several major chroniclers of the later fifteenth century, were directly indebted to the anonymous author of the "2034," as critical research has shown.[52] It may be difficult to prove that Sanudo also consulted the version of the *Cronaca Pre-Dolfina* represented by "87.1." But the narrative sources of the early fifteenth century became accessible to Sanudo also by being partially included in later fifteenth-century chronicles. He drew upon Antonio Morosini by using Pietro Dolfin, and similarly upon the author of the "2034" by leaning heavily on Giorgio Dolfin. The latter, however, as we have seen,[53] had consulted a chronicle of the "87.1" type. Thus Giorgio Dolfin gave Sanudo access to those portions of the "87.1" which had been incorporated into Giorgio's own chronicle. Of this we can cite the following example.

From Monticolo's apparatus to Sanudo's *Vite*[54] we learn that Sanudo, in narrating the Venetian occupation of Rhodes in 1125, is in general agreement with "2034," but that Sanudo says that the Venetians "*smontati su l'isola andòno verso la terra e quella* per forza *prese*," whereas the phrase in "2034" runs, "*questi Venyziany de l'oste* armata manu *desmonta in terra.*" Did Sanudo italianize *armata manu*, rendering it by *per forza*? When we compare "87.1," we find that Sanudo's *per forza* was there already a part of the text: "... *i uenenziani*

---

in the Attila section. That the subsequent chronicle, too, is identical with the text of "87.1" can be established by a second clue in Gar's description. In this Vienna manuscript, he says, "si trova tutto il trattato di pace tra Filippo Visconti e la Signoria di Venezia nel 1428." The treaty is found *in extenso* in "87.1" as well, fol. 190v–191v.

[51] On the manuscripts Paris 337 and 1192, cf. Prost, *op. cit.*, p. 539; on the manuscripts Marc. It., VII. 31 and 45, cf. Mazzatinti, *Inventari*, pp. 11, 15.

[52] See above, note 8.   [53] See above, pp. 182 ff.

[54] Monticolo, in his edition of Sanudo, pp. 189–90.

dela dita armada desmonta in terra per forza" (fol. 28v). Consequently, if Sanudo had not seen a manuscript of the "87.1" type, the "87.1" version of this paragraph of the *Cronaca Pre-Dolfina* would seem to have reached him by way of Giorgio Dolfin's chronicle.

It is likely that Sanudo got in touch with the "87.1" form of the *Pre-Dolfina* through other channels as well. Some of them are complicated to prove,[55] but in at least one instance the indirect influence seems to be as obvious as it is surprising. Among the more recent chroniclers from whom Sanudo borrowed was Donato Contarini,[56] who about 1500 or even a little later composed a *Cronaca Veneta*, which carried the history of the city only to 1433/34. A comparison of its *incipit* and *explicit*, published from a Foscarini manuscript in Vienna,[57] with the text of "87.1" shows that the opening of Contarini's work is entirely different from the "87.1" chronicle, but that Contarini ends with a sentence nearly identical with one in the concluding paragraph of "87.1" (fol. 217v). The kinship of the two texts at this point is close enough to permit a correction of a corrupt sentence in the younger work. For whereas Contarini's *Cronaca* has the overly compressed wording "*el quale ritornava da Roma dalla presentia del Papa, in 8 zorni a Venetia,*" we may learn from "87.1" that this sentence originally had run quite smoothly: "... *dala presenzia del papa e*

---

[55] One, though with due reservations, may be briefly explained. We mentioned at one point that there exists an autograph volume (the manuscript Marc. It., VII. 760) in which Sanudo collected certain materials needed in the composition of his *Vite,* among other pieces a *Cronachetta della guerra di Chioggia* (1378–80). Since Sanudo's *Cronachetta* is very similar to—and often identical with—Giorgio Dolfin's text and since they show identical passages derived from "2034," Maria Zannoni (pp. 534-37) argued that Sanudo's *Cronachetta* was nothing but a little-changed section of Dolfin's work. When "87.1" is compared with Maria Zannoni's samples, it is found to correspond almost literally with the *Cronachetta,* including virtually all the minor points where Dolfin, in his turn, diverges from the *Cronachetta.* There are two passages, however—one comprising a few words and the other an extensive sentence—where "87.1" coincides with "2034" instead of with the *Cronachetta.* (The few words—"se puo dir"; "87.1," fol. 77v, cf. "2034" in Zannoni, p. 534—have been discussed above, p. 182. The extensive sentence is the passage "et a questa palada lo uene ... et retornar a Malamocho," found in "87.1" on fol. 87r and in "2034" on fol. 249v, as quoted by Zannoni, p. 535.) Since there can be no doubt that "2034" was the earliest of the four texts, the most probable explanation is that Sanudo copied his *Cronachetta* not from Giorgio Dolfin, who in spite of a general affinity with him often differs in detail, but from a manuscript which was similar to "87.1," although it must have been a little farther removed from the "2034" version of the *Cronaca Pre-Dolfina* than is "87.1."

[56] Cf. Foscarini, *Della Letteratura* (Venice, 1854), p. 175 n. 1.

[57] Cf. T. Gar, *Archivio Stor. Ital.* V (1843), 287–88.

venne in oto zorni a veniexia."[58] Thus—directly or indirectly—
Donato Contarini, when writing the later portion of his work,
must have used for his information the *Cronaca Pre-Dolfina* in
its "87.1" form; and through the mediation of Contarini, the
chronicle of the "87.1" type must have reached Sanudo.

V. The establishment of these later dependencies does not
necessarily imply that the "87.1" chronicle exerted a substantial influence on the mind of Marino Sanudo. The outlook
and concerns of the early Renaissance chroniclers were very
different from those of the great encyclopedic collector and
historian of about 1500—so different, indeed, that although
the smaller canvases of the early chroniclers are modest when
compared with Sanudo's broad and colorful world, the former
retain a value of their own. They have not become negligible
just because some major parts of their accounts were merged
in Sanudo's synthesis. A brief, concluding comparison of the
interests of the anonymous author of "87.1" with those
which Sanudo displays in his *Vite* will help to round out our
appraisal of the chronicle preserved in the Newberry manuscript.

Selecting one year of the period most extensively described
by the "87.1" Anonymous—the year 1429—one notices immediately that much of Sanudo's more cosmopolitan information has no counterpart in the Anonymous' report; it must
have reached Sanudo from other sources. Of this kind is some
of Sanudo's news on Turkey; most of his information on new
developments in the relations between the King of Tunis and
the King of Aragon; everything about that exciting event in
France, the appearance of Jeanne d'Arc (facts mainly learned,
though indirectly, from Antonio Morosini); and even some
important data on the reappointment of Carmagnola as

---

[58] Another, perhaps characteristic, divergence between the mid-fifteenth-century author and the writer of about 1500 is that, whereas "87.1" in the cited sentence only
says "che dio e misier san marcho lasa meter tuto in bon achordo," Donato Contarini
makes that sentence include the name of Maria: "che Iddio et Madonna S. Maria et
Missier San Marco lassa metter tutto in buon accordo." One can further observe that
this concluding sentence of Contarini's work is the last but one sentence of "87.1,"
that is, in "87.1" it is followed merely by the incomplete passage in the midst of
which the writer of "87.1" suddenly broke off. This suggests that Contarini used the
"87.1" type chronicle in a text that ended at about the same point as the Newberry
manuscript does.

condottiere of the Republic. On the other hand, there is a large, compact body of information which in composition and phrasing is very near to the account of the Anonymous—so near that one puzzling lacuna in Sanudo's rendering of a request by Florentine ambassadors (*"ch'era chiamato . . . . pe' Castelli ch'egli teneva di ragione di que' di Pisa"*)[59] can be made intelligible from the context of "87.1." For clearly, this passage must be supplemented and interpreted, just as the phrasing on fol. 195r of "87.1" suggests, *"chel dito signor idouese dar zinque castelle che lui tegniua, che iera del chontado de Pixa."*

Not, however, that Sanudo incorporated every important feature found in "87.1." He actually stopped short of certain topics, foremost among which were economic issues. In "87.1," the description of the year 1429 includes in particular three entries on the landings and sailings of ships to which Sanudo's report seems to contain no equivalent: arrivals from Flanders and London, departures of merchant ships to Soria in Turkey (recorded with the names of the captains and the amount of the invested capital), and of men-of-war to Soria and Gallipoli. Moreover, the older source gives detailed accounts (including names, descriptions of locations in the city, agreements with creditors, etc.) of the bankruptcy of two banks, and of the opening of two others, one of which, we are told, was established on the premises of one of the bankrupt firms. There are also two minor records of economic interest not reproduced by Sanudo: one about new small coins, to *"bater in la zecha di Venexia,"* the other about a request, in which the Pope had intervened, for installment payments to the city.[60] This takes us near the horizon of the local chronicle; and, indeed, there are two even more parochial entries passed over by Sanudo: the legitimization by Pope Martin V of a certain bastard, and a detailed description of destructive local inundations.[61] Finally, once or twice an arrival of foreign ambassadors has no equivalent in Sanudo's account. The Anonymous of "87.1" had tried to be scrupulous in this as in

---

[59] Sanudo, *Vite de' Duchi di Venezia*, in Muratori, *Rer. Ital. Script.*, XXII (1733), col. 1006 D.

[60] Newberry Ms. f 87.1, fol. 194r–196v.

[61] *Ibid.*, fol. 194r and 195r-v.

every other reporting of daily comings and goings, although it must be admitted that at times he became entangled in erroneous chronologies, presumably because he did not write his entries concurrently with the events in the manner of a diary, but rather at a later time when he was unable to recall every circumstance correctly.[62]

If these observations for the year 1429 are typical, our estimate of the usefulness of the "87.1"-type chronicle will have to be similar to what Maria Zannoni observed about the not much older chronicle preserved in Cod. Marc. It., VII. 2034. The chronicle in the Da Ponte–Newberry manuscript, too, is the work of an author who "does not miss any opportunity for talking about the expedition of galleys to the East or to the North," while he "lists with great care the arrivals and departures of all the merchantmen in the port of Venice."[63] Despite the comparatively short radius of its world, the *Cronaca Pre-Dolfina* in its successive versions remains of lasting interest, especially for its added information, not in Sanudo's narrative, on economic life in the early Renaissance.

---

[62] As suggested by the inclusion in the text of such cross-references as "quel che segui vederemo avantj"; cf. the citations above, note 21.

[63] Zannoni, "Le fonti . . . ," p. 526 n. 2.

7 AULUS GELLIUS IN THE RENAISSANCE:
His Influence and a Manuscript from the
School of Guarino

I. Aulus Gellius does not belong among the ancient authors who shaped humanistic culture by their personality, artistic perfection, or profundity of thought. He is the earliest of the surviving encyclopedic writers of the late Roman period, whose greatest usefulness was to preserve abstracts and substantial quotations from many ancient books soon afterwards lost. On the other hand, as a son of the Rome of the Antonine emperors, he was still nearer than Macrobius and Martianus Capella, the epitomists of the fifth century, to the Ciceronian and Augustan age, in spirit as well as time. Although to him and his generation (to use the verdict of a modern critic) the question was no longer "how to say a thing in the best way, but what Cato or Gracchus or Cicero said" about it,[1] still, in many respects, he was an heir to Ciceronian culture. We find a fair proportion of the products of Greek literature included in his selections from the best writers in all fields, with numerous quotations in the original Greek. His extracts are often dramatized into dialogues between the epitomized authors, and the discussions occur in the most illustrious places of the ancient world, from Athens to the villa of Atticus and the Forum Romanum, and from the luxurious spa of Pozzuoli to the scenic beauties of Naples. There are descriptions of social events, such as the monthly dinner gatherings which the author in his youth had attended with his fellow students. In spite of many inadequacies in the execution of the artistic scheme, this was still a literary creation which, when read in its entirety, could conjure up an image of ancient urbanity

---

First published partly in *Studies in Philology*, XLVIII (1951), 107–25 (under the title "Aulus Gellius in the Renaissance and a Manuscript from the School of Guarino"), and partly *ibid.*, XLIX (1952), 248–50 ("The Scribe of the Newberry Gellius of 1445: a Supplementary Note"; see note 31, below).

[1] H. Nettleship in his still widely quoted appraisal of "The Noctes Atticae of Aulus Gellius," in *Lectures and Essays on Subjects Connected with Latin Literature and Scholarship* (Oxford, 1885), p. 276.

and social life. Not by chance did the humanists of the Renaissance find one of the most complete and often used definitions of the meaning of *humanitas* in the discussions of the *Attic Nights*.[2] Also, it must be borne in mind that Gellius is one of the classical authors whose work became reasonably intelligible only through the critical efforts of the humanists. The *Noctes Atticae* had not been forgotten in the Middle Ages, but acquaintance with it as an integrated work was usually denied to medieval readers.[3] In Roman times the twenty books of Gellius' encyclopedia were usually copied on two bookrolls Of the Roman manuscripts copied by medieval scribes, one

---

[2] In the famous chapter XIII 17, which reaches the conclusion "humanitatem non id esse . . . , quod . . . a Graecis φιλανθρωπία dicitur . . . , sed . . . quod Graeci παιδείαν vocant, nos eruditionem institutionemque in bonas artes dicimus." I. Heinemann, in his discussion of this Gellian definition in Pauly-Wissowa, *Real-Encyclopaedie der classischen Altertumswissenschaft* (Supplementband V [1931], col. 283 f.), notes that, while it was narrower than Cicero's original ideal of *humanitas*, it rather accurately foreshadowed the later humanistic usage. K. Brandi, *Das Werden der Renaissance* (Göttingen, 1908), p. 21 and *passim*, traces the actual influence of Gellius' concept on the Italian humanists of the early Quattrocento. J. Niedermann, *Kultur. Werden und Wandlungen des Begriffs und seiner Ersatzbegriffe von Cicero bis Herder* (Florence, 1941), gives supplements and also stresses the significance of Gellius' definition for Erasmian and German humanists ("immer wieder wird auf Cicero und Gellius zurueckgegriffen"); cf. esp. pp. 30, 76 ff., 91, 95 f.

Other influences of Gellius: H. Baron, "Cicero and the Roman Civic Spirit in the Middle Ages and the Early Renaissance," *Bulletin of the John Rylands Library* (Manchester), XXII (1938), 89, for an example, dating from about 1400, of the role which the information drawn from Gellius played in the humanistic rediscovery of ancient citizenship. More recently it has also been established that in the ideas on education formed by Matteo Palmieri and Maffeo Vegio, during the 1430's and 1440's, everything connected with the mother's behavior during pregnancy and nursing of the child at the breast was taken from Gellius; cf. L. Rainaldi, "Di una fonte comune di Matteo Palmieri e di Maffeo Vegio," *Giornale Storico della Letteratura Italiana*, CXXX (1953), 495–507. In the late Renaissance, the phrase *veritas temporis filia* from *Noctes Atticae* XII 11.7 was used by Leonardo, Machiavelli, Bruno, Galileo, and Bacon as a catchword to express the notion of the progress of human knowledge; see L. Olschki, *Galilei und seine Zeit* (Halle, 1927), pp. 279 f., and G. Gentile, *Il Pensiero Italiano del Rinascimento*, 3d ed. (Florence, 1940), pp. 342 f.; now also H. Baron, *Journal of the History of Ideas*, XXI (1960), 142.

The literary and historical qualities of the *Noctes Atticae* have in recent years been evaluated more positively than by Nettleship (cf. preceding note) and by A. Hosius (in Pauly-Wissowa, *Real-Encyclopaedie*, vol. VII [1912], col. 998) in an article by V. Ussani in the *Enciclopedia Italiana*, XVI (1932), 485 f.

[3] For the Middle Ages (but not for the Renaissance, for reasons explained later) the manuscript material was collected by M. Hertz and (together with a valuable survey on the acquaintance of the principal medieval writers with Gellius) is analyzed in the fundamental "Praefatio" to Hertz's edition of *A. Gellii Noctium Atticarum Libri XX*, vol. II (Berolini, 1885), pp. xii–lv. This preface has remained the only study on the influence of Gellius which approaches a monograph; it forms the basis for the following remarks.

roll must have contained Books I–VIII and the other the remaining books, for these two sections of the work remained apart in the medieval codices which replaced the ancient rolls. It evidently happened rarely, down to the end of the fourteenth century, that the separate halves of the *Noctes* were found together in one locality, much less that they were united between two covers. Although some exceptional students of antiquity, such as John of Salisbury and Petrarch, were familiar with the entire work, the fact that all surviving pre-fifteenth-century manuscripts are limited either to the first or to the second part implies that ordinarily a medieval reader would not have known more than a fragment of Gellius' enterprise. A fourteenth-century polyhistor such as Richard of Bury could still be limited in his knowledge to the first part.[4] Moreover, the closing portions of the surviving rolls had been seriously mutilated at the beginning of the Middle Ages. As a consequence, even a John of Salisbury and a Petrarch had no means of guessing how the thread of the narrative was continued through the eighth book, which was entirely lost from the first section; nor did they ever see the last passages of the twentieth book beyond chapter 10.6. Last but not least, ignorance of Greek caused most of the Greek quotations (an integral part of the text) to be misspelled to the point of obscurity, or to be indicated merely by an abundance of blank spaces.

From all this one should expect that with the coming of the Humanism of the Renaissance Gellius was bound to arouse increasing interest, and eventually to gain an influence equal to that exerted by Macrobius and Martianus Capella upon medieval Humanism. In fact, we find that from the early fifteenth century onward forgotten copies which combined Books I–VII and IX–XX were recovered, and soon there ap-

---

[4] On John of Salisbury: Hertz, *op. cit.*, vol. II, p. xxviii. On Petrarch: *ibid.*, p. xlii, and R. Sabbadini, *Le scoperte dei codici latini e greci ne' secoli XIV e XV* (Florence, 1905), p. 92, n. 28. On Richard of Bury's *Philobiblon:* Hertz, *op. cit.*, p. xliii; R. Sabbadini, *Le scoperte dei codici latini e greci ne' secoli XIV e XV. Nuove ricerche* (Florence, 1914), p. 9. Robert Holcot's knowledge of Gellius may have resulted from his use of Richard of Bury's copy, as Beryl Smalley has recently suggested (*English Friars and Antiquity* [Oxford, 1960], p. 153). In the thirteenth century, it is true, Vincent of Beauvais reproduced quotations from both parts (Hertz, *op. cit.*, p. xli); but he is known to have drawn generously on secondary sources. See B. L. Ullman's general warning in *Speculum*, VIII (1933), 321 f.

peared the first complete manuscripts, "complete" as far as the state of transmission allowed. For although the text of the eighth book proved to be irretrievably lost, one or a few manuscripts were rediscovered that contained the complete table of the summary-like chapter headings, including those of the eighth book. Again, although the end of the twentieth book was not entirely regained, copies were found that reduced the extent of that second lacuna by adding paragraphs 10.7–11.5.[5] And by the middle of the fifteenth century, thanks to the revival of Greek studies, a satisfactory understanding of the Greek passages was achieved.

Two recently discovered illuminated manuscripts from the middle and second half of the Quattrocento indicate how Gellius thenceforth served as a cicerone to the ancient treasures. One of these manuscripts, the Codex "Scotti" (now in the Biblioteca Ambrosiana in Milan), was copied at Bologna in 1448 by a scribe who praises Gellius as a source from which one should drink deeply; the manuscript was decorated by Guglielmo Giraldi of Ferrara, a famous miniaturist who worked for such patrons as the Este, Gonzaga, and Montefeltro. The picture at the beginning of the text shows a *piazza* bordering on the sea and surrounded by architecture in the Quattrocento manner but representing a square in the *"civitas Athenarum"*; on its edge we see, through the windows of a house marked *"Auli Gelii hedes,"* the author of the *Noctes Atticae* working in his library, a typical Quattrocento study. Again we find him outside in the square in brisk debate with the writers, statesmen, and orators of his age whom he had met, according to his work—a reflection of the keenness with which humanistic readers responded to Gellius' literary device of substituting for bookish expositions animated dialogues

---

5 On the recovered portions of the *Noctes Atticae*: Hertz, *op. cit.*, pp. lxxxi–lxxxiv and xcvi f. For other traces of what was then called an "Agellius totus" or "integer," in Salutati, Poggio, and Nicolaus Cusanus, see Sabbadini, *Scoperte*, p. 92, and *Scoperte* . . . *Nuove ricerche*, pp. 24, 183. A. M. Bandini, *Catalogus codicum latinorum Bibliothecae Mediceae Laurentianae*, vol. II (Florentiae, 1775), col. 681 f., describes Cod. Laur. LIV c. 30, written 1425 in Florence by Antonio di Mario and containing Books I–VII and IX–XX. Hertz, in his preface and edition, does not consult this early complete copy by a particularly reliable scribe, nor does he explain the omission. According to Bandini, it includes the Greek, but by a different hand; so this may have been inserted later.

between men of flesh and blood.[6] The other manuscript, to which attention has lately been called, is a superbly illuminated transcript from the library of the kings of Aragon at Naples (now in the University Library of Valencia); the text is written by the most outstanding Florentine copyist of the 1470's and 1480's, Antonio Sinibaldi. Here, in a splendid example, we see the *Noctes Atticae* entering the group of classical writings copied in the Renaissance in sumptuous editions for princely libraries.[7]

In the thirteenth century, even Aquinas, who read and consulted many of the authors later used by the humanists, seems to have known nothing of Gellius but the occasional passages quoted in patristic works.[8] From the mid-fifteenth century

---

[6] The Gellius manuscript of the Duke Tommaso Gallarati Scotti, after having been given as a gift to the Biblioteca Ambrosiana, was described by P. Libaert in "Un' opera sconosciuta di Guglielmo Giraldi," *L'Arte*, XIV (1911), 401 ff. It has also been described briefly by Mgr. Giovanni Galbiati, former prefect of the Ambrosian Library, in *Miscellanea Leo Van Puyvelde* (Brussels, 1949), pp. 259–61. The colophon indicates that the manuscript was written at Bologna. The date in the colophon is reported by Libaert as 1408, an error by Libaert or the scribe. The indiction is given as the eleventh, which fits 1448, as do Libaert's findings about Giraldi's artistic activities and the occurrence of an epidemic at Bologna in 1448. The volume opens with the note: "Repertorialis summula totius operis Doctissimi et clarissimi viri Aulu-Gellii Noctium Atticarum felicissime incipit: confecta lungo sudore et maximis vigiliis in amoenissima et delectabili villa Scannelli ad quam secesseramus devitandi contagii opportunitate." On the last leaf we read: "Aulu-Gellii Doctissimi et clarissimi viri et labiis totis absorbandi [*sic!* at least in Libaert] . . . Noctium Atticarum Liber . . . ultimus felicissime finit." It is not known for whom the manuscript was executed. On Giraldi see P. D'Ancona and E. Aeschlimann, *Dictionnaire des miniaturistes*, 2d ed. (Milan, 1949), pp. 93 f. The miniature at the beginning of the text was reproduced by Libaert, *loc. cit.*, F. Wittgens in *The Burlington Magazine for Connoisseurs*, LXIII (1933), 63, Bibliothèque Nationale, *Trésors des Bibliothèques d'Italie IVᵉ–XVIᵉ Siècles* (Paris, 1950), Plate 14, and in color by M. Salmi in *Tesori delle Biblioteche d'Italia*, I (1932), 338.

[7] The fact that Antonio Sinibaldi copied the *Noctes Atticae* was not known until recently; the Valencia manuscript referred to is not mentioned in the list of Sinibaldi's transcripts by J. P. Elder in *Studies in Philology*, XLIV (1947), 138–39. It was identified from its script and assigned to Sinibaldi by T. De Marinis in his *La Biblioteca Napoletana dei Re d'Aragona*, II (Milan, 1947), 76, 150. I am indebted for this reference to the late Mr. Stanley Morison.

It should be mentioned that since the first appearance of this study, a third precious manuscript of this type, which once belonged to the library of King Matthias Corvinus, has been identified. It is now manuscript no. 27900 of the Chetham's Library, Manchester. According to A. R. A. Hobson, "A Binding for Matthias Corvinus, King of Hungary and Bohemia, ca. 1480–90," *The Book Collector*, VII (1958), 267 f., "the manuscript is clearly Florentine and resembles those supplied by Vespasiano da Bisticci," "with Greek quotations added in red by a different hand." The magnificent binding for the king was made in a Hungarian atelier at Buda.

[8] According to L. Sorrento's recent statistical observations on Aquinas' use of classical authors (*Medievalia. Problemi e Studi* [Brescia, 1943], p. 372), only one direct reference to Gellius is found in Aquinas' works, and this reference is to a passage quoted by Augustine.

onward, Gellius belonged among the widely printed and re-printed writers. When the first classical works appeared in print, at Sweynheym and Pannartz' press in Rome, Gellius (published in 1469) was preceded only by Cicero and Apuleius. A reprint became desirable as early as 1472, and in the same year the *Noctes Atticae* was also among the pioneer Venetian editions of classical texts printed by Nicolaus Jenson. Six more Gellius editions appeared in Venice before Aldus Manutius brought out his well-known one in 1515. Even prior to that date the *Noctes Atticae* had appeared at Brescia (1485), Bologna (1503), and Florence (1513); the latter edition, print-ed by the Giunta press, was represented in the collections of the Medici by an illuminated luxury copy on vellum leaves, now in the British Museum. Before long, Gellius was also printed in the northern countries. On the Rhine, he was pub-lished in Basel, 1519, in Strassburg, 1521; and frequently in Cologne from 1526 onward. In France, Lyons saw at least eight editions from 1512 to 1566. The *Attic Nights* eventually became one of the steadily studied and emended classical works in Paris. More than a dozen editions appeared from Paris presses between 1508 and 1585, the year when Henry Estienne there produced the first enduring landmark in the modern critical reconstruction of the text.[9]

The judgment of the foremost scholars of the sixteenth cen-tury confirms the impressiveness of this publication history. Erasmus in his *Adagiorum Chiliades* (I 4.37) stated that the *Noctes Atticae* contained stores of information *"quibus nihil fieri potest neque tersius neque eruditius."* No doubt, the human-ists under his influence shared this appreciation. From Petrus Mosellanus we have a commentary on the *Attic Nights* which was repeatedly published in Cologne and Paris from 1526 on-

---

[9] These (and some of the following) bibliographical data can be collected from the catalogues of printed books of the British Museum (under: Gellius, Aulus) and the Bibliothèque Nationale at Paris (under: Aulu-Gelle), as well as from the *Bibliothèque des impressions et des oeuvres de Josse Badius Ascensius, imprimeur et humaniste, 1462–1535,* by Ph. Renouard, II (Paris, 1908), 463–70. Another means for a wide circulation of one chapter of Gellius was the early printed editions of Aesop's *Fabulae,* to which *Noctes Atticae* II 29, containing an (otherwise unknown) *Apologus* by Aesop, was often added. This appendix, under Gellius' name, is found in the Aldine edition of Aesop of 1505, according to the catalogue of the Bibliothèque Nationale, tome 48, col. 136. The catalogue of the British Museum lists ten Aesop editions with the Gellius appendix for the period 1516 to 1600.

ward. The Strassburg Gellius of 1521, on the other hand, appearing at the time when Ulrich von Hutten was a central figure in German Humanism, shortly after the publication of the *Epistolae Obscurorum Virorum* and the beginning of the Reformation, carried a Latin poem addressed to Hutten by an Alsatian poet, Ottmar Luscinius—a eulogy which extolled Gellius as a messenger of knowledge and light, fit for Hutten's struggle against darkness and obscuration.[10] It is this Strassburg edition which, half a century later, served as a basis for the study of the *Attic Nights* by Joseph Justus Scaliger, whose copy, filled with copious notes from his hand, has been preserved in the British Museum. That other great humanists of the Netherlands and France also paid active attention to Gellius' work is testified by the surviving working copies of scholars of the rank of Passerat, Puteanus, Cujacius, and Huet in the Bibliothèque Nationale in Paris.[11]

The seriousness of this attention can be gathered from the animated critique and praise of the *Noctes* found among these humanists. Gellius, as is well known, had adhered to a tendency of literary archaism and, in its wake had disparaged one of the foremost writers of the period directly preceding his own: Seneca. In the sixteenth century, he was passionately taken to task for this disparagement by Juan Luis Vives, a Spaniard like Seneca; but a friendly advocate arose in Henry Estienne. The latter's 1585 edition of the *Noctes Atticae*, besides including a running commentary from Estienne's pen (planned to continue a previous commentary fragment by a Flemish philologist, Carrion), set forth a comprehensive defense of Gellius against Vives' reproaches. Estienne's forceful apology formed part of a general discussion of Gellius and his works. It was an appraisal which had grown out of conversations between Estienne and Pasquier, was dedicated (among others) to De Thou, and was punningly entitled *Noctes aliquot Parisinae, Atticis A. Gellii Noctibus seu Vigiliis*

---

[10] *Ottomari Luscinii Argentini iuris consulti de Auli Gellii laudibus ad Ulricum Huttenum equitem virum doctissimum et Germaniae nobilitatis praecipuum ornamentum Carmen* has been reprinted from the Strassburg 1521 edition of the *Noctes Atticae* in *Ulrichs von Hutten Schriften*, ed. E. Boecking, II (Leipzig, 1859), 6–8.

[11] See the catalogues of the British Museum and the Bibliothèque Nationale.

invigilatae. This was the final tribute of the humanistic era to the Roman writer's work.[12]

When seen against the background of this bibliographical history, there can be no doubt concerning the incision of the change that came about in the history of Gellius' influence with the Renaissance. One of the facets needed in our picture of the *renaissance des lettres* is an adequate account of the reviving acquaintance with the *Attic Nights*, of the critical reconstruction of its text, and of the various effects of Gellius on the literature of the fifteenth and sixteenth centuries.

II. Yet the investigation of Gellius' fortunes in the Renaissance has not progressed much beyond a modest start; no monograph has been written on the reviving interest in Gellius after the end of the Middle Ages. To a degree, it would appear, this failure is due to our ignorance of the textual history—to the incompleteness of our information about the humanistic manuscripts which must provide the indispensable documentary basis.

In the study of most ancient writers, the collection and collation of the copies made by the humanists of the early Renaissance has been a by-product of the labor of modern editors, who have had to identify and survey the manuscripts of their respective authors. But for the *Noctes Atticae* the fifteenth-century manuscripts and printed editions are of little value to a present-day editor. For although some humanistic manuscripts must be consulted for the chapter headings of the lost eighth book, for the supplementary paragraphs at the end of Book XX, and for a few minor supplements, all the rest of a Renaissance text of Gellius gives more embarrassment than help to the modern critic. Whereas humanists often paved the way to the final evaluation and selection of variants in the case of works whose basic manuscripts they rediscovered in the fifteenth century, this applies to the *Noctes Atticae* at the

---

[12] Cf. the information on Henri Estienne's Gellius edition of 1585 and on his *Noctes Parisinae* in M. Maittaire, *Stephanorum historia, vitas ipsorum ac libros complectens,* I (Londini, 1709), 429–33; L. Feugère, *Essai sur la vie et les ouvrages de Henri Estienne* (Paris, 1853), pp. 188–90; *Nouvelle Biographie Générale,* vol. XVI (Paris: Firmin Didot, 1856), col. 542–43 (article "Estienne, Henri"). After 1600, the *Noctes Parisinae* were repeatedly republished in Frankfurt-am-Main. On Louis Carrion: *Nouvelle Biographie Générale,* vol. VIII (1855), col. 881 f.

most in regard to the few recovered sections.[13] For the remainder of the text the modern *recensio* must be built on a multitude of fragmentary medieval manuscripts dispersed all over Europe and not available to scholars in the early Renaissance. The latter, in the absence of such help, chiefly depended on the methods of conjecture and emendation open to their times: they freely ventured upon corrections, relying on the new familiarity with Greek and Latin usage; they supplemented defective quotations (especially many from the Greek) by consulting Gellius' sources. Judged in the light of Renaissance needs, this was a happy short cut to the reestablishment of a work formerly unintelligible in large parts; but it would often arbitrarily restore quotations beyond the extent to which they had been known to Gellius himself and normalize the text in a manner which is the despair of the modern critical reader.

As a consequence, the wealth of surviving Renaissance manuscripts (of which more than fifty were counted by the 1880's)[14] has practically been left a *terra incognita* by modern editors of the *Attic Nights*. The fifteenth-century manuscripts used in the critical reconstruction of the text are often those that were and are the least satisfactory of all, both to the humanists themselves and to our own study of their activities— copies in which humanistic philology had not yet tampered very much with the medieval imperfections. One of these better-known favorites of the modern editors of Gellius is what may be the earliest collection of the surviving nineteen books and rediscovered supplements between two covers, made in Florence as early as 1418 and still without a mastery of Greek. Another is a fragmentary text (beginning with the sixth book) carefully copied in 1431 by Niccolò Niccoli, with the assistance of Ambrogio Traversari for the Greek, from a

---

[13] That is, with the one, not important, exception of the *Codex Buslidii*. This medieval manuscript, available about 1500 and now lost, contained a number of otherwise unknown variants and phrases filling lacunae; the readings saved from it by some sixteenth-century humanists (notably Canter and Carrion) have, therefore, remained useful. But references are generally limited to the first book, are often suspect, and only of minor significance. See esp. H. M. Hornsby, *op. cit.*, note 15, below, pp. xix f., xxii.

[14] Hertz says that he examined over fifty manuscripts more or less carefully (*op. cit.*, vol. II, p. lxvii).

newly discovered medieval manuscript.[15] As to the vast remainder of fifteenth-century manuscripts and early editions, the critics of Gellius' text have agreed that here was a potential storehouse of information on the influence of this author on the Renaissance; but for the editorial tasks in hand the humanistic transcripts were left aside and grouped together in the neglected category of the more recent and inferior manuscripts.[16] We would in fact not even have a tentative idea of what happened to the text of the *Noctes Atticae* in the hands of the early humanists, were it not for the fundamental observations made by Remigio Sabbadini in his various studies on Guarino da Verona.[17] From these we have learned that it was only one year after Niccoli and Traversari had regained some of the formerly unfamiliar parts and had begun to improve upon the readings that a critical revision of the entire text was published by Guarino in Ferrara. This was the climax of ten years of work during which Guarino used manuscripts from all over northern Italy and labored in contact with the Florentine humanists. "I think it would be a shame," he had said as early as 1422 with Gellius and Macrobius in mind, "that authors who daily improve my mind should remain unimproved in my house."[18] During the following years manuscripts were

---

[15] The Florentine manuscript of 1418 has not been preserved, but Hertz found a derivative of it in Breslau, Silesia; *op. cit.*, pp. lxxx f. Niccoli's copy of 1431 is Cod. Florence Bibl. Naz. Magb. 329; it includes the chapter headings of the lost eighth book and XX 10.7–11.5. Cf. Hertz, *op. cit.*, pp. lxiv f.; H. M. Hornsby (ed.), *A. Gellii Noctium Atticarum Liber I* (Dublin, 1936), p. xx. The manuscript has now again been used in the reconstruction of Books IX–XX by L. Meagher, "The Gellius Manuscript of Lupus of Ferrières" (Ph.D. diss., University of Chicago, 1936).

[16] That is, the s group of manuscripts. For their evaluation: Hertz, who calls them interesting only for the purposes of the "traditionis Gellianae historia"; C. Hosius, in the preface to his edition of Gellius (Lipsiae, 1903), p. xv, and in his article on Gellius in Pauly-Wissowa, *Real-Encyclopaedie*, vol. VII (1912), col. 998. Cf. G. Wissowa, in *Goettingische Gelehrte Anzeigen* (1907), p. 728, who in appraising Hertz's attainments says: "Nicht für die Rezensio, wohl aber für die Textgeschichte wäre eine eingehendere Würdigung der das ganze Werk umfassenden Handschriften des 15. Jahrhunderts (s) am Platze gewesen."

[17] R. Sabbadini, *La scuola e gli studi di Guarino Guarini Veronese* (Catania, 1896), pp. 118–19; *Le Scoperte*, pp. 97, 128, 138; *Storia e critica dei testi latini* (Catania, 1914), pp. 331, 435. Later on most of the source material was published, or republished, in Sabbadini's critical edition of Guarino's *Epistolario*, 2 vols. (Venice, 1915 and 1916) and a commentary volume (Venice, 1919), published in *Miscellanea di Storia Veneta*, ser. III, vols. 8, 11, 14.

[18] "Indignum enim censeo ut qui me in dies meliorem faciunt, ii apud me inemendati maneant." *Epistolario di Guarino Veronese*, vol. I, no. 224.

continually borrowed and loaned (Cosimo de' Medici, for instance, consulted a manuscript in Guarino's possession during the year 1425); and interest was especially directed to the Greek citations and the list of chapter headings, as is seen from Guarino's letters.[19] When the laborious enterprise reached its goal in 1432, Guarino claimed he had performed "a work deserving immortality"; when asked to lend his working copy of the corrected version, he replied that in its shabby external garb it was a treasure which he would not exchange for any wealth.[20]

The fortunes of his revision proved him right. With the Greek parts accessible again, Gellius (as we have seen) was among the first classical authors to be printed by Sweynheym and Pannartz in Rome as early as 1469. In introducing this first edition, the learned editor Andrea de' Bussi said that the *Noctes Atticae* was one of the most necessary of all ancient works because of its comprehensive sweep of classical erudition, Greek and Latin alike; it was a monument to the surpassing value of bilingual culture, although, unfortunately, nowadays Greek had become the privilege of few erudites and so rare that the new edition of Gellius was to have an adequate Latin translation following the Greek. This Latin translation was in fact the only far-reaching innovation added to the Guarinian text in this first and in many subsequent printed editions.[21]

So much is sure: Guarino's revision was the ranking event in the early history of Gellius' revival and Renaissance influence. Yet when it comes to the details we can no longer speak with commensurate assurance. Unfortunately, neither Guarino's working copy nor the final transcript made by Niccolò Pirondolo in 1432 has survived; nor has the early manuscript of a complete Gellius (possibly a reproduction of Guarino's text), which was in the famous Florentine library of S. Spirito

---

[19] *Epistolario*, vol. I, nos. 305, 315, 322, 324, 351, 363, 365; vol. III, p. 185.

[20] ". . . opus immortalitate dignum." "An Gellium habeam quaeris? habeo quidem sordidum, veste pannosa et bombicina indutum tunica, sed adeo veridicum et magna ex parte emendatum, ut eum pro Croesi opibus et auro Midae mutaturus non sim." *Epistolario*, vol. II, nos. 631 (1432) and 649 (1434).

[21] Andrea de' Bussi's preface is reprinted in B. Botfield, *Praefationes et epistolae editionibus principibus auctorum veterum praepositae* (Cantabrigiae, 1861), pp. 80 ff.

in 1451, to perish there, in 1471, by fire.[22] Until now the only manuscript basis for reconstructing the Guarinian revision has been a copy penned in 1432 (probably in Ferrara) by Guarino's friend Giovanni Lamola and preserved in the Vatican Library (Cod. Vat. Lat. 3453). This early transcript, to be sure, is and will always be a most authoritative source. But its scribal notes merely state that it was written by Lamola, without any indication of its relationship to Guarino's efforts; and Lamola is known to have been active in his own right in emending classical authors in those years. A precondition for any further steps, therefore, is the identification of other copies of the Guarinian revision which could serve as counterparts to Lamola's text and determine how far the latter's readings accurately reproduce Guarino's labor.[23]

It may be hoped that the illuminated Gellius written at Bologna in 1448 and now in the Biblioteca Ambrosiana will eventually prove to be such a transcript.[24] Meanwhile an even earlier offspring of Guarino's text has come to light in a manuscript acquired by the Newberry Library in Chicago from the Libreria Antiquaria Hoepli in Milan.

III. The significance of the Newberry manuscript (Ms. 90.5), which seems to have remained unknown to students until its removal to Chicago in 1949, is not immediately apparent because it is mutilated, presumably at the beginning, and certainly at the end. Otherwise the vellum volume is well

---

[22] The note on the Gellius in S. Spirito is found in the inventory of 1451, published by A. Goldmann in *Centralblatt fuer Bibliothekswesen*, IV (1887), 143; on the loss by fire in 1471, cf. *ibid.*, 138. Since the manuscript is described as "agellius Noctium aticharum . . . , cuius principium est 'Plutarchus in libro.' Finis vero 'Inueniri q3 possit', " it must have contained the text from the first chapter of the first book up to the preface which in many manuscripts of the Quattrocento follows the twentieth book (see below, p. 213).

[23] On Lamola's manuscript as a transcript from Guarino and as the only source giving access to Guarino's revision, cf. Sabbadini, *Scuola*, p. 118; *Epistolario*, III, pp. 307, 310. The scribe's notes in this manuscript run: On the fly-leaf: "Iste liber est mei Johannis Lamolae quem propria manu tamen scripsi"; the end-subscription: "Auli Gellii Noctium Atticarum liber vigesimus et ultimus feliciter explicit. MCCCCXXXII, pridie Kalendas novembrias."

[24] Until now the manuscript has only been studied for its illumination, without attention to the text. But since it was written in a region near Ferrara, is introduced by the table of chapter headings (see the citation above, note 6), begins with the first chapter of the first book (as shown by the photographic reproductions listed in note 6), and ends with the twentieth book, one should expect a reproduction of the Guarinian text.

preserved and remarkably beautiful. Its technical accuracy, indicated by conscientious insertion of arabic numeral pagination, arabic numeral signatures, and signature references to the next following words at the end of each quire; the calligraphic evenness of the humanistic hand, in Greek as well as Latin; and the perfection of the decoration, including finely illuminated initial letters—all bespeak, if not a professional scribe, at least a copyist trained in a distinguished writing school. The manuscript contains the list of chapter headings, including those for the eighth book; the text of Books I–VII and IX–XX (to 11.5), with all the Greek quotations in place; the preface-epilogue (on which more will be said later); and an extensive alphabetic index from the scribe's hand. This index, after running from fol. 245r to 272v, breaks off in the middle of the letter T, so that one or more leaves must have been lost at the end. Moreover, the manuscript is not in its original case but in a seventeenth- or eighteenth-century binding, and the margins are slightly clipped—apparently as a result of the rebinding. The original flyleaves probably disappeared on the same occasion, and with them all direct marks of provenance.

Consequently, the origin and history of the manuscript must be inferred from other indications, especially by interpreting the scribe's subscription found between the preface-epilogue and the incompletely preserved alphabetic index: "Per Milanum Burrum 1445."[25]

A family of the Borro, or Borri, latinized Burri, is well known at Milan. From the twelfth to the seventeenth century they contributed many prominent figures to the ruling group of that city and to the ranks of army captains, scholars, and scientists. Otherwise the name seems to be rare in Italy. True, in Arezzo in Tuscany we find another branch of the family, which had emigrated there from Milan during the Middle Ages. And in the fifteenth century we also meet Borro in Parma, then a Milanese dependency, and in Venice: namesakes, whose relationship to the Milanese family is still *sub judice*. But the Parmese Borro, throughout the fifteenth century, consisted of one single family line, the members of which

---

[25] Fol. 244v.

are known from documents; as to Venice, merely one person of this name is known there, a learned monk who may or may not have immigrated from Milan.[26] So we seem to be left with an alternative between the Milanese line and the Aretine branch of the Borro family. We have three further criteria available to help us decide.

One can be taken from the first name of our scribe. If the family name of the Borro is rare in Italy, the form Milanus, which would demand the Christian name of Milano as its equivalent in the Italian vernacular, is so unusual that it does not seem to be listed in historical dictionaries of Italian names. Yet this uncommon praenomen appears precisely among the Milanese Borro. In 1386, according to a legal document,[27] Johannes Franciscus (called Caesar) Burrus, from whom some of the famous Borro in the seventeenth century were descended, bought the family house in the Milanese suburb Borgo Corbetta from one Dominus Franceschinus Burrus, son of the late Dominus Milanus. We may infer that the Milanus Burrus who wrote the lately acquired Newberry manuscript in 1445 hailed from a branch of this fourteenth-century family.

The second clue in our volume also points persuasively to the Milanese region. In the leaf design illuminating the first page, one encounters a coat of arms which is identical with that of the Finardi, a patrician family of Bergamo; this city at the foot of the Alps is only about thirty miles to the northeast of Milan.[28] Of course, early ownership is not necessarily

---

[26] On the Borro family in Milan and Arezzo: P. Argelati, *Bibliotheca Scriptorum Mediolanensium*, tom. I, pars 2 (Mediolani, 1745), col. 237 ff.; *Enciclopedia Italiana*, VII (1930), 510 f. Borro in Parma: I. Affò, *Memorie degli scrittori letterati Parmigiani*, IV (Parma, 1793), 14 f. Borro in Venice: F. G. degli Agostini, *Notizie istorico-critiche* . . . *degli scrittori Viniziani*, II (Venezia, 1754), 600 ff.

[27] Printed in "Genealogia illustrissimi domini Francisci Josephi Burri, ex instrumentis publicis," published in *Nova Librorum Rariorum Conlectio*, fasc. II (Halis Magdeburg, 1709), p. 259.

[28] The coat of arms of the Finardi of Bergamo is reproduced in *Enciclopedia storico-nobiliare Italiana*, ed. V. Spreti, III (1930), 182. (I owe this reference to Mr. J. Wolf, head of the Department of Genealogy and Local History in the Newberry Library). The only, though improbable, alternative to be considered would seem to be the armor of the Fenaroli, whicn exhibits the same heraldic elements, but shows a somewhat different proportion between the upper and the lower part of the shield and an additional small crown above the eagle. Since the branches of the Fenaroli lived in Milan, Modena, and especially Brescia, the neighbor town of Bergamo (*ibid.*, pp. 116–18), the early home of the Borro manuscript would be in Milan or the surrounding region in any event.

identical with local origin; a manuscript may well have been bought from another region. But the Finardi in provincial Bergamo were not great patrons who had *desiderata* copied in faraway lands or manuscripts purchased by agents abroad. A book in this out-of-the-way library in the northernmost corner of the peninsula is likely to have come from some place in the neighborhood, most probably from Milan, the nearby metropolitan center. In a case in which the name of the scribe is Milanese, it would seem safe to assume an origin from (roughly speaking) the same locality.

Now the heraldic mark of ownership in the Borro copy was not put in simultaneously with script and page decoration; consequently, it does not indicate the first owner. For, in spite of evident execution in the fifteenth century, the colors of the coat of arms differ from those used in the borders, and a part of the decoration was apparently erased to make room for the coat of arms. So the sequence of events must have been this: The manuscript, having been written and (presumably) owned by a Milanese, was subsequently acquired by a citizen of nearby Bergamo. And since the volume was still in the Milanese region recently (the firm of Hoepli bought it from the Biblioteca Molza, the property of an old patrician family of Modena, about a hundred miles southeast of Milan),[29] we shall not be far from the truth if we assume that the manuscript, until its recent transoceanic trip, never left the boundaries of central northern Italy.

The last and most important evidence derives from our recently acquired knowledge of three other manuscripts written by the same scribe. These manuscripts were first discussed by Dorothy Miner in *The Princeton University Library Chronicle* of 1949-50[30] and were still unknown to me when I published the present study for the first time in 1951.[31] Two of the three manuscripts in question were written by Milanus Burrus in the years immediately preceding the Newberry Gellius—a

---

[29] This information has been kindly given by Dr. E. Aeschlimann, former *consigliere delegato* of the Libreria Antiquaria Hoepli.

[30] Miner, Dorothy, "The Manuscripts of the Grenville Kane Collection," *Princeton University Library Chronicle*, XI (1949-50), 41-44.

[31] The appraisal of Miss Miner's valuable findings which follows appeared first in *Studies in Philology*, XLIX (1952), 248-50.

Suetonius of 1443, now in the McLean Collection of the
Fitzwilliam Museum in Cambridge, and a copy of Bruni's
De Primo Bello Punico dated 1444, now in the J. F. Lewis Collection of the Free Library of Philadelphia. The third manuscript is another Suetonius, written as early as 1433, which
formed part of the Grenville Kane Library acquired by Princeton University. Like the Newberry Gellius, all these manuscripts show no place name beside the words *"per Milanum
Burrum"* and the date, but provide indications of patrons and
early owners, not easy to identify, however, because of
erasures. Miss Miner, tacitly correcting or reinterpreting the
information given in De Ricci's *Census of Medieval and Renaissance Manuscripts* and in M. R. James's *Descriptive Catalogue of
the McLean Collection*, concludes from an examination of the
illuminations and badges in the manuscripts, first, that all
three, not excepting the Kane-Princeton Suetonius, in which
the patron's insignia on the title page have been entirely
effaced by a later owner, were written at the request of members of the Visconti family, though not the Duke himself; and,
second, that Milanus Burrus must be classed as one of the
scribes who "worked during the 1430's and 1440's in an
atelier supplying books for the powerful Visconti family of
Milan and Pavia."

A brief comparison of these findings with the facts established for the Newberry Gellius suggests the following conclusions: As long as no copies by Milanus Burrus are found
among the manuscripts stemming from the Pavia Library of
the Visconti and Sforza (the known copies point to side
branches of the Visconti family), we should, perhaps, not go
so far as to associate Burrus directly with the copyists whom
the dukes "set to work," as Miss Miner puts it, for their
library; since the Gellius manuscript exhibits none of the
features indicating Visconti patronage, we are prompted to
presume that Milanus Burrus also worked for other patrons.[32]
On the other hand, the data now available do prove: the
patrons or early owners of all four known Burrus manuscripts

[32] The only trait in the Newberry Gellius that might possibly reveal a trace of the
Visconti atmosphere is the serpent or dragon motif in the large colored initial P at
the beginning of the first book; but this decorative motif need not have anything to do
with the patron of the manuscript.

must be sought in the Milanese region;[33] the name "Milanus Burrus" was used in the Milanese family of the Borro; and, as Miss Miner has pointed out, the contemporaneous illuminations in some of Burrus' copies show a close relationship to the illuminations in some manuscripts from the Pavia Library of Filippo Maria Visconti. The combination of all these facts allows us to say with certainty that the scriptorium indicated by the hand of the scribe of the Newberry Gellius was in or near Milan. In other words, the manuscript was written in a place not very far from Guarino's Ferrara; it was copied there with great care only thirteen years after the completion of the Guarinian revision of the *Noctes Atticae* and equipped with a full run of the Greek quotations. In these circumstances, it is difficult to believe that the scribe was following any model but Guarino's text.

When placed in this setting, the following observation carries conviction. Of the two deviations of the Lamola manuscript from Gellius' *textus communis* to which Sabbadini has drawn attention,[34] the more important one is also encountered in the Borro transcript. In *Noctes Atticae* XIII 7.2, where other Gellius manuscripts in a citation from Herodotus write ἰσχυρόν, Lamola's copy has ἰσχυρότατον, that is, it uses the reading known from the text of Herodotus' work. In addition, while the citation in other Gellius manuscripts stops at the word μήτρας, in Lamola's copy it is continued for several more lines, until ὑγιές οὐδέν. "In 1432," Sabbadini comments, "this familiarity with the Greek text of Herodotus could hardly be expected to be found in anyone but Guarino, who had had in his possession a copy of Herodotus since 1427." Now, precisely the same substitutions from Herodotus' original text that can be credited only to Guarino are found on fol. 156v of the Borro transcript. On the other hand, the latter does not go along with Lamola's copy in the case of Sabbadini's second example. In *Noctes Atticae* XX 5.11, in a quotation of Alexander's letter to Aristotle, Lamola replaces the ἀκροατικούς of the Gellius Vulgate with the word ἀκροαματικούς found in the

---

[33] If the Viscontean origin of the Kane-Princeton Suetonius should be considered open to question, still, the later owner who erased the patron's armorial bearings, Guiniforte della Croce, also resided at a place in the Milanese region—in Vigevano near Pavia, or in Milan itself. See *Enciclopedia storico-nobiliare Italiana*, II (Milan, 1929), 580 f.

[34] In *Scuola*, p. 119.

reproduction of the same letter in Plutarch's *Vita Alexandri;* and here Borro retains the customary ἀκροατικούς. Does this indicate that Lamola made a more extensive change in following Gellius' source than Guarino had done? Since Alexander's letter in the Lamola copy (according to Sabbadini's description) is written *in rasura* and also across the margin of the page, a subsequent alteration of Guarino's phrasing seems to be the most likely explanation. But if Lamola did not feel bound to respect Guarino's reading in this place, can we expect him to have been a faithful copyist everywhere else? In any case, after our observations we can no longer take for granted the identity of the Lamola copy with the Guarinian revision, the repeatedly affirmed basis of Sabbadini's evaluation of the Vatican manuscript.[35] Only a full comparison of Lamola's readings with Borro's transcript, as well as with the Bolognese manuscript of 1448 if this proves to be another copy of Guarino's text, will decide whether and where Lamola's transcription may have swerved from Guarino's diction.

At one point, it is true, a doubt may arise whether the Borro transcript can really have followed the Guarinian text. The latter, as far as is known, never included Gellius' preface,[36] whereas the Borro manuscript does contain it, although appended as an epilogue (a form encountered in many Gellius transcripts in the fifteenth century). But we need not look far to discover that this difference does not refute derivation of the Borro copy from Guarino. Its preface-epilogue, in striking contrast to the usage in the preceding parts of the manuscript, entirely omits Greek quotations, leaving blank spaces even for the few Greek words which one finds in the reproduction of the preface-epilogue in the Roman incunabulum some decades later. This inconsistency is open to one explanation: Milanus Burrus followed the Guarinian text as far as it went, and, consequently, for the preface-epilogue was forced to rely on a medieval copy (or a derivative thereof) devoid of Greek.[37]

---

[35] "Il codice . . . del Lamola, vale a dire il guariniano." *Scuola*, p. 119.

[36] Cf. Sabbadini, *Scoperte*, p. 128.

[37] Comparison of the Borro manuscript in the Newberry Library with the preface-epilogue of the incunabulum of 1469 was first made possible by the courtesy of Mr. H. R. Mead of the Henry E. Huntington Library, who sent me a photostat of fol. (s6)v and information about other parts of the 1469 text of the preface. More recently, a copy of the incunabulum has been acquired by the Newberry Library.

IV. Finally, Milanus Burrus' Gellius will henceforth be a help in establishing the text in which the *Noctes Atticae* was transmitted to Renaissance England.

Although the influence of Gellius on English writers has been as little systematically explored as the history of the humanistic interest in Gellius in Italy, we know enough to infer that his encyclopedia must have been an often consulted source of reference on the English bookshelf of the Renaissance. In William Painter's *Palace of Pleasure*, that storehouse of classical knowledge for so many English authors of the later sixteenth century, including Shakespeare, Gellius ranks high as a source, together with Herodotus and Livy;[38] and in the early seventeenth century, the same is true of Ben Jonson and Robert Burton.[39]

When tracing the history of English familiarity with the *Noctes Atticae* to its beginning, we are eventually carried back as far as the first half of the fifteenth century, when Duke Humphrey of Gloucester made the first large-scale acquisitions of Renaissance manuscripts for English libraries. As early as 1439, in his first major gift of books to the University of Oxford, we find included an "Aulus Gellius 'Noccium Atticarum'."[40] This manuscript, however, did not satisfy the great patron, for soon afterwards, in 1441, he requested a complete Aulus Gellius ("*Aulumgelium perfectum*") from Italy. Many years ago Sabbadini advanced the hypothesis that the Gellius which thereupon entered the English literary scene (the manuscript has not been traced) was not merely a volume combining Books I–VII and IX–XX between two covers, but the revised and completed text from Guarino's pen.[41]

The agent from whom Duke Humphrey requested the complete Gellius text was the Milanese humanist Pier Candido Decembrio.[42] The members of the scholar-family of the

---

[38] Cf. *Cambridge History of English Literature*, IV (1909), 6.

[39] *Ibid.*, pp. 249, 348.

[40] The list of Duke Humphrey of Gloucester's gift of 1439 is published in *Epistolae academiae Oxoniensis*, ed. H. Anstey, vol. I (Oxford, 1898), p. 183; cf. also *Bodleian Quarterly Record*, I (1914–16), 132.

[41] *Scoperte*, p. 138.

[42] Humphrey's request to Pier Candido Decembrio is published in the *English Historical Review*, XIX (1904), 524 (ed. Borsa, with the correct date, 1441), and in *Scoperte* (1905), p. 205 (with an incorrect date, 1451).

Decembri in Milan were particularly well acquainted with the recent restoration of the *Noctes Atticae;* they also had intimate relations with Guarino's Ferrarese circle. From the pen of Pier Candido's younger brother, Angelo Decembrio, we have, under the title *Politia Litteraria,* a series of dialogues describing social intercourse and intellectual exchange at Ferrara. This idealizing account of humanistic conversations was shaped on the model set by Gellius, as the author himself says. When the same Angelo traveled to Spain in 1465, he carried with him a Gellius manuscript which, we hear, was written *cum optimo greco.* If this was a reference to Guarino's revised version (which seems most probable), the text in Pier Candido's possession was presumably also a specimen of the Guarinian revision.[43]

The implication is that in the Borro manuscript we have obtained a document that should help more than any other text of the *Noctes Atticae* in forming an idea of the Gellius that came to England from Milan in the middle of the fifteenth century. With this new transcript as a guide, it should be possible to determine the nature and relationship of such Renaissance manuscripts of Gellius' encyclopedia as have survived in the British Isles, beginning with the volume in Robert Flemmyng's important fifteenth-century library to which attention was recently drawn.[44]

Thus we are able to add another useful page to the history of Gellius' influence on the Renaissance—and of the humanistic scholars' devoted efforts to recover the ancient authors.

---

[43] On Angelo Decembrio and Gellius see *Scuola,* p. 153; *Scoperte,* p. 138; and A. della Guardia, *La politia litteraria di Angelo Decembrio* (Modena, 1910). On Angelo's role as a kind of middleman who "divise il suo tempo fra Ferrara e Milano," particularly in the 1440's when he "tenne scuola" at Milan and was under the patronage of Leonello d'Este at Ferrara, see R. Sabbadini, *Classici e umanisti, da codici Ambrosiani* (Florence, 1933), p. 99; and G. Bertoni, *Guarino da Verona tra letterati e cortigiani a Ferrara, 1429–1460* (Geneva, 1921), pp. 77 f.

[44] The reference to this Gellius manuscript, now MS. Lincoln College Oxford no. 59, is in R. Weiss, *Humanism in England during the Fifteenth Century* (Oxford, 1941), p. 104. On "Sir Thomas More's use of Aulus Gellius' *Noctes Atticae*" we now have some observations by R. J. Schoeck, *Renaissance News,* XIII (1960), 127–29, who has also collected some further notes on Gellius' use by English and French sixteenth-century authors, *ibid.,* pp. 232 f.

APPENDIX

BRUNI'S
LAUDATIO FLORENTINAE URBIS
FIRST PRINTED EDITION

INTRODUCTION TO THE EDITION

Bruni's Spelling: the *Michi-Mihi* Controversy
and the Use of Diphthongs

Even a text of the *Laudatio* that does not purport to provide
the final critical edition demands careful consideration of
Bruni's spelling, which to some extent also means his way of
pronouncing Latin. According to present custom, editors normally use the medieval mode of spelling—replacement of the classical diphthongs by a uniform *e ; michi* and *nichil* instead of *mihi* and
nihil; and the medieval writing and enunciation of the consonants—for all humanists of the Trecento, including Salutati.
For humanists of the Quattrocento, on the other hand, Bruni
included, ancient and modern practice is followed. We find
the classical system adopted in the texts of Bruni's *Historiae*
and *Commentarius Rerum Suo Tempore Gestarum* as edited in the
"Rerum Italicarum Scriptores"; in all modern editions of the
Dialogi, including the last one by E. Garin; and in my own
1928 collection of the rarer works of Bruni. To be sure, by the
time of Bruni's death the classical manner had been revived;
but it took fully as long as that (about forty years) before
the transformation was reasonably complete. At the time of
the composition of the *Dialogi* and the *Laudatio*, Bruni must
still have written in the medieval and Trecento manner.

Exactly how the first copies of these works were written,
we will, of course, not know until their autographs, or at
least autographs of Bruni's contemporaneous letters, are
found; and, until now, there has been no trace of them. But
we can infer roughly the type of text they must have presented. That the problem of the lost diphthongs was already
heatedly discussed among the younger members of Salutati's
circle, we know from the complaints of a contemporary,
Cino Rinuccini, who tells us that those young "prattlers"
loudly and arrogantly argued in public on the *piazza* "how
many diphthongs had existed in the language of the ancients,

and why today only two of them are used."[1] But were these critics capable of drawing the consequences in their own writing and in their copying of manuscripts? About the usage of their master, Salutati, we are better informed because we have the autographs of a few of his letters. Although he had become aware of the medieval origin of the elimination of diphthongs as early as the beginning of the 1390's, he did not draw practical consequences from his insight except for using the letter-character $ę$ to indicate the diphthong *ae*, though very sparingly as yet. Thus we find in a letter of 1392/93 an occasional *meę* and *quę* among many instances of the traditional *e*, sometimes even in the same words.[2] After 1400, *suę*, *vestrę*, *sacrilegę*, *adęquare*, *cęlesti*, etc., appear more often in the few available autographs in the same unsystematic fashion.[3] But they are not used according to any consistent rule and have left no traces in the modern editions of Salutati's works. It is important for us to know these facts when dealing with the reconstruction of Bruni's early writings, because they make it highly improbable that Bruni, even if he was familiar with Salutati's hesitant attempts and occasionally tried something similar, can at that time have worked out any systematic innovations.

There are a few direct indications that Bruni did not yet use any diphthongs in those years. One is the spelling in a manuscript in the Biblioteca Comunale of Siena, in which an early admirer of Bruni copied, in the order in which they became known to him, some of Bruni's letters from the first decade of the Quattrocento.[4] From Novati's edition in Salutati's *Epistolario* of one of these texts, a letter by Bruni addressed to Salutati,[5] one learns that this contemporaneous

---

[1] "... gridano a piaza quanti dittonghi avevano gli antichi e perchè oggi non se ne usano se non due." Cino Rinuccini, *Invettiva contro a cierti calunniatori di Dante e di messer Francesco Petrarca e di messer Giovanni Boccaci*, ed. in A. Wesselofsky, *Il Paradiso degli Alberti*, vol. I, part 2 ("Scelta di Curiosità Letterarie Inedite o Rare," disp. LXXXVI, 2 [Bologna, 1867]), p. 306.

[2] For Salutati's awareness of the problem from the early 1390's, cf. R. Sabbadini, *Il Metodo degli Umanisti* (Florence, 1929), p. 5; for Salutati's autograph letter to Pope Boniface IX of 1392/93, see his *Epistolario*, ed. Novati, vol. IV, pp. 255-59.

[3] Cf. *Epistolario*, vol. III, pp. 665 f., 667 f.

[4] According to the observations by F. P. Luiso in *Raccolta di Studi Critici dedicati ad Alessandro D'Ancona* (Florence, 1901), p. 94.

[5] Letter of Bruni to Salutati, Nov./Dec., 1405, in Salutati's *Epistolario*, vol. IV, pp. 375-78. For this letter, see *Leonardo Bruni Aretino: Humanistisch-philosophische Schriften*, ed. H. Baron (Leipzig, 1928), pp. 217 f.

copyist not only used *michi-nichil* but also failed to write any diphthongs. A second test can be made by comparing a very early dated manuscript of the *Dialogi*, cod. Augiensis 131 of the Badische Landesbibliothek, Karlsruhe, written about 1410 by a scribe who must have been in personal contact with Bruni because he includes one of Bruni's poems, otherwise unknown, and gives us the author's own opinion on it. No diphthongs at all are found in this copy. The manuscript shows some inconsistency in the use of *michi* or *mihi*, but here the scribe must have deviated from Bruni's persistent *michi*, as will be seen presently.[6] Third, these results chime with the fact that only those manuscripts of the *Laudatio* which stem from the middle or second half of the Quattrocento show diphthongs.[7]

How much depends on whether we remain close to Bruni's original intentions in these formal and linguistic matters? Here we should give heed to an episode from his later life which shows his deeper motivation. In an undated letter, probably written as late as the latter part of the 1430's,[8] Bruni tells his correspondent, who had wondered why he "sometimes" continued to follow the custom of saying *michi* and *nichil* instead of returning to classical usage, that he had done so not only occasionally but quite systematically throughout his entire scholarly life. He had, he said, followed the custom of Dante, Petrarch, Boccaccio, and Salutati. These "*doctissimi homines*" had rightly adhered to the "common usage"; only "certain ostentatious classicists [*quosdam qui ostentare volunt se antiquarios esse*]" were trying to re-establish a fashion which, as usage testified, had proved to be repugnant to the Latin-speaking people of the West, who have a propensity to guttural pronunciation, that is, to form aspirates not deep down in the breast as the Chaldeans and Jews do, but to form them with their tongue, lips, and throat. "For usage is the teacher and lord of our speech," not "reason and consistency."[9] The ancient Latin writers who preferred

---

[6] Regarding the Karlsruhe Ms., see *Humanistic and Political Literature*, pp. 138 f., 147.

[7] See pp. 226 f. below about the Mss. used for our edition.

[8] Bruni, *Ep. VIII 2*, ed. L. Mehus (Florence, 1741), vol. II, p. 108. For the date, cf. *Bruni: Humanistisch-philosophische Schriften*, p. 213.

[9] "Usus nempe magister, et dominus est sermonis nostri, . . . qui non tam ratione, et via, quam pro arbitrio moveatur." *Ep. VIII 2*, ed. Mehus, vol. II, p. 108.

mihi-nihil were themselves following a contemporary custom, because reason and consistency would have demanded *mihi*, not *mihi*, in consonance with *tibi* and *sibi*. "Accordingly, usage [*usus*], which was the master then, is the master today; it can disprove what had once been considered right. Otherwise words would never alter, and so much that was agreeable to the ancients would not have changed. . . . *Usus*, therefore, was the decisive factor for them. Why should the same *usus* not have the same potency for us?"[10]

Two basic characteristics of Bruni's Humanism, then—his defense of the pre-classicist tradition in the Florentine Trecento and of the right of modern Florentines to do as the Ancients had done—are profoundly intertwined with what appear to be mere technicalities of spelling and pronunciation. Differing with Bruni's adherence to Salutati's position in the *michi-mihi* controversy, a more "classicistic" humanist like Poggio criticized this position even during Salutati's lifetime;[11] and by the time of Bruni's quoted defense, most of the Italian humanists had learned to prefer the classical *mihi*. When consulting the ultimate word in this quarrel, the theory developed during the second half of the century in Giovanni Pontano's *De Aspiratione* (1481), one senses that this had been a struggle not only for grammatical correctness but also between different humanistic attitudes. For what Pontano criticized most had been dearest to Bruni. "Leonardo should not have had recourse to either Petrarch, Dante, Boccaccio, or Salutati as authorities," said Pontano; "for the writings of these men (I speak of their Latin works) show so little knowledge of the Latin language that, very often, they not only barely speak Latin, but do not even speak grammatically."[12] What has entirely disappeared in

---

[10] "Usus ergo, qui tunc dominus fuit, etiam hodie dominus est, et potest improbare, quod tunc probavit; alioquin variatio nulla foret in verbis, nec essent mutata tot antiquorum placita. . . . Usus ergo apud illos haec potuit: cur igitur idem usus apud nos idem non possit?" *Ibid.*

[11] As we know from Salutati's last letter, of March 26, 1406; *Epistolario*, vol. IV, pp. 162 f.

[12] "Neque a Petrarcha neque a Dante neque a Boccaccio neque a Colutio auctoritas quaerenda erat Leonardo; quorum scripta (de his enim quae latine scripserunt loquor) tam parvam prae se ferunt latinae linguae cognitionem ut non modo parum latine sed ne grammatice quidem saepenumero loquantur, quod qui non credit eorum libros inspiciat." Giov. G. Pontano, *Opera Omnia*, vol. II (Venice, 1519), fol. 31v.

Pontano's review of the controversy is Bruni's historically minded interpretation of the changing needs of *usus* and of the right of the Moderns to do what the Ancients had done. If we allow Bruni to say *michi* and *nichil*, as we must, it would be inconsistent and misleading to make it appear that he used a system of diphthongs which we know he did not use. We would thereby remove the *Laudatio* from the intellectual atmosphere in which Bruni's first writings were conceived and would help to destroy the image of the historical continuity which Bruni himself defended and tried to preserve.

In these circumstances it seems much better to reconstruct at least the early writings before Bruni's departure to the Curia according to the spelling familiar from Salutati's latest writings. I have, therefore, in all essential points taken Novati's edition of Salutati's *Epistolario* as my guide, not only for the diphthongs and the vocalism, but also for the writing of consonants, consonant combinations, division of words, and wherever Salutati's usage seemed to provide more reliable guideposts than could individual manuscripts of the *Laudatio* whose scribes and whose relationship to the author are unknown.[13]

As is usual today (Novati's edition being no exception), consonant *v* and vowel *u* have been distinguished despite the fact that humanistic usage confused them.

Punctuation and capitalization have been freely used in the accepted manner, and the text broken into paragraphs, in order to facilitate understanding and to bring out the structure of the work. For the same purpose I have divided the text into four sections with subtitles whose phrasings are taken from the text itself. Since, unlike the rest of the work, these section titles are printed in italics and placed in square brackets, the reader will not be able to mistake them for Bruni's own.

---

[13] Following Salutati's usage, I have in particular eliminated one striking and embarrassing feature found in several of the best and oldest *Laudatio* manuscripts—their adherence to the medieval use of mixed forms for both the pronouns *hic* and *is*: *hii* for *hi* and *ii*; *hiis* for *his* and *iis*; *hee* or *hec* for *hae* and *eae*. Since these perversions are no longer found in Salutati's writings, and had also been rejected by Petrarch, I find it difficult to believe that Bruni would have been more "medieval," in this respect, than his Trecento masters. Since the scribes of the late manuscripts usually dissolved these bastard forms, breaking them down into forms of either *hic* or *is*, I have chosen in such cases one of the possible alternatives while leaving it to the critical apparatus to show the distribution of the *hii* and other forms among the manuscripts.

The Manuscripts
and the Arrangement of This Edition

The text of the *Laudatio* which follows was reconstructed from five manuscripts—two in the Biblioteca Laurenziana and three in the Biblioteca Vaticana—during 1948–49, when, in preparing *Humanistic and Political Literature* and the first edition of *The Crisis of the Early Italian Renaissance*, I needed a complete and reasonably reliable text of Bruni's work, which had never been printed *in extenso*.[14] Sizable paragraphs of the text thus reconstructed were printed in the second volume of *Crisis*, but publication of the whole was delayed, for reasons that will be explained presently.

Since it was not possible for me to visit Italy during the immediate postwar years and to base my text on a comprehensive inspection of manuscripts, I had to rely on notes made during prewar visits to Florence and Rome, and, on this basis, in 1948–49 had the selected five manuscripts and a few others partly photostated and partly microfilmed, thanks to the helpfulness of Paul O. Kristeller and the late Theodor E. Mommsen. Without their assistance in locating the needed material and obtaining reproductions of it, and the ready cooperation of the administrations of the two libraries, this edition could not have been prepared. If I venture to publish it now essentially unchanged, after so many years have passed since it was first used for my studies, it is because I am still persuaded that each of the selected five manuscripts deserves the attention which it here receives, and that the text emerging from their collation leaves so few and relatively insignificant variant readings that, for most purposes, no enlargement of the manuscript basis will be needed until the time when the final text can be built upon systematic examination of the constantly growing number of known manuscripts.[15]

---

[14] Only fragments had been published previously in E. T. Klette's *Beiträge zur Geschichte . . . der italienischen Gelehrtenrenaissance*, II (Greifswald, 1889), 84–105, and G. Kirner's *Della 'Laudatio Urbis Florentinae' di Leonardo Bruni: Notizia* (Leghorn, 1889), *passim*.

[15] This will hardly be the case before we reap the rich harvest in Paul O. Kristeller's rapidly growing *Iter Italicum* and in the increasing number of manuscript catalogues of libraries now being published.

The five manuscripts on which the present reconstruction is based are the following:

G = Laur. Gadd. 90 inf. c. 13, a miscellany *Saec. XV. ineuntis.*[16] Apparently the oldest manuscript known thus far; of Florentine origin. Except for the equally valuable Ms. *L*, it is superior to all other collated texts and also to those referred to by earlier scholars.[17] The leaves containing the *Laudatio* (fol. 54r–61r) (used in photostat) are in a *bastarda* hand, the Italian cursive, which is normally not found much later than 1400 in copies of humanistic works. At the end of the *Laudatio*: "*Liber mei Angeli Zenobii de Gaddis de Florentia XLVIII.*" Angelo Gaddi, who belonged to a patrician Florentine family, was the collector, and sometimes the copyist, of numerous manuscripts which came to the Biblioteca Laurenziana later in the century; a manuscript copied by him (a Boccaccio item in Ms. Laur. 90 sup. 104) dates from 1414.[18] The remainder of Laur. Gadd. inf. c. 13 consists of various writings by humanists of the Trecento and of humanistic and diplomatic correspondence from the years 1404 to 1413, all Florentine. On the last page is an "*Elenchus Decem Baliae civitatis Florentine,*" a list of 1414.[19]

Although these features all point to an origin not later than the second decade of the fifteenth century, such an early transcription is not fully assured because the manuscript was written by various hands, and the *bastarda* hand that copied the *Laudatio* is found in none of the datable pieces.[20] Furthermore, Angelo Gaddi was still purchasing and collecting books as late as around 1440.[21] Consequently, the possibility cannot be entirely excluded that the *Laudatio* text was added to the

---

[16] See A. M. Bandini, *Catalogus Codicum Latinorum Bibliothecae Mediceae Laurentianae*, III (Florence, 1776), col. 723.

[17] Especially Klette and Kirner (see n. 14, above).

[18] On Angelo di Zanobi Gaddi as a collector and copyist of manuscripts, see Mehus, *Vita di Traversari, passim* (listed in index); R. Sabbadini, *Le Scoperte dei Codici Latini e Greci* (Florence, 1905), p. 86; V. Rossi in his introduction to the *Epistolae Familiares* of Petrarch ("Edizione Nazionale"), vol. I, pp. lviii ff.

[19] Identifiable through consultation of the survey of the successive *Decem Baliae* in *Delizie Degli Eruditi Toscani*, ed. Ildefonso di San Luigi, vol. XIV (Florence, 1781); see p. 296 for 1414.

[20] According to the examination of the manuscript kindly made at my request by Signorina Teresa Lodi and Dr. J. M. Edelstein in 1950.

[21] Mehus, *Vita di Traversari*, pp. cclxxvi and ccccxxxi.

miscellany at a somewhat later time than 1404–14, although the *bastarda* script makes such a hypothesis improbable.

L = Laur. 65 c. 15, a collection of several works by Bruni, with the *Laudatio* on fol. 133v–156r. In view of the mature humanistic hand, a copy of the mid-Quattrocento. Like *G*, of Florentine provenience. Subscription: *"Iste Liber est Monasterii S. Salvatoris de Septimo Cisterc. ordinis et Florentine diec."* In spite of Bandini's assertion *"diligenter exaratus, sed parum correcte,"*[22] the text is free of most of the corruptions found in all other mid-Quattrocento manuscripts I have seen, and seems to have been carefully rechecked and corrected by the scribe. It shows none of the occasional mistakes and omissions encountered in *G* and may, therefore, be considered a second close derivation from the archetype, of hardly less authority than *G*.

C = Vat. Chig. J 215, a miscellany of humanistic texts from the latter part of the fifteenth century, to judge from the script, the replacement of *michi* and *nichil* by *mihi* and *nihil*, and the sustained rendering of diphthongs by means of the sign *ę*. Despite the late date, however, this is a collection of "good texts of Bruni," already acknowledged by earlier scholars.[23] The text of the *Laudatio*, while inferior to *G* and *L*, is related to *G*, though not derived from it. An excellent help in the identification of slips and omissions in the text of *G*.

O = Vat. Ottobon. Lat. 1901, another good collection of a large number of Bruni's works, probably from the middle of the century.[24] Diphthongs are not indicated and *michi-nichil* remains unchanged. Related to *L*, though not derived from it. An excellent help in the identification of slips and omissions in the text of *L*.

P = Vat. Palat. Lat. 1598, a collection of many of Bruni's major works from Giannozzo Manetti's humanistic library, with the note at the end of the *Laudatio* copy: *"Finit MᵒCCCCXXXVIIIIᵒ."* This volume has proved valuable and reliable for editions of other works by Bruni.[25] For the

---

[22] *Catalogus Codicum*, II, col. 734.
[23] See L. Bertalot in *Archivum Romanicum*, XV (1931), 308 n. 3.
[24] Cf. *Bruni: Humanistisch-philosophische Schriften*, p. 231.
[25] *Ibid.*, p. 20; L. Bertalot, *Historische Vierteljahrsschrift*, XXIX (1935), 387; C. C. Bayley, *War and Society in Renaissance Florence* (Toronto, 1961), stemma on p. 361.

Laudatio, it transmits a considerable number of obviously correct readings also found in *G* and *L*, but not in *C* and *0*. On the other hand, just as it changes *michi-nichil* to *mihi-nihil* in the classicistic manner (while it does not introduce diphthongs), so it has a number of variants which are nearer to classical usage than those found in any of the other four manuscripts.[26] In general, *P* is more closely related to the *G-C* group of manuscripts than to *L* and *0* and is often helpful in deciding between divergencies of the other four manuscripts; also, in some details it points to an independent tradition that deserves consideration. But the conformity, not shared by the other manuscripts, to classical usage, especially in the sequence of words, warns one to use caution. An earlier manuscript which agrees with some of *P*'s readings will be described later (p. 231 below).

Another relative of *P* is the copy of the *Laudatio* in the Ms. Vat. Lat. 1560, an interesting collection, probably from about the middle of the fifteenth century, of many of Bruni's writings (cf. *Bruni: Humanistisch-philosophische Schriften*, pp. 5, 82, 228). The copy of the *Laudatio* in this volume is disfigured by too many lacunae and corruptions as to warrant its use in reconstructing the text.

Working on the basis of our five manuscripts, I have been guided in the presentation of the text by the following rules: (1) Wherever the two closest derivatives from the archetype, that is, *G* and *L*, are identical, and the support of at least one other manuscript reassures us that this identity is no mere coincidence, we assume that we have the authentic text before us and need not quote any variants. This applies to the overwhelming majority of divergencies between the manuscripts. (2) If *G* and *L* agree but are not backed up by any of the other

---

[26] These variants often look like changes by a later hand, and this is confirmed by the following observation. At one point (p. 242, line 3, below) *P*, supported only by the related Ms. *A* (which will be discussed presently), has the more classical-sounding name *Janua* for Genoa, whereas all our other Mss. have *Genua*. Now, Salutati at about the same time explained in a letter (*Epistolario*, vol. IV, pp. 96 f.) that, though *Janua* had been the original name, the city was already called *Genua* among the ancients. In these circumstances, the fact that our manuscripts are almost unanimous in writing *Genua*, not *Janua*, can mean only that Bruni followed Salutati in preferring the modern name, and that the *Janua* variant found in *P* and few related manuscripts is the work of a classical-minded copyist. This also chimes with the fact that Bruni, in later years, continued to write *Genua*, not *Janua*, in his *Historiae* and *Rerum Suo Tempore Gestarum Commentarius*, according to the texts in RR.II.SS.

three manuscripts, the common reading of *G* and *L* has usually been accepted, but all variations of the manuscripts are noted in the *apparatus criticus*. (3) If *G* and *L* differ, all five manuscripts are quoted, and the choice among them remains a matter of discernment according to the conditions of the case. (4) In each case where variants are provided, the *apparatus criticus* confronts all five manuscripts with each other. First the form which has been chosen is listed, followed by the letters of the manuscripts in which it appears; this is followed by a square bracket. The alternative readings and their sources are given after the bracket.

Throughout the edition, evident mistakes of scribes proved by the testimony of other manuscripts have been tacitly eliminated. Similarly, if the form of a personal or geographic name is identical in *G* and *L*, other readings have normally been discarded, since scribes are liable to vary the form of names *ad libitum*. On the other hand, our listing of variations occasionally includes information that helps to throw light on the nature and relationship of the consulted manuscripts. For instance, the erasure of an original phrasing known from other manuscripts is usually noted.[27]

It remains for me to explain why the edition of the *Laudatio* prepared in 1948–49 has not been published until now. Delay became advisable when, as already mentioned,[28] I learned in 1950 that the *Laudatio* copy in *G* (Ms. Laur. 90 inf. 13, from Angelo Gaddi's library) was written by another hand than the remainder of the volume, and that, therefore, we cannot be absolutely sure that even this manuscript, the oldest copy of which I was aware at the time, was written before the mid-1430's when Bruni, then Florentine chancellor, sent his youthful work to the Church Council in Basel for purposes of Florentine propaganda.[29] We must assume that only then was the *Laudatio* widely circulated, because all known imitations of the work fall into those very years, or are even later; and the same is true of all manuscripts, except *G*, known to me

---

[27] I wish to mention here, with warm thanks, that Professor Herbert Bloch of Harvard University gave me most valuable advice in some cases where oddities in Bruni's Latin usage made consultation with a philological authority advisable.

[28] Pp. 225 f., above.   [29] Cf. p. 152, above.

about 1950. Unless, therefore, another manuscript could be found that was beyond a doubt written before the 1430's or copied from a pre-1430 manuscript, the possibility could not be ruled out that Bruni might have made changes in the text during the 1430's and that the five manuscripts of our edition might not represent the form phrased in Bruni's youth. When I learned that Paul O. Kristeller was collecting a vast body of manuscript material for his *Iter Italicum*, I postponed publication until I could discover whether Kristeller's lists of uncatalogued manuscripts would reveal any text datable before the 1430's.

The first volume of the *Iter* (London, 1963) located two formerly uncatalogued manuscripts which fulfil this requirement.[30] One of them is Cod. Ashburnham 1702 in the Biblioteca Laurenziana, a miscellany which includes several of Bruni's works, among them the *Laudatio* whose copy ends with the scribe's subscription "*Scriptum Constancię pridie idus februarii milleximo CCCC°XVII° P S A I* [probably instead of the more usual P A I S, i.e., *Post Annum Incarnationis Salvatoris*]." The other is a separate copy of the *Laudatio*, Ms. 126 of the "Biblioteca della Fraternità dei Laici" at the Biblioteca Comunale di Arezzo; it ends with the scribe's subscription "*Scripsit Constantie pridie idus februarij 1418.*"[31]

Have we succeeded in locating a text of as early as 1417 or 1418? The first question, of course, concerns the relationship of the two new manuscripts: it would be an odd whim of chance if two copies had both been completed in Constance on February 12 of the same year or of two successive years. Evidently, the two manuscripts must in some way be related. As a comparison of the two subscriptions shows, the one in the Arezzo manuscript must be a later phrasing, changed by a later scribe. For its odd wording "*scripsit Constantie*" can be explained only by the assumption that the scribe of the Arezzo manuscript had somewhere seen the line "*scriptum Constancie*," as it is preserved in the Ashburnham manuscript,

---

30 P. O. Kristeller, *Iter Italicum*, I (London, 1963), 2 and 97.

31 During 1966, Miss Ruth Prelowski most helpfully examined the Laur. Ashburnham Ms. for me, and Drs. Roberto Abbondanza, Director of the Archivio di Stato, Perugia, and John Tedeschi, Bibliographer of the Newberry Library, Chicago, kindly helped me eventually to secure microfilms of both manuscripts.

but had misunderstood it to mean that it was the author who wrote (*"scripsit"*) his work in Constance on February 12, 1418. Similarly, it is easily understandable that a scribe who found *"milleximo CCCC°XVII° [anno]"* in a manuscript would render this more simply with an arabic numeral, whereas it would be almost impossible to imagine that a scribe who found "1418" in his model could in his copy have written *"milleximo CCCC°XVII° P S A I"*. As for the difference in year, a scribe who knew that the Florentines did not begin the new year until March 25 and who assumed that *scriptum milleximo CCCC°XVII° [anno]"* referred to composition by the Florentine author, can easily have concluded that, in the ordinary calculation of years, this meant February 1418.

The Arezzo manuscript, then, was undoubtedly not written in Constance during 1418, but rather is a copy (or copy of a copy) of a manuscript written in 1417 or 1418. Yet, Ashburn. 1702 can also not be the actual manuscript written and dated by the scribe in Constance in 1417/18 and afterwards copied in the Arezzo manuscript, for we find several lacunae in the Ashburnham manuscript—for instance absence of the entire line *"sunt, permulta . . . necesse. Plato"*[32]—that are not found in the Arezzo manuscript. This difference would not be possible if there had not been a preceding, complete copy, dated 1417/18, from which both the Ashburnham and Arezzo manuscripts are derived.

Even though Ashburn. 1702 is merely a copy (or copy of a copy) of a manuscript executed in Constance in February 1417 or 1418, this derivation suffices to assure us that the text recopied in the Ashburnham and Arezzo manuscripts existed as early as 1417/18 and, consequently, preceded the critical time of the 1430's. Now, a collation shows that the text of the *Laudatio* in both copies of the Constance manuscript is fully identical with the text in the other known manuscripts, except for the usual minor variations and omissions of the copyists. We are, therefore, assured that the text constructed on the basis of our five manuscripts is earlier than the 1430's; and, consequently, there is no reason to doubt that it represents the form of the *Laudatio* as written in 1403 or 1404.

---

[32] P. 240, lines 31–32, in our edition below.

Since, as copies, the two Constance manuscripts are inferior to the five initially selected manuscripts, there is no cause for changing the original text or *apparatus criticus* of our edition. The Arezzo copy is seriously corrupt, lacks a title, and its first part has been badly damaged (probably by water); it has been completely disregarded for our edition. I have added references to the Ashburnham manuscript (under the sigla *A*) in certain cases. This manuscript is of some textual interest because both it and the defective Arezzo manuscript prove to be closely related to *P*, the Manetti library copy of 1439; they demonstrate that a number of the peculiar readings of *P*, listed in our *apparatus criticus*, can be traced back to a much earlier time than 1439. I have therefore, noted the readings of *A* wherever *P* is cited in the *apparatus*.

The ever-increasing information, during recent years, about formerly unknown manuscripts of the *Laudatio* reveals an unexpected and impressively wide circulation of Bruni's youthful work. One day this growing material will allow us to lay the basis for a complete history of the influence of the *Laudatio*, as well as for the final critical edition of the work. Until that time, it may be hoped, the present reconstruction of the text will satisfy most needs.

LEONARDO BRUNI'S
LAUDATIO FLORENTINAE URBIS[1]

LEONARDI ARETINI
ORATIO DE LAUDIBUS FLORENTINE URBIS.

Vellem michi a deo immortali datum esset ut vel Florentine urbi, de qua dicturus sum, parem eloquentiam prestare possem, vel certe meo
5   erga illam studio meeque voluntati. Alterutrum enim, ut opinor, abunde esset ad illius magnificentiam nitoremque ostendendum. Nam et ipsa urbs eiusmodi est ut nichil neque luculentius neque splendidius in toto orbe terrarum inveniri possit, et voluntas quidem mea, ut ego de me ipso facile intelligo, nulla in re unquam fuit ardentior: ut nullo
10   modo dubitem, si quodvis illorum adesset, me de hac precellenti et formosissima urbe cum elegantia et dignitate verba facere posse. Verum quia non omnia que volumus eadem nobis et posse concessum est, quantum poterimus id in medium afferemus, ut non voluntas nobis sed facultas potius videatur defuisse.
15   Admirabilis quidem est huius urbis prestantia et quam nullius eloquentia adequare possit. Sed nonnullos et graves et bonos viros etiam de ipso deo videmus locutos, cuius glorie ac magnitudinis ne ad

---

1/2 Leonardi . . . Urbis] Domini Leonardi aretini Laudes florentine urbis incipiunt *G;* Leonardi Arretini Oratio De Laudibus Florentine Urbis *L;* Leonardi Aretini Oratio De Laudibus Florentine Urbis incipit *0;* Oratio Leonardi Aretini [?] de laudibus Florentie [?] *C;* Leonardi arretini de laudibus florentine urbis incipit feliciter *P;* Leonardi Aretini viri eloquentissimi Oratio De Laudibus Florentie incipit *A.*   17 de ipso deo *L 0 P A*] de deo immortali *G C.*

---

[1] None of the manuscripts cited on this page uses the form *Laudatio*, and no other early manuscript has it according to my knowledge. Yet the title *Laudatio Florentinae Urbis* was Bruni's own final choice, as we know from his letter *Ep. I 8* of 1403 or 1404 where (ed. Mehus, vol. I, p. 17) he tells Niccolò Niccoli: "Orationem, in qua laudes Florentinorum congessi, *Laudatio Florentinae Urbis* inscribi placet, eamque ut Colucius videat, curabis." In agreement with this decision, Bruni referred a few years later, in *Ep. II 4* of 1406, to "*Laudationi Florentinae Urbis*, quam nuper edidi" (ed. Mehus, vol. I, p. 36). The manner in which the speakers in *Dialogus II* are made to mention Bruni's earlier work is also in full harmony with the statement of *Ep. I 8*; for Salutati is there made to talk of Bruni's opinions expressed "in oratione illa in qua laudes florentinae urbis accuratissime congessit," whereas the person who answers Salutati in the dialogue, Pietro di ser Mino, uses Bruni's formulation: "cum istam *laudationem* legerem" (*Dialogus II*, ed. Garin, p. 76). In the text of the *Laudatio* itself, Bruni uses the expression "*hec mea Laudatio*" several times (see p. 249 below). In later years, too, Bruni talked of his *Laudatio* (see p. 152 n. 2, above).

Presumably the recurrent desire of contemporary humanists and copyists to follow strict classical usage eventually suppressed this personal coinage in favor of more classical-sounding phrasings. But modern scholarship has duly returned to Bruni's own appellation of his work, which, moreover, recommends itself as the best quotable form.

minimam quidem partem quamvis eloquentissimi hominis aspirat
oratio; nec deterrentur tamen ob eiusmodi excessum quominus, quantum anniti queunt, de tam immensa magnitudine loquantur. Et ipse
igitur satis fecisse michi videbor, si, quantum studio, disciplina, ex-
ercitatione dicendi, multis denique vigiliis assecutus sum, id omne in   5
laudanda hac urbe potissimum conferam, etsi plane intelligo id eiusmodi esse ut nullo modo cum tanto splendore civitatis sit comparandum.

Quod igitur a plerisque oratoribus dictum est: nescire se unde initium sumant, id profecto nunc michi evenire non verbis, quemadmo-   10
dum illis, sed re ipsa intelligo, non solum enim quia multe sunt res et
varie inter se ultro citroque connexe, verum etiam quia ita preclare
omnes et quodammodo egregie sunt ut inter se ipsas de excellentia
certare videantur, nec facilis sit deliberatio quenam in dicendo sit
anteponenda. Sive enim pulcritudinem ac nitorem urbis intueare,   15
nichil dignius videri potest de quo quam primum enarretur; sive potentiam atque opes, illud omnino censebis preferendum. At si res
gestas vel in nostra etate vel superiori tempore contempleris, nichil
tanti videri potest ut illis anteponatur. Cum vero mores institutaque
consideres, nichil omnino arbitraris prestantius.   20

Hec me dubium tenent, sepeque de altero dicere parantem alterius
recordatio ad se revocat, nec deliberandi permittunt facultatem. Ego
tamen unde aptissimum et congruentissimum putabo, inde initium
dicendi sumam; quod quidem credo etiam ceteros non esse improba-
turos.   25

[I]

[*Qualis urbs ipsa est*]

Ut enim non nullos filios videmus tantam habere cum parentibus
similitudinem ut in ipso aspectu manifestissime cognoscantur, ita
huic nobilissime atque inclite urbi tanta cum suis civibus convenien-   30
tia est ut neque eos alibi quam in illa habitasse nec ipsam alios quam
huiusmodi habitatores habuisse summa ratione factum videatur.
Nam quemadmodum ipsi cives naturali quodam ingenio, prudentia,
lautitia et magnificentia ceteris hominibus plurimum prestant, sic et
urbs prudentissime sita ceteras omnes urbes splendore et ornatu et   35
munditia superat.

Principio igitur, quod prudentie maxime est: nichil ad ostentati-
onem facere nec periculosam et inanem iactantiam sequi potius quam
tranquillam stabilemque commoditatem, hoc Florentiam quidem
cernimus observasse. Neque enim summis in montibus collocata est   40
ut inde se preclare ostentare posset, nec rursus in latissimo camporum
equore ut quoquo versus esset aperta. Prudentissime quidem utrunque
et optimo consilio ab hac urbe factum. Neque enim in summis monti-

bus habitare licet sine adversa celi intemperie, sine ventis, sine procellis, sine summa habitatorum incomoditate atque molestia; nec rursus in immensa vastaque planitie absque uditate soli, absque impuritate aeris, absque caligine nebularum. Has igitur incomodi-
5 tates fugiens, prudentissima urbs eo in loco posita est ut, quod in omni re maxime probatur, medium sit inter extrema sortita et procul ab iniquitate montis et fastidio planitiei remota. Sic tamen utrunque complectitur, ut neutrius utilitatis sit expers et mira celi suavitate fruatur. Obiecti enim ad septentriones Fesulani montes, quasi pro-
10 pugnacula quedam urbis, ingentem vim frigoris et borree aquilonisque furentes impetus repellunt. Ad austrum vero, cuius vis minor est, humiliores muniunt colles. A ceteris autem partibus apricissimi se explicant campi, ad zephiros tamen magis aperti. Itaque plurima in his locis tranquillitas est summaque temperies, a quibus cum discedis,
15 quocumque progrediare, aut te frigora maiora excipiunt aut solis ardores.

Ipsam vero urbem, quantum vel montis vel planitiei sua magnitudine occupat, speciosissima murorum sepit corona, non tamen tanto apparatu ut timida aut diffidens suis viribus videatur, nec rursus ita
20 neglecta ut petulans aut inconsulta possit haberi. Quid dicam de frequentia populi, de splendore edificiorum, de templorum ornatu, de totius urbis incredibili admirandaque lautitia? Omnia, me hercule, conspicua sunt et egregia pulcritudine ornata.

Sed ea melius ex comparatione aliarum quam ex se ipsis licet cog-
25 noscere. Itaque ii qui aliquod tempus abfuere, cum Florentiam reveniunt, soli ferme intelligunt quantum hec florentissima urbs ceteris omnibus longissime prestet. Nulla est enim in toto orbe terrarum cui non aliquid maximarum rerum ad pulcritudinem desit. Hec populo caret, illa edificiorum ornatu, alia vero harum quidem rerum minime
30 inopiam patitur, verum sita haud salubri celo. Non nulla autem ita immunda est ut, quicquid sordis noctu factum est, id mane ponat ante oculos hominum et pedibus per vias calcandum subiciat, quo nichil fedius excogitari potest. Iam enim etsi mille ibi sint regie, si inexhauste divitie, si infinita populi multitudo, contemnam tamen
35 fetidissimam urbem nec multi unquam existimabo. Quemadmodum enim in deformi corpore, etsi cetera omnia preclara habeat, felicitas tamen esse non potest, ita in urbibus, si immunde sint, etsi cetera omnia assint, pulcritudo esse nullo modo potest. Cui autem urbi pulcritudo deest ei summum maximumque ornamentum deesse quis
40 non videt?

Florentiam vero usque adeo mundam atque abstersam cernimus ut nusquam aliquid reperiatur nitidius. Unica quidem hec est urbs, et in

14 his *L C O A*] hiis *G P*.   25 ii *L C O*] hii *G P;* hi *A.*

toto orbe terrarum sola, in qua nichil fedum oculis, nichil tetrum naribus, nichil pedibus sordidum offendas. Summa diligentia habitatorum cuncta eiusmodi cauta ac provisa sunt ut, omni turpitudine procul semota, ea tantum incurras que letitiam ac iocunditatem sensibus queant afferre. Itaque magnificentia quidem eas fortasse omnes que nunc sunt, splendore autem atque lautitia et eas que sunt et eas que unquam fuerunt urbes sine controversia superat. Est enim inaudita tanta munditia, et incredibilis iis qui nunquam Florentiam viderunt, quippe nos ipsos qui eam habitamus quotidie hec habet admiratio, nec consuetudine satiari possumus. Quid enim mirabilius quam in populosissima urbe nichil usquam limi apparere, imbrem autem quamvis maximum nichil impedire quominus siccis plantis urbem perambules, cum prius ferme opportunis rivis aqua pluvia absorta est quam in terram fuerit delapsa. Ex quo fit ut ne splendidarum quidem domorum thalami aliis in urbibus adeo mundi atque abstersi sint ut huius urbis vie atque platee.

Neque vero munditiam habet, non autem ornatum edificiorum; nec ornatum edificiorum, non autem salubritatem celi; nec salubritatem celi, non autem multitudinem ac frequentiam populi. Sed de primo ad extremum omnia assunt que beatam urbem possunt efficere. Sive enim antiquitate delecteris, permulta invenies vel in publicis vel in privatis edibus antiquitatis vestigia. Sive novitatem queris, nichil novis exedificationibus magnificentius aut splendidius est. Amnis vero, qui per mediam fluit urbem, difficile dictu est plusne utilitatis afferat an amenitatis. Quatuor enim ex lapide quadrato magnifice structi pontes fluvii ripas utrinque coniungunt, ita percommode inter se dimensi ut nulla celeberrimarum viarum interventu alvei abruptionem patiatur, nec minus comode per urbem incedas quam si a nullo prorsus amne esset divisa. Hinc atque hinc splendissime platee et nobilium familiarum ornatissime porticus et semper cetibus hominum frequentia compita. Domus autem prope amnem site partim undis preterlabentibus abluuntur, partim tantum a fluvio recedunt quantum vie intermedie spatium relinquatur, qua frequentissima multitudo vel negotii obeundi vel voluptatis gratia possit incedere. Nichil est enim deambulationibus per hec loca suavius, aut meridianis si hiems sit, aut vespertinis si estas.

Sed quid ego in uno aliquo urbis loco occupatus sum? Quid iuxta fluvii ripas ceu piscator quidam obversor? Quasi vero hec duntaxat regio splendida sit, ac non universe totius urbis partes simili aut etiam maiori pulcritudine niteant! Quid est in toto orbe tam

8 iis *L O P A*] hiis *G;* his *C.*   19 ac *G O A*] et *L;* atque *C;* nec *P.*   25 structi *G*] instructi *L C O P A (cf. "monasterium structum lapidibus", Salutati, Ep. XI 3, ed. Novati, vol. III p. 340).*   31 prope *L C O P*] propter *G A.*

splendidum aut tam magnificum quod cum edificiis huius sit comparandum? Pudet me profecto ceterarum urbium, quotiens huius rei comparatio michi venit in mentem. Ille enim, una aut summum duabus viis in tota urbe ornatis, in ceteris omnibus ita ornamentorum
5 vacue sunt ut ab advenis conspici magnopere erubescant. In hac vero nostra nulla est via, nulla urbis regio, que non amplissimis atque ornatissimis edificiis sit referta. Que enim, deus immortalis, domorum instructiones, que ornamenta! Quam magnus edificatorum animus in his structionibus cernitur, quam magne eorum qui inhabitant
10 delitie! Inter cetera tamen urbis edificia augustiori quadam amplitudine ac magnificentia prestant sacra templa atque delubra, que frequentissime per urbem sparsa ac distributa, ut divina decet loca, mira a suis queque tribubus coluntur pietate, mira religione observantur. Itaque nichil est illis ditius, nichil ornatius, nichil magnifi-
15 centius. Non enim profana tantum loca cure fuit ornare, verum etiam sacra; nec modo viventium habitacula preclara esse voluerunt, verum etiam defunctorum sepulcra.

Sed redeo ad privatorum domos, que ad delitias, ad amplitudinem, ad honestatem maximeque ad magnificentiam instructe, excogitate,
20 edificate sunt. Quid potest esse pulcrius aut amenius, quam cernere domorum vestibula, atria, pavimenta, triclinia ceteraque domorum penetralia! intueri laxitatem edium multitudinis capacem! intueri proiecta, fornices, laquearia, tecta supra modum ornata, et (quod in plerisque domibus est) estiva habitacula ab hibernis divisa! ad hec
25 vero preclara cubicula, ditissimam supellectilem, aurum, argentum, stragulam vestem pretiosaque peristromata! Sedne ego stultus sum qui hec enumerare aggrediar? Non michi si centum lingue sint, oraque centum, ferrea vox, omnem magnificentiam, ornatum, gazam, delitias, nitorem possem ostendere. Sed si quis ea nosse cupit, huc ac-
30 cedat, urbem peragret; nec velut festinus hospes aut citatus viator pertranseat, sed insistat, inquirat, contempletur. Nam ceterarum quidem urbium valde interest ne quis in ea peregrinus trahat moram diutius. Nam si quid ornamenti habent, id quidem omne in propatulo est atque in primo (ut ita dicam) cortice, quod simul atque urbem
35 ingressi sunt advene homines intueantur. At si celebriora loca relinquant, si non domorum cortices sed medullas perscrutentur, nichil erit quod ei quam ante conceperant opinioni respondeat: pro domibus enim edicule sunt, proque externo decore interne sordes. Florentia vero nisi intus inspiciatur, omnis eius pulcritudo cognosci non potest.

2/3 rei comparatio *P A*] rei *G L C O*.   9 his *L C O A*] hiis *G P*. structionibus *G*]
instructionibus *L C O P A*.   11 atque delubra *L C O A*] ac delubra *G P*.   16 nec
modo *P A*] nec *G L C O*.   25 cubicula *G C P A*] cubilia *L O*.   27 aggrediar *G C P A*]
aggredior *L O*.   29 nosse *G C P A*] noscere *L O*.   38 Florentia *C O P A*] Florentiam
G; Florentiam (*signo addito fortasse corruptionem litterae* m *indicante*) *L*.

Itaque quod aliis damnum existimationis affert, huic summe auget existimationem. Non enim intra parietes minus ornamenti aut magnificentie habet quam extra; nec una aut altera via decora aut nitida est, sed universe totius urbis partes. Nam velut sanguis per universum corpus, sic ornamenta delitieque per universam urbem 5 diffuse sunt.

Per media vero edificia superbissima insurgit arx ingenti pulcritudine miroque apparatu, que ipso aspectu facile declarat cuius rei gratia sit constituta. Ut enim in magna classe pretoria navis eiusmodi esse solet ut facile appareat in illa vectari ducem qui ceterorum sit mode- 10 rator et princeps, sic huius arcis ea species est ut quivis iudicare possit in ea habitare viros qui gubernatores sint rerum publicarum. Sic enim magnifice instructa est, sic precelsa insurgit, ut omnibus que circa sunt edibus latissime dominetur, appareatque eius plus quam privatum fastigium. 15

Quamquam vereor equidem ne hec simpliciter 'arx', verum 'arx arcis' appellari debeat. Tam multa enim, statim atque menibus extuleris pedem, undique tibi occurrunt edificia, ut illa quidem 'urbs', hec autem que menibus cingitur rectius 'arx' appellanda videatur. Quemadmodum enim de nive scribit Homerus:[2] illam celitus delapsam 20 montes occupare et colles iugaque montium et pinguia culta, ita hec extra urbem edificia universos circum montes collesque et planitiem occupant, ut potius e celo delapsa quam manu hominum facta videantur. At quanta horum edificiorum magnificentia est, quantum decus, quantus ornatus! Sunt enim ampliora etiam quam urbana, 25 utpote latioribus in locis constituta et maiori cum licentia ad delectationem amenitatemque edificata. Quamobrem nemo in his laxitatem requirit, nemo porticum, nemo hortos, nemo viridaria. Nam quid ego de cubiculis aut tricliniis loquar, quibus nichil est magnificentius aut ornatius. Inter hec vero frondosi luci, florida prata, letissimi 30 rivi, nitidissimi fontes et, quod omnia superat, natura ipsa locorum ad letitiam nata. Videntur enim colles ipsi ridere et quandam a se diffundere iocunditatem, qua intuentes expleri non possunt nec videndo satiari: ut universa hec regio paradisus ⟨quidam⟩ recte haberi et nominari queat, cui nichil vel ad pulcritudinem vel ad letitiam in 35 toto orbe sit par. Obstupescunt certe homines qui Florentiam adveniunt, cum procul ex aliquo montis vertice tantam molem urbis, tantam amplitudinem, tantum ornatum, tantam frequentiam villarum conspicantur.

1 existimationis *G C*] extimationis *L O P;* estimationis *A.* affert *L P A*] aufert *G C O.*
2 existimationem *G C P*] extimationem *L O A.*   34 quidam] quedam *codices.*

---

2 *Iliad,* M (lib. XII), 278–86.

Nec vero procul conspecta speciosa sunt, cum autem te illis admiscueris sordescunt, quod in non vera pulcritudine evenire solet. Sed ita omnia comparata sunt, ita non simulato nitent decore, ut, quanto propius intueare, tantum magnificentie tibi crescat opinio. Quare et ville longinquos aspectus, et suburbia villas, et urbs ipsa suburbia pulcritudine vincit. Quam cum ingressi sunt advene, iam externi nitoris ornatusque obliti tantum splendorem urbis velut attoniti admirantur.

Volo preterea unum narrare quod michi in primis argumentum videri solet magnitudinis huius urbis ostendende. Gessit hec civitas complurima bella, contra potentissimos hostes reluctata est. Stravit crescentes et formidolosas potentias. Consilio, opibus, magnitudine animorum eos superavit quibus nec par quidem fore nec resistere posse ullo pacto credebatur. Nuperrime vero adversus potentissimum et opulentissimum hostem ita summa vi per multos annos contendit ut omnium mentes in admirationem converteret. Eum enim ducem,[3] cuius opes atque potentiam et transalpine gentes et reliqua omnis formidabat Italia, spe elatum, victoriis exultantem omniaque miro successu quasi tempestatem quandam occupantem hec una civitas inventa est que non solum invadentem reprimeret cursumque victoriarum retardaret, verum etiam post longum bellum affligeret. Sed de rebus quidem ab hac urbe gestis paulo post erit tempus facultasque dicendi; nunc autem quod intendimus agamus.

Dico igitur omnes homines sic esse admiratos magnitudinem contentionis et diurnitatem belli, ut secum ipsi obstupescerent unde huic uni civitati tante vires, tante opes, tante ad bellum suppeditarent pecunie. Sed hec tanta admiratio, hic tantus stupor, tam diu apud homines est quam diu hanc pulcerrimam urbem non aspexerunt neque viderunt eius magnificentiam. Ceterum ubi illam intuiti sunt, omnis talis evanescit abitque admiratio. Videmus hoc quidem inter omnes constare, nec ullus Florentiam advenit qui non id sibi evenisse fateatur. Nam simul atque urbem conspicati sunt, cum occurrat oculis tanta moles rerum, tanta edificiorum collatio, tanta magnificentia, tantus splendor, cum precelsas turres, cum marmorea templa, cum basilicarum fastigia, cum superbissimas domos, cum turrita menia, cum villarum multitudinem, cum delitias, nitorem, ornatum intuentur: illico omnium mentes animique ita mutantur ut non iam de maximis atque amplissimis rebus ab hac urbe gestis obstupescant, non!

---

11 complurima *L C P A*] quam plurima *G;* complura *O.*   20 inventa *G C P A*] reperta *L;* inventa *om. O.*   26 suppeditarent *L O P*] suppeditarentur *G C A.*   38 obstupescant, non *G C A*] obstupescant *L O;* non stupescant *P.*

---

3 That is, Duke Giangaleazzo Visconti of Milan.

238

sed potius sufficientem autument ad totius orbis dominium imperiumque adipiscendum. Ex quo intelligi potest maxime admirabilem esse hanc urbem, de cuius pulcritudine ac magnificentia nemo satis digne vel concipere animo vel enarrare verbis potest. Sed tantum audita a visu superantur, quantum ab auditis vincebatur opinio. 5

Equidem nescio quid ceteri existiment, sed michi ita perurgens videri solet eiusmodi argumentum ut vel hoc uno abunde putem huiusce urbis incredibilem quandam prestantiam confirmari posse. Neque enim illa tanta et tam communis admiratio ita facile, visa urbe, ex animo deleri et extirpari posset, nisi esset in ipsa urbe vis 10 quedam maior ingenuitatis atque decoris, que illum animi stuporem pre magnitudine rerum gestarum conceptum non attenuaret modo, verum etiam obrueret. Velut enim si quis michi narret inaudita quedam et incredibilia virium facinora a pugile quodam in certaminibus edita; si alios pugno contritos, alios cestu prostratos ab eo predi- 15 cet; si multos ab uno victos ac precipites datos, si citatas quadrigas stetisse aut vivum taurum per stadium tulisse (quod Milo Crotoniates fecisse dicitur) aut, cum in uncto staret clipeo, nullius vi depelli potuisse (quod a Polidamante factum legimus); et deinde michi super his rebus obstupescenti addat hec quidem audita incredibilia 20 videri, ceterum si quis hominem videat contempleturque corporis robur, fore ut non amplius quisquam admiretur, sed et hec que narrata sunt et maiora etiam eum facere posse confidat; hec, inquam, si quis michi narret affirmetque, continuo michi fortissimi viri imago succurrat necesse est que generosam quandam habitudinem corporis 25 et membrorum letitiam roburque ostentet: sic, cum hec prestantissima et ornatissima urbs omnem admirationem de se conceptam, simul atque visa est, continuo expellat in contrariumque mentes hominum reformet, necesse est infinitam quandam vim magnificentie, ornamentorum opulentieque in se habere. Quid enim aliud dici 30 potest in tam manifesta mutatione mentis, sententiarum, opinionum, quam esse tantam huius urbis amplitudinem ac maiestatem quantam nec lingue narrantium significare poterant nec mentes audientium concipere. Nam laudant illam quidem laudabuntque semper omnes, nullus tamen inventus est ⟨cui⟩, cum eam cerneret, non multo precla- 35 rior quam audiens sibi finxerat videretur. Itaque non vereor equidem quin permulti sint qui me temeritatis audacieque condemnent, qui eiusmodi rem fuerim aggressus. Sed neque ego poteram tam inclitam urbem aspiciens non admirari neque admirans laudes eius reticere. Quod si eam non assequor, quam nulli unquam assequi valuerunt, 40 ignosci michi quam succenseri equius est. Sed iam ad rem redeamus.

---

6 perurgens *L O P A*] perurguens *G;* peringens *C.*   20 his *L O C A*] hiis *G P.*   35 cui] qui *codices.*   41 michi *G C P A*] *om. L O.*

Post villas autem castella sunt. Castella autem, imo vero nichil
est ex omni illa regione que villas cingit, que non splendidissimis
ac celeberrimis referta sit oppidis. Urbs autem media est tanquam
antistes quedam ac dominatrix; illa vero circum adstant, suo queque
5 loco constituta. Et lunam a stellis circumdari poeta recte diceret
quispiam; fitque ex eo res pulcerrima visu. Quemadmodum enim in
clipeo, circulis sese ad invicem includentibus, intimus orbis in um-
belicum desinit, qui medius est totius clipei locus: eodem hic itidem
modo videmus regiones quasi circulos quosdam ad invicem clausas
10 ac circunfusas. Quarum urbs quidem prima est, quasi umbelicus
quidam totius ambitus media. Hec autem menibus cingitur atque
suburbiis. Suburbia rursus ville circumdant, villas autem oppida;
atque hec omnis extima regio maiore ambitu circuloque complectitur. Inter oppida vero castella sunt arcesque in celum minantes et
15 agricolarum tutissima refugia.

Multitudo autem incolarum tanta est ut omnes saltus facillime
compleantur. Quid dicam de suavitate atque abundatia fructuum?
Quid de agrorum splendidissima cultura? Hec quidem omnibus nota
sunt et ante oculos exposita, nec demonstratione ulla indigent. Hoc
20 tantum dico: non facile reperiri posse agrum qui tantam multitudinem incolentium nutriat. Neque enim plereque urbes tam frequentes
habitatores habent, quam Florentinus ager. Hos tamen omnes una
cum populosissima urbe ita pascit ut non modo ad victum, sed ne ad
delitias quidem externi cuiusquam indigeat auxilii. Quamobrem urbs
25 quidem ipsa talis est, vel intra menia vel extra, ut nulla beatior sit
existimanda.

Quod si quis est qui propterea deesse aliquid huic urbi arbitretur
quod maritima non sit, is meo iudicio longissime errat et quod laudare debet id in vitium vertit. Est enim maris vicinia vendendis com-
30 parandisque rebus forsitan utilis, ceterum salsa atque amara nimis.
Permulta sunt quippe incomoda quibus maritime urbes obnoxie sunt,
permulta pericula quibus subiacere habent necesse. Plato Athenien-
sis, omnium philosophorum longissime princeps, cum civitatem que
bene ac beate viveret in suis libris institueret et que adesse queve
35 abesse oporteret diligentissime perquireret, in primis quidem illud
censuit ut procul a mari esset remota. Nec putavit sapientissimus vir
eam urbem ullo modo beatam esse posse que aut in litore posita foret
aut maris fluctibus esset propinqua. Narrat multas clades, multa ad
beate vivendum impedimenta que maris porrigit affertque vicinia.[4]

1–3 *sententia forse obscura, sed talis in G L et omnibus aliis codicibus consultatis.*   6 enim]
om. L O.   8 desinit] desinit *P A;* desinit (s *in rasura*) *L;* definit *G C O.*   13 extima]
extrema *L O.*   22 omnes *L O P A*] omnis *G C.*

---

[4] Bruni, therefore, must have known Plato's *Leges,* 704–7 (the beginning of lib. IV).

The Text

Et profecto si recte considerare volumus, pergrave quiddam est urbem
eo in loco esse positam, ut a Tanay atque Tribisonda Gades adusque
sit pertimescendum; ubi non solum quid vicine agant gentes, quid
finitimi populi consilii capiant, quid moliantur, quemadmodum erga
nos fuerint animati perscrutari sat est et eorum vel latentes insidias   5
vel apertos impetus cavere, sed Egiptii, Phenices, Colchi, Scyte,
Mauri, Gaditani, barbare et maxime inter se disiuncte nationes, sunt
formidande. Atqui finitimarum gentium consilia nonnunquam fal-
unt: quid facient igitur longinquarum? Terrestres impetus, qui tar-
diores esse solent, nonnunquam prius assunt quam quicquam tale   10
potuerit presentiri: quid igitur a celeritate classium est expectandum?
Non enim si hec in presenti non fiunt, ideo sperare possumus aliquando non fore; et fuisse olim certissime scimus. Est autem perstultum,
cum secure tranquilleque possis degere, te ipsum sponte periculis
obiectare.   15
Quodsi rationes minime istos movent qui fluctus ac litora tantopere
amant, atne antiquitatis etiam commovebunt exempla? Lege Latinas,
lege Grecas historias, et in his animadverte quam multi sint casus,
quam crebra excidia urbium maritimarum, quam multe civitates,
cum florerent opibus, viris, pecuniis, a classe hostium prius fuerint   20
capte quam quicquam tale potuerint suspicari. Hec si illi reputabunt,
iam incipient credere nichil huic urbi deesse quod maritima non sit,
sed contra, ut cetera omnia, ita et hoc summa providentia factum.
Troya, nobilissimum totius *Asie culmen* et *celitum* (ut inquit ille)[5]
egregius labor, bis classe capta et diruta est; primo Herculis et Tela-   25
monis repentino adventu, secundo Agamenonis et Ulixis fraude.
Capi florentissima civitas nullo modo poterat, nisi vicinum mare
prebuisset facultatem. Decennium terrestribus preliis frustra erat
consumptum. Ad classem denique atque undas decursum est, aptis-
simam ad insidias tendendas materiam; et cum cives se diuturna   30
obsidione liberatos arbitrarentur, cum nichil hostile usquam appareret, nichil suspicarentur, *ast Argiva falanx instructis navibus ibat a
Tenedo tacite per amica silentia lune.*[6] Et paulo post: *Alii rapiunt incensa*

2 Tanay G] Tanai L C O; athanai P; Athanay A. Tribisonda G C P A] Tribusunda O;
Trapezonda L.   6 Egiptii G L C P A] Egyptii O. Phenices G O] Phoenices C; Fenices
L P; phenices A. Scyte G] Scite P; Scythe L O; Sythe C; Scite A.   10 quicquam L C
O P A] quidquam G.   16 tantopere G C O P A] tanto opere L.   18 his L C O A] hiis
G P.   21 potuerint G C P A] potuerit L O.   24 Troya G P A] Troia *ex* Troya *corr.*
L; Troia O C.   25 et G] ac L C O P A. diruta] diructa G; diruta O A; dirupta C P;
direpta (e *in rasura*) L.   25/26 Telamonis G] Thelamonis L C O P A.   32 ast] at (a
in rasura duarum litterarum) L; at G C O; ast P A.

5 Seneca, *Troades*, 7–8.
6 Virgil, *Aeneid*, II 254–55. (The correct beginning of the passage is neither *ast* nor *at*,
but *et etiam*.)

241

feruntque Pergama; vos celsis nunc primum a navibus itis?[7] Hec sunt maris premia! hec laudanda propinquitas! Sed quid ego tam longinqua commemoro? Genuam, nobilissimam Italie urbem, secundo bello Punico a Magone, Hamilcaris filio, ex improviso captam et ad solum dirutam legimus. Quid Phocensium eversionem commemorem, quid Syracusarum, quid Alexandrie, quid Athenarum? Quid, populo Romano maxime florente et orbi terrarum imperante, nonne ita per multos annos a predatoriis classibus infestatum est mare ut complures populi Romani urbes extremam cladem paterentur? Nec is populus, qui totum subegerat orbem, a classium incursionibus maritimas urbes valuit illesas prestare. Adde crassitatem aeris, adde inconstantiam celi, adde pallentes morbos, id est insalubritatem litoree plage et totius maritime confinitatis inclementiam. In his tot tantisque adversis rebus minime mirandum est si prudentissima urbs effugit portum, ut se tranquillitatis conferret in portum, et maris fluctibus maluit carere quam tot tantisque fluctibus subiacere.

Quid autem si ne portu quidem caret? Quamquam vereor quomodo hoc quis sit accepturus, sed tamen dicam quod sentio. Ut enim cetera omnia, ita et hoc summa providentia optimoque consilio factum ab hac urbe videtur. Nam cum a litore tantum remota sit ut omnium illarum calamitatum quas maris propinquitas affert omnino sit expers, ita tamen portubus vicina est ut nulla maris utilitate privetur. Itaque in his dumtaxat rebus a maritimis urbibus Florentia superatur in quibus vinci victoria est. Illis enim portus ac litora non nullam sane prebent utilitatem, sed tamen eam ipsam multis implicitam calamitatibus multisque permixtam molestiis; Florentia vero ita propinquo fruitur mari ut puram ex illo capiat utilitatem, nullis adversis rebus perturbatam nullisque calamitatibus imminutam. Nichil ex hac comoditate pestilens celum, nichil crassus atque impurus aer, nichil undarum humiditas, nichil autumnales perturbant ac detrahunt morbi; sed tota illa quantumcunque est pura ac minime periculosa minimeque infecta utilitas est.

Michi vero solet videri illa etiam de causa ab infero mari Florentia recessisse, ut superi quoque maris opportunitatem haberet, quod quidem consilium satis laudari non potest. Nam si in alterutro litore constitisset, preterquam quod multis variisque molestiis propter maris adherentiam premeretur, illud etiam accederet incomodum

---

3 Genuam *G C L O*] Januam *P A*.   6 Syracusarum *L O P A*] Siracusarum *G C*.   7 Athenarum *L C O P A*] Hactenarum *G*.   18 quidem caret *C A*] quidem caret (caret *ex* carere *corr. esse videtur*) *L;* caret *G P;* quidem carere *O*.   19 hoc *L C O P A*] hec *G*.   30 atque impurus *G C A* (atque improprius *P*)] et impurus *L* (tam crassus quam impurus *O*).

---

[7] *Aeneid*, II 374–75.

quod nimis ab altero esset remota; ex quo illud fieret, ut in duobus extremis eodem tempore peccaret, vel longinquitate nimia vel propinquitate. Nunc autem sic ab utroque litore remota est ut non altero ipsorum videatur fuisse contenta, sed utrunque simul in suos usus convertere voluisse. Sedet enim media inter Tyrenum et Adriaticum 5 mare quasi regina quedam Italie, purissimo ac saluberrimo celo constituta nec planitiei nec montis expers. Hinc apricissimi campi, illinc letissimi insurgunt colles. Amnis vero per media fluens menia, cum maximo est ornamento, tum multo maiori utilitati. In ipsa vero urbe mirande lautitie, incomparabilis nitor, stupendi ornatus, sum- 10 ma omnium rerum magnificentia est; villarum autem immense inauditeque delitie, amenitas vero plus quam terrena, omnia plena letitie, plena suavitatis, plena decoris. His tot tantisque bonis ornamentisque referta, non solum Italie sed omnium provinciarum urbes longissime antecellit. 15

Verum me pulcerrimarum rerum affluentia, et dives ac semper sponte sua se offerens ad dicendum materia, impetu quodam et violentia huc usque me rapuit, nec ullam consistendi prebuit facultatem. Et forsitan parum diserte facere visus sum, qui de ornamentis huius urbis disserens ea que sunt prima ac maxima ornamenta pretermise- 20 rim. In cetero enim splendore ac magnificentia huius inclite urbis referenda occupatus, quasi oblitus mei, de multitudine populi, de virorum copia, de virtute, industria, humanitate civium dicere effugerat, que maxima quidem ornamenta sunt in primisque memoranda. Redeundum est igitur unde exieram, et his, qui hanc incolunt 25 urbem, partes suas reddendum. Quin potius quod errore factum est id nos ad oratoriam reducamus; et aliquando nos ipsos colligamus, despiciamusque de quibus rebus iam dictum est de quibusve deinceps simus dicturi, ne diutius in hoc errore versemur.

[II] 30

[*Quibus parentibus populus Florentinus ortus est*]

Qualis igitur urbs ipsa sit, demonstratum est. Nunc, cuiusmodi habitatores eius sint, consideremus. Volumus igitur, ut in privatis hominibus fieri solet, ita et hunc populum ab initio inspicere, et quibus parentibus ortus sit, queve eius per omnem etatem fuerint 35 opera domi forisque, considerare. *Sic opinor; a principio* (ut inquit Cicero)[8] *ordiamur.*

Unde igitur huic populo genus est? qui fuerunt eius parentes? a

---

5 Tyrenum *G C P*] Tyrrenum *L;* Tirrenum *O;* tyrenum *A.*   15 antecellit *G C P A*] antecedit *L O.*

---

[8] Cicero, *In M. Antonium Oratio Philippica II,* 44.

quibus mortalibus hec inclita urbs fundata est? Cognoscite, viri
Florentini, cognoscite stirpem ac prosapiam vestram! reputate quam
omnium gentium sitis clarissimi! Ceteri enim populi aut profugos aut
extorres patriis sedibus aut agrestes aut convenas obscuros atque
5   incertos habent auctores. Vobis autem populus Romanus, orbis
terrarum victor dominusque, est auctor. O deus immortalis, tantane
in hanc unam urbem bona contulisse, ut omnia que ubique sunt
queve optare fas est ad eius ornamenta convenisse videantur!
Nam quanti hoc primum est: ut a populo Romano Florentinorum
10   genus sit ortum! Que gens in toto orbe clarior, que potentior, que
omni genere virtutis prestantior populo Romano unquam fuit? Res
geste cuius adeo illustres sunt ut maxima ceterorum hominum facta
pre illorum magnitudine pueriles ludi videantur; cuius imperium,
terris adequatum, ita summa ratione per multa secula gubernatum
15   est ut plura ex illa una urbe extent virtutis exempla, quam omnes
cetere res publice omni tempore ediderint; in qua innumerabiles viri
ita eximia virtute extiterunt, ut nulli unquam in terris fuerint pares.
Nam ut ceteros omittam summos ac prestantissimos duces et senati
principes, ubi tu gentium Publicolas, ubi Fabritios, ubi Corrunca-
20   nos, ubi Dentatos, ubi Fabios, ubi Decios, ubi Camillos, ubi Paulos,
Marcellos, Scipiones, Catones, Gracchos, Torquatos, Cicerones
extra urbem Romanam invenies? Atqui si nobilitatem in auctore
queris, nichil in toto orbe terrarum nobilius populo Romano poteris
invenire; si divitias, nichil opulentius; si amplitudinem ac magnifi-
25   centiam, nichil omnino clarius neque gloriosius; si magnitudinem
imperii, nichil intra Occeanum est quod non armis subactum in eius
fuerit potestate. Quamobrem ad vos quoque, viri Florentini, dominium orbis terrarum iure quodam hereditario ceu paternarum rerum
possessio pertinet. Ex quo etiam illud fit, ut omnia bella que a populo
30   Florentino geruntur iustissima sint, nec possit hic populus in gerendis bellis iustitia carere, cum omnia bella pro suarum rerum vel de-
fensione vel recuperatione gerat necesse est, que duo bellorum genera
omnes leges omniaque iura permittunt. Quod si parentum gloria,
nobilitas, virtus, amplitudo, magnificentia filios quoque illustrat,
35   nichil est in toto orbe quod Florentinorum dignitati possit preferri,
quandoquidem ex huiusmodi parentibus nati sunt qui omni genere
laudis cunctos mortales longissime antecellunt. Quis enim est hominum qui se a populo Romano non fateatur servatum? Quis autem
servus vel libertus cum domini vel patroni liberis de dignitate con-
40   tendat, aut se preferendum censeat? Non parum igitur ornamenti

---

19 tu *L O*] tum *G A; om. C;* nam *P.*   19/20 Corruncanos *L*] Coruncanos *G;* ubi Corruncanos, ubi Dentatos, ubi Fabios *om. A.*   21 Gracchos *L O P*] Graccos *G A;* Gra-
chos *C.*   37 enim est *G C P A*] est enim *L O.*

est huic urbi, tam claros ipsius ac sue gentis conditores auctoresque
habuisse.

At quo in tempore Florentinorum gens a Romanis est orta? Hoc
enim plurimum arbitror referre, quod et in regiis successoribus ob-
servari aiunt ut is tandem regis filius recte appelletur qui eo tempore   5
natus sit quo eius parens regiam habuerit dignitatem; qui autem vel
ante vel postea nati sunt, eos neque regis filios esse nec in regno pa-
terno successionem habere. Et profecto, ut quisque maxime floret
maximeque sublimis est, ita maxime preclara opera maximeque
egregia molitur. Videntur enim ipse secunde res nescio quo pacto   10
animos tollere ingentesque spiritus adhibere, ut nichil nisi altum
atque magnificum amplissimi viri queant moliri, et que eo tempore
fiant ea maxime prestare contingat.

Hec igitur splendidissima Romanorum colonia eo maxime tempore
deducta est quo populi Romani imperium maxime florebat, quo po-   15
tentissimi reges et bellicosissime gentes armis ac virtute domite
erant: Carthago, Numantia, Corinthus a stirpe interierant; omnes
terre mariaque omnia in potestatem eius populi venerant; nichil
calamitatis populo Romano ab ullis hostibus inflictum erat. Nondum
Cesares, Antonii, Tiberii, Nerones, pestes atque exitia rei publice,   20
libertatem sustulerant. Sed vigebat sancta et inconcussa libertas,
que tamen non multo post hanc coloniam deductam a sceleratissimis
latronibus sublata est. Ex quo illud evenire arbitror, quod in hac
civitate egregie preter ceteras et fuisse et esse videmus: ut Florentini
homines maxime omnium libertate gaudeant et tyrannorum valde   25
sint inimici. Tantum, ut opinor, odii adversus invasores imperii et
rei publice eversores iam ex illo tempore Florentia concepit ut nec
hodie quidem videatur oblita, sed si quod illorum vel nomen vel
vestigium adhuc superest id hec res publica dedignatur et odit.

Non sunt nova in Florentino populo hec partium studia, nec nuper,   30
ut quidem arbitrantur, incepit: altius hec concertatio suscepta est.
Cum nefarii homines, per summum scelus rem publicam adorti, populi Romani libertatem, splendorem dignitatemque sustulere, tunc
hoc ardore incensi, tunc hec concertatio atque hec partium studia a
Florentinis suscepta, quas ad hanc diem constantissime retinet. Nec   35
si alio atque alio nomine diversis temporibus he partes appellate sunt,
ideo tamen diverse fuere. Sed una fuit semper atque eadem causa
contra invasores imperii, ab initio suscepta et usque ad hec tempora
constantissime conservata. Iustum, me hercule, odium et antique

3 est orta *G C*] orta est *L O;* sit orta *P A*.   4 successoribus *G C*] successionibus *L O P A*.
17 Carthago *L O P*] Cartago *G C A*.   26 ut opinor *G C P A*] opinor *L O*.   34 hoc
G C P A] eo *ex* ego *corr. esse videtur L;* ergo *O.* tunc hec *G C P A*] hec *om. L O (in O signo
affixo fortasse corruptionem indicante).*   35 quas *G L O C*] que *P A*.   36 hee *G (aut* hec
G?) C P A] he *L O*.

patrie plus quam debita pietas! Quis enim ferat Romanorum imperium, tanta virtute partum, quanta Camillus, Publicola, Fabritius,
Curius, Fabius, Regulus, Scipiones, Marcellus, Catones aliique innumerabiles sanctissimi et continentissimi viri prestitere, id in C.
5 Caligule aut eiusmodi immanium ac scelestium tyrannorum manus
nutumque pervenisse, quibus nulla virtus, nulla a vitiis redemptio.
Unum dumtaxat, et id quidem summum, erat illis certamen, quo
totis viribus inter se contendebant.

Ita enim in trucidandis civibus Romanis omni crudelitatis genere
10 intenti erant, quasi summum premium fuisset expositum si in ea urbe
nullam nobilitatem, nullum ingenium, nullum omnino civem reli-
quissent. Itaque C. Caligula, cum tantam fecisset stragem, quantam
potuisset maximam, innumeri tamen cives ut in magna urbe superes-
sent, fessus iam necando ac trucidando, cum satiare crudelitatem
15 animi nullo modo posset, nefariam illam emisit vocem que testis
esset suae immanitatis: O utinam, inquit, populus Romanus unam
cervicem haberet, quam uno ictu possem avellere! Et plane ita fecit.
Nunquam enim sanguine civium satiatus est, vacue fecissetque omnino urbem si paulo longior ei vita fuisset. Adactus est gladius per
20 senatorium ordinem, trucidati clarissimi atque optimi cives consu-
lares et triumphales, familie funditus delete, plebs duntaxat in urbe
relicta, quam tamen quotidianis cedibus veluti pecora turmatim
concidebat. Huic immanissime crudelitati immaniora etiam flagitia
adiungebat, non vulgaria illa quidem neque usitata, sed omni seculo
25 inaudita et nunquam sine detestatione memoranda. Tres ab illo
sorores per ordinem stuprate et pro concubinis palam habite. Hicine
imperatores, hi preclari Cesares, quos non nulli homines laudandos
putant! Que flagitia sunt hec, que monstra hominum! Pro quibus
quidem rebus quis mirabitur si hec civitas tantum odii adversus eas
30 partes concepit ut etiam ad hec tempora conservet?

Nam que indignatio unquam iustior? Aut quem magis tangebat
iste dolor quam Florentinum populum? cum cerneret populum Romanum, parentem atque auctorem suum, qui paulo ante omnibus
terris summa virtute domitis imperabat, tunc adempta libertate
35 propria a facinorosissimis hominibus crudelissime lacerari, qui, si
res publica valeret, in ultima fece civitatis fuissent. Quid autem
Tiberius Cesar? quamquam is ante Caligulam regnavit. Sed minime
per ordinem referendi sunt in quibus neque ordo neque ratio ulla fuit.
Quid enim tetrius, quid flagitiosius usquam visum aut auditum est
40 quam aut Tiberii crudelitates in torquendis ac necandis civibus Romanis apud Capream expresse, aut eiusdem imperatoris pisciculi

---

14 ac *G C P A*] atque *L O*. trucidando *G C P A*] detrucidando *L O*.   26 hicine *ex* hiccine *L;* hicine *O A*] hiccine *G C P*.   31 unquam *G C P A*] *om. L O*.

atque spintrie, nefanda et inaudita libidinum genera, ut michi quidem pudor Italie videatur talia flagitiorum exempla aliquando in ea extitisse. At si hi teterrimi et pernitiosi, tamen qui postea secuti sunt meliores fuere. Quinam isti? Nero scilicet et Vitellius et Domitianus et Heliogabalus? Ita profecto. Neque enim dictu facile est 5
quante virtutis quanteve humanitatis fuerit Nero. Agrippina mater pietatem filii miris laudibus in celum tollit, nec qui tanta pietate in matrem fuerit in alios fuisse impius aut inhumanus putandus est; qui etiam, ne cives frigore lederentur, misericordia ductus urbem ipsam incendit. 10
O Cai Cesar, quam plane tua facinora Romanam urbem evertere! Sed comprimam ipse me. Sunt enim qui Lucanum, doctissimum et sapientissimum hominem, vera de te scripsisse permoleste ferant. Nec fortasse carent ratione: etsi enim multa ac magna in te vitia erant, multis tamen ac magnis virtutibus obumbrabantur. Quam- 15
obrem de te silere tutius erit. Et simul filium tuum eadem illa ratione preteribo; quamquam non ignoramus, cuius tu rei gratia ut illum adoptares allectus es. Sed totum pretereo, neque eius laxam crudelitatem nec proscriptiones cedesque innocentium civium neque proditionem senatus neque adulteria stupraque eius memorabo. Fuerunt 20
enim in illo, ut in patre quoque fuerant, vestigia quedam virtutum que vitia quoque tolerabiliora faciebant. At hec monstra, quibus imperium tradidistis, nulla virtute redempta erant a vitiis, nisi forte virtus est omni conatu rem publicam delere nec ullo flagitio quantumvis maximo abstinere. Quare etsi cetera vestra obliviscar, illud 25
tamen neque oblivisci neque ut vobis non succenseam adduci possum, quod viam tantis malis tantisque sceleribus patefecistis, quanta successores vestri omni genere impietatis nequitieque ediderunt.

Sed quorsum hec? dicet fortasse quispiam. Utriusque videlicet gratia: primum, ut ostenderem non iniuste hanc civitatem eiusmodi 30
partes suscepisse; et simul intelligeretur eo tempore hanc coloniam deductam fuisse quo urbs Romana potentia, libertate, ingeniis, clarissimis civibus maxime florebat. Nam posteaquam res publica in unius potestatem deducta est, preclara illa ingenia (ut inquit Cornelius)[9] abiere: ut plurimum intersit tunc an inferiori tempore colonia 35
hec fuerit deducta, cum ita iam omnis virtus ac nobilitas Romane

---

11 Cai *L C O*] Gai *G; C P A*.   18 laxam *L O*] lassam *G*; lapsam *C P A*.   19 civium *G C P A*] *om. L O*.   27 tantisque sceleribus *G C P A*] sceleribusque *L;* sceleribus *O*.   32 Romana *G L C*] Roma *O P A*.

---

9 Tacitus, *Historiae*, I 1. For the importance of this dictum of Tacitus, which had been discovered not long before the composition of the *Laudatio*, to Bruni and to contemporary humanists, cf. *Crisis*, rev. ed., pp. 58 ff.

urbis extirpata erat ut nichil preclarum neque egregium qui ex ea migrabant secum possent efferre.

Nunc vero, cum Florentia eiusmodi habeat auctores, quibus omnia que ubique sunt virtute atque armis domita paruerint, et cum eo tempore deducta sit quo populus Romanus liber atque incolumis potentia, nobilitate, virtute, ingeniis maxime florebat, a nullo profecto dubitari potest, quin hec una urbs non solum pulcritudine et ornatu et opportunitate loci, ut videmus, sed etiam dignitate et nobilitate generis plurimum prestet.

Sed iam ad reliqua pergamus.

[III]

[*Quibus artibus Florentia de principatu in Italia certavit.—De virtute urbis qualis foris fuit*]

Ab his igitur parentibus orta, civitas non secordia atque ignavia se corrumpi passa est, nec paterna vel avita gloria contenta molliter tranquilleque vitam agere decrevit, sed, quanto clariori loco nata esset, tanto maiora a se exigi ac postulari putans, ita auctores suos omni genere virtutis imitata est ut omnium iudicio haud indignam se prestiterit tanto nomine tantaque successione.

Neque enim prius certare destitit, quam se antistitem quandam Italie prestitit. Eamque amplitudinem atque gloriam adepta est non sedendo atque oscitando, nec rursus sceleribus accincta et fraudibus, sed magnitudine consilii, susceptione periculorum, fide, integritate, continentia maximeque tenuiorum causa patrocinioque suscepto. Neque enim divitiis solum prestare studuit, sed multo magis industria atque magnificentia; nec potentia tantum superare pulcrum duxit, quantum iustitia atque humanitate. His illa artibus de principatu certavit, his auctoritatem gloriamque nacta est. Quibus nisi uteretur, se plane a maiorum suorum virtutibus degenerare intelligebat, nec sibi nobilitatem parentum plus honori esse quam oneri, sapienter id quidem ac verissime cogitans. Nam dignitas et amplitudo maiorum ita demum filios quoque illustrat, cum illi sua quoque nitent virtute. Enimvero si ignavi sint vel dissoluti vel alio modo a virtute degeneres, maiorum splendor non tam vitia eorum tegit, quam detegit. Nichil enim sinit esse occultum paterne glorie lumen, convertitque omnium oculos expectatio et quasi repetitio hereditarie virtutis; que spes si fallat, ob claritatem quidem generis non tam nobiles illi fiunt quam noti. Sed quemadmodum maiorum amplitudo minime eis prodest qui degeneres sunt, sic, cum generosos succes-

---

14 secordia *G C*] socordia *C O P;* secordia *ex* socordia *corr. A.* 24 patrocinioque *G O P A*] patrocinioque *ex* patrocinio *corr. L;* patrocinio *C.* 26 atque *G C P A*] quam *L O.* 30 esse *G P A*] fore *L; om. C O.*

sorum animos nacta est, quasi multiplicato lumine vehementer illustrat. Augetur enim dignitas et gratia, tollunturque in celum homines cum in uno eodemque loco et propria virtus et maiorum nobilitas conglutinata perpenditur. Quod quidem videmus huic civitati contingere, cuius et clarissime res geste et permulta ac maxima   5
virtutis extant exempla, in quibus Romana illa virtus et magnitudo animi perfacile recognoscitur. Quare cum ob generis claritatem prestantiamque decoratur, tum multo magis ob proprias virtutes propriasque res gestas.

Sed de generis quidem claritate satis, ut opinor, dictum est, quan-   10
quam id latius per se ipsum patet. De virtute autem urbis, id est, qualis ipsa foris domique fuerit, restabat dicendum; quod faciam equidem brevissime. Neque enim historiarum descriptionem presens oratio patitur. Loca igitur tantum perstringam.

Sed antequam ad rem veniam, optimum simul ac necessarium mihi   15
visum est aliquid prefari ac premonere, ne quis falsa opinione ductus me aut impudentie aut inscitie condemnet, quorum alterum stultitie crimen est, alterum levitatis, utrunque vero pariter fugiendum. Non dubito igitur quin non nullis stultis hominibus suspectus sim, ne gratiam quandam popularem ex hac mea laudatione captare velim et,   20
dum benivolentiam inire cupio et mentes hominum quam maxime conciliare michi studeo, terminos veritatis longe sim pretergressus falsaque cum veris ornandi causa miscuerim. Qui mihi docendi sunt, vel potius dedocendi, ut hec putare desinant et omnem eiusmodi suspitionem deponant. Ego enim, etsi cupio me carum acceptumque   25
omnibus esse, quod quidem me plane gliscere atque optare profiteor, non tamen unquam adductus sum ut blanditiis atque assentando id consequi vellem. Virtute equidem semper putavi carum esse oportere, non vitiis; nec ex hac laudatione gratiam ullam expecto neque expostulo. Perstultus quippe essem, si ex hac tantula re numerosissimi   30
populi gratiam comparare mihi posse existimarem. Sed ego, cum hanc pulcerrimam urbem viderem, cum eius prestantiam, ornatum, nobilitatem, delitias, gloriam magnopere admirarer, tentare volui possemne dicendo tantam pulcritudinem ac magnificentiam explicare. Hec scribendi causa fuit, non benivolentie aucupatio nec captatio   35
popularis aure. Tantum autem abest ut gratie conciliande causa hoc negotium susceperim, ut semper arbitratus sim preclare mecum agi si non plus malivolentie ex hac laudatione adversus me contraheretur. Periculum enim videbatur ne omnes eos, qui hanc rem publicam florere dolent, propter eam rem haberem infensos, nec id quidem etiam   40
nunc vereri desino. Iam omnes invidi, omnes adversarii, omnes qui vexati, fracti, superati, aut ipsi aut maiores sui, ab hac civitate unquam fuerunt, omnes (inquam) huiusmodi homines hec mea laudatio michi faciet inimicos: ut valde equidem verear ne magnum onus

malivolentie michi sit subeundum. Sed proferam condicionem, quam
nemo iuste repudiare queat. Si aliquid false aut cupide aut petulanter
dixero, iure michi infesti inimicique sunto. Sin autem vera erunt que
loquar, et in his ipsis dicendis moderationem quandam servabo, ne
5   illi michi irascantur. Quid hac condicione potest dici equius? Quis
usque adeo perversus atque iniquus est ut succensendum michi putet
quod suis ac veris laudibus civitatem ornare cupio?

Ex omnibus igitur predictis intelligi potest me neque gratia ad
scribendum adductum, nec esse omnino aliquem qui michi iuste
10   queat irasci. Sed cum tam varia sint ingenia hominum, non ambigo
equidem quin permulti inveniantur apud quos rationes mee parum
roboris sint habiture. Aliis quidem enim odiosa ipsa per se ac molesta
est veritas; alii vero, sive malignitate nature sive ignoratione rerum,
nichil verum esse volunt nisi quod ipsis fuerit gratum. Hi me vanita-
15   tis insimulabunt et nichil sinceri scripsisse calumniabuntur. Quibus
ego denuntio ne astute mecum agant, neve temere ad accusandum
prosiliant, sed etiam atque etiam videant quid putent reprehenden-
dum, maximeque illud meminerint me non privatim de singulorum
civium virtute aut prestantia loqui, sed de universa re publica. Quare
20   non, si unus atque alter in hac urbe minus probatis moribus fuere, id
communiter ad calumniam civitatis referri par est, que malorum
civium facta non tam sequi quam persequi ac vindicare consuevit.

Nulla unquam civitas adeo bene morata aut instituta fuit ut malorum hominum esset omnino vacua. Sed quemadmodum recte pauco-
25   rum mentes stultam ac perversam multitudinem non liberant ab
infamia, ita perversitas ac malitia paucorum universam rem publicam
recte factorum laudibus privare non debet. Alia sunt delicta publica,
alia privata, eaque inter se plurimum distant. In privatis animus
agentis spectatur, in publicis universe civitatis voluntas. In qua
30   quidem re quid unus aut alter sentiat usque adeo non attenditur, ut
legibus ac moribus sancitum sit; quod maior pars populi fecerit, id
quidem a tota civitate factum videri. Sed in aliis quidem populis
maior pars sepe meliorem vincit; in hac autem civitate eadem semper
videtur fuisse melior que maior. Quamobrem ne me illi falso accusent,
35   neve michi privatorum hominum facta obiciant, non magis quam aut
Romanorum continentie Verrina furta, aut Atheniensium fortitudini
Chersili ignaviam. Quod si intelligere volunt quanta sit civitatis

---

4 his *G C O A*] iis *L;* hiis *P*.   7 ornare cupio *L*] ornari *G;* ornarim *C O P A*.   12 enim
G C P A] *om. L O.*   19/20 quare . . . urbe *G C P*] *om.*, *sed* neque enim si qui cives *insert.*
in margine, L; om. O; atque alter in hac urbe minus *om. A.*   31 ac *L O P A*] atque *G* et *C*.
33 maior *G C O P A*] minor *in rasura L*.   37 Chersili *G C A*] Chersili *ex* Chersilii *corr.*
esse videtur L; Chersilii *O P.* (For identification Thersites comes to mind, whose somewhat similar name appears in certain late manuscripts [cf. Th. Klette, *Beiträge zur Geschichte und Literatur der italienischen Gelehrtenrenaissance*, II (Greifswald, 1889), 96]. But
Thersites is said to have been an Aeolian, not an Athenian as is required by the context.)

The Text

huius prestantia, nec a me sine ratione tot verbis laudari, perscrutentur orbem terrarum et quamlibet ex eo eligant urbem, quam cum hac
nostra in comparationem adducant non splendoris atque ornatus (qua
in re nulla sibi in toto orbe est par) neque nobilitatis (qua in re cetere
omnes sine controversia cedunt), sed rerum gestarum atque virtutis. 5
Hoc si illi facient, iam intelligere incipient, quantum inter hanc urbem ceterasque intersit. Nullam enim invenient que in omni genere
laudis huic nostre respondere queat.

In *omni* dixi; propius accedam. Si quam inveniunt urbem que in uno
aliquo genere virtutis opinione hominum putetur excellere, in illo 10
ipso in quo prestare dicitur periculum faciant. Nulla invenietur que
vel in ipso suo genere huic non succumbat. Neque poterit ulla prorsus
in ullo genere laudis inveniri par, non fide, non industria, non humanitate, non magnitudine animorum. Adducant in certamen quam
velint urbem: nullius congressum Florentia reformidat. Per univer- 15
sum orbem querant civitatem que in una aliqua specie virtutis gloriam maximam putetur consecuta. Fiat contentio egregiorum facino-
rum vel in eo ipso in quo videatur excellere: nullam profecto reperire
quibunt, nisi ipsi plane se velint decipere, cui hec civitas non sit longe
superior. Est enim admiranda huius urbis virtus, et in omni genere 20
laudis invictum exemplar.

Nam ut prudentiam pretermittam, que omnium iudicio huic uni
civitati maxima conceditur et per quam cuncta omni tempore summa
industria ab hac re publica videmus provisa, cuius unquam tanta
beneficentia audita est quantam huius civitatis et fuisse et esse con- 25
spicimus? Semper enim id quidem meditata videtur, ut prodesset
quam plurimis omnesque sentirent eius liberalitatem, maxime autem
hi qui maxime indigerent. Itaque omnes qui aut seditionibus pulsi
aut invidia deturbati patriis sedibus extorres aguntur, ii se Florentiam universi recipiunt quasi in unicum refugium tutamenque cunc- 30
torum. Nec ullus est iam in universa Italia qui non duplicem patriam
se habere arbitretur: privatim propriam unusquisque suam, publice
autem Florentinam urbem. Ex quo quidem fit ut hec communis quedam sit patria et totius Italie certissimum asilum, ad quod omnes
undique, cum sit opus, confugiunt recipiunturque cum summo inco- 35
lentium favore summaque benignitate. Tantum enim studium beneficentie et humanitatis in hac re publica est, ut clara voce clamare
videatur et palam omnibus attestari, ne quisquam patria se carere
putet donec Florentinorum supersit urbs. Hoc benignitatis preconium
facta etiam maiora quam professio sequuntur. Neque enim solum 40

25 est *G C P A*] est *ex verbo longiore corr. L O.*   33 Florentinam *G C P A*] Florentinam
fortasse ex Florentiam *corr. L;* Florentiam *O.*

leta fronte recipiuntur, verum etiam, si non penitus indigni videantur, opibus pecuniisque adiuvantur, quibus illi freti vel manere cum dignitate, si ita malint, vel reditum sibi ad proprios penates recuperare possint. An hec vera non sunt? an quisquam malivolorum negare audebit? At sunt huius rei testes infiniti pene mortales qui, cum rei familiaris angustiis premerentur, cum iniuste suis urbibus essent eiecti, pecuniis publicis adiuti sunt et beneficio huius urbis in patrias sedes restituti.

Testes sunt etiam permulte civitates que, cum vicinorum conspiratione aut tyrannorum violentia opprimerentur, consilio, opibus, pecuniis, sustentate sunt et difficillimo tempore conservate. Mitto federa inter discordes populos ab hac urbe coniuncta; mitto legationes ad conciliandos animos, ubicunque ira efferbuit, demissas, qua quidem in re hec civitas suam promptissime semper interposuit auctoritatem. Potest igitur que hec tot tantaque pro alienis comodis susceperit non beneficentissima appellari? aut satis digne pro tanta virtute meritisque laudari? Nunquam enim tulit iniurias aliarum urbium, neque otiosam spectatricem se prebuit aliene calamitatis. Sed primum omni studio conata est verbis et auctoritate rem componere inimicitiasque sedare et pacem, si fieri posset, suadere. Quod si convenire non potuit, ei semper parti opitulata est cui a potentioribus inferebatur iniuria. Sic enim imbecilles omni tempore defendit, quasi ad curam suam pertinere existimaret ne quis Italie populus excidium pateretur. Itaque non otii cupiditate nec formidine ulla potuit unquam adduci ut ad eas quibus aliqua respublica lacesseretur iniurias conniveret; nec putavit se in tranquillitate aut otio esse oportere, cum aliqua urbs aut socia aut amica aut saltem non inimica laboraret. Sed continuo exurgens et causas aliarum suscipiens mediam se adversus impetum opposuit, protexitque eos qui perditum iri videbantur, copiis, opibus pecuniisque adiuvit.

Quis igitur hanc pro tanta beneficentia ac liberalitate satis abunde unquam laudabit? Aut que civitas est in toto orbe, que in hoc genere laudis possit conferri? que tot pecunias absumpserit? tantos labores pro alienis comodis susceperit? tam multos in periculis protexerit? Atqui que civitas in periculis alios tutatur, eam fateantur patronam necesse est. Que autem patrona sit, dignitate, potentia, industria, auctoritate precellere quis negabit?

Huic beneficentie ac liberalitati admirabilis fides coniuncta est, quam semper hec res publica summa constantia inviolatam servavit.

15 que hec *G O*] hec que *L P A;* que *C.*   20 inimicitiasque sedare *G C A*] inimicitias
sedare *L O;* inimicitias . . . sedare *om. P.*   28 exurgens *G L C A*] exsurgens *ex* exurgens
corr. O; exsurgens *P.*   29 perditum iri *G C*] perdituri *L O P A.*

Semper enim ita animata fuit ut putaret, antequam promitteretur, diligentissime providendum, ubi vero promissum esset, nullo modo retractandum. Quod cum a principio vidisset et ita iustum esse censuisset, ob nullam utilitatis speciem adduci unquam potuit ut pacta, conventa, federa, iusiurandum, promissa violaret. Nichil enim 5 dignitati rei publice magis convenire arbitrata est, quam in dictis factisque omnibus observare constantiam, nichil autem alienius, quam promissa mentiri; id quidem esse facinorosorum hominum, qui maxime inimici sunt rerum publicarum, de quorum numero est ille* qui ait 'iuravi lingua, mentem iniuratam gero', quod iustissima 10 civitas nunquam sibi licere putavit. Itaque in omni quidem re multa cum maturitate ad promittendum descendit; quod autem semel promisisset, id non magis a se mutari posse arbitrata est quam ea que non forent in eius potestate.

Usque autem adeo fides et integritas in hac civitate plurimum 15 valuit, ut iura etiam hostibus religiosissime servarit, nec unquam vel in hoc genere inveniatur mentita. Ex quo factum est ut ne inimici quidem unquam dubitarint huius rei publice fidem sequi, sed etiam apud eos civitatis nomen maximam semper habuerit auctoritatem. Huius autem rei manifestissimum est argumentum quod non nulli 20 homines, cum antea inimici eius manifestissime fuissent, liberos et fortunas suas in tutela huius populi esse voluerunt, secuti civitatis fidem atque humanitatem, quarum altera ad remittendum iniurias et suscipiendum munus promptissima videbatur, altera ad id quod suscepisset summa cum iustitia adimplendum. Nec spes eos fefellit. 25 Nam ita res summa cum diligentia administrate iis quibus debebantur restitute sunt, ut non solum non errasse putarentur qui fidem huius populi fuissent secuti, sed etiam ceteri homines allicerentur exemplo. Semper enim hec civitas cure habuit, ut suum cuique ius diligentissime tribueret et in omni re honestatem utilitati anteponeret, imo vero nichil utile, quod non idem honestum foret, arbitrata 30 est.

Ex multis tamen et preclaris virtutibus quibus hanc civitatem preditam invenio, nulla michi neque maior neque prestabilior videri solet, neque in qua magis Romanum genus virtusque recognoscatur, 35 quam magnitudo animorum periculorumque contemptio. Nam cuius virtutis esse potest nisi Romane, per omnem etatem bello contendisse et maxima quidem certamina maximasque dimicationes suscepisse et, quod etiam rarius atque admirabilius est, in maximis periculis

---

3 esse *G C P*] *om. L O.* et ita iustum esse censuisset *om. A.*   26 res *L O*] res eorum *G C P A.*   36 contemptio *L*] contētio *G;* contentio *C O P A.*

---

* In Euripides' *Hippolytus*, quoted in Cicero's *De officiis* III 108.

difficillimisque temporibus nunquam mente concidisse nec remisisse aliquid de magnitudine animorum. Cesar[10] iratus fuit ad portas, faces atque exitium huic urbi portendens; hunc omnis inimicorum factio, stricta, parata neci, sequebatur. Castra erant intra primum lapidem; omnia circa urbem loca ferro atque hostili clamore reboabant. Nec infestioribus signis Hannibal quondam ad Portam Collinam profectus est, quam illud tunc monstrum in Florentina menia ruebat. Accedebat ad hec, quod ea pars urbis que maxime castris erat opposita parum munita eo tempore videbatur; itaque nullus putabatur fore civis qui vel arma capere vel mente consistere valeret. At vero fortissima civitas usque adeo minas illius furoremque contempsit ut, cum ille extra urbem multos dies perbaccharetur, nusquam intra urbem sit trepidatum. Sed ita gerebantur omnia, quasi nichil pericli immineret nec ulla vis hostium esset propinqua. Omnes officine, omnia horrea per vias patebant; nulla remissio operum, nullum omnino erat iustitium. Que cum Cesari nuntiarentur, admiratus civitatis prestantiam et magnitudinem animorum, ab oppugnatione recessit.[11]

Nec solum in resistendo fortis hec civitas fuit, sed etiam in inferenda vi, hoc est in ulciscenda iniuria, formidabilis. Nam etsi nunquam alicui nocere voluit nisi prius lacessita, tamen, ubi quid iniurie inflictum est, vehementissimam pugnatricem se prestitit pro sua dignitate. Illud enim omne tempus habuit, ut incredibili quodam amore laudis glorieque flagraret. Itaque semper res maximas et vehementer arduas aggressa est, nec in illis gerendis aut periculorum magnitudinem aut laborum formidavit. Possum commemorare munitissima oppida manu capta, innumerabilia pene trophea de finitimis populis ab hac urbe constituta, egregia rei militaris facinora edita ipso populo Florentino exeunte atque armis fruente. Sed non est presentis

6 Hannibal *L O*] Anibal *G;* Hanibal *C A;* Hanybal *P.* collinam *L O P A*] capenam *G C.* 12 multos dies perbaccharetur *G C O A*] multos dies pervagaretur *P;* per multos dies perbaccharetur *L.*

---

[10] That is, Emperor Henry VII, who pitched the camp of the imperial army before the city gates of Florence in 1312.
[11] This should be compared with Bruni's later description of Henry's siege in the *Historiae Florentini Populi* (ed. Santini, p. 109) where the same motif—the continuation of ordinary conditions in the city during the siege—reappears, no longer in rhetorical magnification, however, but as a factor in an objective analysis. Two armed camps, we now learn, were facing each other for a long time, until that of the Florentines, opposing the Emperor from within the walls, thanks to its constant reinforcement by allies became too strong for the imperial army; thus protected, the larger part of the city remained in a position to carry on its daily life. ("In his [i.e., castris Florentinis] armati cives sociique perstabant; caeterae vero urbis partes sic tranquillae erant, ut ne sentire quidem obsidionem viderentur. . . . Tandem, cum frustra teri ab eo tempus appareret, et quotidie magis in urbe crescerent amicorum auxilia, . . . [imperator] retro castra movit, ac transmisso Arno, duobus passuum millibus ab urbe super Emam fluvium castra fecit.")

temporis tot varias bellorum contentiones tantasque res gestas posse
referre; proprium illa desiderant opus, et quidem magnum, quod nos,
ut spero, aliquando aggrediemur et, quo pacto singula ab hoc populo
gesta sunt, litteris memorieque mandabimus. In presentia vero unum
aut alterum exempli gratia referemus, ut ex illis intelligi possit quan-   5
ta in ceteris quoque fuerit civitatis virtus.

Vetustum est Etrurie oppidum nobileque Volterre, sed tamen ita
summis montibus positum, ut vix expediti homines eo queant adire.
Hanc urbem oppugnare Florentini aggressi sunt.[12] Virtus enim,
durissima omnia superare consueta, neque asperitatem loci neque   10
iniquitatem certaminis verebatur. Cohortes igitur ad ea loca deducte
cum montem capescere cepissent, et oppidani a summis arcibus ir-
ruissent, acerrime utrinque pugnatum est. Numerus quidem bella-
torum erat pene par, magnitudo autem animi et peritia pugnandi
dispar, sed multum natura ipsa loci pro Vulterranis pugnabat. Cer-   15
neres illos e superiore loco non solum pilis atque gladiis ascensum
prohibentes, sed etiam grandia saxa per declivia devolventes. Florentini autem per ipsas asperrimas rupes sursum versus annitebantur, nec
ferrum nec saxa nec hostes nec asperitas ulla montis contra eorum
conatum quibat resistere. Itaque superato contra vim hostium pede-   20
tentim monte, et oppidanis intra menia compulsis, ipsam quoque
urbem, que munitissima erat menibus, primo impetu ceperunt.[13]
Atque hec fecit populus Florentinus nullis extraneis auxiliis, sed ipse
militans et pro dignitate atque gloria promptissime certans.

Sed cum ceteris hoc factum preclarum videri debet, tum ii maxime   25
obstupescunt qui Volterras viderunt. Constat enim inter omnes
nullum Italie oppidum esse munitius. Tunc autem erat refertum
multis atque audacibus viris, qui pro aris atque focis acerrime pug-
nabant. Attamen maiori virtute superati sunt. Quis igitur non admiretur tam validissimam urbem una die captam? quis non virtutem   30
eorum qui ceperunt tollat in celum? Eiusmodi sunt huius civitatis res
geste, huiusmodi virtus et fortitudo eius. Hac illa magnitudine animi
sepe Senenses prostravit, sepe Pisanos delevit, sepe potentes hostes
tyrannosque contrivit.

Illud tamen preclarum est, quod magnos labores magnasque dimica-   35
tiones non tam pro sua quam pro aliorum utilitate suscepit. Hoc enim

---

2 opus *G L C O*] tempus *P A*.   15 Vulterranis *G C O*] Volterranis *P;* Volaterranis *ex*
Volterranis *altera manu corr. L;* Volateranis *A*.   32 hac illa magnitudine *G P A*] hec
illa magnitudine *C;* illa hec magnitudo *L;* hec illa magnitudo *O*.

---

[12] Anno 1254.
[13] These contentions, too, should be compared with the later objective narrative in
Bruni's *Historiae*. Cf. the confrontation of the two versions p. 154, above.

maxime convenire arbitrata est sue amplitudini sueque dignitati, si pro aliorum salute ac libertate pericula adiret multosque suo patrocinio tutaretur. Pisani, gens huic urbi male pacata, Lucenses, Florentinorum socios atque amicos, bello lacessebant.[14] Tandem vero, collatis signis cum utrique dimicassent, et in eo prelio Lucensium copie fuissent delete multique capti ducerentur, Florentini, qui forte per id tempus in agro Pistoriensi castra habebant, nuntiata amicorum clade, nequaquam mente conciderunt nec formidaverunt elatos victoria homines. Sed relicto castro quod obsidebant, rapto post victores agmine, prius illorum aciem consecuti sunt quam Pisas se recipere potuissent; illatisque in eos signis, ita victoriam illorum commutaverunt, ut Lucenses ipsi, qui captivi ducebantur, maximum Pisanorum numerum qui a cede superfuit caperent, eosque in vinculis Lucam adducerent. Ita Florentinorum virtus Lucenses servavit, Pisanorum autem victoriam repressit, sibi vero gloriam laudemque comparavit.

Sed quid magis laudet quispiam in hoc preclaro civitatis facinore? An virtutem, quod vicerunt? an magnitudinem animorum, quod victores secuti fuerunt? an beneficentiam, quod pro salute amicorum tantam contentionem subierunt? Michi quidem tria in uno eodemque facto summe laudanda videntur. Sed nequeo singula suis laudibus prosequi; nam et vereor ne longior sim, et maiora etiam impellunt.

Non enim privatim duntaxat huic vel illi urbi benefica fuit hec civitas, sed universe simul Italie. Angusti quidem animi putavit esse, pro suis duntaxat comodis sollicitudinem capere; contraque illud gloriosum, si suorum laborum fructus complurime sentirent atque caperent gentes. Que cum ita esset animata, pro incolumitate vicinarum urbium se pugilem prestitit, et quotiens vel finitima aliqua tyrannis vel avara potentia populis immineret, ita adversus eam se opposuit, ut cunctis mortalibus palam faceret sibi patrium esse pro libertate Italie dimicare. Neque ipsa quidem ita fuit animata, non autem perfecit, sed pie iusteque voluntati plurimus dei annuit favor. Nolo nimis antiqua referre, sed ea dicam que nostra ferme vidit etas; quanquam constare video inter omnes, non semel ab hac una urbe totam Italiam a servitutis periculo fuisse liberatam. Sed nos cetera omittamus et ea que nuperrime gesta sunt consideremus.

An quisquam tam absurdus ingenio aut tam a vero devius reperiri poterit, qui non fateatur universam Italiam in potestatem Ligustini hostis[15] perventuram fuisse, nisi hec una urbs suis viribus suoque consilio contra illius potentiam restitisset? Quis enim erat in tota

---

37 ligustini *L C O*] ligustrini *G;* ligustici *P A.*

---

[14] Anno 1252.
[15] That is, Giangaleazzo Visconti, whose empire included Liguria.

Italia, qui aut potentia aut industria cum illo hoste comparari potuisset? Aut quis eius conatum pertulisset, cuius nomen ipsum cunctis mortalibus erat terrori? Iam enim non Italiam solam, sed transalpinos quoque populos eius fama terrebat. Opibus, pecuniis virisque, sed multo magis consilio astuque valebat. Potentiam habe- 5 bat maximam atque formidandam: omnes Gallie cisalpine tractus, omnes ferme civitates que ab Alpibus ad Etruriam atque Flaminiam inter duo maria continentur, in eius potestate erant dictoque pare- bant; in Etruria vero Pisas, Senas, Perusiam, Assisium tenebat, tandem etiam Bononiam occuparat.[16] Multa preterea oppida, multi 10 potentes ac domi nobiles, seu metu seu rapinarum spe seu etiam fraude adducti, nomen fortunasque illius sequebantur. His tantis tamque amplis opibus consilia non deerant. Sed felix ille, felix inquam, nimium esse potuit, si suam industriam, vigilantiam, so- lertiam in bonis artibus exercuisset.[17] Nullo unquam in homine cal- 15 lidiora consilia neque acriora. Omnibus in locis aderat, nichil inte- grum esse sinebat, nichil intentatum relinquebat. Alios pecuniis, alios largitionibus, alios caritatis specie promissisque adsciscebat. Omnes Italie populos seminatis discordiis ad invicem collidebat, et ubi satis afflicti erant ipse sua potentia superveniens occupabat. Omnibus 20 denique locis eius artes dolique pululabant.

Sed cetere quidem res publice tantas vires intuentes perterrite erant temporibusque cedebant. Florentina autem magnitudo animi terreri non potuit, neque remittendum aliquid censuit de pristina dignitate. Sciebat enim generis esse Romani, pro libertate Italie 25 contra hostes pugnare. Sic maiores suos contra Cimbros, contra Teutones, item contra Gallos audiebat pugnavisse, neque Pirri fero- ciam aut Hannibalis fraudulentiam formidasse, nec ullos unquam labores pro tuenda dignitate atque amplitudine sua vitasse, sed in maximis periculis maximam sibi gloriam peperisse; quod sibi quoque 30 putavit faciendum, si splendorem sibi a maioribus traditum con- servare vellet. Hec populus Florentinus secum reputans, ita magno et elato animo ad bellum profectus est, ut putaret aut cum gloria vi- vendum aut pro illa ipsa oppetendum. Ita autem pulcrum duxit locum sibi a maioribus traditum tueri, ut nunquam divitias ullas pluris 35

---

7 Flaminiam *G C P A*] Flamminiam *L O.*   9 Perusiam *G L A*] Perusium *C O P.*
18 adsciscebat] adscidebat *G;* asciscebat *L C O A;* ascistebat *P.*   26 Cimbros *G O P*]
Cymbros *L C A.*   28 Hannibalis *L C O*] Hanibalis *P;* Anibalis *G;* Hannibalis *ex*
Annibalis *corr. A.*   nec *G C P A*] neque *L O.*   34 oppetendum *L O P A*] oppetien-
dum *G C.*

---

[16] Giangaleazzo occupied, or received the homage of, Pisa early in 1399, Siena during the summer, Perugia at the beginning of 1400, Assisi in May 1400, Bologna in June 1402. Cf. the discussion of this passage p. 116, above.

[17] Giangaleazzo died September 2, 1402.

fecerit quam dignitatem, sed et pecunias et vitam ipsam abicere paratus fuerit pro libertate, prudenter simul et fortissime decernens. Nam et divitie et pecunie et eiusmodi omnia victorum sunt premia; quibus in bello si quis parcit et, cum illis se tutari posset, illa mavult, 5 hostium negotium magis gerit quam suum. Sic igitur hec civitas animata cum potentissimo et opulentissimo hoste ita summa virtute congressa est, ut, qui paulo ante toti Italie imminebat nec quenquam sibi resistere posse arbitrabatur, eum et pacem optare et intra Ticini menia trepidare coegerit, et tandem non solum Etrurie ac Flaminie 10 urbes relinquere sed etiam Gallie maximam partem amittere.

O incredibilem magnificentiam virtutemque civitatis! O vere Romanum genus stirpemque Romuleam! Quis iam Florentinum nomen pro tanta mentis prestantia tantaque rerum gestarum magnitudine cum summo favore non excipiat? Nam quid potuit maius, quid pre-15 clarius hec civitas edere, aut in qua magis re maiorum suorum virtutem in se conservatam ostendere, quam universa Italia suo labore suisque facultatibus a servitutis periculo liberata? Ex quo quotidie ab omnibus quidem populis gratulationes, laudes, gratie huic urbi acte, ab hac vero urbe ad deum immortalem reiecte. Semper enim ea 20 modestia fuit ut mallet has preclaras res dei beneficio quam sue virtuti ferri acceptas. Itaque non intumuit illa in secundis rebus, nec ira victoriam comitata est, nec adversus omnes quibus iure potuit succensere excanduit, sed summam humanitatem adversus victos servavit, ut qui fortitudinem eius in bello cognoverant iidem in victoria 25 experirentur clementiam. Nam et hec una est ex summis virtutibus civitatis, ut in omni tempore retineret dignitatem; nec maiori cure fuit res magnas gerere, quam in ipsis gerendis decorem servare. Itaque neque successibus ultra modum exultavit, neque adversis rebus prostrata est. Ex modestia autem in secundis, constantia in adversis, 30 iustitia vero ac prudentia in omnibus, preclarum apud omnes mortales nomen maximamque gloriam consecuta est.

[*IV*]

[*Quare Florentia disciplina institutisque
domesticis admirabilis est*]

35 Sed cum foris hec civitas admirabilis est, tum vero disciplina institutisque domesticis. Nusquam tantus ordo rerum, nusquam tanta elegantia, nusquam tanta concinnitas. Quemadmodum enim in cordis convenientia est, ad quam, cum intense fuerint, una ex diversis

8 Ticini *G C P* (Thicini)] Ticini *in rasura novem litterarum L;* Thycini *A;* Mediolani *O.* 9 Flaminie *G C P A*] Flamminie *L O.* 21 illa *G C P A*] *om. L O.* rebus *G C O P A*] urbs *L.* 24 iidem *L O P A*] idem *G;* hidem *C.* 31 consecuta est *G C O*] est consecuta *L P A.*

tonis fit armonia, qua nichil auribus iocundius est neque suavius, eodem modo hec prudentissima civitas ita omnes sui partes moderata est ut inde summa quedam rei publice sibi ipsi consentanea resultet, que mentes atque oculos hominum sua convenientia delectet. Nichil est in ea preposterum, nichil inconveniens, nichil absurdum, nichil vagum; suum queque locum tenent, non modo certum, sed etiam congruentem: distincta officia, distincti magistratus, distincta iudicia, distincti ordines. Ita tamen hec distincta sunt ut ad summam rei publice, tanquam tribuni ad imperatorem, conveniant.

Primum igitur omni cura provisum est ut ius in civitate sanctissimum habeatur, sine quo nec civitas esse nec nominari ulla potest; deinde ut sit libertas, sine qua nunquam hic populus vivendum sibi existimavit. Ad hec duo simul coniuncta, quasi ad quoddam signum ac portum, omnia huius rei publice instituta provisaque contendunt. Et iuris quidem gratia magistratus sunt constituti, iisque imperium datum est et in facinorosos homines animadversio, maximeque ut provideant ne cuius potentia plus valeat in civitate quam leges. Magistratibus ergo privati, itemque inferioris gradus homines, parere omnes et obedire coguntur eorumque insignia vereri. Sed ne ipsi legum vindices in summa potestate constituti arbitrari possint non custodiam civium sed tyrannidem ad se esse delatam, et sic, dum alios cohercent, aliquid de summa libertate minuatur, multis cautionibus provisum est. Principio enim supremus magistratus, qui quandam vim regie potestatis habere videbatur, ea cautela temperatus est, ut non ad unum sed ad novem simul, nec ad annum sed ad bimestre tempus, deferatur. Eo enim modo preclare rem publicam administrari existimavit, cum et pluralitas sententiarum errorem consilii et brevitas temporis insolentiam auferret. Urbe igitur in regiones quatuor divisa, ne cui illarum suus unquam deesset honos, ex singulis partibus bini viri eliguntur, nec ii quidem fortuiti sed iudicio populi iam dudum approbati et tanto honore digni iudicati. His octo civibus ad gubernandam rem publicam unus vir, prestans virtute et auctoritate, ex illis iisdem partibus per vicissitudinem adicitur, qui sit in collegio princeps et pro iustitia exequenda contra turbulentos homines ferat vexillum. Hos igitur novem viros, quibus rei publice gubernacula commissa sunt, neque alibi quam in publica arce habitare voluit, quo ad rem publicam gerendam paratiores forent, neque sine lictorum pompa prodire, quo amplior ipsorum haberetur maiestas. Verum quia nonnunquam accidunt tempora ut maiore consilio opus esse videatur, additi sunt duodecim viri boni, qui cum novem prioribus rei publice consulerent. Additi preterea iuventutis signiferi, ad

15 iisque *L O A*] hiisque *G P;* hisque *C.*   31 his *L O P A*] hiis *G;* hisdem *C.*   33/34 in collegio *G C P A*] in illo collegio *L O.*

quos, cum armis pro tuenda libertate opus est, universa concurrit sequiturque multitudo. Hi et in consilio assunt, et (ut superiores magistratus) ex quadrantibus deliguntur, et quatuor menses tenent potestatem.

5 Sed neque omnium rerum decernendarum hec tria collegia habent potestatem; sed pleraque, cum ab illis approbata sunt, ad populare consilium communeque referuntur. Quod enim ad multos attinet, id non aliter quam multorum sententia decerni consentaneum iuri rationique iudicavit. Hoc modo et libertas viget et iustitia sanctis-
10 sime in civitate servatur, cum nichil ex unius aut alterius libidine contra tot hominum sententiam possit constitui.

Sed hi quidem homines rei publice consulunt, iura sanciunt, leges abrogant, equitatem decernunt. Iuri autem ex legibus dicendo gladi-oque exequendo minores presunt magistratus; nec ii quidem cives,
15 sed peregrini ad hoc ipsum ex longinquo ad civitatem vocati, non quia cives id facere nescirent (nam quotidie in alienis id factitant urbibus), sed ne iurisdictionis causa odia atque inimicitie inter cives nascerentur. Plerique enim, nimia sui caritate decepti, plus iuris sibi tribuunt quam leges patiantur. Qui, etsi recte iudicetur, adversus
20 magistratum exercent querelas. Grave preterea visum est in libera civitate civem de capite civis ferre sententiam; eum enim qui id fecisset, etiam si iustissime fecerit, pollutum tamen et abominabilem inter cives videri. Ea de causa ex longinquo accersiti iudices, iisque leges prescripte sunt, a quibus discedi nullo modo licet. Nam et
25 iurati illas suscipiunt, et magistratu abeuntes quasi institores quidam rationem administrationis sue populo reddunt. Ita in omni re populus libertasque dominatur.

Quo autem cuique facilius esset in amplissima civitate suum ius consequi, nec, dum aliis occuparentur magistratus, aliis iustitia
30 legesque deessent, data est quibusdam collegiis inter suos homines cognoscendi iudicandique potestas; veluti mercatoribus, numulariis, item quibusdam aliis, quorum non nulli etiam suorum hominum cohercendorum ius habent. Sunt item alii magistratus, aut publi-carum rationum gratia aut pietatis causa constituti; quorum in
35 numero sunt magistri vectigalium et prefecti erario, item pupil-lorum pupillariumque rerum protectores; qui magistratus publice et privatim utilis est et a beneficentissima civitate pie salubriterque excogitatus.

Sed ex omnibus magistratibus, qui multi atque amplissimi in hac
40 urbe sunt, nullus neque illustrior est neque a pulcriori initio causaque

---

5 decernendarum *G C P A*] gerendarum *L; om. O.*   6 illis *G C P A*] aliis *L O.*
14 ii *G*] hi *L C O A;* hii *P.*   16 nescirent *G C P A*] nescierint *L O.*   21 eum *G C P A*]
eum *ex* cum *corr. esse videtur L;* cum *O.* qui *G C P A*] qui *in rasura (insert. esse videtur)*
L; om. O.   32 etiam *G C P A*] *om. L O.*

profectus quam optimarum partium duces; de quorum origine non ab re forsitan erit aliquid referre, quo melius amplitudo eius possit intelligi. Erit autem brevissima digressio, nec inutilis, ut opinor, neque indigna cognitu.

Accepta enim apud Arbiam calamitate, cum propter ingens rei 5 publice vulnus nullo pacto urbs defendi posse videretur, omnes cives qui alto ac generoso erant animo, ne eos in urbe dominantes viderent qui patriam suam manifestissime prodiderant, relictis patriis laribus cum coniugibus ac liberis Lucam se contulerunt, imitati Atheniensium illud preclarum et laudatissimum factum, qui secundo Persico 10 bello urbem ipsam reliquere ut aliquando in ea liberi habitare possent. Hac igitur mente egregii cives qui a tanta clade supererant urbe egressi sunt, putantes eo modo maiorem ulciscendi facultatem habituros quam si inclusi menibus famem aut interitum urbis operirentur. Lucam itaque delati, et suis qui propter prelii fortunam dispersi 15 erant in unum convocatis, ita se armis, equis et omni apparatu belli comparavere ut universi homines eorum animi prestantiam promptitudinemque admirarentur. Post multa igitur fortitudinis opera per Italiam edita, cum sepe amicis auxilium tulissent, sepe inimice factionis homines sua virtute et audacia contrivissent, omnibus 20 denique ex locis ubi pugnaretur victoriam reportassent, tempus venisse rati quod illi maxime optabant, ut patrie notas maculasque delerent, contra Manfredum Sicilie regem (quoniam is diversarum partium princeps in Italia erat et milites suos ad Arbiam miserat) profecti sunt, secuti prestantissimum atque optimum ducem quem 25 ad comprimendam Manfredi insolentiam pontifex maximus ex Gallia accersierat. Postquam ergo in Apuliam ventum est, quantam illi virtutem singulis in locis ostenderint libentissime equidem referrem, si hic locus tantam narrationem pateretur. Ut autem brevissime dicam, tales se prestiterunt ut etiam acerbissimus hostis decorem ac 30 prestantiam eorum laudare cogeretur. Subacta igitur Apulia, hosteque trucidato, magnifice laudati donatique a rege in Etruriam revertuntur. Pulsisque ex urbe iis qui malo rei publice regnabant, itemque vicinis hostibus magnifice ultis, collegium sibi statuerunt virosque primarios prefecerunt qui essent duces optimarum partium principes- 35 que legitime incliteque conspirationis.

Ab huiusmodi initio hic magistratus profectus, plurimam in urbe habet auctoritatem. Positus est enim quasi in vigilia quadam atque custodia, ne res publica e curriculo a maioribus observato deflectat, neve ad homines diversa sentientes administratio rei publice defera- 40

---

13 eo modo maiorem *G C O P A*] eo modo se modum *in rasura L.*   26 comprimendam *G C O A*] comprimendum *L P.*   28 illi *G C P A*] illam *L O.* equidem *G C P A*] quidem *L O.*

tur. Quod igitur Rome censores, Athenis areopagite, Lacedemonie ephori, hoc sunt in Florentina civitate partium duces, id est, ex his civibus qui bene de re publica sentiunt primarii viri electi ad rem publicam tuendam.

5 Sub his igitur magistratibus ita diligens et preclara est huius urbis gubernatio ut nulla unquam domus sub frugi patre familias maiori disciplina fuerit instituta. Quamobrem nemo hic iniuriam pati potest, nec quisquam rem suam nisi volens amittit. Parata semper iudicia, parati magistratus, patet curia, patet summum tribunal. 10 Querele adversus omne genus hominum in hac civitate liberrime sunt, iura autem prudenter et salubriter constituta et semper opitulari parata. Nec est locus ullus in terris in quo ius magis equum sit omnibus. Nusquam enim viget tanta libertas et maiorum cum minoribus exequata condicio. Nam in hoc quoque cognoscere licet 15 civitatis huius prudentiam, nescio an maximam omnium civitatum. Cum enim potentiores, suis opibus confisi, tenues ledere aspernarique viderentur, causas eorum qui minus poterant ipsa res publica suscepit, maiorique pena res illorum personasque munivit. Rationi quippe consentaneum arbitrata est ut disparem condicionem hominum dis- 20 par pena sequeretur, et qui magis indigebat ei plus auxilii tribuere sue prudentie iustitieque putavit. Itaque ex diversis ordinibus facta est quedam equabilitas, cum maiores sua potentia, minores res publica, utrosque vero metus pene defendat. Ex quo nata est illa vox, quam adversus potentiores frequentissime iactari videmus; cum enim quid 25 minantur, promptissime aiunt: ego quoque Florentinus sum civis. Hac illi voce attestari videntur et palam admonere, ut nemo se propter imbecillitatem contemnat nec sibi iniuriam propter potentiam minari pergat; parem esse condicionem omnium, cum eos qui minus possint ipsa res publica polliceatur ulcisci.

30 Quanquam non cives duntaxat hec res publica defendit, sed etiam peregrinos. Nulli enim patitur fieri iniuriam, sed sive civis sive peregrinus sit suum cuique ius ut tribuatur laborat. Hec eadem iustitia equabilitasque civitatis cum facilitatem et humanitatem inter cives parit, cum nemo magnopere inflari aut alios aspernari possit, 35 tum vero erga omnes homines benignitatem.

Iam vero de honestate vite et, ut in hoc tempore, sanctimonia morum quis satis digne possit referre? Maxima quidem in hac urbe

1 Lacedemonie *G O P A*] Lacedomone *L;* Lacedemonia *C.*   2 partium *G C*] Guelforum *L O P A.* his *L C O P A*] hiis *G.*   3 sentiunt *L O P A*] statuunt *G C.*   5 his *L C O A*] hiis *G P.* igitur *G C A*] *om. L O P.*   13 enim *G C P A*] *om. L O.*   15 maximam *G C P A*] maximam *ex* maxima *corr. esse videtur L;* maxima *O.*   18 rationi *G C P A*] rationis *L;* rationis (*sed cum signo in margine fortasse indicante corruptionem*) *O.* 31/32 sive civis sive peregrinus sit *L C*] si civis sive peregrinus sit *G;* sive civis sit sive peregrinus *P A;* sive civis sit sive peregrinus sit *O.*   33 equabilitasque *G C A*] equabilitas *O;* equalitasque *L P.*   36 et ut in *G C P A*] et in *L O.*

ingenia sunt et, quamcunque rem agere pergant, modum ceterorum
hominum perfacile excedentia. Sive enim arma sequantur, sive ad
rem publicam gubernandam se conferant, sive ad studia aliqua
rerumve cognitiones, sive ad mercaturas, in omni denique re obeunda
omnique actione cunctos mortales longissime anteeunt, nec ulli 5
penitus genti cuiusquam excessus locum relinquunt, patientes laborum, presentes in periculis, glorie avidi, pollentes consilio, industrii,
liberales, magnifici, iocundi, affabiles, maximeque urbani.
Nam quid ego de orationis suavitate et verborum elegantia loquar?
in qua quidem re sine controversia superat. Sola enim hec in tota 10
Italia civitas purissimo ac nitidissimo sermone uti existimatur.
Itaque omnes qui bene atque emendate loqui volunt ex hac una urbe
sumunt exemplum. Habet enim hec civitas homines qui in hoc popu-
lari atque communi genere dicendi ceteros omnes infantes ostenderint. Littere autem ipse, non mercennarie ille quidem neque sordi- 15
de, sed que maxime sunt liberis hominibus digne, que in omni
principe populo semper floruerunt, in hac una urbe plurimum vigent.
Quo igitur ornamento hec civitas caret, aut quid sibi ad summam
laudem atque amplitudinem deest? Num generis claritas? que a populo Romano sit orta! num gloria? que preclaras res tanta virtute et 20
industria domis forisque gesserit et quotidie gerat! num splendor
edificiorum, num ornatus, num lautitia, num divitie, num multitudo
populi, num salubritas atque amenitas locorum? Et quid est preterea
quod ulla civitas possit optare? Nichil profecto!
Quid igitur iam dicemus, aut quid agendum superextat? Quid 25
aliud, quam summum numen pro tanto beneficio venerari eique
preces porrigere: Tu igitur deus omnipotens atque immortalis, cuius
delubra atque aras hic tuus populus religiosissime colit; tuque sanc-
tissima parens, cui ingens templum ex puro ac nitido marmore in hac
urbe absolvitur, que tuum dulcissimum complexa natum eadem mater 30
es et intemeratissima virgo, tuque Iohannes Baptista, quem sibi
patronum hec civitas adoptavit: hanc pulcerrimam et ornatissimam
urbem populumque eius ab omni clade maloque defendite!

5 cunctos *G C O P A*] ceteros *L*.   11 ac *G C A*] atque *L O P*.   16 sed que *L O P A*]
sed ille que *G C*.   19 atque *L C P A*] atque ad *G O*.   25 iam *C P A*] iam dudum *G;*
iam *om. L O*.   29 ac *G C A*] et *L O;* atque *P*.   31 Baptista *L C O P A*] Batista
G.   33 defendite] defendite. Deo gratias amen. Leonardi aretini Laudes florentine
urbis explicunt *G;* defendite. Finis. Laus Deo *C;* defendite. Finit *L O;* defende. Finit
MᵒCCCCXXXVIIIIᵒ *P;* defende. Scriptum Constancie pridie idus Februarii milleximo
CCCCᵒXVIIᵒ *P S A I A*.

INDEX

Index

Index